Literary M

and Socic

Literary Methods and Sociological Theory

Case Studies of Simmel and Weber

Bryan S. Green

The University of Chicago Press • *Chicago & London*

BRYAN S. GREEN is associate professor of sociology at York University. He is the author of *Introduction to Sociology* and *Knowing the Poor*.

The University of Chicago Press, Chicago 60637
The University of Chicago Press, Ltd., London
© 1988 by The University of Chicago
All rights reserved. Published 1988
Printed in the United States of America
97 96 95 94 93 92 91 90 89 88   54321

Library of Congress Cataloging-in-Publication Data

Green, Bryan S.
   Literary methods and sociological theory : case studies of Simmel
and Weber / Bryan S. Green.
      p.   cm.
   Bibliography: p.
   Includes index.
   ISBN 0-226-30612-7   ISBN 0-226-30613-5 (pbk.)
   1. Sociology. 2. Simmel, Georg, 1858–1918—Criticism, Textual.
3. Weber, Max, 1864–1920—Criticism, Textual. I. Title.
HM24.G69 1988   87-30256
301'.01—dc19   CIP

Contents

v

Preface

This study grew out of long-term teaching of classical sociological theory, pondering its awkward status in the discipline, and seeking appropriate terms through which to analyze and evaluate it. By awkward I mean the scientifically unaccountable cultivation of theory as a separate area of study, the obsessive and seemingly insatiable interest in reading long-ago, faraway authors, and the accumulation of exegetical commentaries apparently fed by nothing more than a desire to interpret. My appraisal of the situation is that there must be more to theory than official disciplinary accounts of its purposes and functions can grasp. More particularly, I believe that the de facto work of theory is being missed in de jure accounts of it and in the conventional reading habits to which those accounts are tied. In other words, we need to see theory as a real-world activity—a feature of social life—and characterize it in terms of what it is and what it does in that context rather than the normative context of serving the discipline.

The proposal advanced in this study is that sociological theory is a form of literary activity which belongs to a ubiquitous social practice: the simultaneous representation and construction of social life in determinate ways of word use. It is a written extension of mundane theorizing, working with and upon its linguistic resources. In this perspective, theory is a performative activity in language whose operative methods are ways of writing through which specifiable reading responses are composed. In short, the missed de facto work of sociological theory is text work.

The study proceeds empirically, rather than programmatically, by analyzing the performative practices of particular theorists. In particular, I attempt to identify in textual detail the compositional methods and performative styles of Georg Simmel and Max Weber. With the eventual aim of formulating critical standards of good theory, though in the spirit of cultural appreciation rather than legislative prescription, I have chosen to analyze work whose classical status attests to a value in them. The value is to be sought, however, in generic styles exemplified in the work—here that of Simmel and Weber—not assigned indiscriminately and reverentially to famous names. An author may, after all, fail to live up to the performative standards of the genre which informs his work. We will, in fact, show this to be the case for both authors studied.

Finally, I should emphasize that I am not analyzing original texts but translated ones. Thus when I refer to Simmel or to Simmel's work, I mean the English-translated Simmel, and so on. My observations are limited then to their effective existence in Anglo-American sociology. The translated work is a textual phenomenon worth analyzing in its own right. However, I do assign the work to the proper names Simmel and Weber; and although this is a standard convention accepted for ordinary discussions of content, it might be thought to need special justification where the concern is with the linguistic styling of content. Certainly if it could be shown that a particular translator had imposed another style upon a particular body of work this would at least demand a renaming of the author to avoid improper attribution. My analysis includes three safeguards against such misattribution: no single translator is relied upon; readers of the original texts are used to suggest and check stylistic characteristics; and for the most part, characterization is not made to depend upon very precise details of wording. In the one place (an indicated section of chapter 5) where precise wording was an issue, I checked with the translator. I am reasonably sure, then, that the literary methods discerned here in the translated works of Simmel and Weber are operative also in the original texts.

Part One: The Work of Sociological Theory

Introduction

There is a continuing uncertainty about the place of theory in the sociological enterprise and a persisting inability to normalize it, either scientifically or humanistically, which cannot any longer be attributed to the immaturity of the discipline and is certainly not understandable as a shortcoming of its members. Rather, the situation suggests that prevailing concepts of what theory is, despite their diversity, are inadequate to grasp theoretic work. There is an excess of deed over disposition. In the literature this is symptomatically registered in vain repetitions of standard complaints, diagnoses, and remedies. My argument is that current ways of treating theory miss its actual work because they are constrained by inappropriate precepts of what theory should be. Observation of the work is limited to what the precepts provide for.

The dominant precept is that the proper role of theory is to go into service: the disciplinary service of empirical research. This is why standard complaints revolve around the phenomenon of what can be called autonomous theory: that is, theorizing carried out in apparent independence of empirical inquiry. I will begin by examining the complaints.

Autonomous Theory as a Deviant Activity

The cultivation of sociological theory as a substantive subarea in its own right, replete with specialized courses, publications, and practitioners, is a notable feature of contemporary sociology. In the 1950s it was possible to ask students to discuss Whitehead's dictum, "A science which hesitates to forget its founders is lost," in a spirit of scientistic bravado. Today the burgeoning prosperity of a theory subarea based upon continual interpretive renewal of classical texts requires us to ask openly (not contemptuously or dismissively) what kind of science this is that cannot forget its founders—that turns their writings into an area specialty.

Standard (in the sense of standardizing) responses to autonomous theory are as various in tone as those of schoolteachers to an unruly class member: stern reproof, mild admonition, making allowances, and qualified encouragement of liveliness. The cogency and accountability of all such responses, however, depends on the operation of a strong conformity-deviance schema. Even tolerance of creative difference presupposes an eventual return to normal inquiry. The operation of the schema and the limitations it imposes can be seen in three common topics of concern: the theory-research gap; the unclear separation between the history and systematics of theory; and the uses of studying classical theory.

The Theory-Research Gap

The existence of the theory-research gap as an occasion for concern is provided for by a discipline norm that theory and research should be integrated. Menzies (1982:1) describes the concern and urges clearer definition of the norm behind it: "In accord with their ideology, sociologists condemn this gap for leading to research which is formulated in a vacuum. . . . Usually this complaint about the theory-research gap is made ritualistically. What is meant by a theory-research gap, and how it manifests itself, is unspecified." In search of a more rigorous standard, Menzies proposes that since research is always to some extent theoretically formulated, the ritualistically decried gap is actually between "theoreticians' theory" and "research theory." The regulative ideal appropriate to their relationship is a combination of symbiotic exchange, critical correction, and stimulating tension: "Some divergence between theoreticians' theory and research theory is beneficial to sociology. Without a gap between them, neither could clarify, force reassessments, suggest extensions or stimulate new directions for the other. The contention of this book is that the gap is now so wide that there is little possibility of interplay between theory and research in many areas" (Menzies, 1982:4). From this it might seem that the two forms of intellectual activity are equal partners. This is not the case. Whereas research cannot detach itself entirely from theory and therefore has salvation from emptiness built into it, theory can proceed independently and become valueless. Independence is displayed in discursive enclosure and autoreferential writing: "Theoreticians' theory in several areas . . . working on a different set of problems from research theory. . . . Theoreticians tend largely to be concerned with, and to cite, other theoreticians rather than research" (Menzies, 1982:188).

The twin fault here is that autonomous theory places itself beyond the bounds of science and in doing so stigmatizes the community it is associated with: "When theoreticians' theory does not correspond in substantial measure to research theory, then, in one crucial respect it lies outside science. If science is seen not as a body of ideas, but as the outcome of a social process, then a theory-research gap indicates that

THE WORK OF SOCIOLOGICAL THEORY

this process is inappropriately integrated: sociology is not the collective enterprise it should be" (Menzies, 1982:2).

Within the disciplinary conventions of sociology, theoreticians' theory can achieve value only in exchange relations with a particular activity outside itself: research. It is not construed as an activity which might be imbued with value simply by virtue of being a part of social life.

Interestingly, Menzies raises that possibility, but only as a limitation of his study. He says that Marxist journals were considered to be beyond his definition of "theory in use" because Marxism represents a concern for praxis that places it beyond the theory-research distinction. More specifically, its location in an extradisciplinary social practice— "political action"—places it on a different plane from other theory.

My position, to be amplified subsequently, is that all social theory is part of a social practice—the interactive construction of social reality in language use—and needs no service to research to confer value upon it. If postpositivist sociology, under such headings as labeling theory, critical theory, ethnomethodology, and social phenomenology, has done nothing else, it has amply demonstrated the pervasiveness of social theorizing in mundane social life and in the political interplay of public language, individual conduct, and organizational order. Sociological theory reflects and in critical turn reflects upon socially constitutive forms of language use. In the critical turn, where sensitivity to socially good language use about society is paramount, attention to the language of sociological theorists is warranted and indeed necessary. If sociological theory is a formalized extension of mundane social theorizing, then "theoreticians' theory" would be an essential element in establishing and sustaining a critical-reflexive return of mundane theorizing to itself.

A comparable return of language to itself occurs in fictional writing. The counterpart there of "theoreticians' theory" is literary criticism. This also involves an interpretive renewal of classical texts in the interest of good language use, but there the interest is aesthetically rather than socially conceived. In a revealing passage, Menzies notes the similarity, but can make no more of it than a stigmatizing gibe:

> Many books on sociological theory are undertaken largely on the basis of the author's reading of other books and articles on theory. The author defines precisely what other theorists mean in their works—obscurities are clarified and concepts redefined. Next, the author produces his own statement of the relationship between the various concepts he has analysed. . . . The result, to overstate

the case, reads like a cross between literary criticism and philosophy of science written by a fortune teller turned sociologist. (Menzies, 1982:ix)

What the gibe reveals is conventional blindness to the active work place of sociological theory, namely, the reading experience, and the intrinsically literary character of that work. The actual work of sociological theorizing takes place in determinate reading-writing processes. The operative methods of sociological theory are ways of writing, that is, literary methods. Theoreticians' theory includes reflection upon the worth of particular theoretical writings. Therefore it cannot help being, if only latently, a kind of literary criticism; a special kind, however, because it answers to the linguistic demands of appropriately representing social life rather than those of creating aesthetically satisfying experiences in cultural artifacts. Sociological theory is a fashioning and refashioning of collective self-representations in the light of critical reason. Theoreticians' theory is the bringing of that process to conceptual awareness. It can never then be "mere" theory, divorced from reality, because social life, social knowledge, and social reality alike are generated in a coexistent linguistic medium. Sociological theory, even when turning in upon itself, is working in and upon the constitutive materials of society: descriptive vocabularies, classificatory schemata, explanatory recipes, enunciative rules: in short, the word ways through which a continuing social order with a definite identity is represented and reproduced. The practical value of theoreticians' theory inheres in the dual fact that word ways delimit what is normal/abnormal, possible/impossible, proper/improper, contingent/necessary for those living in them, and that the limits, while beyond willfully planned alteration, are mutable by critical awareness.

The History, Systematics, and Proper Study of Theory

Whereas Menzies finds the reprehensible deviance of autonomous theory in a separation from research, Merton (1967: chap. 1) finds it in a certain scholastic, commemorative, and mimetic relation to past theories which is scientifically useless: "The study of classical writings can either be deplorably useless or wonderfully useful. It all depends on the form that study takes. For a vast difference separates the anemic practices of mere commentary or banalization from the active practice of following up and developing the theoretical leads of significant predecessors" (Merton, 1967:30). Or, again:

THE WORK OF SOCIOLOGICAL THEORY

> Sociologists in our time must continue to behave unlike their
> contemporaries in the physical and life sciences and devote more of
> themselves to close familiarity with their not-so-distant predeces-
> sors. But if they are to be effective rather than merely pious, if they
> are to *use* earlier formulations of theory rather than simply com-
> memorate them, they must distinguish between the scholastic
> practice of commentary and exegesis and the scientific practice of
> extending antecedent theory. (Merton, 1967:37)

The question facing us is what forms of theory study lie within "the
scientific practice of extending antecedent theory," and whether our
proposal to treat theory as literary work can find a place in the realm of
the wonderfully useful.

The scientific purpose of studying past theory is "obliteration by
incorporation," or a full absorption of past into present thought. The
reason why sociologists, relative to their natural science contemporaries, must devote more of themselves to studying classic texts is,
Merton says, because of the still imperfect retrieval of past theories in
their discipline.

Merton's distinction between the systematics and the history of theory
allows for two retrieval operations. First, bringing good ideas, conceptual tools, methodological rules, and other resources into contemporary
theory construction. This corresponds to Menzies' normalizing concept
of research activity and need not detain us. More interesting is the
operation performed by "authentic," which is to say, sociologically
grounded, histories of sociological theories:

> They would take up such matters as the complex filiation of so-
> ciological ideas, the ways in which they developed, the connections
> of theory with the changing social origins and subsequent social
> statuses of its exponents, the interaction of theory with the chang-
> ing social organization of sociology, the diffusion of theory from
> centers of sociological thought and its modification in the course of
> diffusion, and the ways in which it was influenced by changes in the
> environing culture and social structure. (Merton, 1967:2)

Clearly the outward direction of inquiry dictated by this historical
sociology of ideas is contrary to my determination to stay within textual
bounds, yet there is an almost identical point of departure. Merton
observes a "rock-bound difference between the finished versions of
scientific work as they appear in print and the actual course of inquiry
followed by the inquirer" (Merton, 1967:4). Authentic histories would
penetrate below the "immaculate appearance" of scientific papers and

reconstruct the "actual course of scientific developments" that do not appear in the public record of science—"the ways in which scientists actually think, feel and go about their work" (Merton, 1967:4).

The aspiration I share with Merton is to retrieve the hidden work glossed over in the "immaculate appearance" of finished products in print. However, his references are to research reports and the inquiry events excluded from them—untidy adaptations, guesswork, false starts, happy accidents—not to theoretical texts and the hidden work they include. Here the work would have to be found in the printed product, in its literary structure, rather than behind the scenes in pre-, sub-, or con-textual happenings. Thus, while Merton's rationale for an authentic history of science can be adapted to my project, its program does not satisfy my analytic requirements.

There is one more feature of Merton's essay worth commenting on. It asserts values in classical theory that exceed anything allowed for in either historical or systematic retrieval operations: values, moreover, which being immanent and inexhaustible are beyond the goal of complete incorporation into ongoing science; values suggesting a possible nonscientific and noninstrumental interpretation of Merton's claim regarding the functions of reading the classics, that each function "derives from the imperfect retrieval of past sociological theory that has not yet been fully absorbed" (Merton, 1967:37). It may be that absorption refers to something other than incorporation into research theories, and that "imperfect retrieval" is a virtuous sign of hermeneutic richness rather than a confession of scientific immaturity. If so, the classics might be studied independently of research without incurring the stigmata of being piously commemorative, thoughtlessly mimetic, and deplorably useless.

Merton marks a possible place for autonomous theory in a contrast between newer and older practices of sociological writing: "Past sociological papers and particularly books were written in a style in which the basic concepts were seldom strictly defined, while the logic of procedure and the relationships between variables and the specific theory being developed remained largely implicit, in keeping with the long-established humanist tradition" (Merton, 1967:14). The humanist tradition might then be used as a legitimating place-name for autonomous theory to be undertaken. Disappointingly, Merton cites it only to explain the difficulties of historians of theory in distinguishing genuine prediscoveries, rediscoveries, and the like, from verbal similitudes. Yet the door is not completely closed. In a footnote "to keep the record straight," he denies either the newer scientific format or the older humanistic style a privileged relationship to sociological truth, adding: "the issue here is not the relative scientific merit of differing styles of sociological writing" (Merton, 1967:14). For me, this is precisely the issue (provided we suspend the prescriptive term "scientific") that underlies the unsettled and unsettling position of theory in sociology. For his part, Merton describes the pathos of a discipline caught between scientific and humanistic ideals, tough-mindedly urges a commitment to science, and ambivalently retains other commitments as private convictions and personal pleasures:

> Sociology retains its kinship with the humanities. It is reluctant to abandon a firsthand acquaintance with the classical works of sociology and presociology as an integral part of the experience of the sociologist *qua* sociologist. Every contemporary sociologist with a claim to sociological literacy has had direct and repeated encounters with the works of the founding fathers. . . . Since I have long shared the reluctance to lose touch with the classics, even before finding a rationale for it, and since to a degree I continue to share it, this may be reason enough for speculating about its character and sources. (Merton, 1967:29)

Merton's justificatory explanation of sociologists' reluctance to shelve the classics takes the form of describing functions for members of the discipline. As such it suffers from the methodological weakness of all functionalist explanations. A demonstration of subsequent utility in a phenomenon once it has appeared does not explain its initial appearance. The origins remain unexplicated. My argument is that they lie in the transdisciplinary status of social theorizing as a reflexive and constitutive element of everyday society (one needs ungrammatically to say "societying"). However, more needs to be said about conventional reasons for reading the classics and the values we are invited to find in them.

The Uses of Classical Theory

Merton's list of the functions of repeated readings of the founding fathers includes not only benefits to scientific research but some that are personal, regenerative, and almost spiritual in nature. They constitute a sublimation of the same extrascientific aspects of theory study which in reverse are stigmatic signs of waste and waywardness. A rhetoric of life-in-death communion is invoked to turn unacceptable tendencies into collective values:

It is often assumed that to cite an earlier source necessarily means that the idea or finding in that citation first came to mind upon the reading of it. Yet the evidence often indicates that the earlier passage is noted only because it agrees with what the reader has developed on his own. What we find here is that unlikely sounding event: a dialogue between the dead and the living. These do not differ much from dialogues between contemporary scientists in which each is delighted as he discovers that the other agrees with what was until then an idea held in solitude and perhaps even suspect. (Merton, 1967:35)

The metaphors of life in communion and death in solitude return, though in a different structural arrangement, on the next page. Merton argues the necessity of regular rereading because "part of what is communicated by the printed page changes as the result of an interaction between the dead author and the live reader." Nor is it enough to simply read again literally or ritualistically: "This process requires intensive reading of the classics—the kind of concentration evidenced by that truly dedicated scholar (described by Edmund Wilson) who, interrupted at his work by a knock on the door, opened it, strangled the stranger who stood there, and then returned to his work" (Merton, 1967:36).

The dedicated scholar renews himself through preserving what seems to be his solitude but is actually a communion, though invisible to strangers. The intrusion and sacrifice of strangers is, however, crucial to the intensiveness needed to sustain a community carved out from immanent solitude. From this it is clear that the sociological scholar, unlike natural scientists, cannot even begin to forget his founders. They will turn up again and again, either as dialogical communicants or as intrusive strangers serving the sacrificial function.

It should not be thought that such excessive life-in-death metaphors are peculiar to Merton. They appear repeatedly in the literature and typically in conjunction with scientifically defined uses of the classics. The conjunction reinforces my claim that they are sublimatory restorations of theoretic activities alien to science but essential to sociology.

For example, Smelser and Warner (1976) offer two "complementary treatises" on theory, the former showing the critical incorporation of ideas from the classics through scientifically constructed theories, the latter combining textual exegesis with contextual and biographical interpretation.

Warner's essay is instructive in this respect because in the jointly written introduction he subscribes with Smelser to scientific sociology,

THE WORK OF SOCIOLOGICAL THEORY

but his reverent, elegiac concern to preserve classical texts as originally written is in total contrast with Smelser's selective reconstruction of concepts and propositions into suitably scientific forms—forms in which original writings have no particular value as such and are incorporated without trace, except for footnote references.

Warner is sensitive to the antagonism between interpretive preservation and extractive absorption; he shows it in a highly pertinent question: "And yet, if such discrete propositions can be extracted from the classics, why should we bother to read the originals? Why is it not enough to codify these propositions, to assess them in the light of the current evidence, and to consign the original studies to the student of history?" (Smelser and Warner, 1976:6). Warner answers himself unconvincingly through conventional metaphors of value that say nothing of the reader-writing process even though his opening question suggests its operations as the place to look. The nearest he gets is in asserting that the classics repay study "partly because the matrix in which the nuggets are embedded adds greatly to their appreciation" (Smelser and Warner, 1976:7). At most, the original writing appears here as an aesthetic setting that adds to our appreciation of valuable contents. Beyond this the contents are valued because of "the sociological wisdom" of the classic authors, their inspiring example, and the fact that they address big issues that still concern us. In these ways of wisdom, relevance, and inspirational example, "the classic authors richly deserve our attention, not merely as historical phenomena but as living colleagues" (Smelser and Warner, 1976:11).

What I would emphasize is that these images of inexhaustible treasure, ageless wisdom, ethical propensity, and collegial immortality are retroactive glosses that leave their topic virtually untouched. What, as Donald Levine asks, accounts for this "phenomenal quest for the classics today?" (Rhea, 1981:62). Why, as Warner asks, does the quest have to proceed through the original texts? If they provide inspiring examples, as every apologist claims, what actually, in practice, do they exemplify? Merton talks of the classics providing "a model for intellectual work," but can only figuratively describe the nature of that work as forming "standards of taste and judgment in identifying a good sociological problem," or serving to "sharpen the faculties of exacting readers who give them their undivided attention" (1967:36). The actual basis for all such reader-response values, namely, methods of textual composition, is hidden in a conventional preoccupation with content—extraction of content being the regulative ideal by which our normal reading habits are governed.

Rather unexpectedly, of the authors reviewed above, it is Smelser, pursuing a selectively scientistic interest in the classics, who comes closest, as least verbally, to my way of seeing them. For example, referring to the traditional separation between courses on theory construction and those on the history of sociological thought: "I am going to cut through this troublesome distinction by adopting the following strategy. I shall assume that there is such an activity as sociological theorizing and that in pursuing this activity a thinker has to face a definite number of issues or problems" (Smelser and Warner, 1976:138). I too wish to think of sociological theorizing as a definite activity. However, it is to be construed as a social activity of language use involving individuals as reader-writers rather than just thinkers. The quiddity of theorizing is to be found in what happens in reading-writing experiences, not inside thinkers' minds. Moreover, I do not wish to follow Smelser in presupposing a normative model of theory to which all theorizing is held regulatively accountable (as in saying the thinker must explicitly define concepts, avoid logical contradictions, and seek empirical tests of ideas). Rather, I begin with certified samples of valuable theory (certified by their status as classics) and ask naively, What reading responses are evoked here? and What literary methods of composition underlie them? In this, I honor the spirit of Durkheim's first rule of method, that we must consider social facts as things and not as ideas we already have of them: "The definition [of a phenomenon for investigation] must deal with phenomena not as ideas but in terms of their inherent properties. It must characterize them by elements essential to their nature, not by their conformity to an intellectual ideal" (Durkheim, [1895] 1938:35). Smelser's shortcoming—and it is a typical one—lies in equating sociological theory with an intellectual, in this case a scientistic, ideal. The exclusionary effects, destructive of inquiry into the phenomenon of theory as it is, are spelled out by Smelser himself:

> To evaluate this theoretical aspect is to consider but one facet of any scholar's thought. There are other aspects as well—literary elegance, ideological potency, social utility, and so on—which can be assessed by multiplying canons other than those of theoretical adequacy. Furthermore, if and when we discover theoretical omissions and flaws in a body of thought, we are not necessarily scolding the scholar for not measuring up to his objectives. It may be that he did not intend to create a sociological theory in the full sense we now conceive it. Nevertheless, it is still possible and profitable to inquire in what ways his work does and does not

qualify as sociological theory. (Smelser and Warner, 1976:138–39)

In contrast, I approach classical texts in terms of their manifest existence as literary organizations of reading responses, not their ideal existence as approximations to normative preconceptions of theory. Standards of good "theoretician's theory" are to emerge from examinations of what canonical theorists have done in textual practice, not laid down in advance, and they are to be intrinsically, not extrinsically, warranted.

To take our bearings more carefully, we will next consider the topic of writing style and its treatment in sociology.

1   The Treatment of Writing Style in Sociology

The methodological relevance of style for creating truth effects in a community of knowledge seekers has been raised by Amelie Rorty (1983). Although she speaks only of philosophy, her remarks are directly pertinent to sociological theory.

Like Merton, Rorty contrasts older with newer practices of inquiry, but with a closer concern for the relation between style and truth:

> Sobriety, attention to detail, care without obsession, the right balance of generality and attention, an easy rather than a relentless use of imagery and metaphor—these are integral to philosophical legitimation. But these matters are themselves set by fashion, by the genres of the time. Someone writing now with Hobbes' historical allusions and imagery, Hume's evasive turns of phrase . . . would not qualify as a professional philosopher. And in reading these philosophers now, we gloss over their reliance on history and classical allusion, ignoring the role of style and genre in their arguments. (Rorty, 1983:546)

Such matters are glossed over and screened out because the professionalization of philosophy in the nineteenth century rested upon a strong distinction between rational and rhetorical persuasion—the former depending exclusively on the interior power of validly organized arguments to carry conviction, thus separating philosophers from moralists, orators, reformers, and the like. As in sociology, however, this confinement of authentic inquiry to particular rules of writing has proceeded without benefit of proper critical justification: "We philosophers have avoided openly discussing our own problems of style and genre, taking evasive action to assure respectability by following the pervading fashions. And not without reason: To whom can we speak about the difficulties of stylistic choice, and in what voice?" So it is with sociologists. How, within the present conventions of sociology—its rules of method, its ways of reading and writing—can writing style be discussed? What does its discursive system allow for in the way of address and voice on the topic of style? The literature suggests that it allows only for marginal concern: marginal in a double sense. First, writing style is an occasional, secondary, and peripheral topic: one sometimes mentioned in passing in prefatory remarks, footnotes, supplementary comments, and other marginalia. Even when noted more fully or made an issue, it is typically in a negative voice only: reactions against breaches of stylistic rules whose authority to govern sociological theorizing is left methodologically unexplicated. For example, critiques of jargon (Runciman, 1965; Kirk, 1974), verbosity (Mills, 1959), and obscurantism (Rex, 1974). I have attempted elsewhere to provide a methodological rationale for such complaints and will not pursue the question here (Green, 1977). Of more immediate concern is a second sense of marginality.

Whenever sociological writing style is made a matter of discussion, it is typically in terms of evaluative criteria belonging to other areas of language use—in particular, natural science, literary art, and standard public language. The last refers to norms of proper usage, instilled especially through formal education, and serving to maintain a common medium of communication and control in the face of regional dialects, in-group argot, colloquialisms, vernacular, slang, and other babelish elements (see, for example, Mueller, 1973; Bernstein, 1975; Labov, 1970; Balibar and Laporte, 1974).

Marginality here has the connotation of being at a boundary. Evaluative concepts of good writing are imported across the boundaries of sociology from other language realms. They meet no strong scrutiny because there is no indigenous, discipline-specific concept of good writing to oppose them. Consequently style is methodologically marginal in the sense of being extrinsically and imitatively derived. When we speak of stylistic choice it is in the voices of others.

To extend the argument and further pursue the consideration of style as integral rather than marginal to the work of sociological theory, I will examine two samples of import-based discussions. The first represents natural science imitation, the prevalent standard of the discipline (Reynolds, 1971); the second, emulation of literary art (Nisbet, 1976). Although these are in some ways opposing tendencies, they similarly blank out the question of the generic specificity of sociological writing. What is sociological work conceived as a literary practice sui generis? What are its particular compositional possibilities and performative demands?

Natural Science Rules of Sociological Writing

Paul Reynolds's textbook openly expresses its commitment to a natural science normalization of sociology. The prefatory page states: "This book is designed to provide a general introduction to the philosophy of science as it can and should be applied to social and human phenomena." Within this scientistic perspective, theory is assigned certain well-known tasks: to organize and categorize things, to articulate causal processes, to predict future events, and to explain past ones. Our interest is in the rules of writing thus legislated.

All theories consist of abstract statements, but not any syntagmatic arrangement will do. Reynolds specifies three allowable forms that theory statements may take: a set of laws (i.e., well-supported empirical generalizations), an axiomatic model, or a causal-process model.

Whichever enunciative form theory writing takes, there are certain semantic requirements placed upon its statements. The concepts entering into them should be defined in explicit, communally shareable terms; their meaning should be independent of historical, situational, or other contingent circumstances; and they should be translatable into empirical research results.

Behind such familiar rules of method is a conventional attitude to language that must be suspended in order that we may pursue our line of inquiry. It assumes that there are ideas in the mind and facts in reality prior to any words chosen to represent them. This assumption is expressed in metaphors of language as container, carrier, conduit, and viewing instrument. On this metaphorical base scientifically minded philosophers such as Hobbes and Locke mounted their polemics against the use of figurative words in writing intended to be truthful.

Hobbes says the general use of writing is to "transfer our mental discourse into verbal; or the train of our thoughts into a train of words" (1968:102). Figurative language is criticized because its words have no constant meaning and "inconstant names can never be true grounds of rational thought." They lack instrumental utility because they possess a protean changeability. John Locke ([1690] 1964:2:105–6) urges: "If we would speak of things as they are, we must allow that all art of rhetoric . . . all the artificial and figurative application of words eloquence has invented, are for nothing else but to insinuate wrong ideas, move the passions, mislead the judgement, and so indeed are perfect cheats . . . and wholly to be avoided in all discourses that pretend to inform and instruct."

Constancy of meaning is the central semantic value in the instrumental attitude to language. Reynolds says, "the most important feature of any term, used to indicate a concept, is the degree of agreement about its meaning" (Reynolds, 1971:48). He observes as an endemic problem in social science the tendency of its readers to supplement even carefully defined words with their own interpretations, thus changing the meaning of a statement. Such interpretive excess can only be curbed by abstract symbols, neologisms, and technical inventions: the antithesis of figurative, poetic, rhetorical words. The reward for such discipline is a language of truth and reason: one capable of describing things as they are and conveying the meaning originally intended.

The latter point reminds us that ideas as well as things are assumed to preexist their expression in language. Theory construction is said to begin with a scientist having an idea which he then expresses in terms of a shared vocabulary. Its effect depends upon its incarnation as written theory, but "the written theory is only a reflection of the new orientation or idea" (Reynolds, 1971:21). The mimetic metaphor of reflection, no less than vehicular metaphors of container and conveyor, asserts the secondary and separable status of linguistic form in relation to content.

Accepting that sociology is an interpretive community whose members share compositional strategies of the above kind, we can identify certain interlocking reading conventions that uncritically bound, or frame, normal work in the discipline:

1. The content of sociological writing is separable from its style. It is taken for granted that things as they are and originally intended ideas provide two external references for extracting empirical and discursive content, respectively.

2. The scientific value of sociological writing (its truth value) is to be found in content, not style. Style can obscure truth value through bias and "noise," but cannot positively possess it. Good style is that which does not get in the way of empirical and discursive content.

The power of these conventions is apparent in contemporary accounts of the continuing value of the sociological classics, even those undertaken by readers averse to scientistic reductionism.

Editing a volume of essays on classical theory, Buford Rhea explicitly invited contributors to show "how the classics are contemporary and important" (Rhea, 1981:x). Rhea's commission suggests content-oriented topics, like a theorist's conceptualizations of problems and his major hypotheses, but he also mentions "becoming familiar with the style of a master craftsman," and in any case invites the contributors to feel free to deal with the issue as they see fit. In short, there was no instruction to dwell upon content alone. Nonetheless, all nine essays unquestioningly treat the exemplary "how" of the classics' worth in this way—yet not quite totally. There are places where style, if only implicitly, appears as another basis for addressing the issue of worth.

For example, Dennis Wrong separates the "subfield" influence of Weber's ideas on bureaucracy, religious ethics, and so on, from his status as "one of a small group of 'classical' nineteenth and early twentieth century social thinkers who are regarded as *general* sociological theorists" (Rhea, 1981:39). In this capacity, Weber has contributed to the search for a "unified general perspective on human nature, society and history"; a search answering to a need "independent both of specific investigations and of the history of sociology or social thought considered as a special subfield of sociology devoted to recounting the achievements of illustrious ancestors" (Rhea, 1981:39).

Where, however, is this general theoretical value of Weber to be found? Wrong himself emphasizes that Weber examined social reality through "individualizing" as opposed to "generalizing" concepts, and that he was opposed to comprehensive systems like those of Comte and Spencer. However, since that kind of theorizing also seeks a unified perspective on human nature, society, and history, it cannot be the mere fact of searching for a unified perspective that makes Weber an exemplary general theorist. Nor, we should recall, is his worth as a general theorist dependent upon the scientific value of his specific investigations.

Where it is to be found, I would suggest, is in the style of Weber's texts—that is, in certain literary ways of turning words from the linguistic medium of social life into representational knowledge of it; those ways being characteristic of the texts, original and translated, to which the name Weber is attached. This awkward formulation is not intended to signify allegiance to the recently fashionable notion of autonomous, authorless texts, but to reinforce my strategic decision to seek a theorist's style in the writing work, not (quoting Wrong), in "the man behind the work" (Rhea, 1981:57). This confinement of attention is, I believe, necessary to explicate style as a methodologically central feature of sociology.

Certainly there is no such explication in Wrong, or in the other contributors to Rhea's collection. Consequently they fall uncritically into content-oriented accounts of what is valuable in the classics. Levine, for example, seeking to explain what he calls the phenomenal and unique quest for the classics in sociology, appeals to their integrative value for a fragmented discipline and to their intellectual relevance in helping sociologists respond "to the expectations both of those who entered the field and of the larger intellectual community that sociology, as prescriptive heir to theology and moral philosophy, may have something worthwhile to say about the human condition in 'modern' society" (Rhea, 1981:64).

There is a normal content-centered bias carried in the innocuous phrase at the end of that passage. The bias is confirmed in Levine's subsequent account of Simmel's vitality where, in spite of accepting Simmel's principle of giving form analytic priority over content, he nonetheless makes the content of Simmel's work the locus of its value. When Levine comments on Simmel's writing style—calling it "essayistic rather than rigorously expository, full of detours and distractions, and anything but overtly systematic" (Rhea, 1981:67)—it is a bothersome epiphenomenon, something to be overcome by revision: "An effort is required to introduce a greater degree of systematic order to his thought than Simmel himself provided. We can do this by formalizing what is only implicit in the full range of Simmel's sociological writings. . . ." (Rhea, 1981:67).

To show what is needed, Levine abstracts six general research questions to be asked of any form of association and six universal variables through which to begin answering them. However, he is too close a reader of Simmel to simply abandon without trace the topic of writing style. It is recalled obliquely as "one other feature of Simmel's sociological approach" deserving mention, and labeled "the principle of dualism" (Rhea, 1981:70).

Though only an additional point contained in a list, it is potentially disruptive for the orderliness of Levine's exposition, that is to say, for the reading conventions forming the sociological discipline and governing his local disciplining of Simmel. The principle of dualism could be heard as a description of Simmel's style: one which (*a*) refers to his literary working method; (*b*) makes his lack of systematic orderliness crucial to the point, purpose, and value of his work; and (*c*) challenges the formalizing, systematizing style of work that Levine has recommended and performed.

Levine cannot take it this way. Sociology's conventions of reading, like an immune system, defend against intrusion. The principle of dualism is reduced to the kind of content found in particular social forms: fashion combines conformity and individualization, trust in another is formed somewhere between complete knowledge and total ignorance, and so on. Dualism is seen as the definitive "what" of a social life real beyond words, not a particular method of world making within words. The principle of dualism is, then, taken to mean that social scientists should acknowledge this ontological fact in their normal procedures of concept formation, description, and interpretation. It is not considered as a style or stance, conducted through language, which members, not merely observers, need in order to place themselves in a maximally true relationship to social life. Thus when Levine comes to appraise the value of Simmel's *Philosophy of Money,* he does so entirely in terms of thematic contents: for example, what it says about the positive and negative implications of money for individuality, and not at all in terms of how it styles thematic materials to produce certain reading experiences. In contrast, I would give full weight to Simmel's apparently frivolous remark in his textbook, *Sociology,* that although it contains factual examples, he could just as well have used fictitious ones (Frisby, 1984:15). I take this to mean that Simmel himself located the value of his work in its composition rather than its content.

Levine notes a contrast between Simmel's dualistic approach and "the prevailing orientation in American sociology [which] looks for dominant patterns, univalent metrics and unilineal logical derivations" (Rhea, 1981:71). A judgment echoing Caplow's observation of "a discrepancy between Simmel's style of thought and the prevailing sociological idiom" (quoted by Frisby, 1984:15). If we add to this the idea of complicity between standard social science practices of knowledge and institutional practices of "rational" management and control advanced, for example, by Michel Foucault (1977, 1980) and critical theorists like Schroyer (1973), then Simmel's contrary style of thought might be valuable to us in itself as a performative example of how to think differently. However, this is a possibility that cannot be considered within the content-centered conventions of normal reading. The idea of sociology as a natural science is tied to those conventions and cannot therefore breach them. We must see now if the idea of sociology as an art form can do so.

Art, Literature, and Sociological Writing

I have chosen Robert Nisbet (1976) as the protagonist here because, first, he is one of the few top-ranking sociologists to have seriously addressed the issue of style; second, his starting point is similar to mine; and third, consequently, the weaknesses and gaps in his treatment are especially instructive for us.

Nisbet's starting point is the thought that none of the founding themes of sociology were formulated through anything resembling textbook accounts of theory construction and empirical methodology. His second and third thoughts suggest a strategy for giving this fact a positive interpretation. The same themes appear in early sociology as in

THE WORK OF SOCIOLOGICAL THEORY

nineteenth-century art and literature, and scientific discovery is akin to artistic creation. Consequently one can depict sociology as an art form without abandoning its commitment to science. More specifically, Nisbet makes his case by claiming an affinity between actual science (as opposed to regulative idealizations of it) and the artistic creation of meaningful structures and interpretive images, then demonstrating similarities, parallels, and homologues between artistic works and classical sociological writings. In sum, Nisbet incorporates sociology into a unitary art-and-science through analytic conflation, reading them all as exercises of creative imagination, and asserting analogical equivalences between sociological and artistic means of representing reality.

Undoubtedly this unitarian strategy draws renewed attention to writing style. However, it does not decisively separate the question of stylistic value in sociological writing from that of the substantive value of its contents, nor can it address the generic specificity of sociological writing: its particular demands and limits as contrasted with natural science and novels or other literary forms. Let us consider in more detail how Nisbet's procedure distorts and silences pertinent questions.

To place painters, poets, novelists, and sociologists on the same plane, Nisbet claims that all have relied strongly upon landscapes and portraits to convey perceptions of reality:

> what Tocqueville and Marx, and then Toennies, Weber, Durkheim, and Simmel give us in their greatest works . . . is a series of landscapes, each as distinctive and compelling as any to be found among the greater novels or paintings of their age. . . . The same holds with portraits. What artist of the period gave us role-types in his novel or painting more evocative than what we draw from Marx about the bourgeois and worker, from Weber about the bureaucrat, or from Michels on the party politician? (Nisbet, 1976:7)

Let us, for a moment, accept the loose metaphorical equation of landscapes and portraits in paint with counterparts in words, and the contention that the classical sociologists rivaled great artists in the evocative power and truthful insights of their images. What grounds are there for asserting this as a reason for the intellectual longevity of their texts? Is it the quality of their characterizations of places and human types that has drawn successive generations of social scientists to read and reread them? Nisbet refers to *Capital* as containing Marx's "richest landscape," where "the poverty of the worker, the inescapable subjection to the machine, the desolating conditions of work in factories, mills and mines . . . are set forth in commanding detail" (Nisbet, 1976:59).

But is it the detail that has commanded attention and generated readerships? Judging by the secondary literature, the commanding features of Marx's text are not the occasional concrete depictions of poverty and suffering but the theoretical formulations of dialectical materialism and the capitalist mode of production. In any case, if Nisbet's artistic criterion of good sociology had validity we would expect the depictively powerful works of, say, Charles Booth and Seebohm Rowntree on poverty and urban life to have become active classics. But who now reads Booth or Rowntree?

By literary criteria the most fertile parts of the classic texts are depictively impoverished and singularly prosaic. Nisbet's unitarian formulation ignores the question of the specificity of artistic compared to scientific and other representations of meaningful order and in doing so ignores the specificity of social science work compared both to that of art and natural science. Having decided that the artist's imagination is the common factor in all discovery and interpretation, Nisbet can only recommend that sociologists abandon the normalizing ideal of scientific work presently ruling their discipline and commit themselves instead to an incorporative ideal of art-science: "How different things would be, one cannot help reflecting, if the social sciences at the time of their systematic formation in the nineteenth century had taken the arts in the same degree they took the physical sciences as models. . . . The really distinguished and seminal minds of the century in the social sciences . . . clearly recognised the affinity between the sources of science and art (Nisbet, 1976:16).

Ordinary minds, however, missed the affinity and built sociology around rules of inquiry separated from "the real heart, the psychological heart," which is to say the artistic core, of "physical science at its very best" (Nisbet, 1976:16). Thus a false model was followed.

Now it might be agreed that sociology lost itself in copying a false model of natural science, but it does not follow that it would find itself by means of a truer copy. Suppose that sociology's founding purpose is fashioning statements true to social life, and further, that this requires an autonomous discourse governed by indigenous rules of inquiry. This is a supposition making sense of the omnidirectional methodological battles marking the history of the discipline: the critiques of common sense and scientism, value commitment and objectivity, intuitionism and positivism, subjectivism and objectivism, philosophical idealism and materialism, historical explanation and homological explanation, and all kinds of reductionism. In this case it would be a betrayal

THE WORK OF SOCIOLOGICAL THEORY

from other factual genres like newspaper stories, administrative memo-randums, and government reports.

Since the analytic focus of the present study is on the work of individual theorists rather than the discipline as a whole, we will be directly concerned with style rather than genre, even though the latter is an indispensable framing concept. However, style and genre are analyt-ically alike in that both focus attention on how semantic materials are organized and transformed rather than on their abstractable and ex-tractable content. Stated in loosely Foucaultian terms (especially Foucault, 1972), the search for style, like genre, points toward an account of rules governing the deployment of words in concepts and statements: the regulation of their introduction, elaboration, transfor-mation, withdrawal, combination, separation, and so on, such that a definite compositional identity is created. The distinction between style and genre is, then, a difference between levels of analysis, not between substantive entities. Style refers to individual ways of deploying words. Since no author can be an island, however, a textual area will display shared literary methods in definite clusters which can be called genres. In the case studies we will seek stylistic companies of texts to move from one level to the other.

Within the second level it is necessary to distinguish between lower-order and higher-order genres; as, say, between the detective story and the novel, or between a Weberian form of theorizing and sociological writing. For our purpose, the latter serves as an analytic outer limit, a generic frame with regulatory significance, within which lower-order formations can be critically compared. This is illustrated in the conclu-sion of my study. The critical position taken there is close to that outlined by Ronald Dworkin with respect to purely literary criticism: "An interpretation of a piece of literature attempts to show which way of reading . . . the text reveals it as the best work of art. . . . Interpreta-tion of a text attempts to show *it* as the best work of art *it* can be, and the pronoun insists on the difference between explaining a work of art and changing it into a different one" (Dworkin, 1982:183).

Informing sociological writing too is a constitutive ideal making possible immanently grounded critique: not art, but truth to social life. The identification of compositional methods in styles and genres of theory writing points irresistably toward the critical question of what interpretation of a given text reveals what is the best the text can be in terms of the constitutive ideal of this kind of writing.

2   Strategies for
Studying Style

I want to conceptualize style as a compositional activity. To begin, let us separate it from two other and more common meanings, both of which appear in Nisbet's treatise: style as a taxonomic category and style as typical thematic content.

The former usage is illustrated in a passage close to the distinction I am trying to establish: "It should be observed that the artist's concept of 'styles' is also appropriate to our understanding of this history of philosophy and science. I refer here not so much to the 'style' of the individual artist or scientist but rather to those patterns or configurations of intellectual and artistic activity which we are able to see successively manifesting themselves in the history of a given discipline" (Nisbet, 1976:28).

The second sentence adequately defines the taxonomic meaning of style and I would add only two minor qualifications for the sake of clarity. First, particular stylistic configurations, such as baroque art, are not simply self-manifesting patterns we are able to see. Rather they are observers' categories through which work is selectively reconstructed and made manifest. They are generic concepts with which we are able to see. Second, with reference to the first sentence, the taxonomic concept of style appropriate for historical reconstruction is not a practitioner's concept. I set it aside here because my concern is with doing sociology more adequately, not with writing a history or an overview of the discipline.

The thematic concept of style appears in a passage that attempts to escape the static connotations of classificatory analysis: "At the center of any given style lies what can only be called a theme, or a cluster of themes. Theme carries with it a more active, positive, and dynamic character than does the word style. Implicit in any theme is at once a question being answered, more or less, and also an ordering of experience and observation in a special focus" (Nisbet, 1976:31). I share the intent to analyze style dynamically but do not believe that it can be achieved through a thematic focus. It is the way thematic materials are worked up and upon that constitutes stylistic activity. The analytic fault both of thematic and taxonomic treatments of style is that they deflect attention from the real, situated, existence of the phenomenon.

THE WORK OF SOCIOLOGICAL THEORY

Robert Jones, in the context of a polemic against "presentist" (mis)readings of past texts, echoes a dictum attributed to John Dunn, which I would also endorse: "If we wish to make true statements about Durkheim's thought, we must first grant it status as a real activity" (Jones, 1977:289). Application of the dictum, however, requires that a certain kind of "real activity" be specified. Jones takes it to mean the activity of authorial engagement with ideas, debates, and the intellectual coinage of his writing situation. The strategic key to interpretation here is recovery of what the author could have intended. (For critical elaboration, see Seidman, 1983:79–93.)

Along comparable lines, Michael Overington (1981) has proposed reading classic texts as rhetorical activities. The key to interpretation in this case consists of identifying attempts at persuasion aimed at authorially significant audiences within a certain structure of communicative possibilities and limitations. Again, analysis centers around authorial consciousness and an original writing context.

For me, the real activity in which "Durkheim's thought" is grounded consists of textually propelled and constrained reading experiences, where the text is construed as an enactment of sociological theorizing rather than of authorial consciousness or rhetorical strategy. Thus, I would not ask, What did Durkheim intend, and why? but What reading experiences do these words elicit, and how? The proposal to treat sociological theory as a particular form of literary work makes the stylistic *how* of writing—what the work is doing in the course of composing descriptive and expository content—crucial instead of marginal.

Style and Content

Stanley Fish (1980:21–67) has argued the merits of an interpretive shift from *what* to *how* analysis in literary criticism and has provided a "magic question" through which to accomplish it:

> The concept [of the method] is simply the rigorous and disinterested asking of the question, what does this word, sentence, paragraph, chapter, novel, play, poem, *do*? And the execution involves an analysis of the developing responses of the reader in relation to the words as they succeed one another in time. . . . The category of response includes any and all of the activities provoked by a string of words: the projection of syntactical and/or lexical probabilities; their subsequent occurrence or nonoccurrence; attitudes toward persons, or things, or ideas referred to; the reversal or questioning of those attitudes; and much more. (Fish, 1980:26–27)

For example, Milton's twentieth sonnet, after twelve straightforward lines in which a Roman youth is invited to eat, drink, and be merry on a sullen winter's day, closes with a troubling couplet:

> He who of those delights can judge, and spare
> To interpose them oft, is not unwise.

The trouble lies in the ambivalence of the word "spare" between often making time for pleasure and only doing so sparingly. Content-oriented readers, supposing that the correct meaning (and thus the intended judgment of pleasurable pastimes) is lodged in the text, have undertaken rigorous internal and contextual semantic investigations, involving reviews of Latin as well as English syntactic conventions. (For a full discussion, see Fish, 1980:149–52.) The balance of scholarly opinion has trembled toward the restraint interpretation, but Fish's argument is that the entire quest for a decision is misguided because it ignores, indeed methodologically obliterates, the actual locus of meaning in the reading experience. What the sequence of words does is draw the reader into a judgmental attitude ("he who of those delights can judge") which is frustrated by the textual indeterminacy of the judgment itself. Instead of being able to assent or dissent with a stable opinion, the reader experiences an unstable oscillation that defies objective fixity. The couplet's last two words, "not unwise," compound the experienced frustration of a normal desire to settle ethical questions by appeals to moral formulas. It is in such experiences, in the structure of the reading act rather than in the objectively conceived language structures of the poem itself, that meaning is located. The latter are significant only in the context of the former.

With respect to our methodological concerns, Fish's strategy enjoins an active and processual against a formal and structural concept of style. The latter, referred to polemically as stylistics, has been the target of a sustained critique. (Fish, 1980:68–96 and 246–67.) Stylists identify formal features of texts through statistical-grammatical processing techniques. The fatal flaw of the method, according to Fish, is that the extracted structures are hermeneutically empty. Consequently the graphs, tables, diagrams, and charts must have interpretive significance read into them. This interpolation gives rise to redundant "discoveries" of prior interpretive opinions, circular paraphrases in technical terms, and arbitrary, farfetched linkages of formal structure to substantive meaning.

As an example, Fish cites Louis Milic's conclusion, based on the numerical frequency of grammatical classes of words in Jonathan

Swift's writings, that "the low frequency of initial determiners, taken together with the high frequency of initial connectives, makes [Swift] a writer who likes transitions and made much of connectives" (quoted in Fish, 1980:71). In another conclusion, circularity gives way to arbitrary linkage when Milic interprets Swift's habit of piling up words in series as evidence of a fertile, well-stocked mind.

Similarly, with regard to Richard Ohmann's use of transformational grammar to specify Faulkner's style, Fish, though admitting the superiority of grammatical to statistical techniques for "fingerprinting an author," argues again that there is no way of making nontrivial interpretive inferences from revealed formal structures. It may be true that Faulkner's prose relies distinctively on three related grammatical transformations, but to call this the basis of his style makes unwarranted assumptions about their connection with authorial purpose, semantic values, and reading effects.

Critical considerations of the above kind are sufficient to cast strong doubt on the fruitfulness of the formalist strategy, and I will avoid it. This does not mean, however, that I will be thrown back into a thematic, content-dominated analysis. One virtue of Fish's "affective stylistics" is that it breaks open the dichotomous form-content classification of possible methods and provides a third direction to go in. When, therefore, Jules Prown, in an important article on cultural fingerprinting in material artifacts, asserts: "The way in which something is done, produced, or expressed is its style. Style is manifested in the form of things rather than in content" (Prown, 1980:200), we can nod agreement to the first sentence but hesitate at the second. Following Fish's lead (and thinking now specifically of literary artifacts), I can say that style does not exist either in form or content but in reading experiences and response patterns—in a produced styling of reading responses. If reader-registered patterns are projected back onto a text (as its style) or an author (his style), these are to be understood as secondary attributions and not confused with the place where style manifestly exists, which is to say, where styling of response takes place: in the person who reads.

Style as Personal Composition

Depersonalized concepts of reader-writers as nothing but constructed objects, enactors of collective patterns, and extensions of interpretive communities, or more exotically, the idea of authorless texts, are to be considered as cognitive conceits invaluable for suspending individualistic preconceptions, but not as descriptive truths. It needs to be stressed, developing a theme from my earlier discussion of the uses of classical theory, that sociological theory, considered in its own right, is a literary genre which indispensably demands the adoption of a personalized reading relationship. One cannot read a text as pure sociological theory except within a personalized reading attitude. As soon as that attitude is abandoned, a text will start turning into something else, say an instruction manual, a research theory, or a science monograph. Anonymization is incompatible with the constitution of the genre. This is evidenced in the stubborn centering of interpretation around individual names (a practice vainly satirized in references to the Weber industry, Durkheim Inc., Habermas Ltd., and the like). Even joint authorship is generically rare and is adjusted for when it occurs. The joint texts of Marx and Engels, for example, are read as if exclusively by Marx. Team writing is as inconsistent with the genre of sociological theory as it is with the novel.

Previously I cited descriptions of the personalized reading attitude as dialogues between live readers and dead authors, or conversations with past yet somehow present colleagues, but rejected them as too fanciful to grasp the phenomenon. This obliges me to provide a more adequate account.

A beginning appears in Berel Lang's critique of instrumental concepts of style on behalf of what he calls a transitive concept (Lang, 1978). In effect, this means abandoning the notion of style as formative additions to a substantive core, external accretions around an inner meaning, or a unilateral modification of materials given separately and in advance. Instead there is an integral styling process moving between the modalities of *what* and *how,* with no separate core of content:

> The transitive model of style is shaped, then, by the premise that the categories or predicates of style are not auxiliary or accidental features of an otherwise integral object but rather—transitively— precisely those features which determine that integrity for the object or work of art; there is no space between those features and the object or process itself, no internal spirit or power of which style is then a mere instrument. (Lang, 1978:725)

To move beyond these merely programmatic contrasts, we must take up the linked notions of personal style and the integrity of the object in the context of seeking the generic features of sociological theory.

Although style is carried in observation units as various as brush strokes, commas, chords, and teapots, there is a basic unit common to all stylistic analysis: "The least unit of style, like the least unit of ex-

THE WORK OF SOCIOLOGICAL THEORY

pression, is not any single figure of speech or gesture or statement or emotion (however small or large), but a concept of the person—without whom none of the other expressive designations, whatever their scope, would be intelligible" (Lang, 1978:726). We need to be clear regarding the epistemological status of a concept of the person in stylistic analysis. I take it to be a constitutive concept indispensable for that immediate recognition of stylistic identity which underlies interpretive analysis. Extending the thought, the concept of person has the same a priori status in understanding social theory that Simmel claims for it in studying history (1977).

For Simmel, following Kant, knowledge of anything is a synthetic apperception of unity in multiplicity based upon formative capacities of thought. Knowledge of all kinds is made possible by the synthetic activities of a priori constitutive categories. Simmel modifies Kant's stern adherence to a single, natural science model of knowledge, as well as abandoning his purely transcendental view of the categories, by positing distinct forms of knowledge based on variations in (*a*) the materials given for apperception, (*b*) the dynamics of the synthetic function, and (*c*) the kinds of constitutive concepts involved. The latter are specified to actual knowledge projects and have therefore only a quasi-transcendental status.

Historical knowledge, Simmel argues, is founded to a unique degree on the same conceptual presuppositions through which we synthesize social knowledge in everyday life. Fundamental to both is the projection of integral identity ahead of words and actions so that the latter are, to use a semiotic phrase, encountered as indexical expressions of the former. Not that integral identity is always confirmed in the event, but it is always projected before, and perhaps in spite of, events as a condition of knowledge. Simmel says of the production of historical knowledge objects:

> The existence of personal and group identity is an a priori presupposition of all historical research. In the case of the individual person, this presupposition entails that his actions and ideas seem to be produced by a single, integral self, an entity that varies only as a result of organic changes. Such an entity amounts to a mere unknown; nothing further can be said about it. Therefore to say that a person has an identity is to say that his ideas are susceptible to mutual explanation and derivation. (Simmel, 1977:58)

It is precisely in this sense, I would say, that the reading of words as pure sociological theory presupposes personal identity. Reading in this way is undertaken by a person within the attitude that the words signify an integral vision of social life formed by another person. This is the interpretant through which a unity of ideas is recognized. Of course as we saw earlier in comparing Smelser's "formal" reading of the classics with Warner's collegial reading (Warner and Smelser, 1976), there is another way of synthesizing the words. With Smelser, the interpretant changes from a presupposed person to a presupposed structure of reality, but then scientific research theory rather than autonomous social theory is read: unity of consciousness rather than unity of nature is the presupposition of the latter.

In Lang's account of stylistic recognition, as in Simmel's account of historical knowledge, the presupposition of identity in the interpreting subject passes over into the interpreted object as its principle of unity. Hence the term transitive in Lang's model. Again, it must be emphasized that the identity posited is open, indeterminate, and projected, not biographical and historical. Only so could there be an integration of oncoming contingent signifiers into an emergent meaning. Having accepted the principle, however, we must recall that our interest lies in characterizing actual styles rather than accounting for the possibility of stylistic recognition as such. Accordingly, we need concepts for gearing down to the empirical level.

A promising lead appears in Lang's observation that the signature of style is "distinctive consistency," involving a "protocol of repetition." This is not to be understood as the repetition of themes, motifs, and the like, so much as the recurrence of compositional principles:

> Consistency . . . involves the concept of stylistic transformation: the movement by the artist from the solution of one artistic "problem" (e.g. the rendering of an arm) to the address of another (e.g. the rendering of facial features). It is not, in such cases, that the specific results of the transformation can be predicted beforehand . . . but that retrospectively, as the viewer of a new artistic "event" reconciles his expectations with the present, a consistency is evident which reflects a common generative principle. (Lang, 1978:726–27)

An artist's, or a theorist's, work might be seen then as a record of how a person successively generated and solved compositional problems in a material medium (much as Gregory Bateson [1979:13] views a conch shell as a snail's record of successive solutions to a formal problem in pattern creation). Of course where linguistic materials are concerned, their physical aspect is of minor importance. The compositional problems set by written symbols arise primarily from compositional conventions: that is to say, the rules of local language games. For example, the suitability of a line to end a sonnet involves the sonic rhythm of candidate words, but this material feature does not itself form compositional problems in the strong sense that, say, the physical properties of marble do for a sculptor or concrete for an architect. Thus we understand the compositional problems and solutions in which the style of a theorist can be recognized as records of an encounter within (and against) generic conventions of writing social theory.

In order to confirm and sharpen the idea of style as person we will consider illustrations of what might be called transitive stylistics.

Examples of Person-in-Style Analysis

We will look at three examples: Norman Holland on Robert Frost, various authors on Nietzsche, and Charles Cooley on Herbert Spencer. In each case we seek instruction, positive or negative, for the guidance of our own project.

1. Holland's (1984) characterization of Frost allows me to specify two prerequisites for all stylistic analysis and also to pinpoint three kinds of evidence in which style can be detected.

Frost is a doubly appropriate subject (and object) of stylistic inquiry for Holland. First, Holland has through prolonged study worked himself into Frost's work. Second, he can rely upon familiarity with Frost in his anticipated reader. These are analytic prerequisites because transitive stylistics (and this is a point implied but not properly brought out by Lang) is at least a three-way process. Here I endorse Charles Peirce's principle that meaning is irreducibly triadic: "I define a Sign as anything which is so determined by something else, called its Object, and so determines an effect upon a person, which effect I call its Interpretant, that the latter is thereby mediately determined by the former" (Peirce, 1966:404). Holland represents effects upon himself of written artifacts grasped as determinations of an object (Frost's identity): "Frost's identity is a function of my identity. A unique me uses shared codes of interpretation and language to arrive at a theme and variations identity for Frost. Therefore I want to . . . include in my definition of identity the *language* one subject, me, uses to represent another subject, Frost" (Holland, 1984:380).

Holland is not actually interpreting as a completely singular person but as a member of English-language and literary communities of convention. It needs to be added that in order for his words to be realized as stylistic analysis, they in turn must produce interpretant effects in another reader. Stylistic analysis draws at least four elements into a transitive network: artifact, artificer, interpreter, and an interpretant reader of that triad. This point is not made to invite regressive dizziness but to underline the open-endedly involving nature of cultural artifacts: a feature absolutely essential to the status of sociological theory as a real-world activity in its own right.

Regarding evidence, Robert Frost not only created poems but left interpretations of other's creations, thus allowing himself to be characterized in how he read poetry as well as wrote it. Within any observed set of composition practices, it is possible to isolate interpretive from creative transformation as a distinct activity providing separate evidence of stylistic identity. Such activity will have a special compositional importance in sociological theory because it is a genre that rests upon cumulative reappraisal of others' work.

A third source of evidence drawn upon by Holland consists of the kinds of linguistic materials that Frost typically selected for compositional transformation: those with which he displayed an elective affinity. Again, this is a subset of compositional practices worth isolating because it promises extra observational purchase on stylistic identity. Holland's analysis illustrates the promise, even though it is weakened by its drift towards a thematic instead of performative specification of style.

Frost's poetic identity includes a reiterative tracing of cosmic themes in homely details. Crucial here is the kind of detail, the semantic materials, that Frost elected to transform: "He used the language and materials of small New England farms to grasp the largest issues human beings can face. That is, he used folksy language to talk about big themes, small knowns to manage big unknowns" (Holland, 1984:367). Frost's preoccupation with finding limited things snugly at home in the limitless, his pleasure when "something small succeeds in holding something larger to a point of balance," extends into his reading style (Holland, 1984:369). In reading Edwin Arlington Robinson's "Miniver Cheevy," Frost records that the magical, "intolerable" touch of poetry came to him in the seventh stanza:

> Miniver scorned the gold he sought
> But sore annoyed was he without it:
> Miniver thought, and thought, and thought,
> And thought about it.

The key for him is the surprise encounter with yet another "thought"

THE WORK OF SOCIOLOGICAL THEORY

on rounding the corner of the third line. As if the line might, yet does not, go on forever. The conventional limits of the stanza are exploited by the extra repetition to evoke limitless possibility.

In the same way, Frost finds the beauty of Robinson's "Mr. Flood's Party" in the fact that when the drunken Mr. Flood pours out his sorrow in singing "Auld Lang Syne" on a hilltop at night, there are two moons listening (as on Mars). One moon would have made the grief too stark, more than two would have dispersed it. A perfect sympathy of response is held in that small detail.

The methodologically useful point I would retain here is that a certain protocol of repetition can be found in how Frost read, how he wrote, and in his choice of materials. In such a protocol, style is made evident.

2. Nietzsche has long been an object of interest for those fascinated by the twilight zone between philosophy and literature. In the 1930s, Kenneth Burke, writing of the dialectical interplay of pious conservation and impious shattering in art, science, and social life, observed a "Nietzschean method" in the poetic madness of his later style: "Nietzsche establishes his perspectives by a constant juxtaposition of incongruous words, attaching to some name a qualifying epithet which had heretofore gone with a different order of names" (Burke, 1954:90).

Given that piety is a traditional sense of what properly belongs with what, it may be said that disruptive reconnections of words (as in startling new metaphors) are impious communicative acts. In Nietzsche's case, Burke discerns a protocol of repetition that justifies speaking of a method or style of disruptive incongruity. Although Burke does not pursue the matter, the same style might be seen in Nietzsche's reading preferences. Some of these are given in a discarded draft for a section of the essay "Why I Am So Clever" (Nietzsche, 1967b:339–40). He praises Emerson for his liberating skepsis, Sterne for the anarchic humor of *Tristram Shandy,* and most of all, Petronius for his freedom from conventional morality and his readiness to leap "with grace and malice" across normal limits of linguistic good taste: mixing educated with vulgar Latin, prose with poetry, philosophy with earthiness.

What Burke calls the Nietzschean method has proved difficult to preserve within the interpretive conventions—the reading methods—of professional philosophy. There, as Allison has observed, the disciplinary concern to systematize ethical, epistemological, and ontological arguments has led interpreters "to modify if not sacrifice what they consider to be the stylistic excess of his writing" (Allison, 1982:199).

Elsewhere, Allison criticizes the exclusionary preoccupation of professional philosophy with discursive content in terms I have already used against sociology. Still speaking of Nietzsche: "Nowhere, then, has the *style* of a philosopher's expression so forcefully reflected its content. What he says and how he says it are so much the same (Allison, 1977:xiii).

In philosophy as in social theory, there are writers such as Nietzsche whose stylistic excess makes for a certain awkwardness or indigestibility in their reception history that can be turned back upon the incorporative conventions of a discipline as a critique of adequacy. The classics of sociological theory can be shown to have this characteristic. It needs to be added, however, that for such a critique to be effective, it must persuade discipline members that present conventions are screening out meanings crucial for the intellectual interests of their discipline. Otherwise practitioners would be perfectly justified in saying, study it that way if you wish but literary style is none of our concern. In this respect, Allison issues what is for us a significant warning against becoming "lost in an exclusive, if not rhapsodic concern with style alone" (1982:199).

Certainly I do not wish to engage in a poetic rhapsodization of style in itself, nor to idolize any particular style. My intent is to valorize the stylistic dimension of theorizing and identify potentially fruitful ways of constructing theory that might otherwise pass unnoticed. I seek a supplementary and perhaps more appropriate procedure for analyzing the practice of theory than is provided by standard classifications based upon philosophical schools, root metaphors, and social movements (for example, Martindale's classification of theory into positivistic organicism, conflict theory, social Darwinism, neo-Kantian sociological formalism, humanistic holism, symbolic interactionism, and other categories [1981]).

3. Lang's concept of style as person is nicely illustrated in an essay on Herbert Spencer by Charles Cooley (1930:263–79). The essay is directly relevant to our goal in that Cooley suggests the existence of stylistic requirements for truthful writing about social life: requirements that Spencer, in his life-and-writing style, is said to lack. To grasp the criticism it is necessary to recall Cooley's premise that life grows in organic patterns and this should be reflected in scientific representations of life. The idea will be more fully considered in chapter 3. At this point it is sufficiently described in a passage from another essay, "Case Study of Small Institutions":

THE WORK OF SOCIOLOGICAL THEORY

It seems to me that this organic or behavioristic point of view involves some revision in our criteria of scientific knowledge. We are accustomed to think of scientific exactness as a matter of measurement in small units of time and space. But behavioristic knowledge is essentially organic, must exist in wholes or it does not exist at all. Even in the simplest forms it deals with conformations, patterns, systems, not with mechanical units. For this reason the phenomena of life are often better distinguished by pattern than by quantity. Those who are striving to make sociology an exact science might well give more attention to the method of pattern comparison. Starting, perhaps, from the use of finger prints to identify criminals, it might conceivably be carried, by the aid of photography and phonography into very subtle regions of behavior. Measurement is only one kind of precision. (Cooley, 1930:314)

The particular references to photography and phonography need not concern us, except to note from the suffix that they, like interpretive commentary, are forms of writing. Subsequently, in my analysis of Simmel, I will take up the notion that repeated adjectives attached to a body of work can be treated as imprints, or graphic impresses, of its style. Cooley's position is by no means idiosyncratic. It is, for example, close to that of Gregory Bateson (1972, 1979). His cybernetically derived account of life forms also asserts that because living patterns cannot properly be reduced to quantitative variables, truthful representation cannot be achieved in the standard way of exact measurement, linear connection, and causal modeling. Bateson's affinity to Cooley is clearly marked in his introduction to *Mind and Nature*. It dwells upon a division between "the world of the living (where *distinctions* are drawn and *difference* can be a cause) and the world of nonliving billiard balls and galaxies (where forces and impacts are the 'causes' of events)" (1979:7). The distinctive principle of living things is further expressed by Bateson as "the pattern that connects."

Since pattern connects all living things, including those who know them as such, it follows that transitivity is as much built into the study of life forms as, recalling Lang, the study of writing style. The life scientist too needs an aesthetic sensibility, where aesthetic means responsiveness to "the pattern that connects." Truthful inquiry into living things must be through mutual "recognition and empathy" because that is how they are constituted (Bateson, 1979:9).

For Cooley, it is precisely a lack of empathy that incapacitates Spencer and ruins his sociological writings. From Spencer's autobiography and other sources, a deficiency in those "sympathetic qualities," which alone give us direct knowledge of others, is observed. This is shown in a "lack of tact . . . accentuated by a somewhat censorious and unreconciliatory way of expressing himself" (Cooley, 1930:265). He addressed others in a unilateral manner, tending to read them lectures rather than to converse: "Spencer's disregard of personality is curiously illustrated by his essay on 'The Philosophy of Style.' In this he does not appear to be interested in the fact—if indeed he perceives it at all—that at least half of style is the communication of personal attitudes, and this by means so subtle as to defy the rather mechanical analysis which he employs" (Cooley, 1930:266).

Even Spencer's organic concept of society (which might in name seem congenial to Cooley's point of view) suffers from translation into lifeless, mechanistic formulas. It is not that Spencer is unable to see patterns; on the contrary, he sees them everywhere and in every detail of existence. The trouble is that they are impersonally derived and externally imposed on life, rather than empathically perceived through connective participation in it. In "society," for example, he can see nothing but egoistic striving, willing, and seeking in a framework of biological imperatives. Spencer's blindness to style as personal communication is duplicated in a characteristic blindness to social life:

> Spencer . . . has little perception of a *social* organism continuous with the past. His organism, so far as he has one, is biological in its process, transmitted to the individual by the direct inheritance of mental states created by use . . . the individuals thus generated unite into a differentiated and co-ordinated society, but this is conceived almost as if it were continually reproduced from biological roots, like the annual foliage of a perennial herb. (Cooley, 1930:273)

> Human life is perceived not directly but through mechanical analogies. The higher and more distinctively human part of it is hardly perceived at all. (Cooley 1930:275)

> This lack of insight into other minds, whether in face-to-face intercourse or through works of literature and art, was nothing less than a lack of the perceptions indispensable to any direct study of social phenomena. (Cooley 1930:267)

Spencer can think cosmic patterns and subordinate social life to them, but he cannot directly perceive the patterns that are social life itself. His personal disconnection from others means that he lacks what Lang calls the least unit of style and expression—the concept of personal identity—and therefore the capacity to synthesize social knowledge objects through transitive identification with actions, works of art, and so on.

As a methodological corrective to what might seem an overly personalized approach, I should stress Cooley's observation that as much as half of style is something other than the communication of personal attitudes. He does not say what the other half of style might be, but for my purpose—a literary analysis of sociological writing—it is an essential question. Provisionally it can be said to consist of a characteristic record of how a text, or body of texts, has resolved problems of literary composition in sociological theory—understanding that these are not simply set in advance, like an examination paper, but take shape as instigative, reactive, and emergent problems within a textual process. It should be added that if a realized text is a transitive reader-writer phenomenon, the problems may be construed doubly as those of reader response and authorial creation. I make no strong distinction between the two.

Finally, it must be emphasized that the problems in question are not individual difficulties contingently experienced by particular readers, but are constitutive features of a genre of writing. Such problems cannot therefore be revealed by empirical studies of readers, only by literary and semiotic analyses of texts. Performative problems are to be conceived as formative and defining elements of sociological theory.

The governing problem of every work of sociological theory, within which performative problems emerge, is to produce truth and knowledge effects in the course of a generically appropriate treatment of generically appropriate materials. The materials include discipline disputes, current typologies, scholarly terminologies, relevant intertexts, social issues, and ideological vocabularies. However, the same elements can appear also as means of appropriating materials and as contexts of composition. Where linguistic materials are being worked upon within linguistic structures, distinctions between materials, means, and contexts of composition can only refer to shifts of analytic standpoint.

As a basis for appreciating the performative problems and compositional structure of works of theory, we need a stronger specification of the structure and dynamics of theory writing than has so far been achieved. To this end, chapter 3 develops a concept of theory writing as text work.

3   The Concept of Text Work

The analytic challenge I wish to confront here is how to conceptualize a text in such a way that a question like What is it about? will be heard as a request for the dynamics of a compositional process, not for a summary of thematic content. It is helpful (cf. Bloom et al., 1979:1) to recall the physical meaning of "about" as on the outside of something. We are led then to think of the something that a given text, or genre, forms around, and to think of this as an active process. We ask, What is this text, or genre, formed about? in the sense that an astronomer might ask for the inner stresses, parameters, pushes, and pulls that give a definite structure to the ice rings of Jupiter and are the something actively informing it. The same sense appears colloquially when a person's actions are addressed by the question What was that about? In those cases, however, the request is for motives, beliefs, and inner springs of conduct, whereas I seek the inner necessities of a certain form of writing (sociological theory) and generic and stylistic variations of them. A text is to be conceived as a dynamic structure of signification rather than as a container of subjective content.

For conceptual aid I return to Charles Cooley, one of the very few sociologists to have seen that the truthfulness of writing about society is not exhausted by the logical and empirical validity of its propositions, but depends also upon its style.

Tentative Process and Text Work

Robert Cooley Angell has drawn attention to the isomorphy asserted by Cooley between social life, methods of social inquiry, and sociological writing. The key idea is that since the life process of individuals, groups, social movements, institutions, and all social entities is characterized by a "tentative method of growth" rather than the realization of rational will and prior plan, methods of recording and representing it should have the same character:

> Cooley was so persuaded of the virtues of the tentative process that he applied it to his own habits of thinking and writing. He did not believe in creating a sociological system. He felt that spontaneity of insight was the main thing and that those who developed a system were tempted to fill it out with uninspired observation and analy-

sis. A serious work should have a natural structure which the reader can discover if and when he pleases. It is good to display a subject with unity enough to make it intelligible, and yet not without an alluring unfinality! (Reiss, 1968:9)

The tentative method is most fully described in the first chapter of *Social Process* (1918). Given that Cooley typically worked close to home, drawing upon personal and domestic experiences, it is not surprising that he found the ideal image of the method in his own backyard: a wild grapevine growing along a fence.

> This vine has received from its ancestry a certain system of tendencies. There is, for example, the vital impulse itself, the general bent to grow. Then there is its habit of sending out straight rapidly growing shoots with two-branched tendrils at the end. These tendrils revolve slowly through the air, and when one touches an obstacle, as a wire or branch, it hooks itself about it and draws up in the form of a spiral spring, pulling the shoot up after it. A shoot which thus gets a hold grows rapidly and sends out more tendrils; if it fails to get a hold it by and by sags down and ceases to grow. Thus it feels its way and has a system of behavior that insures its growth along the line of successful experiment. (Cooley, 1918:8–9)

Is it too far-fetched to suppose that a text is like this? That syntagmatic chains, propelled by a system of tendencies, turn around themes, issues, topics, and resistances to form a system of meaning? Cooley would probably not have thought it was. His examples include stories, natural languages, and book writing:

> One may sometimes discover in his own mind the working of complex tendencies which he has not willed or understood. When one first plans a book he feels but vaguely what material he wants, and collects notes somewhat at random. But as he goes on, if his mind has some synthetic energy, his thought gradually takes on a system, complex yet unified, having a growth of its own, so that every suggestion in this department comes to have a definite bearing upon some one of the many points at which his mind is striving to develop. Every one who has been through anything of this sort knows that the process is largely unintentional and unconscious, and that, as many authors have testified, the growing organism frequently develops with greatest vigor in unforeseen directions. (Cooley, 1918:15–16)

The unifying concept through which Cooley draws together natural, social, and linguistic forms of life is that of "working." His specification of it is sufficiently precise that one might refer to a Cooleyan process of text work.

The general process includes three elements:

1. That which is latently ready to work (as grape must, for example, is ready to work when yeast is introduced). Cooley calls this "an antecedent system of tendencies."

2. Stimulants, initiations, or incitements to working (which include, importantly, obstacles and barriers to extension). They might be referred to collectively as tensing elements. Cooley's less obvious examples include a glance, a word, the quality of a voice, a poetic passage in a book, and a striking metaphor.

3. An emergent organization of latent tendencies and tensing elements, forming a system of activities.

With textual analysis in mind, there are two crucial features of all such systems: their deceptive appearance of planned design and the illusion they convey of having a center. From this position it is not far to the contemporary semiotic notion of the autonomous text striving vainly, (in modern parlance, deconstructively), to anchor itself in objective meaning.

In the first three chapters of *Social Process,* Cooley undertakes a critical dissolution of our cultural confidence in the dominant role of intended design in social life. The following passages (from chapter 2, "Organization") are typical:

> The social processes, though they result in a structure which seems rational, perhaps, when it is perceived, are for the most part not planned at all. Consciousness is at work in them, but seldom consciousness of anything more than some immediate object, some detail that contributes to the whole without the actor being aware of the fact. . . .
>
> We do not know when—for obscure reasons that even the psychologist can hardly detect—we use one word rather than another, or use an old word in a new sense, that we are participating in the growth of the language organism. (Cooley, 1918:21, 23)

Our interpretive habit of attributing pattern to the operation of prior design and conscious will belongs to a broader predisposition to see in a whole entity a single origin and central organizing principle. If Cooley is heard to be talking of texts and author-centered practices of interpretation, there are passages that will sound strangely familiar to readers of deconstructive literary analysis. (For examples, see Young,

THE WORK OF SOCIOLOGICAL THEORY

1981. A systematic exposition of the deconstruction project is attempted by Culler, 1982.)

Cooley dismisses all theories of history and social life that assign a privileged shaping function to some part of the whole: "The fallacy of all such ideas lies in supposing that life is built up from some one point, instead of being an organic whole which is developing as a whole. . . . Nothing is fixed or independent, everything is plastic and takes influence as well as gives it" (Cooley 1918:44). The lack of fixity applies even to origins: "there is no beginning; we know nothing about beginnings" (Cooley 1918:46). Similarly, deconstructive literary criticism regards any search for an originally present meaning in a text as a chimerical pursuit. Interpretation cannot, for example, be grounded on the meanings originally intended by a historical author, because the author is a changing internal function of interpretation, not a fixed external origin to which a text can be traced. In Cooley's terms, a text is an emergent organization of meanings within which nothing is fixed and where origin is absent.

Let me say, by way of summary, that the force of Cooley's model is to withhold interpretive efficacy from authorial will, design, consciousness, and intent. A worrisome possibility that follows is the opening of an interpretive vacuum that would cast critical judgment into a void. If a text has no original or objective meaning against which to hold interpretations, if "everything is plastic" and a text is nothing but what is made of it by an interpretation, then how can interpretations (or texts) be judged as better or worse, richer or poorer? Is it a case of every sovereign reader for himself in a state of radical pluralism bordering on critical nihilism? Some such concern seems to have prompted the attack of Foucault (1973: appendix) on his former student Derrida, the citational "founder" of deconstructionism, for reducing a text to nothing but the "traces" of its textuality upon a reader. Foucault, marking a position close to that established in my introduction via the thesis of linguistic reality construction, locates texts in power-knowledge networks that pass in and out of writing: networks that have an institutional, historical, and somatic, as well as semiotic, reality. (For a strong contrast between Foucault and Derrida along these lines, see Said, 1978.)

From the viewpoint of a desire to evaluate theory as writing, Foucault's virtue is to gear writing into the world (specifically, the political-administrative world), thus allowing something more for commentary, of which sociological theory entirely consists, than an indefinite Derridaian process of textual redoubling, where words are placed at one remove from previous words in an empty endeavor to catch their truth, real meaning, or other transcendent content. If, following Foucault, texts enter social life as conductors, mediators, exchange points, and relays between power and knowledge, normative evaluation could examine texts in terms of their political complicity.

I have argued elsewhere (Green, 1983, chap. 6) that Foucault provides a link between textual analysis and neo-Marxian critiques of self-alienation in society. Whereas, however, neo-Marxians talk macroscopically of capture in false consciousness, distorted communication, cultural hegemony, and instrumental reason, Foucault has preferred to focus on local practices of objectification (testing, diagnosing, classifying, reporting, recording, and the like) through which embodied subjects are made into something docile and useful. Theory writing is reasonably open to evaluation in terms of its implications for promoting or resisting such practices.

To this it should be added, as a point for later consideration, that there is more to social life (and so to the demands upon social theory) than the "political" dimension of capture and emancipation. Its quality includes broadly aesthetic assessments of coherence, pattern, meaning, and stimulation, the ritual and recreational aspects of life, that have more to do with what is called interpretive than with critical theory. (For a preliminary attempt to work out the literary demands of interpretive theory as a distinct form of sociology, see Green, 1977.)

I accept that the introduction of extratextual considerations is ultimately indispensable for making evaluative judgments of theory, yet too fast a move in that direction would leave behind my analytic, I might say technical, interest in literary composition methods, threatening a degeneration into nothing but normative exposition. To obtain an analytic hold on texts, it is vital to postpone extratextual considerations as long as possible. I must focus upon them initially in an attitude of severe inwardness, as if there were nothing outside the text. Edward Said has taken this to be the value (a heuristic one) of Derrida's denial that there is anything other than textuality in texts: "Derrida wants us to see—if not to understand—that so long as we believe that language is mainly a representation of something else, we cannot see what language *does*" (Said, 1978:689; italics in original). The attitude of severe inwardness means that any search for methods of composition, by which is meant discernible rulings or constraints of word use, must be conducted as a search for limitations internal to a text or body of texts. Cooley's model specifies two possible kinds of inner limitation: obstacles or difficulties to an emergent organization of meaning and an antecedent system of tendencies.

Suggestions as to what the former might be in a reading can be drawn from an argument by Nehamas that interpretation, by its nature, places limits on the meanings that can be accountably attributed to a text; in short, interpretation need not, indeed cannot, be radically indeterminate (Nehamas, 1981).

Tensing Elements in Text Work

Internal Limits to Organizations of Meaning

Modern reflections on knowledge have relativized all, even scientific, perceptions of "what there is" to theoretical-linguistic-methodological standpoints. Literary interpretation is no exception; indeed it has suffered (and prospered) greatly from relativity and its discontents. Thus Nehamas reports that Kafka's *Metamorphosis* has generated at least 148 different interpretations, with no end in sight (making the story title singularly apt for the topic).

The fate of Kafka's text illustrates the universal fate of writing described so poignantly by Derrida:

> It must continue to "act" and to be legible even if what is called the author of the writing no longer answers for what he has written, for what he seems to have signed. . . . This essential drifting, due to writing as an iterative structure cut off from all absolute responsibility, from consciousness as the authority of the last analysis, writing orphaned, and separated at birth from the assistance of its father, is indeed what Plato condemned in the *Phaedrus*. (Derrida, 1982:316)

What is there to hold and organize the exegetical growth of a text if the real author (his meaning) is irretrievably absent? According to Nehamas, it is a postulated author, a provisionally hypothesized agent to whose actions a text may be completely attributed; an ideally conceived agent "who may not coincide with the actual writer's self-understanding, fragmentary and incomplete as it probably is" (Nehamas, 1981: 147), but is bound by the principle of historical plausibility. That is, the meanings attributed to the text must have been possible ones for the actual writer. It is in this binding, which amounts to evidential checks on interpretive hypotheses, that counterparts to Cooleyan tensing elements can be detected. At one level, that of history, biography, philology, social anthropology, and so on, there are circumstantial limitations on what the author could have meant. For example, it has been said that the hours on Gregor's clock in *The Metamorphosis* correspond to years in Freud's theory of ego development, but to sustain that reading it would have to be shown that Kafka could have known the theory. However, our interest is not in externally conceived limits on what an author could have intended, but in internal limits on what a text can become. Nehamas's discussion suggests three possibilities: (1) conventions of language, giving a normal content; (2) generic conventions of a type of composition; and (3) textual details. I wish to postpone discussion of generic conventions for a while and will begin by considering the other two.

The idea that there is a subinterpretational bedrock of meanings, given to members of a language community in obvious, normal, "first" readings (which are always being returned to), is exemplified by the argument of Meiland (1978) that there are basic, agreed-upon "textual meanings" which place negative limits on the validity of interpretive claims. They can rule out, but not rule in, claimed "literary meanings."

Given this entirely negative view of the role of language conventions, it is hardly surprising that Nehamas finds them too weak to discriminate between conflicting interpretations and looks instead to textual details. Even a cursory consideration of his own examples reveals, however, that the choice is artificial, because textual details capable of checking interpretive claims can be given by nothing but the language in which the text is read—read, that is to say, obviously, normally, and the first time through.

Returning to the metamorphosis of Gregor into a giant cockroach, Nehamas states that a psychoanalytic interpretation of the father kicking the monstrosity when it gets stuck in a doorway, calling it an act of libidinal aggression, would run foul of a textual detail, namely, that the story itself requires the kicking to be Gregor's salvation.

An interpretive claim always has this general form: the meaning of X is Y. The point I would make is that the details entering the first space can come from nowhere but the words grasped through the conventions of a natural language community. The possibility of a text being an analyzable, interpretable, disputable object depends upon a resistant tension between the meaning of the identification terms entering the first space and the predicative terms entering the second. Since the latter derive from interpretive schemata of some kind, the former, to be really resistant, must come from a prior, subinterpretive level of language: one, at least, where interpretation is an implicit process rather than an explicit account applied to prior words. Such is the natural language community which grounds not simply particular interpretations but the possibility of interpretation as such.

The above amounts only to an amendment of Nehamas, showing how language conventions secure textual details as resistances in an emergent growth of interpretation. There is, however, another feature of his argument with which I must take stronger issue, because it forces me to a conceptual choice concerning the nature of text work. I refer to the monistic model of meaning served by the principle that everything in a text reflects authorial intention. Nehamas states that "monism of content" allows methodological pluralism to thrive constructively, and that "critical monism" must be accepted as a regulative ideal in order to compare the validity of interpretations. In one guise or another, this represents a mainstream position in literary criticism.

One might well challenge the adequacy of authorial intention to ground interpretation (as the next section of the chapter will show, I am unwilling to confine the antecedent tendencies propelling a text to just this one category), but the objection I want to make here is to the monistic ideal itself. My objection is that its regulative concept of a text as an already-constituted object waiting to be examined obscures the nature of interpretation as a projective, tentative process through which a text emerges.

At this point, as a counterpoise to monism, I would like to introduce a bipolar, dialectical model of interpretation developed by Paul Ricoeur (1976). It is congenial to the Cooleyan image of text work and offers a closer specification of its elements.

Ricoeur proceeds through a series of oppositions, of which the first pole is typically active and performative, while the second is objective and structural. In Cooleyan terms, everything like an antecedent system of tendencies would be at the first pole and everything like a tensing element at the second. I will emphasize the latter.

Ricoeur begins with a general dualism between discourse as event and discourse as meaning that applies both to speech and writing, then works through, via a series of subordinate oppositions, to a dialectic between understanding and explanation that is only made manifest when interpreting texts.

As event, discourse is situated and localized: someone's utterance to someone else in a context. As pure meaning, discourse is transsituational, transferable, translatable, and there for anyone who knows the language. The minimal unit for carrying meaning is a sentence. It consists of a predicate—a typical quality, quantity, relation, action—

attached to a singular identity term like a noun, pronoun, or proper name. The interplay of predication and identification in a sentence forms a propositional content. This may also be thought of as utterance meaning, in contrast with utterer's meaning.

An important point here is that utterer's meaning is not a psychic substance transported from one mind to another, but arises entirely through indexicals contained in the structure of sentences. Linguists call them "shifters." They include all kinds of open-ended terms through which propositions can be fastened to a situated subject: personal pronouns, adverbs of time and space, demonstrative adjectives. The importance of this for textual interpretation is that the inclusion of the subjective, intentional side of meaning requires no recourse to the psychology of the author: "The mental meaning can be found nowhere else than in discourse itself. The utterer's meaning has its mark in the utterance meaning . . . we are able to give a nonpsychological, because purely semantic, definition of the utterer's meaning. No mental entity need be hypothesized or hypostatized" (Ricoeur, 1976:13).

A psychologizing hermeneutic mistakes meaning for nothing but event. It is most plausible in spoken discourse, where meaning and event are closely merged, but its effect in literary analysis is to construe a text as nothing but transcribed speech, thus losing the particularity of writing. The detachment of meaning in writing, its exteriorization, escapes the grasp of interpretation oriented to the utterer. The problem persists in intentionalist revisions of psychologizing hermeneutics like that of Nehamas. He distinguishes the postulated author, which is a hypothesis, a "formal cause" read into the text as its necessary and sufficient agent, from the actual historical writer. In practice, however, given that the postulated author must be historically plausible to achieve interpretive efficacy, the distinction collapses and a psychologizing hermeneutic reenters.

In this situation it might be tempting to turn to an opposite hermeneutic, a semiotic analysis of propositional elements. Ricoeur, however, resists such a switch because it would reduce human discourse to combinatorial systems of signs, thus missing its communicative aspect and therefore its specificity. This is why Ricoeur insists that a science of semantics based upon the sentence must be distinguished from a science of semiotics based upon the sign. It is also why he advocates a dialectical hermeneutic: one responsive to the dual status of sentences as communicative events and linguistic objects. Monism must surrender to one or the other side of discourse, thus falsifying it.

Ricoeur traces the dialectic of event and meaning into texts. There the event aspect of discourse is expressed in interpretation, and the linguistic meaning or objective-sense aspect in explanation. When we are reading a text, interpretation is initiated by the irremediable absence of the utterer and the consequent necessity of guessing his meaning. Interpretation is, if we recall Cooley's imagery, a tentative reaching into a space that the original utterer, the author, cannot fill. Ricoeur regards this as a genuine substitution and not a recognition or recovery of what the author intended:

> The surpassing of the intention by the meaning signifies precisely that understanding takes place in a nonpsychological and properly semantical space, which the text has carved out by severing itself from the mental intention of its author. . . . The problem of understanding can no longer be solved by a simple return to the alleged situation of the author. The concept of guess has no other origin. (Ricoeur, 1976:76)

For clarity it should be noted that interpretation is regarded as a special case of understanding when applied to written signs. Here, explanation takes the form of checking and validating by scholarship and close reading. Normal practices of reading theory in sociology cluster fixedly around this pole: practices like extracting models, correlating arguments within and between texts, collating references to the same topic by the same and different authors, drawing out empirical implications, confronting data, mapping onto types of theory, and explicating the structure of a discursive field.

According to Ricoeur's model, full comprehension, or the realization of the full meaning value of written words, cannot be achieved except by a return movement from explanatory assessment to interpretive participation in the text. Arguably there are forms of writing where this is a trivial consideration, say science reports, but the entire force of the position taken in the present study is to deny that sociological theory can be one of them.

Writing has a paradoxical relation to the dialectic of full comprehension. On the one hand, by exteriorizing meaning it sets up the explanatory pole and allows for confinement there. On the other hand, by severing words from located usage, so that referencing is no longer anchored in situated pointing and showing, it renders immanently problematic the fixing of words to things. Complementing the problem of the lost author is the latent problem of the lost referent. This can be cultivated polemically to denounce referential theories of language and promote visions of unfettered word play. Ricoeur, however, prefers to stress its strategic value in making room for nonreferential explanations of the interior structure of texts, as in structuralist, poststructuralist, and formalist literary studies. The explanatory retreat from referential to semiological accounts has a dialectical value in that it shifts interpretive guessing onto a new ground, that of a deep semantic script underwriting textual details. From here a significant new question takes shape. If referential words do not represent external things standing next to language, then what in the world of the interpreter might they represent?

Ricoeur says that texts project or disclose possible worlds and ways of being in them, which entails virtual selves corresponding to possible worlds. I would add, in line with the main thesis of this study, that possibilities of social life are projected also in the styling of reading experiences, not just in verbal contents. If we think of sociology texts, it is not enough to identify projection with utopias, plans, or other images of the future, nor even with sense-making devices and cultural codes through which accounts of social life are accomplished. The status of a text as an exemplary event, an enactment of possibilities of language, must also be considered.

This injunction is based on the premise that since social life is linguistically constituted, its possibilities depend upon what language can provide for. Ricoeur's argument suggests that the constitutive power of language is especially marked in writing, because of its release from situated containment and subservience to the ostensive function of pointing and showing. I take this to be the meaning of his description of the non-ostensive function of language in writing, thanks to which discourse transcends what exists or is happening, so that "showing is at the same time creating a new mode of being" (Ricoeur, 1976:88). I would balk at the heroic substitution of "new" for "possible," but otherwise accept this as an attitude in which to ask what the literary methods in classical texts show us.

Reality and Representation

To fill out this sketch of tensing elements in text work, I will introduce some recent commentary on a seemingly esoteric problem in literary theory: how to salvage the ancient concept of mimesis from the ruins of classical, world → mind → word theories of representation. Mimesis is the simulation of something real: an imitative resemblance. To the extent, however, that reality is thought of as constituted in and by representation, ideas of imitative resemblance are confounded. So the problem of mimesis returns us to the question broached by

Ricoeur: What is being represented in realistic representations of reality?

Where writing is concerned the question gains maximum force in fictional literature (cf. Smith, 1978). But extensions of referential uncertainty to the writing of knowledge, a movement unraveled in exquisite detail by Rorty (1980), now make it pertinent to science, especially the science of social life, where the object of knowledge is so intensely entwined with language.

Within literary theory a kind of answer is gaining credence in a middle ground between the extremes of linguistic autonomy and objective reference that is interestingly similar to conceptual positions worked out by sociologists between collective nominalism (i.e., methodological individualism) and collective realism, and between voluntarism and determinism. Indeed the sociological literature is being directly cited, and there is a continuity of vocabulary evidenced in common paradigmatic appeals to games and performing arts. Lima (1985) and Prendergast (1985) offer convenient statements.

A prime case of literary mimesis is the realistic narrative novel. Prendergast uses Fredric Jameson's (1971) observation that the raw materials of narration are meanings preformed in a sociocultural matrix to re-think mimesis as a representation of collective representation: "The primary relation involved in mimetic literary practice is not the relation 'word/thing,' 'text/world,' but a relation of representations. . . . In other words, mimesis is a re-presentation (in the terms of the generic requirements of the given literary form) of a representation that is itself socially and historically produced" (Prendergast, 1985:35, 36). A possible way of developing the thought is through Wittgenstein's idea of language games played in (and playing out) "forms of life." The latter are conceived as cultural sets of practical activities like telling a joke, reporting an event, and presenting an argument. A serious problem here is that Wittgenstein analyzes language in general and does not make the explicit distinction, which I found valuable in Ricoeur, between speech and writing. Consequently it is not at all clear how forms of life enter the reading process or what a set of practical activities might look like there. For me, an appealing answer, to be amplified subsequently, lies in the concept of literary genres. Prendergast hints parenthetically at some such solution in the quote above, and again in talking of a "mimetic contract," presumably a conventional reading attitude, entered by the reader of that type of text. However, they remain only hints, because his Wittgensteinian formulation confines him to a broad language-game approach where the play of words is limited by public categories of meaning, shared recognitions, tacit knowledge, language habits, and similar elements of pragmatic consensus. No specifically literary analysis is pursued, even though that is the sphere in which the problem of mimesis arose, and which, recalling Ricoeur, could not arise except in writing.

Lima follows the same track but with more explicit sociological references. Instead of "forms of life," the meaning of utterances is said to be grounded in "social ceremonials," the staging of scenes, and giving shows. Erving Goffman (1975) has proposed the term "frame" to denote a primary framework of premises and expectations within which a "strip of activity," including (we must suppose) a sequence of words, is first grasped. Finer specifications of meaning are achieved through "keying." Keys include make-believe, contests, and documentary illustration. Their function is to allow items to appear in a strip of activity with a sense different from that conferred by the primary framework—for example, reading out offensive words in an obscenity trail. From the standpoint of defining mimesis, the important key is make-believe, or play: it is discourse set up in that key, though only, Lima claims, to begin with. In its course, withdrawal from real world truth conditions is complemented by a serious return to the constitutive base of the real world, representation itself:

> A particularized form of play, mimesis can be distinguished from other forms by the fact that its playfulness is only a starting point that soon changes into a seriousness of its own: the serious request that one thinks about what one is playing. . . . A representation of representations, mimesis presupposes between representations and its own scene a separation that makes it possible to appreciate, know, and/or question representations. Therefore, this separation, while precluding any practical action upon the world, permits one to think of it, to experience oneself in it. (Lima, 1985:461)

While the pleasure of a make-believe artifact, or "mimema," resides in identification with its ways of world making and experiencing self-recognition in them, the element of separation or reflexivity in mimesis gives it an analytic quality. Indeed Lima observes that a mimema defined by separation alone could easily be mistaken for an attempt to interpret the world analytically, let us say for sociological theory. Difficulties in the reception of Shaw's more didactic political plays illustrate this problem of boundary confusion: a problem which is not merely a matter of boredom and enjoyment, but of the mimetic contract being broken so that meanings are missed or misunderstood.

THE WORK OF SOCIOLOGICAL THEORY

The closeness of mimesis, which playfully redoubles collective representations, to sociological theory, which seriously reflects upon them, by means of them, forces forward again the question of the generic distinctiveness of theory. Using Lima's terms, sociological theory to be readable as such cannot be mimetic. This enables us to identify certain internal limitations organizing that kind of text work. First, it cannot be written in the play, or make-believe, key. It must, as serious rather than fictive discourse, be construed as continuous with the world it represents: something inferentially extended from the life world and promising practical contact with it; a working guide, or an operational mock-up, rather than a fictional imitation. Play can be inserted into theory—for example, the use of the man-from-Mars perspective to put our institutions in a new light—but cannot be its defining frame. The example also makes it clear that "serious discourse," to which theory belongs, describes an interpretive posture, the way words and so on are to be taken, not a type of semantic unit. Fictions can be read fictively or seriously.

A second limitation shaping sociological theory derives from its association with the scientific mode of seriousness—a mode distinct from, say, philosophical, ethical, or theological seriousness. To objectify social life scientifically, theory is constrained not just to be separate from collective representations, as Lima says of mimesis, but to be critical of their cognitive adequacy. The constraint can be seen in the constant concern of sociological theory to distance itself from ideological and from commonsensical accounts of society. Both might be seen as forms of inadvertent mimesis whereby analysis relapses into merely imitative duplications of accounting practices already operative in social life. The social-scientific problem is how to think, describe, explain, and write outside such practices, yet without abandoning them or the medium of natural language in which they and therefore social facts exist.

Emile Durkheim—whose idea of collective representations making up both social life and our cognitive faculties is aptly used by Lima to open the topic of mimesis—conceived the science of society as a consciously critical representation of representations. The second chapter of his treatise on rules of sociological method (Durkheim, [1895] 1938) opens with a rationale for the most fundamental rule: to approach social facts as things. The attitude is required to suspend the hegemony of commonsense concepts, built into ordinary language, through which everything in society has an already-known character, threatening to make methodical inquiry redundant. Durkheim says that such concepts are like a veil between ourselves and social facts, "concealing them from us the more successfully as we think them more transparent" (Durkheim, [1895] 1938:15). To this we can add Durkheim's observation, from the extraordinary conclusion to his study of elementary religion, that "the great majority of the concepts which we use are not methodically constituted; we get them from language, that is to say from common experience, without submitting them to any criticism" (Durkheim, [1912] 1915:486).

The first paragraph of Durkheim's analysis of suicide, his demonstration of social science at work, finds him grappling critically with the paradoxical opacity of transparently clear collective concepts:

> Since the word "suicide" recurs constantly in the course of conversation, it might be thought that its sense is universally known and that definition is superfluous. Actually, the words of every day language, like the concepts they express, are always susceptible of more than one meaning, and the scholar employing them in their accepted use without further definition would risk serious misunderstanding. Not only is their meaning so indefinite as to vary, from case to case, with the needs of the argument, but, as the classification from which they derive is not analytic, but merely translates the confused impressions of the crowd, categories of very different sorts of fact are indistinctly combined under the same heading, or similar realities are differently named. (Durkheim, [1897] 1951:41)

In themselves the above quotations could easily be assimilated to a scientistic, positivistic methodology; indeed this is the legend through which Durkheim has been read into the discipline. Elsewhere, however, he expresses a constitutive relationship between collective concepts and social reality that makes it difficult to talk straightforwardly of "similar realities" being "differently named," as if social reality could be known independently of how it is named. Certainly the relation between scientific and pre- or subscientific concepts is not as straightforward as the metaphor of removing the veil suggests. If social science, everyday language, and social reality are entwined in constitutive complicity, there can be no simple relation of exclusion and substitution between scientific concepts and collective representations. This is most strongly and starkly expressed in Durkheim's posthumously published lectures on pragmatism and sociology, especially lectures 17–19, where he distinguishes prescientific and nonscientific from scientific truths (Durkheim, [1955] 1983:82–92).

The constitutive complicity of collective representations and social reality is stated uncompromisingly at the end of the seventeenth lecture:

THE WORK OF SOCIOLOGICAL THEORY

"In the last analysis, it is thought which creates reality; and the major role of the collective representations is to 'make' that higher reality which is society itself" (Durkheim, [1955] 1983:85). By collective representation, Durkheim triply means collective source, collective reference, and collective effect. Significantly for our purpose, scientific ideas about society are included within collective representations, not set above them as judgments of their truth. The relation between them is not one of truth to error, but of different forms of truth: "In the history of human thought there are two kinds of mutually contrasting truths, namely, mythological and scientific truths" (Durkheim, [1955] 1983:86).

Although Durkheim uses the term mythology, it is clear from his inclusion of "democracy," "progress," and "class struggle" as examples that ideology, the myriad "isms" of modern culture, and all the implementive and oppositional categories of public rhetoric are to be included in this type of truth.

The ground of mythological truth is not, like that of science, methodically tested correspondence between combinatories of signs and combinatories of things designated by them, even though any representation, to become collective, must possess some adaptive efficacy. It is what Durkheim calls the creative power of its ideas (including images, symbols, concepts, and other representations). By virtue of their origin in collective activities and sentiments, these representations possess a power over individual thought that enables them to create reality effects, to constitute an objectively existent and pragmatically coherent world for individuals: "Collective representations carry with them their objects and entail their existence" (Durkheim, [1955] 1983:86).

Durkheim locates sociology somewhere between the two forms of truth. He might have argued that it must be Janus-faced because it is caught up in an elusive redoubling of linguistic representation and objective reality. The problem of composing truthful representations of real forces and structures whose reality is entirely carried by prior representations compels its turning between scientific and "mythological" truth. Instead he advances a pragmatic explanation. Sociology has an urgent mission of social transformation with only as-yet limited means of accomplishment. Comte's positivist program anticipated an era in which conduct would be entirely guided by scientific truths and questioning guided by rational doubt. Durkheim demurs:

> I accept that this is so with regard to knowledge about the physical world, but it cannot be the case so far as the human and social

world is concerned. In these areas, science is still in a rudimentary state. . . . In that world we have to act and live; and in order to live we need something other than doubt. Society cannot wait for its problems to be solved scientifically. It has to make decisions about what action to take, and in order to make these decisions it has to have an idea of what it is. (Durkheim, 1983:90)

A dilemma appears in this passage. Societal self-representation is needed to take action, existing "mythological" representations are inadequate, yet sociology is not in a position to decisively replace them with scientific truths. What, then, can it do?

Durkheim proposes the cultivation from within of existing representations to a higher level: a procedure of education and edification rather than government by objective knowledge: "[Society] must conduct itself with reference to a representation of the same kind as those which constitute mythological truths" (Durkheim, [1955] 1983:90).

Durkheim concludes this, the nineteenth, lecture with a reference to the task of "speculative truth," which I interpret to mean theoretical reflection, in providing "nourishment for the collective consciousness" (a task spelled out fully in his lectures on moral education; see Durkheim, [1925] 1961, especially the introduction and part 1). Of interest here is his comment that a truthful "copy" of reality is not a redundant duplication. It adds something to reality, a specifically human and social addendum: "Truth is the means by which a new order of things becomes possible, and that new order is nothing less than civilisation" (Durkheim, [1955] 1983:92).

Putting these pieces together, I infer that sociological theory, to fulfill itself, must incorporate and extend prescientific formulations such as mythologies, ideologies, and commonsense accounting schemes. Taking this back toward literary composition, we can say that they are indispensable tensing elements in this form of writing. Such schemes provide semantic elements which must be (*a*) worked into a theory text to provide appropriate content; (*b*) worked against to yield analytic gain and scientific knowledge effects; and (*c*) preserved to sustain pragmatic relevance and edificatory value. A major goal of my case studies will be to identify different styles of performing these demands.

In conclusion, I would note that while the view of sociological text work drawn from Durkheim is in perfect accord with his theory of collective representations, it is contradicted by the several gestures toward scientism made in his theory of method. For example, in the lecture quoted above, having said that there must always be room in social life for mythological truth, he speaks as if this were only a temporary condition, with scientific truth gradually winning out, and he refers to the survival of mythological truth as a great obstacle obstructing the development of sociology. Clearly a removable obstacle is radically different from an indispensable tensing element, and such passages are irreconcilable with my interpretation. I would argue, however, that they are also out of line with Durkheim's ideational concept of social reality and the constitutive power of its representations. Consequently they can be treated as extraneous growths or vestigial remnants of Comtean positivism and cut away without damage. That is, of course, for my present purposes. From another standpoint, the scientistic passages are themselves textual details tensing emergent organizations of Durkheim's meaning. That, however, entails a switch of attention from their propositional content to their nonreferential function as discourse events. Here I am recalling Ricoeur's distinction between verbal meanings and textual events, reinforcing his point that interpretation cannot be simultaneously conducted in both modes at once.

Emergent Organization and Generic Recognizability

Reading cannot procede, nor an organization of meaning emerge, through natural language conventions alone. Also necessary are expectations associated with particular types of text. The term genre is as useful as any here. All writing is performed under the constraint of being a recognizable genre of writing within some cultural array. Let us call it the constraint of generic recognizability.

Ricoeur is helpful here also. He describes genres in terms close to Cooley's concept of organic forms growing by "working":

> The function of these generative devices is to produce new entities of language longer than the sentence, organic wholes irreducible to a mere addition of sentences. . . . Language is submitted to the rules of a kind of craftsmanship, which allows us to speak of production and of works of art, and, by extension of works of discourse. . . . The generative devices, which we call literary genres, are the technical rules presiding over their production. (Ricoeur, 1976:32–33)

For me, it would be a normal cultural bias to equate production entirely with writing and to understand technical crafting to be purely writer's work. However, the therapeutic import of interpretation theory is to show text work to be a double-sided activity. A text is not simply a produced, done, and finished object but something creatively reproduced in reading performances. Analytically this warrants an option to locate generative devices on whichever side of text work one pleases. I choose the reader's side, because this is where the social interest of texts lies, and social interest is the ultimate judgmental ground of sociological writing.

In line with my choice, Peter Rabinowitz (1985) has proposed treating genres as performative strategies for reading rather than objective features of writing. By this definition, a genre would correspond to a definite reading posture or attitude. Rabinowitz uses terms like sets of operations, reading conventions, and bundles of rules to define genres. An indicator of their existence is that interpretive questions appropriate within a given genre sound satirical, silly, or otherwise inappropriate when applied beyond its bounds. For example, within the generic category of serious novels a title can be expected to have symbolic significance and be worth exploring, whereas popular fiction titles are only expected to be descriptive identity tags. Thus it would be appropriate to ask about the symbolic and metaphorical meanings of William Faulkner's *Sanctuary* but not Erle Stanley Gardner's *The Case of the Howling Dog*.

The idea can be specified by breaking down rules (which are also expectations and appropriate questions) into types. Thus Rabinowitz identifies rules of notice (what kind of detail to watch for); rules of signification (ways of framing salient detail); rules of configuration (forming framed details into units, patterns, and the like through inserting openings and closures); and rules of coherence (ways of fitting the parts into a whole so that a meaning is comprehended). Since Rabinowitz concentrates on generic differences between popular and serious fiction, saying nothing of nonfictional genres, his particular examples do not aid us. I would, however, stress the connection he makes between generic recognition and full comprehension.

This arises with respect to rules of coherence. The most general constraint here is that the details and patterns of a text are to be read in the "best" way possible. Reading for the best can readily be understood as a regulative ideal, an ideal evident in the endless revisions and interpretive disputes of literary scholars. More strongly and deeply, however, it is an a priori condition for any actual reading to proceed. By this I mean that in order to enter a text, to be able to start reading, we must always already have accepted that a structure of meaning is there which we can in principle fully occupy. One cannot read at all except within the presupposition that there is a possible place from which everything in the text is completely clear: a perfectly fitting place of comprehension.

A more particular constraint, especially relevant for nonfiction, concerns the tolerability of generic mixing in a text. Even in fiction, where the juxtaposition of diverse genres is often associated with artistic creativity (for example, in James Joyce's *Ulysses*), a critical line is drawn against mere heterogeneity. Christine Brooke-Rose (1980) has said against Tolkien's *Lord of the Rings* that it cannot be read coherently or therefore satisfactorily, because the composition falls structurally between two incompatible sets of reading expectations: those of the realistic narrative novel, and those—following Todorov (1973)—of a species of fantastic tale called the marvelous.

In nonfiction, generic multiplicity is scarcely tolerable at all, leading readily to perceptions of dishonesty. This is well illustrated by Gibson's (1982) critique of the *New York Herald Tribune* and *Time* magazine for using devices from Hemingway-style narrative fiction to impart false authenticity to reports of street riots. A general limitation on the emergent organization of meaning in nonfictional work can be advanced here: the more seriously reality representation is intended, the stronger is the constraint toward generic homogeneity.

Riffaterre (1984) has expressed essentially the same thesis, but in broader semiotic terms: "The more faithfully a text is supposed to reflect the manifold aspects of reality, or the more it proclaims itself a mirror, the more total the subordination of the mimetic multiplicity to a single message, to a semiotic oneness" (Riffaterre, 1984:159).

His meaning becomes clearer if we recall that in semiotics each lexical item is seen as surrounded by a set of synonyms, antonyms, figurative substitutes, and conventionally associated terms, called a paradigm. Riffaterre is saying that literariness, or literary artifactuality, depends upon the insertion of words that somehow disrupt or disturb the paradigmatic unity of a piece of writing. A wonderfully economical example is William Carlos Williams's poetic description of a wheelbarrow:

> so much depends
> upon
> a red wheel
> barrow
> glazed with rain
> water
> beside the white
> chickens

So plain is the vocabulary that the poetry is hard to see. Riffaterre argues, convincingly I think, that it resides in a single word, "glazed." That word belongs to a paradigm of delicate objects, including porcelain dogs and other such ornaments, that contradicts the sturdy, utilitarian associations of the wheelbarrow as tool. With this one artfully disruptive word, Williams' almost literal description is turned into a literary creation. Conversely, this is something that nonfictional representation, to be fully readable as such, needs to avoid.

A further specification, placing the homogeneity thesis in an even broader context, is offered by Robert Scholes's (1977) account of literariness in the reading experience. Drawing upon Jakobson's well-known breakdown of a communicative act into six components—addresser, addressee, message, contact medium, code rules, and referential context—Scholes proposes that we experience literariness when any of the components loses its simplicity. Simplicity meaning unity, wholeness, and integrity. By implication, literal-reality representation requires a single, nonduplicitous author; a simple, single reading posture; a consistent code, including what I have called generic homogeneity; and a semiotic oneness of message and context. (In accordance with the orientation adopted throughout this study, the referential context is understood to be a semiotic one consisting of semantic associations and linguistic conventions, rather than things existing outside language.) I have omitted contact simplicity, involving the boundary between written and spoken communication, because it seems to me that sociological theory is such an inescapably literary enterprise that the issue of contact duplicity does not arise here (not, for example, as it may in research reports when verbatim transcriptions are used to supposedly allow respondents to speak in their own voices).

Returning now to the Cooleyan process of text work, we can say that the emergent organization of meaning in sociological theory, in that form of text work, is constrained to be generically, semiotically and interpretively homogeneous. There is no doubt, factually speaking, that homogeneity operates as a normative rule in sociology, as in all putative sciences. It underlies norms like plain prose, scholarly referencing, standard article formats, and lexical standardization. We shall find it underlying negative receptions of Georg Simmel's work. The question an overt investigation of theory as a genre sui generis can raise, however, is whether all homogeneity rules are to be accepted, and if not, what possibilities are offered by classical theory to rethink our standards.

THE WORK OF SOCIOLOGICAL THEORY

What Is It That Works in a Text?

A Cooleyan process begins with an antecedent system of tendencies which then works itself, through stimulants, obstacles, and other tensing elements, into an emergent organization. The task must now be addressed of identifying the antecedent system underlying the text work of sociological theory. Cooley provides a strange and searching question that will direct my efforts: "Just what is it that 'works'?" (Cooley, 1918:13).

An overwhelmingly obvious answer, but one that I, following Cooley's lead, have been trying to resist, is an author's intentions. Preferable, because less likely to exchange textual for psychological, biographical, or other extratextual investigation, is an answer from the other side of interpretation: the reader and his projections. Wolfgang Iser describes the position in terms very close to Cooley's: "As the reader uses the various perspectives offered him by the text in order to relate the patterns and the 'schematized views' to one another, he sets the work in motion, and this very process results ultimately in the awakening of responses within himself. Thus, reading causes the literary work to unfold its inherently dynamic character" (Iser, 1974:275).

I have no quarrel with the formulation; it nicely matches the proprosals for studying style through reader response made in chapter 2. There are, however, strategic reasons for not accepting it as a sufficient account of what "works" in text work. First, I have already included the reader's interpretive activities under tensing elements and emergent organization. Consequently, to make them the meaning of antecedent tendencies as well would render that category analytically redundant; it would also let us too easily off the hook of Cooley's question. We need to be seeking tendencies antecedent to style and to author-reader transactions: tendencies inherent in the very act of writing sociological theory and formatively antecedent to the genre.

If I may reinforce the point, the reader, even if called implied or ideal, is still open to a personalized, psychologized interpretation; again, short-circuiting a thoroughly textual inquiry. The pull of that kind of account is so powerful in our culture that strong counterconcepts are needed to allow any kind of social or cultural inquiry full orbit.

Cooley's warning is apposite:

> When we speak of human life we are apt to assume that the existing tendency is some conscious purpose, and that whatever goes to realise this is "working" and everything else is failure to work. In

other words we make the whole matter voluntary and utilitarian. This is an inadequate and for the most part a wrong conception of the case. The working of a man, or of any other human whole, in a given situation is much more nearly analogous to that of the vine than we perceive. Although conscious purpose may play a central part in it, there is also a whole organism of tendencies that feel their way about in the situation, reacting in a complex and mainly unconscious way. (Cooley, 1918:14)

What might the tendencies be in the writing and reading of sociological theory? Another kind of answer than author's intentions or interpreter's strategies would be the structure of a field of discourse. It is feasible to posit a topical matrix in which all sociological theory grows. For example, the entire corpus could be shown to be a working of the following set of questions:

1. (Under the general heading of a theory of sociological method.) What are the defining, distinctive properties of social reality? How are we to gain valid knowledge of it? What is the prospective value of such knowledge? Knowledge for what?

2. What are the defining properties of modern society? What are its dominant institutions, characteristic structures, and determining dynamics?

3. What shape, direction, or meaning can be seen in the record of human history, conceived from the presentist standpoint of the emergence of modern society?

4. What are the defining, distinctive properties of human nature? What are its interests, demands, and dynamics in relation to society and history?

The shortcomings of such a list are obvious. Even if it were shown to exhaust the entire literature, it would still possess only descriptive validity and lack analytic interest.

To go further, one might think of the describable content of theory texts as the surface expression of an underlying structure of concepts. For illustration and by critical reaction to push forward, it is worth examining Paul Hirst's analysis of Durkheim's theory of method.

Discourse Analysis and Literary Analysis

A discourse is not a thing, but a way of reading. Hirst describes his way as follows:

> Conceptual reading entails treating a theoretical text as the product of and the expositional form of discourse. Theoretical discourse

> may be defined as the form in which concepts are deployed in a
> particular mode of reasoning which develops answers to certain
> questions posed in a theory. . . . The conditions of existence of the
> questions and the criteria of validity of those answers, in other
> words the conditions which make discourse possible, are a struc-
> tured set of problems and concepts, the *problematic* of a theory. It is
> this structure which . . . delimits a definite theoretical field with
> specific objects to be explained and specific forms of reasoning.
> (Hirst, 1975:9)

The term "problematic" is taken from Althusser (1969; Althusser and
Balibar, 1970), who himself borrowed it from Jacques Martin. It belongs to an attempt to conceive knowledge as a Marxian production
process. In all production, raw materials are transformed into definite,
realized items (a corkscrew, a cathedral, a wedding ceremony, a cured
patient, a court sentence), by a production apparatus. In knowledge
production, prior concepts and claimed representations (Althusser calls
these materials Generality I) are turned into accredited facts, testable
hypotheses, proper classifications, and so on (Generality III), by appropriate means for fashioning and deploying statements (Generality II).

One of Althusser's early formulations is worth quoting for its startling closeness to Cooley:

> So it is by transforming this Generality I into a Generality III
> (knowledge) that the science works and produces. But *who* or *what*
> is it that works? What should we understand by the expression: the
> science works? . . . It is what I shall call the Generality II, con-
> stituted by the corpus of concepts whose more or less contradictory
> unity constitutes the "theory" of the science at the (historical)
> moment under consideration. (Althusser, 1969:184)

The "problematic" of a discourse works, it should be added, as much
through systematic exclusion and negation as inclusion and affirmation. A telling example occurs in Althusser's reconstruction of the way
Marx read Smith, Ricardo, and the political economists. In his terms it
includes the explication of systematic blanks in their problematic as
revealed by disjunctions between certain of their knowledge statements
and the problems for which they are claimed as answers. Specifically,
political economy claimed that the value of labor, which determines the
real value of all other commodities, corresponds to the goods and
services socially necessary to maintain and reproduce labor. Marx observes a significant disjunction. Whereas the answer, to make sense,
refers to labor power, to a power embodied in the person and life of the

laborer, the concept appears nowhere in the overt theoretical apparatus of political economy. It is present only as a necessary blank. Labor power is a concept that political economy must scan without notice, because blocking it out is crucial to its internal mode of knowledge production.

Comparably, in a study of the 1834 and 1909 Poor Law Reports in England (Green, 1983), I found that the 1834 Report contains no concept of unemployment. Not because there was no such thing, but because its theoretical apparatus was structured around conceptual equations between work, virtue, and reward, idleness, vice, and punishment, and impotence, incapacity, and charity that did not permit the production of the concept. In the 1909 Report the problematic had changed; there was now a schema of system functioning that allowed unemployment to be thought as one of its properties.

Hirst proposes to recover the problematic informing Durkheim's *Rules of Sociological Method*. To this end he maps a discursive space coordinated by positions found in particular philosophies of knowledge and being: vitalism, reductionism, essentialism, materialism, idealism, among others. This enables him to analyze *The Rules* as a series of possible and actual moves within the space. Actual moves involve discursive intentions, but Hirst is especially interested in moves constrained by the structure of the space in spite of intentions. Thus a strong discursive intent of *The Rules* is to escape any reductionist, especially individualist, concept of society. The move is dictated by Durkheim's decision to ground the possibility of a science of society ontologically, in the prior existence of a distinctive form of reality, rather than epistemologically, in the selective construction of thought objects by a methodological community of knowers.

Hirst argues that Durkheim's ontological move against reductionism carries him towards an essentialist, vitalist, group-mind concept of society in spite of his scientific resistance to it. The topography of his terrain (to introduce another Althusserian conceit) determines the movement. Social facts are attributed to a real entity, the collective, which is consequently reified as a source, origin, and supraindividual subject. Collective representations, the core social facts, are attributed to society, the collective consciousness, as if it thought them. Hirst observes: "This mentalism is a necessary consequence of the structure of his problematic. The 'conscience collective' is the generative essence of reality and underlies the particular manifestations of social life" (Hirst, 1975:100).

It should be added, for the sake of accuracy, that no total structural

66

determinism is implied here. Hirst shows how Claude Bernard, located in experimental physiology but within the same philosophical problematic as Durkheim, broke out of the reductionism-vitalism circuit by actualizing various possible moves.

I do not wish to comment on the adequacy of Hirst's application of Althusser, nor on the problems of turning Althusser's singularly ingenious reading of Marx into a general analytic strategy. Let us suppose the viability of a conceptual reading along these lines; it would still only complement rather than satisfy our interest in text work. Its effect is to construe a text as an argument, tracing out movements, immobilities, disjunctions, closed circles, blind spots, and the like in the propositional dimension. An argument, however, is an extraction from a text, a studied setting aside of the events making up the literary dimension. Even if it is admitted that standard reading for content is transcended by Althusser's project, the interpretation still focuses on what words mean as cognitive propositions, rather than on what they do as events in a reading experience. In summary, it might be agreed that a possible answer to the question, What is working in theory texts? is a problematic. But not if it means subordinating the literary to the propositional dimension and reducing text work to nothing but moves in argumentation.

Sociological Theory and the Anxieties of Writing

As a final attempt to answer the question of what is working in text work, I wish to develop a suggestion by Bloom (1973, 1975) and argue that it includes generically specifiable anxieties of writing. I will focus on one, to be called the "anxiety" of ontological emptiness. The quotation marks here signify my concern not to be understood psychologically, as if I were talking about a state of mind in the author. The psychology of writing is not my interest here.

Two more preliminary comments are in order. First, I will treat the concept of anxiety pragmatically. The question is not whether an anxiety of ontological emptiness exists in any absolute sense; but whether the concept, when its implications are spun out, helps us analyze the composition of theory texts, to detect nonobvious compositional structures in the literary dimension. Also, while the answer may at first appear far-fetched, it is grounded in the specific nature of sociological writing and is in that sense an immanent answer rather than one fetched from afar. Nonetheless, we must begin metaphorically, analogically, and marginally, because no other beginning to theory is possible.

The term text work deliberately locates literary composition in a series that includes the Freudian concepts of dream work and wit work. Their common denominator is the idea of a semiotic structure emerging from defensive transformations of an immanent, intrinsic, threatening pressure. In all three cases a describable phenomenon—a dream, a witticism, a text—is construed as the working of a latency, via semiotic materials, into a manifest content.

It would take us too far afield to review Freud, but features of his theory of interpretation of dreams offer instruction, both methodological and substantive, for textual analysis. Starting with method, the uncovering of dream work begins with a recalled dream: a "finished" product already imbued with an evident or face-value meaning. Obviously the dream is not taken at face value; neither, however, is that value simply rejected. It is accepted as a starting point to work from. Something worth stressing here is that detection begins not with a dream but with a recalled dream. The recall and its censoring, ordering, and tidying activities form the first layer of the entire sum of transforming processes called dream work. These overlay the interpolations, running comments, and "cementing thoughts" occurring within the dream itself.

In textual analysis the counterpart would be a distinction between the logic and orderliness enacted by the text itself (through self-monitoring and self-defining elements like prefatory remarks, introductions, organizing statements, headings, subheadings, and summaries) and that established by subsequent exegesis and glossing. The latter will serve later as a strategic point of entry in examining the text work of Weber and Simmel. But whereas Freud gains interpretive leverage by juxtaposing dream elements with deep "dream thoughts" revealed by psychoanalysis (its models), I will do so through juxtaposing text elements with analytic models of genre and style developed in literary theory.

At the substantive level, Freud's most important offerings are a distinction between two forms of dream work—primary limitation and secondary elaboration—and a subsidiary distinction, involving elaboration especially between displacement and condensation. Freud calls these "the two craftsmen undertaking dream-work, the former being the most essential part" (Freud, 1938:338). He adds the important observation that anxiety inheres not simply in the dream thoughts that are repressed but in the act of censorship itself. Elaboration therefore sequentially defends against anxiety invoked by previous defences.

Freud's stress on secondary elaboration and transformation by displacement is readable in Bloom's (1975) homological analysis of the troping maneuvers through which an "anxiety of influence" occasioned by artistic awareness of strong precursive poetry is worked into a new creation. Of the six more-or-less-sequential maneuvers described by Bloom, only the first, the ironic turning of presence into absence, corresponds at all comfortably with primary limitation. The other five, despite Bloom's references to a struggle between limitation and representation played out by them, would seem more clearly thought of as forms of secondary elaboration.

Beyond such terminological amendment, however, it is valuable to retain Bloom's perception of a dialectical process informing text work. In his schema, there is a dialectic of limiting and representing the prior words of strong others, enacted by complementary turns or tropes of language. (He suggests irony-synecdoche, metonymy-hyperbole, metaphor-metalepsis; but the details need not concern us.) Limitation and representation can be taken to refer to dialectical moments of composition in any text. In the kind of writing we are concerned with, some literary moves split, divert, and deflate the aspiration of language to contain reality, while others restore and inflate it.

Consider, for example, Durkheim's *Rules of Sociological Method*. It opens, in the first paragraph of the author's preface to the first edition, with an ironic contrast between common thought and social science:

> If there is to be a social science, we shall expect it not merely to paraphrase the traditional prejudices of the common man but to give us a new and different view of them; for the aim of all science is to make discoveries, and every discovery more or less disturbs accepted ideas. Unless, then, sociology attributes to common sense an authority which it has not enjoyed for a long time in other sciences—and it is impossible to see how such authority could be justified—the scholar must resolutely resist being intimidated by the results to which his researches lead, demanding only that they be conducted scientifically. (Durkheim, [1895] 1938:xxxvii)

This confident affirmation of the ontological fullness of scientific words directly represses the text thought that all words, however formed, are irremediably devoid of intrinsic reality, meaning, and truth. It is ironic, because the science of social reality does not yet exist; consequently the affirmation-denial is being made within or at the margin of empty and false words and depends upon that realm for its own authority. The deflation of language enacted in the opening paragraph is so severe as to be textually disintegrative, and far from binding the anxiety it represses, carries it forward.

The next paragraph, in accordance with Bloom's hypothesis of complementary turns, enacts a reflation of language. The "impulses of common sense" (a metonymic renaming of ordinary language) are said to be deeply ingrained in us, so much so "that it is difficult to eradicate them from sociological discussion." Only "long and special training" (a synecdoche for science) can overcome the strength of ordinary language. Reflation is then amplified by a direct demonstration of the sermonic power of ordinary language. Durkheim addresses "the reader" directly as a repository of the dangerous impulses and loose thought habits of common sense and then delivers a lesson on the scientific normality of crime.

From here it could be shown how successive cycles of deflation and inflation form the literary structure of the book. We could examine the various figures through which the thought of empty words undergoes secondary elaboration: its displacement into a series of objects adjacent to language itself: the "vague generalities" of early sociology, the "voluminous sociology" and "superficial inquiry" of Spencer, "dead letter" formulas, ideological thinking, the "schematic and crystallized representations, the superficial concepts which we employ in ordinary life," "dialectical artifice." Compositionally, *The Rules* consists of a series of deflections of ontological emptiness onto such objects. Each time there is a heightening of anxiety associated with linguistic deflation that is compensated for by a reflationary appeal to the ontological fullness of scientifically ruled words, a process culminating in the introjective-projective imagery of the closing paragraph. Here the emptiness of language is introjected as loud noise and projected as a silence to be obtained when science speaks: A conclusory reworking of the opening irony is achieved: "For, so long as it [sociology] remains involved in partisan struggles, is content to expound common ideas . . . and, consequen⁺ly, presumes no special competence, it has no right to silence passions and prejudices. Assuredly, the time when it will be able to play this role successfully is still far off. However, we must begin work now, in order to put it in condition to fill this role some day" (Durkheim, [1895] 1938:146). The ending is conclusory rather than conclusive, because only a programmatic defence has been achieved and it awaits a working into research to be consolidated. The point about constitutive anxieties, however, whether of dream work or text work, is that the work is never done. There is only renaming, reaiming, displacement, and deferment. In Durkheim's further work, even science turns out to be incapable of settling the anxiety of empty words. This is most apparent in Durkheim's last major work, *The Elementary Forms of the Religious*

THE WORK OF SOCIOLOGICAL THEORY

Life, where society, or the collective consciousness, is now made to bear the burden. All, including scientific thought, is made to stem from it. I will not attempt to document the point but rest content with citing a passage that neatly unravels the defense of anxiety composed by *The Rules:*

> So opinion, primarily a social thing, is a source of authority, and it might even be asked whether all authority is not the daughter of opinion. It may be objected that science is often the antagonist of opinion, whose errors it combats and rectifies. But it cannot succeed in this task if it does not have sufficient authority, and it can obtain this authority only from opinion itself. If a people did not have faith in science, all the scientific demonstrations in the world would be without any influence whatsoever over their minds. (Durkheim, [1912] 1915:238–39)

Far from silencing opinion by its authority, science itself must fall silent unless authority is conferred on it by opinion. Taking *The Rules* and *The Elementary Forms* together, opinion (with its metonyms) corresponds to what Freud called a "nodal point" (Freud, 1938:323) where manifold dream thoughts meet together in an "overdetermined" element of content. In today's literary jargon, it is an "alogical" element inwardly unraveling or "deconstructing" text work (for example, Miller, 1976).

Deconstructionist language analysis is in fact the source of the idea of an anxiety of ontological emptiness advanced here. I wish to specify the rationale and the meaning of the idea more closely.

Frederic Jameson (1972) documents a modern cultural upheaval, variously registered in literature, philosophy, and the human sciences, but crucially articulated in linguistics, consisting of a shift from a substantive to a relational paradigm of language and meaning: a semiotic as opposed to substantialist way of thinking about our world. Near its epicenter (to use a substantialist metaphor) is Saussure's [1916] 1959) theory of the sign, the basic unit of the language systems into which speech acts enter in being understood. Its tenets include the splitting of the sign between a sensory signifier and conceptual (not substantive) signified; the determination of the meaning of a sign by its differences from others in a sign system (in language there are only differences, not names of things); and the essentially arbitrary (Saussure calls it unmotivated) bond between signifier and signified: a bond whose only security is convention and habit.

Certain implications attend the semiotic switch, provocative of the

kind of doubting despair about language witnessed in European intellectuals and artists around 1900–1925 (see Steiner, 1971; Janik and
Toulmin, 1973) and theorized by Derrida as linguistic self-
deconstruction.

First, the meaning of a sign is never anything positive, but is always
negatively determined by irredeemable absences. The signified is never
there except as the other side of the signifier. The meaning value of a
sign is determined in systems by negative and opposite signs, and in
chains by further signs: by difference and deferment. The last point is
made especially clear in Peirce's semiotic principle that the interpretant
of a sign is always another sign (Peirce, 1955). Derrida has attempted to
draw out the insubstantiality of the sign by rejecting the question of its
"formal essence." He does so with the aid of a typographical prop: "The
'formal essence' of the sign can only be determined in terms of presence.
One cannot get around that response, except by challenging the very
form of the question and beginning to think that the sign is that ill-
named thing, the only one, that escapes the instituting question of
philosophy: 'what is'?" (Derrida, 1976:18–19).

A related implication is that there is no inherent limit or closure on
the movement of signification from one interpretant sign to another.
There is no transfer to a transcendent reality, a bedrock presence, only
further rewording that is potentially endless.

Jameson forcefully sums up the situation:

> Language can never really express any *thing:* only relationships
> (Saussure) or sheer absence (Mallarmé). This language has of ne-
> cessity recourse to indirection, to substitution: itself a substitute, it
> must replace that empty center of content with something else, and
> it does so either by saying what the content is like (metaphor), or
> describing the contours of its absence, listing the things that border
> around it (metonymy). (Jameson, 1972:122–23)

We have seen that Cooley conducted a critique of our habitual pre-
sumption that growth processes are governed by a central organizing
principle: a will, design, or plan. In the terms I have been using, Cooley
is registering a tremor that leads back to the semiotic upheaval of
language described above. Looked at psychologically rather than geo-
logically, the tremor is an anxiety of deregulation, of surrender to an
anarchic play of movement:

> The concept of centered structure is in fact the concept of a play
> based on a fundamental ground, a play constituted on the basis of a
> fundamental immobility and a reassuring certitude, which is itself

THE WORK OF SOCIOLOGICAL THEORY

> beyond the reach of play. And on the basis of this certitude anxiety
> can be mastered, for anxiety is invariably the result of a certain
> mode of being implicated in the game, of being caught by the
> game, of being as it were at stake in the game from the outset.
> (Derrida, 1978:279)

Saussure displays awareness of what is at stake in a belated qualification of the principle of arbitrariness. Having in the first chapter of part 1 said simply: "the linguistic sign is arbitrary" (Saussure, [1916] 1959:67), he undertakes a revision of the principle in chapter 6 of part 2: "The fundamental principle of the arbitrariness of the sign does not prevent our singling out in each language what is radically arbitrary, i.e. unmotivated, and what is only relatively arbitrary. Some signs are absolutely arbitrary; in others we note, not its complete absence, but the presence of degrees of arbitrariness: the sign may be relatively motivated" (Saussure, [1916] 1959:131). By "motivation" Saussure means something like structural limitation on degrees of freedom. The clue is given by his use of "minimum organization" (p. 133) to identify the opposite extreme to "minimum arbitrariness." Organization refers to purely linguistic containment: the enclosure of a sign in associative sets and syntagmatic units tied to its own elements and form. Thus the term *dix-neuf* is tied by its two elements and hyphenated form to more numbers and sequences than the term *vingt,* and hence is more organized and less arbitrary. At the macrolevel, Saussure suggests that some languages are less arbitrary, or more "grammatical" than others: Latin more than French, German more than English. What interests us, however, is his insistence that these internal patterning mechanisms are still only "a partial correction of a system that is by nature chaotic" (p. 133). They reflect the attempts of the mind—its cognitive imperative—to introduce order and regularity into a phenomenon that is incorrigibly, recalcitrantly arbitrary, irrational, and chaotic. It is this awareness that is stripped bare when ontological faith is lost.

Grasped as an objective condition of writing, the anxiety of ontological emptiness is a condition of being caught up in the disruptive, distinctively modern event, described by Derrida and Jameson. It need hardly be added, bearing in mind the sociological distinction between objective condition and subjective expression (for example, objective and subjective alienation; objective anomie and subjective anomia), that the event might be registered indirectly and symptomatically rather than by direct reflection: including, perhaps a methodologically overdetermined confidence in the language of science.

I will end with another quotation from Derrida, one which draws together the major themes of this section: the Cooleyan question of just what is working in text work, and the anxiety of ontological emptiness in literary composition.

> This [literary] universe articulates only that which is in excess of everything, the essential nothing on whose basis everything can appear and be produced . . . this excess is the very possibility of writing and of literary *inspiration* in general. Only *pure absence*—not the absence of this or that, but the absence of everything in which all presence is announced—can *inspire,* in other words can *work,* and then make one work. (Derrida, 1978:8; italics in original)

In this passage is explained the secret of sociological theory as a separate undertaking and its necessarily problematic relation to empirical research. The latter announces a ubiquitous presence which the former, from its literary location in language, must render absent, yet without leaving itself nothing to say.

The anxiety of ontological emptiness is tied in sociology to the founding intent of fixing in language a reality (social life) which is open-endedly constituted, through and through, by language. Linguistic reflexivity haunts the enterprise. Its task of making society a stable knowledge object, inescapably forced forward by our rational way of practicing social life, is forever liable to the unraveling effect of reflexive language awareness on its knowledge structures. Sociology is a discipline compelled by its constitution to build upon this fault line between words and reality. Sociological theory, in one way or another, dwells upon it.

Conclusion

I will conclude with some observations on how the case studies of Simmel and Weber will be conducted and on the relevance of the literary method of theory research for regular sociological interests.

First, I do not intend to use their writings merely to exhibit the concepts presented previously. To do so would not only reverse my priorities but risk degeneration into either meretricious show or a Procrustean imposition of categories. The aim is to cultivate responsiveness to the texts, not to shout them into silence.

As to the normal discipline concerns of sociology, it is true that I am not following usual practices like extracting research ideas, reformulating hypotheses, and revealing contradictions. However, there is no question of indifference to referential content about society. Rather, the intent is to comprehend the content more fully by including normally ignored textual features. The stress given them is a countervailing tactic in the face of the exclusionary power of normal reading practices, not a rebellion against the discipline. The aim is the same: a grasp of the requirements of language true to social life. In the case studies following, I will advance interpretive hypotheses about the compositional methods of Simmel and Weber with this aim in mind.

The immediate tests of the hypotheses, simply because they are interpretive, must be local and relative to whatever concerns the readerships gathered by the texts. For example, given the interests, debates, developments and dead ends of an interpretive situation, does a given hypothesis enlighten familiar texts? Does it restore life to texts read almost to death? Does it productively realign perceptions of what is significant in particular works? Does it make better sense of what a theorist was doing? Does it locate a theorist more instructively in relation to others? Such tests can only be administered locally and for the time being within what Gadamer (1975) calls the horizon of a tradition.

Returning to matters of method, my case studies face the analytic problem of how to bring broadly generic concepts to bear upon individual style. The application of the concept of an anxiety of ontological emptiness illustrates the difficulty. No doubt one could document its presence in any text, but this is not necessarily instructive. For example, although I found it revealing to apply the concept to Simmel, this was not the case with Weber. It is as though Simmel was closer to the disruptive "event" described by Derrida and Jameson than Weber was. Its pressures are crucial to his text work and its reception, something not true of Weber. However, this is an interpretive hypothesis to be elaborated later. The point is that one must ask about the closeness and compositional significance of the event for each theorist, not assume significant or equal closeness in advance, as would be done by a schematic application. Along the same lines, a heuristic approach would focus on the specific shape taken by the anxiety in the style of a particular theorist rather than the generic fact of its presence—for example, that it occurs in Durkheim as a redoubling movement around the (in)capacity of words to form binding moral rules, or in Marx as a literary containment of politically (im)potent words.

Of course the idea of generic anxieties of writing is only one of several analytic devices I have reviewed, and it has no privileged standing. Like the others, it will be introduced only to serve my aim: an analysis of the literary methods of particular exemplary works of sociological theory with an eventual concern for adequate methods of critically evaluating sociological writing as such. My contention is that the concern for well-written sociology cannot be sidelined as a mere concern for good style. The complicity between sociological language and the linguistic matrices in which social life is formed and reformed ensures that my approach touches the practical significance of the subject and, I would argue, at a truly deeper level than is provided by established notions of applied and problem-oriented sociology. It is as language that sociology achieves any practicality at all.

Part Two: The Style and Text Work of Georg Simmel

4   Simmel's Style of Writing

Simmel's writings have impressed commentators in diverse ways; yet the impressions are patterned and repeated, not random and scattered. They are recorded in finite sets of adjectives, in what might be called a web of epithets, spun around Simmel's work: more precisely, around the name attached to English-language translations of the work, since it is these which have carried the name into sociological theory and constitute Simmel's effective existence for us. I will treat these incorporative descriptions of Simmel as effects of his text work. They are imprints traced out by his style, his styling of reading responses, from which we might hope to retrace his methods of composition. I will take the fact that some epithets have caught on and been woven into an authorized version of Simmel as prima facie evidence that they have a retrievable truth relation to his work. I would stress retrievable to indicate that no straight read off can be expected, and interpretation is required. The epithets are to be read as endorsed or canonical glosses on Simmel's style of text work. Paraphrasing a wonderfully searching question proposed by Garfinkel and Sacks (1970:352), I will ask, What is the work in the text for which an epithet X is that work's cannonical gloss?

Helpful buttressing for these ideas is provided by Durgnat's (1982) analysis of semantic formations in complex meanings. Like Ricoeur and other modern semanticists, his point of departure is Saussure's severe distinction between pure linguistic possibilities (langue) and individual enactments of them (parole). In order to found a science of language, Saussure shifted all that was performative, contingent, historical, situational, and circumstantial in it to the edge of the field. This left as the site of the new science a realm of signs governed by almost algebraic structural determinacy, where the fixing of one value limits other according to determinable rules of exchange, combination, and exclusion. Parole belongs to what he calls the executive side of the speaker-auditor circuit, langue to the reception side, a shared code existing prior to individual enactments of its possibilities.

The severity of the distinction resides in its banishment of actual speech, including writing, to a peripheral position. Its harm for Durgnat and other critics (Ricoeur, 1976; Hjelmslev, 1971) is that parole is the linguistic locus of social life and individual style. The banishment creates an analytic hiatus which it is the concern of modern semantics and neostructuralist discourse analysis (see Pêcheux and Fuchs, 1982) to fill. More exactly, it is a matter of bringing in from the analytic cold all that belongs to parole, including, for us, the compositional style of particular texts.

Hjelmslev's (1971) proposal envisions a hierarchy of linguistic determinacy with purely semiotic rules of the Saussurean kind at the top, followed by norms of proper usage, then regularities of actual usage. Durgnat follows the same route both in positing intermediate levels of language and in relying upon the idea of social usage to inject determinacy into the active side of language.

His basic idea is that semantic connections grow up around and between nodal words: especially, it would seem from his examples, nouns. This is a social and cultural process, something like walkers wearing pathways in the countryside, not the purely combinatory operation of a sign system: "In this view, semantics is very heavily influenced, indeed dominated, not by language as such, but by culturally (i.e. socially) established concept-networks." . . . (Durgnat, 1982:20).

There are, for example, several word ways leading in and out of the noun "horse," each telling something of the social nature of the beast. Durgnat mentions the English country-set horse (gentry, hounds, fox hunting, jodhpurs), the English agricultural horse (field, plough, harness, farmer), and the Wild West horse (cattle herding, lasso, cowboy). There are, then, locally occasioned properties along with more common extrinsic properties (saddle, rider, reins) and internal ones (mane, hooves, tail). Durgnat wants to be able to treat them all together in mapping the interpretive field of a reader-listener-viewer. Partly for this reason he regards the term connotations as unsatisfactory to describe the elements of a set. It implies only extrinsic—especially emotive and moral—associations, as well as carrying with it the unhelpful assumption of a transsituational stable meaning called, contrastively, the denotation. In the end he chooses "semantic concomitants" as the best option.

The sets of epithets to be discussed can be regarded as semantic concomitants of the name Simmel and his titled works, fashioned by repeated use in his reception history. To this we can add Durgnat's observation that semantic concomitants hang together in larger sets called "conceptual networks." This term loosely designates any and all semantic fields formed around practical, artistic, or scholarly activities: the languages-within-languages of hobbies, crafts, schools of thought, and intellectual disciplines. However, rather than adopt a substantive definition, I would prefer to treat the distinction between conceptual network and semantic concomitant as merely analytic. A conceptual network would be whatever is considered to be the semantic context of items treated as concomitants. Thus, Simmel's work could be considered as a conceptual network within which to locate and make sense of the sets of epithets. It needs to be added, however, recalling the argument of chapter 3, that the literary composition of a network can be distinguished from its discursive structure—a text from an argument—and the former is our priority.

The first use of receptive epithets is to research the literary work of which they are imprints. A second use is to provide clues and evidence of the company of texts to which a work belongs. It is said that you can know a person by the company he keeps. So also with interpreting texts. The problem is how to define companions beyond direct citations (which are themselves only suggestive).

Robert Jones (1977), in an influential advocacy of reading the classics in their formative context, would confine the possible company to works which the author demonstrably knew or could in principle have known, the main force of this being to resist "presentist" and "historicist" impositions of meaning. I would accept this as a guide to the historical reconstruction of arguments (which is Jones's concern) but not literary analysis. For this purpose, the relevant company is determined by the compositional methods and the styling of reading experiences which the target text is held to exemplify: more exactly, by an interpretive hypothesis concerning membership of a stylistic community. The basis for assembling a company of texts will not be topical continuity or the intellectual context of an historicized author, but relevance for outlining and assessing a distinct form of writing: an assessment which must eventually return to the presentist concern to judge between possibilities of doing theory.

My procedure, admittedly tentative and elementary, will be to seek companion texts by following trails of semantic concomitants from one author's reception history to others, on the assumption that uniform reading responses are likely indicators of stylistic communality. I will, as a presentational aid, use technical-sounding terms like "intertext" and "intertextual connections" but make no claim to apply the specific theory of intertextuality developed in literary science by, among others, Michael Riffaterre (1980, 1983, 1984). One reason is that its object, to explain the descriptive power and poetic sense of literary artifacts, is different from mine. In addition, it insists on a strong severance of intertextuality from ordinary concepts of source and influence that recalls Saussure's unduly severe division of pure language from actual usage. For example, Riffaterre contrasts the necessary, obligatory character of intertextuality, as an imperative built into decoding, with merely contingent referencing that depends a reader's knowledge: "Again, it would be wrong to confuse the intertext with allusion or quotation, for the relation between these and text is aleatory—identification depends upon the reader's culture—while the relation of text to presuppositions is obligatory since to perceive these we need only linguistic competence" (Riffaterre, 1980:627–28). Agreed, allusion (direct or indirect) is not the only way to identify an intertext, but in every example Riffaterre provides the textual triggers (excessive words, deficient words, undecidable words, etc.), the presuppositions they elicit, and the intertexts through which a search for the grammaticality of a problem element proceeds are all given and bound by the cultural knowledge of the reader. His typology of intertextual connections, which I will not review here, offers stimulating extensions of orthodox interpretive procedures, but not a radical break.

Nearer my interest and perspective is Riffaterre's supplementary distinction between "sociolect" and "idiolect":

> "Sociolect," in semiotic terminology, is language viewed not just as grammar and lexicon but as the repository of society's myths. These are represented by themes, commonplace phrases, and descriptive systems (stereotyped networks of metonyms around any given lexical nucleus). Sociolect is opposed to "idiolect," an individual's specific semiotic activity, and in the case of literature, the lexicon and grammar specific to a text and whose rules and verbal equivalencies are valid only within its limits. (Riffaterre, 1984:160)

Sociolects correspond to what we have previously called social semantemes, the working materials of sociological theory. As well as being more elegant, Riffaterre's term contains further advantages. Its obverse pairing with idiolect sustains the contrast I have stressed between generic text work and individual styling. Also, his references to "textlike segments" in sociolects and their association with "textual fragments" and texts proper (1984:142) remind us that the semantic materials worked into theory importantly include metaphors, descriptive categories, fashionable phrases, and so on, picked up ready-made from sociology, adjacent disciplines, and the pure and applied sciences in general. This is in addition to textual fragments from the mundane so-

　　　　THE STYLE AND TEXT WORK OF SIMMEL

ciolects of business administration, military technology, government, the mass media, and popular culture. I will then add the term to my vocabulary, yet hope to escape the judgment of Occam's razor.

Receptive Epithets and Simmelian Style

Levine (1971) leads us into the web around Simmel with a fairly full list of the negative terms marking his reception history: "Simmel paid a high price for his nonconformity. He has been damned with many epithets—amateur, exhibitionist, relativist, 'merely' talented, coquettish, empty, aimless" (Levine, 1971:lxi).

The length of the list—the size of the payment—suggests that Simmel wrote in such a way as to put himself at risk. Indeed, the word "haphazard," whose roots combine the notions of chance, fortune, accident, and risk, is another canonical epithet applied to his work (Levine, 1971:xi). Of course Simmel's emergence as a major theorist, one of the classics, shows that his stylistic gamble ultimately made his fortune. I could easily supplement the list with a greater number of positive terms. To avoid wandering around, however, it is important to put some order in the proceedings.

In the research stage, I made a comprehensive collection of epithets commonly applied to Simmel. These fell into seven lexically distinct groups. However, exploration of their stylistic correlates revealed considerable overlaps, and they were amalgamated into three sets. Overlapping was not eliminated, but the sets now formed a roughly cumulative series in which initial impressions were sharpened, deepened, and extended by the next set. There is a progressive movement toward the essence of Simmel's style, culminating in the third set. It is at this stage that the introduction of textual cômpanions becomes crucial for grasping his method of writing. It should be added that the intent of this chapter is to provide an analytic sketch—a development of stylistic hypotheses—in preparation for the systematic analysis of a single text in chapter 5.

In the lists below, the original seven groups are separated within sets by semicolons:

Set 1. Subtle, fine-woven, net weaver, cunning, evasive, secretive; light, airy, frothy, trivial, aimless, empty; brilliant, dazzling, talented, multifaceted.

Set 2. Modern, urban, sceptical, relativistic; aesthetic, poetic, artistic, essayistic.

Set 3. Haphazard, fragmentary, essayistic; marginal, nonconformist, guest, wanderer, stranger, ambivalent, paradoxical, excessive.

Note: The term "essayistic" appears twice because in set 2 it is associated with generic recognizability as art and in set 3 with generic unrecognizability as science.

Sources: Coser (1965); Frisby (1978, 1981); Levine (1971); Spykman, [1925] (1964); Wolff (1950, 1958).

Set 1: All That Glisters Is Not Gold

The stylistic basis for calling Simmel's work brilliant and dazzling is not immediately apparent. His writing is not brilliantly ornamented with rhetorical figures, nor does it dazzle with vivid evocations of social landscapes, characters, scenarios, atmospheres, and dramas. Even when dealing with topics like sociability and fashion—which are, if we have the example of Erving Goffman (1959) in mind, tailor-made for ethnographic brilliance—Simmel's treatment is sublimely (for some, ridiculously) analytic and philosophical. It is in this treatment, however—which, because it is repeated throughout Simmel's work, can be called a stylistic protocol—that we can begin to interpret not only "brilliant" and "dazzling" but the other epithets, positive and negative, making up the first set. The key—the thread—of their meaning is the term "multifaceted." To ground further discussion I will describe the multifaceted protocol at work in Simmel's analysis of fashion (Simmel, 1971: chap. 19).

The various perspectives and standpoints of human knowledge can be conceived as facets of reality for us. Simmel's standard procedure is to turn a selected phenomenon through a series of universal facets, adding local or, as he says, "provincial" variants of them to bring out its specific nature. Whatever the phenomenon, the protocol works, with endless refinement and care, toward a grasp of its essential structure, universal significance, and conditions of possibility. Which is to say, Simmel's investigations are philosophically keyed. This is confirmed by the fact that the philosophical facets observable in the essay on fashion reappear as analytic constants throughout Simmel's work. Sociological and psychological facets serve, in that order, the more provincial function of capturing the specificity of phenomena.

A further feature of Simmel's protocol, worth noting for its relevance to relativism (set 2) and paradox (set 3), is the application of concepts in obverse pairs. Simmel's presupposition is that all actual phenomena take shape at, or as, the boundaries of formally opposite principles.

The facets of fashion, given in the order of Simmel's presentation, are summarized in table 1. It is important to emphasize that the multi-

TABLE 1   Facets of Fashion

Facets	Implementive Concepts
Socio-Philosophical ("the whole history of society")	Socialist adaptation to society/individual departure from its demands
Psycho-Philosophical ("foundations of our individual destiny")	Uniformity/differentiation
Metaphysical	Cosmotheism/inherent separateness of elements
Biological	Heredity/variation
Anthropo-Philosophical ("essential forms of life in the history of our race")	Duration, unity, similarity/change, specialization, peculiarity
Social Psychological	Imitative tendency/individuality; Need for union/need for segregation
Sociological	Group integration/group division
Phenomenological (structure of consciousness)	Purely objective/purely subjective consciousness
Social-Psychological	Inclusiveness/exclusiveness; need for union/need for isolation; socializing impulse/differentiating impulse
Psychological (envy, show)	Object rejection/object desire; Conformity/conspicuousness
Cultural ("spirit of democracy")	Leading/following; ruling/submitting
Philosophical	Destruction/creation
Social-Psychological (female psychology)	Social imitation/individual conspicuousness; submissiveness/affirmation
Anthropo-Philosophical ("subtle impulses of the soul")	External self/internal self
Psychological (shame, freedom)	Ego emphasis/ego withdrawal; Outer dependence/inner dependence
Sociological	Upper- and lower-class conservation/intermediate-class changeability
Philosophical	Ephemeral/eternal; transitory/immortal; content/form; unnatural/natural

ple turns of the topic reflected here occur within the short span of an essay (around 10,000 words). The unit of presentation and the rhythm and range of facet turns within it are entirely characteristic of Simmel's style.

Simmel's writing conforms to what we know of his lecturing style. Kurt Wolff quotes testimony from a hearer: "Just about the time when . . . one felt he had reached a conclusion, he had a way of raising his right arm and, with three fingers of his hand, turning the imaginary object so as to exhibit still another facet" (1950:xvii). The visual image here is of a jeweler turning a stone so that light reflects from one surface or facet to another: hence a dazzling, brilliant show. Semantic connections to other imprints of his style are readily apparent. Facet comes from a diminutive of the French *face*, "face." Multifaced correlates with cunning, subtle, evasive, secretive. Certainly there is a striking contrast between Simmel's fast-shifting movements and the reading experience engendered by, say, Durkheim's scientifically proper demonstration procedures, where the reader is held relentlessly to a single, sustained sifting of alternative hypotheses in terms of their logical coherence and factual adequacy. With Durkheim and the scientific genre, the reader typically has no doubt where he stands with the author: the frame of understanding is secure, the author's identity unproblematic.

Partridge (1966) traces the etymology of "facetious" to the Latin *facetus,* meaning "elegant, witty, and fine-made." Here we might recall that "subtle" derives from *sub*(under) and *tela*(a weaver's web; hence fine-woven). Negatively, "facetious" is a rebuke against being improperly light and airy about a serious subject: making light (*levitas*) of something weighty (*gravitas*). The placement of fashion among cosmic life principles might be an example. It has a humorous effect close to wit. When Simmel applied for a chair at Heidelberg, Professor Schaefer, an establishment scholar at Berlin, wrote a negative recommendation linking his wit to lack of substance: "It would not seem right to me to give official standing to this orientation [sociology] at this early date, especially not at a university which is as important to state and nation as Heidelberg is to Baden and Germany—least of all in the person of one who operates more by wit and pseudo-wit than by solid and systematic thinking" (Coser, 1965:39).

Schaefer argues, with Simmel as a case in point, that sociology combines lack of scientific respectability with disrespect for moral and political authority. It is semantically satisfying to record that in *Chambers Dictionary* (1972) "facetiae" means both witty sayings and a bookseller's term for improper books.

The association of wit with an internal subversion of conventional seriousness is the basis of Sigmund Freud's theory of wit work. It must be admitted that his idiom of psychic energy being stored, displaced, and released is uncongenial to textual analysis, but he makes observations relevant to the imprints of Simmel's style that help confirm the connections I have made.

Part of Simmel's style is to turn a thought object through double-sided concepts, moving with essayistic brevity and minimal explanation from one face to another. Comparably, Freud observes that wit work is inherently two-faced; also, that it must omit explicit connectives to have its effect. These are necessary technical features tied to its diversion of rational structures and logical rules so as to release words and thoughts normally inhibited by them. Even when wit avails itself of extrarational, poetic, dream methods like remote allusion and substitution through symbols, comparisons, or trivia, it respects the limits of conscious thought. It has to, because the process depends upon social, hence conventional, communication. A witticism works by arousing and overriding in another limits which are too strong to override in oneself. The author of wit becomes an agent of pleasure for a recipient—a self-surrogate—in order to achieve a secondhand release of inhibition in himself. Obviously such reciprocity must work through sharing the ordinary limits of a language. In any case, wit does not need the extraordinary displacement methods of dreamwork: "It insists upon retaining the play with words or nonsense unaltered, but thanks to the ambiguity of words and multiplicity of thought-relations, it restricts itself to the choice of cases in which this play or nonsense may appear at the same time admissible (jest) or senseful (wit). Nothing distinguishes wit from all other psychic formations better than this double-sidedness and double-dealing" (Freud, 1938:755–56)

In short, wit exploits that inherent arbitrariness of language discussed previously as the foundation of Saussure's new science and the root idea of modern deconstructionist textual theory. We will return to the implications of this suggestion of textual companionship subsequently.

Recalling Schaefer's complaint against Simmel, Freud links wit with a resistance to the confines of "serious thinking" (Freud, 1938:713), an attempt to rejuvenate old and increasingly lost liberties of language. He refers to the affinity of students, those most rigorously trained in systematic, logical thought, for larks, rags, jests, satires, and witticisms. Wit is placed alongside intoxicants and drugs as a means of relieving "the pressure of logic" (p. 719). It has the advantage, however, of restoring playfulness without abandoning reason. Certainly it would be wrong to call Simmel an antilogical satirist or an anarchic jester. Freud makes a further observation that allows us to specify the sense of Simmel's wittiness. He distinguishes word wit from thought wit: exploitation of the "ambiguity of words" from the "multiplicity of thought-relations." I would say that Simmel trades stylistically on the latter rather than the former and is a witty thinker rather than a witty writer. His reading effect is not so much to make words play (as in puns, poetry, and crossword games) as make thought play multifacetedly around a topic. Essential to the effect is the engagement of the reader in a rational-logical reading attitude. Freud offers further explanation.

The wit process must disarm or suspend rational appraisal of itself, achieving what Freud calls automatic passage. Brevity of expression, reducing possible points of rational appraisal to a minimum, is one aid. More significant, however, are logical "facade formations." For example, "syllogistical facades excellently fulfill the purpose of riveting the attention by an allotted task" (1938:738). Within the hold of the task, the listener is impelled to fill in the omissions and ellipses that mark witty discourse. Along these lines Simmel sets rationally preoccupying tasks. Typically he tells the reader to see the "relational pattern," the "correlation," the "phenomenological formula," the "essential form" running through diverse content. Within a scholarly syntax and lexicon, the reader is led to try to rationally negotiate the unexpected twists of topic and surprising juxtapositions of heterogeneous detail that are features of his style.

Simmel's concern to preoccupy the rational consciousness of the reader is nowhere more explicit than in the preface to the multifaced essays, *Soziologie* (1908), the core of his translated work. True, he warns that "the manner in which the investigation connects phenomena finds no model for its formula in any domain of the recognized disciplines" (Wolff, 1950:xxvi); nonetheless, a rigorous methodological task is projected, that of "giving the fluctuating concept of sociology an unambiguous content, dominated by one, methodologically certain, problem-idea." This is turned into an explicit reading instruction: "The request to the reader to hold on, uninterruptedly, to this one method of asking questions, as it is developed in the first chapter (since otherwise these pages might impress him as an accumulation of unrelated facts and rejections)—this request is the only matter which must be mentioned at the head of this book" (Wolff, 1950:xxvi).

Of course, as Simmel's reception history testifies, the request has proven impossible to comply with, not least because Simmel's text work does not allow the reader to procede uninterruptedly. Does this mean that Simmel failed? By scientific standards of univocal discourse and systematic rules of method, he did. Even by his stated criterion of a single method of questioning, he falls short. If, however, the argument is accepted that sociological theory must be judged in its own terms—and these are linguistic and literary—then Simmel's prefatory statement must be treated as part of a total composition of reading responses, the meanings and value of which may lie precisely in its interruption of a univocal, uniform way of questioning social life. One should not read the preface as a legal contract.

Wolff (1950:xxvi) tries to save face for Simmel by likening the ten chapters of *Soziologie* to "connected nets" (recall again the etymology of "subtle"). Others have described the same texture (in Latin, *texere* means to weave) as weblike. But a web, however finely woven, is a thin metaphor to fit against the discipline demands of scientific demonstration: the cumulative inferential movement between rule, case, and result exemplified so powerfully by Durkheim. And Simmel did work for the discipline.

Von Wiese, reviewing *Soziologie,* mirrors Simmel's prefatory anxiety: "His observations run the danger of ending in scattered fragments. . . . At times the interweaving of his thoughts resembles a spider's web studded with glittering drops of dew; but a substantial breeze can destroy it" (Coser, 1965:55–56).

The unraveling breeze here would be a countervailing assertion of scientific rigor against Simmel's practice of analogically threading observations on general themes. Consider, for example, the amazing collection made on the theme of individuality and group expansion in the first few pages of a chapter translated from *Soziologie* (Simmel, 1971:253–61): the internationalism of aristocrats, social democrats, and early journeymen's unions; master-apprentice differentiation in medieval guilds; role differentiation of merchant from producer under capitalism; sociological differences between those who produce for export and those who produce for domestic consumption; the emancipation of serfs in Prussia; the Indian caste system; the structure of voluntary associations compared to that of guilds; the social order of the Quakers; differences of political structure between Northern and Southern states before the American Civil War; the mania for clubs in Germany; the social functions of adornment; Russian government during the preczarist period; and small-town provincialism in large French cities.

Fast cognitive play across such heterogeneous elements yields, for rationalist critics, an impression of meretricious flashiness and empty show rather than genuine brilliance. It underlies epithets like empty, aimless, and trivial. As before, it can be shown etymologically that the imprints of Simmel run together. We began with the image of a multi-faceted jewel. The word "jewel" derives from Old French *joel,* "plaything or trinket," and *jeu,* "game." Both derive from the Latin *iocus,* "verbal game." The negative image of Simmel's work is of scientifically empty words flashing by in an endless, pointless play of signification. I would note, for subsequent reference, the closeness of this negative impression to the distinctively modern event analyzed earlier as the anxiety of ontological emptiness. We glimpse here circumstantial evidence of Simmel's closeness to it.

Emile Durkheim reviewed *Soziologie* (Coser, 1965:44–49) and, unsurprisingly, could see no system and, therefore, for him, no order in it, only, at best, "subtlety."

> No connection can be discovered among the questions to which he draws the attention of sociologists; they are topics of meditation that have no relation to an integral scientific system. In addition, Simmel's proofs generally consist only of explanations by examples; some facts, borrowed from the most disparate fields, are cited but they are not preceded by critical analysis, and they often offer us no idea of how to assess their value. (Coser, 1965:48)

Without a thread unraveled by rational appraisal, Simmel's observations become scattered fragments and unconsidered trifles. Possibly jewels, possibly valueless trinkets, but not seriously weighed data.

I would add one more stylistic correlate of this first set of imprints, relating indirectly to lightness and aimlessness and directly to evasiveness. Although Simmel relies stylistically on a scholarly lexicon and syntax (however lacking in systematic rigor), his work conspicuously lacks the usual apparatus of footnotes and references through which discourse is conventionally tied to intellectual traditions. Hans Simmel described his father's attitude to his past and that of his family as one of aversion and evasiveness (Frisby, 1981:14). The omission of references to origins, sources, and predecessors in his work follows the same stylistic pattern. Its relevance to lightness is that reading can move quickly from facet to facet and across diverse observations, because there is no stoppage for citation, checking, and weighing up. Putting it another way, Simmel's writing is not weighed down, nor does it weigh the reader down with debts, acknowledgments, warrants, justifications and seals of approval. Coser (1965:3–4) notes that one astute reader,

Ortega y Gasset, caught his spirit exactly in calling him "a kind of philosophical squirrel jumping from one nut to another, scarcely bothering to nibble much at any of them, mainly concerned with performing his magnificent exercises as he leaped from branch to branch (or so it would seem) in the sheer gracefulness of his acrobatic leaps."

Excluding hyperbole and satire, Ortega registers an important aspect of the Simmelian reading experience. Coser adds, no doubt with Professor Schaefer in mind, that one can understand the disquiet of academic colleagues "accustomed as they were to the deliberate movements of professorial pachyderms" (Coser, 1965:4). Once more the etymology of the terms, which are all glosses of reading experiences, is satisfyingly circular. A pachyderm deliberates and is ponderous. The Latin *pensare* means "to weigh up, judge"; it is a cognate of *pondus,* "weight." To call Simmel thoughtless, however, would be a gross slander. It is only that he does not encode thoughtfulness through conventional scholarly writing formats. In terms of the third phase of the Cooleyan model of text work, Simmel's writing lacks generic recognizability, appearing almost sui generis, and to some it is simply disorganized. This is another element to be carried over and amplified in the remaining sets of imprints.

I will conclude with a return to the optical meaning of light, referring to the play of thought across multiple facets and expressed in reading impressions of brilliance and flashiness. Not only jewels (and glass) but gold (and fool's gold) are apt images of light playing on surfaces. A specialist in monetary theory, Knapp, described Simmel's *Philosophy of Money* as "weavings of gold in the carpet of life" (Frisby, 1978:10). In the same vein, Emil Utitz remarks: "His works must be collected, ordered, and minutely indexed, for only then can they become fertile for science . . . which will be able to change all the gold that glitters and shines in his work into its own coin" (Wolff, 1950:xxiii).

The intended reference of "its own" in the quotation is interestingly ambiguous. Is it "science" or "Simmel's work"? Most probably the former. The turning of Simmel's "weavings of gold" into the coinage of science (research hypotheses and theoretical concepts) has been the basis of his reception into sociology. Even dissenters have made little more of this than negative, plaintively "artistic" complaints against the hegemony of scientific method and technical rationality. The question remains, and will be the goal of my inquiry, of what, if it is not scientific, the proper coin and cash value of Simmel's glittering work might be.

Simmel indirectly broaches the question in his essay on the value of adornment and the distinction between mere trinkets and genuine jewels: "Talmi-gold and similar trinkets are identical with what they momentarily *do* for their wearer; genuine jewels are a value that goes beyond this; they have their roots in the value ideas of the whole social circle and are ramified through all of it. . . . Their genuineness makes their aesthetic value—which, too, is here a value 'for the others'—a symbol of . . . membership in the total social value system" (Simmel, 1950:343).

The thesis underlying my case study of *The Philosophy of Money* in chapter 5 is that the specific and exemplary value of Simmel's work as theory is to be found in its status as dialectical writing. This does not refer to its propositional content—I do not claim that Simmel is a dialectical philosopher—but to the kind of reading experience, the experience of language, he composes or, more accurately, which the reader is incited to compose in himself. The concept remains to be worked out through closer analysis and the location of an appropriate company of texts. Meanwhile, Simmel, again talking of adornment, provides a preliminary image of his own reading effect and its involving complicity:

> Beside its formal stylization, the *material* means of its social pur-
> pose is its *brilliance*. By virtue of this brilliance, its wearer appears as
> the center of a circle of radiation in which every close-by person,
> every seeing eye, is caught. As the flash of the precious stone seems
> to be directed at the other—like the lightning of the glance the eye
> addresses to him—it carries the social meaning of jewels, the
> being-for-the-other, which returns to the subject as the enlarge-
> ment of his own sphere of significance. The radii of this sphere
> mark the distance which jewelry creates between men. . . . But on
> the other hand, these radii not only let the other participate: they
> shine in *his* direction; in fact, they exist only for his sake. (Simmel,
> 1950:342)

Set 2: Aestheticism, Modernity, and the Objective Attitude to Life

Simmel's double-sided turning of thought objects from facet to facet already anticipates much of the sense of perspectivism, relativism, and objective distance informing set 2: aestheticism, mod-
ernity, and the objective attitude to life. Three stylistic features, closely related, need to be added:

1. In his sociological work Simmel maneuvers between opposite, usually value-laden terms without making the ethical or political judgments they invite. He withholds commitment to particular ideals or

goals and, in spite of registering strong distaste for the machine age and calculative rationality, offers no positive critique or basis for action. His stance is one of privatized detachment, not collective participation. There is in Simmel's style an intriguing combination of personal presence and absence: personal presence in a distinctive, unconventional shaping of scholarly words, yet absence of a social identity given by beliefs, commitments, and memberships. The combination is nicely captured by two close readers of Simmel:

> His interests in various subjects of study result from a common base, his "temperament," which constitutes the legitimate subjective factor for his cognition. (Hübner-Funk, 1982:2)

> This philosophy is not the world view of a person motivated by powerful ideas but the incursion of a self-less person into the world. (Kracauer, quoted by Frisby, 1981:1)

A "self-less," meaning a socially, politically indefinite person, is one who takes no positive stand against the world, does not strongly organize its features in decisive categories, and cannot therefore propose to reorganize it. Simmel's nearest commitment was to the cultivation, through culture, of unique individuality (the "soul" of the person); it is symptomatically revealing that when he came to analyze its conditions (Simmel, 1968:27–46), it was in terms of a fateful tragedy, an inevitable overwhelming of subjective cultivation by cultural forms and techniques, not sociohistorical-institutional conditions that might be resisted and changed. Simmel locates happenings in the frame of eternal being rather than historical transience; it is not his style to make them available for practical action.

2. Simmel's topical agenda, in contrast to that of most major sociologists, is not dictated by "major" problems and "big" issues of the time. Nor are they introduced when the topic strongly invites them. For example, the essay on conflict (Simmel, 1955), written in a context of Marxian theory and its practice of class conflict, is conspicuously devoid of references to it. Simmel is entirely preoccupied, through his usual protocol, with intricacies of universal form. Here, as throughout his major writings, there is a notable indifference to events of the day (responses to them appear only in occasional journalistic pieces and private correspondence), and to the structure and dynamics of conventionally salient institutions: religious, economic, educational, political, and so on.

3. Simmel's illustrative collections juxtapose "high" and "low," "great" and "small," "scholarly" and "casual" observations in con-

tiguous sentences, as if all were equally significant in principle. The procedure shows a tendency toward analogical merging of usual differences and a disposition to assert odd equivalences, close to the subordination of difference to semiotic free exchange characteristic of wit work and poetry. From the standpoint of scientific reason, rooted in stable verbal boundaries, firm demarcations, secure classifications, and the regulation of linguistic transitions by logical rules, this can only appear as a regrettable regression of language towards play and frivolity. From the comparable standpoint of moral orderliness, the stylistic denial of inherent weight and worthiness to favored objects and topics, the egalitarian respect for "Cinderellas among experiences" (Utitz, in Wolff, 1950:xx) might easily be taken for scepticism.

Durkheim's objection to Simmel's concept of society—"What a strange idea it would be to imagine the group as a sort of empty form of trivial cast that can indifferently receive any kind of material whatsoever!"—might as well have been applied to Simmel's paragraphs and essays (Coser, 1965:47). Relative to the demands of the royal road to science, Simmel's writing might appear reprehensibly like a three-way cross-roads (trivium) allowing any and all traffic through without discrimination. It would be liable to Hamann's judgment against impressionism, cited by Frisby (1981:104)—"The result of this wandering into the unbounded is an intellectual semi-obfuscation that almost borders on frivolity"—even liable to Simmel's own judgment against metropolitan worldliness: "The essence of the blasé attitude is an indifference toward the distinctions between things" (Simmel, 1971:329). "Scepticism," "triviality," and "frivolity" are semantic imprints of Simmel's composition procedures; as such they have a symptomatic, indicative validity. One is entitled to ask, however, whether they possess interpretive validity. The procedures they represent in negative may belong positively to another reading frame. Simmel certainly thought so. His declared intent is not to level what is high, great, and grand, but to elevate what is normally considered low, small, and insignificant: a kind of Blakean aspiration to see the universe in a grain of sand and eternity in an hour:

> The unity of these investigations does not lie, therefore, in an assertion about a particular content of knowledge and its gradually accumulating proofs but rather in the possibility—which must be demonstrated—of finding in each of life's details the totality of its meaning. (Simmel, 1978:55)

> The abstract philosophical construction of a system maintains such a distance from the individual phenomena, especially from prac-

tical existence, that actually, at first sight, it only *postulates* their salvation from isolation and lack of spirituality, even from repulsiveness. Here the achievement of such salvation will be *exemplified* (Ibid.)

> The essence of aesthetic observation and interpretation lies for us in the fact that what is typical is emphasised in the particular, what is normal is emphasised in the accidental, and the essential and significant in things is emphasised in what is superficial and fleeting. (quoted by Frisby, 1981:82)

Obvious problems arise: How, apart from a gradual accumulation of proofs, would it be possible to demonstrate that a totality of meaning can be found in assorted details? What would be the structure of its enactment? Also, if phenomena are isolated from practical existence by intellectual distancing, in what kind of intellectual discourse could salvation from isolation be enacted and exemplified?

My thesis about the linguistic nature of social theory leads me to suppose that the answer to the first question must lie in the demonstrative power of a certain form of reading experience, a certain style of writing, though what that style might be in Simmel's case, I have not yet established. The third quotation above encourages me to look to the term "aesthetic" for an answer to all the questions. Further encouragement is provided by the fact that some outstanding interpreters (for example, Frisby, 1981; Hübner-Funk, 1976) have followed the same signpost. As we shall see, it is ultimately misleading, but instructively so.

Simmel: An Aesthetic Writer?

There is no doubt of Simmel's involvement with aesthetics. He wrote extensively on art and the aesthetic attitude to life. Also, his style of life was marked by aestheticism: exquisite domestic decor, weekly gatherings of gifted and beautiful people, a passion for collecting objets d'art, especially from Japan, and acute sensory sensitivity. From these bases it has proven plausible to claim aestheticism as the definitive characteristic of his work. There it is associated with the collection of detail for its own sake, a "false pathos of distance in relation to all practical life" from which emerges "a powerless hyper-objectivity" (Goldscheid, in Frisby, 1981:86); a sensitive yet uncommitted curiosity about the nuances of human life reminiscent of the urban people watcher, "the *flâneur* who goes botanising on the asphalt" (Benjamin, in Frisby, 1981:78); and a holding back of prior notions and judgmental schemata to allow phenomena to emerge in awareness as they are in themselves:

> From his major writings we know very little of Simmel's own responses and attitudes to the contemporary social, economic and political events of his time. In some way, the author always appears absent from the text and we are left to guess at his own evaluations. It would not be difficult to relate this reticence to an aestheticisation of the world, to that distance from reality which Simmel himself so aptly describes. (Frisby , 1981:10)

Frisby nicely captures this sense of authorial withdrawal in the phrase "a man without qualities," taken from the title of a novel by Robert Musil, once a student of Simmel's. Such a selfless person could not exist (i.e., become textually manifest) except as a transient, taking on the qualities of encountered phenomena. In *The Philosophy of Money*, Simmel contrasts aesthetic "surrender to the object" with making the object surrender to us (as in strong scientific or moral classification). In the same passage he observes, "the specific quality of aesthetic enjoyment is the ability to appreciate and enjoy the object. . . . In place of the former concrete relationship with the object, it is now mere contemplation that is the source of enjoyable sensation . . . whereas formerly the object was valuable as a means for our practical and eudaemonistic ends, it has now become an object of contemplation from which we derive pleasure by confronting it with reserve and remoteness, without touching it" (Simmel, 1978:73).

It seems then that sociological objectivity might be textually enacted through aesthetic writing, an alternative to scientific distancing through conformity to rules of method. However, it carries enough negative connotations to make us hesitate to accept it as the full value of Simmel's work. When Goldscheid (cited previously) speaks of a false pathos of distance and hyperobjectivity, he can be heard to protest that language true to social life, reflecting its specific character, cannot be composed around an author without a social identity. The kind of reading experience styled, the interpretive movements enjoined between reader, imputed author, and subjects of discussion, would be essentially asocial, hence false to socially good language about society. Aesthetic reductionism may be more pleasurable than scientific reductionism, but it is still reductive. The question of Simmel's aestheticism thus gains a certain critical urgency for us.

From the standpoint of literary analysis, it is clear that neither subject matter nor life style is a sufficient basis for calling Simmel's writing aesthetic. Aesthetics can be written about in nonaesthetic modes, and the analogical extension of art collecting to Simmel's collections of examples is only metaphorically persuasive. An adequate basis would have to refer to the selective organization of words on the page and in the reader to a scanning, sense-making principle dictated by the text to decode the words. Reverting to ancient definitions, one might say that aesthetic writing is oriented to effects of beauty rather than to moral goodness or referential truth. However, the criterion terms are too vague and lack any reference to lexical or syntactic features of writing.

For our purpose, the most useful account of aesthetic writing currently available is in Roman Jakobson's (1960) model of the verbal act. There are six base elements of the verbal act and correspondingly six functional types according to which is given primacy or—I would prefer to say—which is the interpretive key of the act.

TABLE 2   Types of Writing

Primary Element	Functional Type
Addresser (author)	Emotive, expressive
Addressee (reader)	Conative, vocative, imperative
Code (language system, genre)	Metalingual, reflexive, glossing
Message (wording, text)	Poetic, aesthetic
Context (referent)	Referential, cognitive
Contact (physical channel, psychological connection)	Phatic, sociational, ceremonial

NOTE: The table is based upon Waugh's (1980) account of Jakobson's model of the verbal act.

In our culture the normal and normalizing type of language is referential. Other types are defined and critically licensed in relation to it. On this point I can cite Ebenezer Cooke, the hero of John Barth's novel, *The Sot-Weed Factor:*

> What I meant was that sundry virtues are—I might say *plain*, for want of proper language, and some *significant*. Among the first are honesty in speech and deed, fidelity, respect for mother and father . . . the second head's comprised of things like eating fish on Friday, resting on the Sabbath, and coming virgin to the grave or marriage bed, whiche'er the case may be; they all mean naught when taken by themselves, like the strokes and scribbles we call *writing*—their virtue lies in what they stand for . . . the first . . . are matters of public policy, and thus apply to prudent men, be

they heathens or believers. The second have small relevance to prudence, being but signs, and differ from faith to faith. The first are social, the second religious; the first are guides for life, the second forms of ceremony; the first practical, the second mysterious or poetic—" "I grasp the principle," Burlingame said. (Pp. 171–72)

A normal scientific or scholarly text is one where the referent context is plainly dominant. Receptive imprints of Simmel's work testify to its deviance from the norm, suggesting a functional imbalance or precariousness; the question is whether it is towards a specifically aesthetic function.

To begin with, there is no case for claiming that the referential function is underplayed in Simmel. If anything, there is a deviance of excess rather than deficit: "Out of this pure aestheticising element of his nature there emerges that excessive cobweb-like feature of his presentation of real circumstances" (Goldscheid, in Frisby, 1981:85). According to Kracauer (see Frisby, 1981:95–97), Simmel conceived the totality of life as a labyrinthine network and sought to reflect the infinite complexity and interrelatedness of its elements in his branching, allusive style. In his texts, propositional content is held together more by claimed similitudes of form, and argument more by analogy than by conceptual definition, logical implication, factual inference, and like chains of reason. The sense of excess is that of a surplus of evidential materials over the normal organizing procedures of referential writing.

Since in literary theory aesthetic (poetic) writing is diametrically opposed to referential writing, the very fact of referential excess rather than deficit in Simmel raises doubt as to whether "aesthetic" adequately names the direction of his deviance. Waugh's (1980) account of "poetic" (versus referential) writing will help weigh the matter more scrupulously.

Aesthetic texts are characterized by a radical internality in that their own structure provides the rationale for their elements. The choice and ordering of words is rendered explicable by architectural demands of felicity and appropriateness. This is most purely apparent in poetry, where the reason for a word's inclusion and placement is contained primarily in its rhythmic, sonic, lexical relations to prior and subsequent words. Waugh, commenting on Mallarmé's dictum that poetry is made with words, not ideas, says "poetry is not about the real world or life, but about itself" (Waugh, 1980:60). It is "autotelic" and "autoreferential" (p. 62).

A second defining feature concerns principles of construction. All messages are constructed through two operations: selection from a stock of possible patterns and lexical items, and combination into utterances. A stock is usually formed by similitude (metaphorical equivalence, analogy, phonetic similarity, grammatical parallel, synonymy, autonymy, and so on), while combination is normally based on contiguity (causal sequence, temporal sequence, logical implication, factual explication). In aesthetic writing, combination is governed by similitude rather than contiguity. Its parallelisms disturb the normal linearity of word chains, folding them back as in a maze or network:

> In the terminology of Roman Jakobson, the poetic function results from a certain formal organization. It relies heavily on internal references, which all have an aspect of repetition or partial repetition: for example, rhyme relies on the repetition of phonemes; rhythm is based on the repetition of fixed units of time and stress; puns, paradox, and parallelism are based on (partial) repetition of certain forms or meanings. . . . The number and strength of these internal references determine the strength of the poetic function. An emphatic poetic function absorbs much of the attention of the reader and diverts it from the cognitive, persuasive and other functions of the text. (Fokkema, 1982:62)

Enough has been said already of Simmel's nonlinear exposition, his presentation of phenomena as paradoxical equations of opposites, to provide plausible links with Jakobson's criteria of aesthetic writing. To this can be added Simmel's "conscious essayism," discussed by Frisby (1981:69–71). The essay is an art form, generically alien to scientific vehicles of writing like the monograph, the treatise, the research paper. No plain writer of referential prose would commit himself and his reader to blatantly literary, hence artificial, limits. Such writing must seem to be shaped by reason and reality, limited otherwise only by extraneous factors like scarce time, energy, and space. Simmel's choice draws attention to the status of his works as an artifactual creation, displaying instead of glossing over its artificiality.

Clearly there is a degree of aestheticism in Simmel's text work, but it would be misleading to make this the interpretive key of his writing. In the first place, the parallelisms are cognitive rather than linguistic. When, for example, Simmel makes the miser the equivalent of the spendthrift (Simmel, 1971:chap. 12), it is not through semantic or semiotic transformations, but through showing both to be instances of the same "demonic formula": means of pleasure (in themselves empty) are treated as ends in themselves. Recalling Mallarmé's distinction, Simmel's texts do not, as their dominant feature, densely fold words back upon themselves through lexical, phonetic, or syntactic parallelisms, but densely fold ideas back upon themselves through formulaic, analogical parallelisms. As I noted before on wit work in Simmel, he trades on the "multiplicity of thought relations," not the "ambiguity of words." In terms of Jakobson's model, his method of combination is still ruled by contiguity rather than equivalence, is analytic and inferential rather than "poetic," but it is set off from plain discourse by the fact that the contiguity is multiple and folds back on itself.

If the message—its linguistic structure—is not the primary element in Simmel's writing, then what, in terms of the Jakobson model (table 2), is? An observation by Richard Hamann provides a clue: "[Simmel] demands a prose style that does not limit itself to the results of thought but also seeks to reflect the movement of thought" (in Frisby, 1981:97). Textually, we can specify the movement of thought to mean the performative conventions of rational explication, inference, and demonstration sanctioned by science and logic: in other words, the code of scientific scholarship. This is the element to which Simmel's style obligatorily draws attention and which defines its function. Jakobson's term "metalingual" is perhaps misleading (for our purpose either reflexive or dialectical will be preferred), but the concept does capture the idea of writing that brings its operative code to the surface by making it densely present in the reading process.

It is, then, misleading to specify Simmel's departure from normal referential writing as aesthetic. The term distorts the basis of his difference and thus the exemplary and critical use it might have in sociological theory. In addition, at the programmatic level it obscures the move in Simmel's work to transcend aesthetic detachment and its attendant immersion in the concrete and particular, in the direction of a philosophy of life. I have already quoted the intent, in the preface to *The Philosophy of Money*, to demonstrate the totality of life's meaning in its details. That this was no move to an aesthetic ideal of totality is shown by his objection against socialism that it promoted not only the calculative rationalization of life but also its aestheticization. Frisby (1981:143) cites an essay where Simmel, discussing socialist ideology, finds it objectionable that "society as a whole should become a work of art in which every single element attains its meaning by virtue of its contribution to the whole . . . there socialist ideas are undoubtedly directed towards aesthetic interests." To this we can add Simmel's observation in "How Is Society Possible?" that the formally, which is to say aesthetically, perfect society would not, indeed could not, be perfect to live in (see Simmel, 1971: chap. 2, especially 20–22). Certainly it is necessary to resist Goldscheid's judgment (in Frisby, 1981:85) that "behind Simmel's whole work there stands not the ethical but the aesthetic ideal." While its informing principle may not be ethical, neither is it aesthetic. Rather, his work moves to incorporate or, in dialectical terms, sublate aestheticism.

The Modern Style

The case for calling Simmel's writing—the direction of its scholarly deviance—reflexive rather than aesthetic, is reinforced by considering the stylistic correlates of another reception category: modern. Valuable aid is given by Fokkema's (1982) analysis of "the period code of modernism." Congenial to our level of analysis, it is conceived as a specific literary code, a secondary and social variant of purely semiotic codes. Simmel's time (turn of the century) and cultural milieu (Berlin) are close to the documented emergence of modernist writing.

An early document is Valéry Larbaud's fictitious compilation of the complete works of A. O. Barnabooth. This imaginary writer, whose metalingual reflexivity is itself an emblem of modernism, is made to speak of "his" work in exactly the way readers have spoken of Simmel. It is willfully paradoxical; it wanders between genres in search of a totality of meaning; it causes the reader "in Nietzschean fashion" to wonder if "everything is relative"; the author is "only a combination of possibilities" which he (the imaginary author, hence the reader who occupies his place) has "every reason to doubt"; his "combination of trivial and sublime elements" yields effects of irony close to scepticism (Fokkema, 1982:70–71).

In his elusive relativism and lack of firm identity, Barnabooth is akin to Robert Musil's modernist anti-hero Ulrich, the "man without qualities," who Frisby (1981) associates with Simmel. Ulrich is a "person without bonds, without a need for a Yes or a No." Because everything is in incessant transformation, the best he can do is live hypothetically and hold aloof, like the scientist, from "facts that are trying to tempt him into over-hastily believing in them." This is why Ulrich "hesitates to become anything" and lives as a "person of possibilities" (Musil, cited in Frisby, 1981:161–62). Simmel exactly expresses the attitude of hesitancy and deferment in *The Philosophy of Money:* "in order to avoid dogmatic thought, we have to treat each position at which we arrive as if it were the penultimate one" (1978:104). Simmel, like Bernard in Gide's modernist novel *Les faux-monnayeurs* (The counterfeiters), enacts an "ethics of relativism" (Fokkema, 1982:76), whereby an ideal of authentic response to the particular forbids the delegation of judgment to any ethical, ideological, or other preemptive schema. Frisby (1981:135) cites passages in Simmel describing the "tendency of modern thought, with its dissolving of substances into functions" and concluding that only a renewed relativism, a recognition of the indispensability of multiple, shifting standpoints for comprehending any part of reality, can save us from "unceasing subjectivism and scepticism." There is then a more-than-aesthetic impulse at work in Simmel's writing: it has an ethical intent.

Simmel's correspondence to modernism extends down to syntactic features of sentence construction. Fokkema observes that the provisional, hypothetical effect of modernist writing is produced in part by typical connectors between utterances: "perhaps," "but," and "yet." Comparably, as Frisby (1981:98–99) relates, Kurt Gassen drew attention to Simmel's "characteristic subtle, hesitant, to some extent hypothetical manner of expression, in which the word "perhaps" . . . played such a prominent role"; Ernst Bloch called him a "philosopher of the 'perhaps,'" and linked that to a characteristic indecisiveness; Richard Hamann cites other typical connectors, "one might say" or "it may well be," and contrasts Simmel's practice with "dogmatically describing the true state of affairs."

To conclude the argument, there are typical semantic imprints of the modern code that exactly match those of Simmel's writing. Central to its semantic constitution are "*awareness, observation* and *detachment*" (Fokkema, 1982:71; italics in original): the noted attributes of the flâneur (botanist of the asphalt) and "man without qualities." A second semantic layer consists of "subtle," "ingenious," "risk," and "refusal" (of final judgments and set boundaries): all regular concomitants of Simmel's work.

Summing up, it is evident that a great deal of what it means stylistically to call Simmel modern can be recovered by placing his writing in the context of a definite literary code of modernism. Its full significance, however, is only realized by examining Simmel's proximity to the linguistic crisis of confidence reviewed in chapter 3, one of the inaugural events of modern consciousness, associated retrospectively with Saussure's new science of language and currently with the "deconstructionist" tendency in language philosophy and literary criticism. Discussion of the third set of epithets will offer further evidence of Simmel's proximity to this company, enough to support it as a plausible hypothesis, textual testing of which will be undertaken in chapter 5.

Set 3: Writing That Refuses Settlement

The question of Simmel's writing I wish to address is its specific exemplary value for social theorizing. The beginning of an answer is that Simmel's writing is, at its best, at its most exemplary, writing that refuses settlement. Previously, in different contexts, three terms have been used to describe such writing: dialectical, reflexive, and deconstructive. They are affiliated at the compositional level but derive from distinct intellectual traditions which it may be advantageous, for both analytic and critical purposes, to retain. However, each carries such a freight of disputed content that a statement of intended usage, narrowing possible meanings, is called for.

Dialectical Writing

I treat dialectical writing first, because it refers to an end product—a type of reading experience—relative to which reflexivity and deconstruction are conceived as particular linguistic means of production, referring to semantic and syntactic structures through which the dialectical effect may be achieved. This ends-means ordering reflects the priority I have given to reader-response analysis in undertaking a literary criticism of sociological theory: the choice of a hermeneutic over a semiotic or linguistic approach.

Dialectical writing is marked by an active engagement with interpretive routines and normal decoding strategies which puts them at risk. More fully, there is a threefold reading experience in which routines and strategies are elicited, then confounded, so as to enforce a higher-level reordering. It would be too grandiose to claim that the self is thus changed, but at least there is a reformation, however small or local, of oneself as interpretant. Dialectical writing conforms to the pattern of all dialectical processes, Socratic or Hegelian: bringing out a higher possibility of integration through enactment, negation, and sublation.

I owe the concept of dialectical writing to Stanley Fish's case studies of "self-consuming artifacts" (1972). Fish contrasts dialectical with rhetorical forms of literary experience, using rhetorical in the pejorative sense of Plato's *Gorgias,* where Socrates calls it a form of pandering because it aims only to flatter the listener (reader) by confirming the truth of existing beliefs, the authenticity of normal value judgments, and the adequacy of normal ways of thinking about the world. In short, the rhetorical form uncritically duplicates prior plausibility structures in the listener (reader), whereas the dialectical form, not by preaching but by performance, makes them questionable. Fish comments that if the characteristic experience of rhetoric is pleasurable flattery, that of dialectic is humiliation: not of the whole self, but of interpretive certitude.

Fish usefully adds another distinction between two ways of making sense of the world: the first through making divisions, classifications, and firm distinctions, the way of logical, rational discourse; the second through holistic intuition of interconnection and interchangeability, the way of imagination based upon what Jakobson calls the principle of equivalence, or what the poet Hart Crane has called the logic of metaphor. Fish's thesis is that in the experience of dialectical writing one is moved away from the first toward the second. The strong premise linking this to the previous distinction is that rational division is the "natural" way of human thought and therefore always the basis of prior plausibility structures. As it stands, this formulation is unacceptable. Comparative historical and cross-cultural studies of cognition have rendered suspect the concept of natural human reason (see, for example, the debates in Hollis and Lukes, 1982). Moreover, the thesis makes incomprehensible the proven capacity of scientific thinking, in its historical emergence, to dialectically disturb established ways of thought. The thesis is only useful then as a suggestion about a probable form dialectical writing will take in a cultural situation dominated by a rationalistic code; however, particular coding rules would have to be specified for analysis to proceed.

Rather than repeat Fish's examples of dialectical writing (see also Fish, 1980:183–96), I will draw an illustration from Simmel: the second paragraph of the preface to *The Philosophy of Money* (1978). Having in the first paragraph argued the indispensibility of philosophy to grasp at the "lower boundary of the exact domain" of science the limits and conditions of cognition, and at the upper boundary, the interpretive significance of "the ever-fragmentary contents of positive knowledge," Simmel proceeds, rationalistically, to distinguish a philosophy from a history of money:

> If there is to be a philosophy of money, then it can only lie on either side of the economic science of money. On the one hand, it can present the pre-conditions that, situated in mental states, in social relations and in the logical structure of reality and values, give money its meaning and its practical position. This is not the question of the origin of money, for such a question belongs to history

THE STYLE AND TEXT WORK OF SIMMEL

and not to philosophy. Moreover, no matter how much we appreciate the gain in the understanding of a phenomenon that is derived from a study of its historical development, its substantive meaning and importance often rest upon connections of a conceptual, psychological or ethical nature that are not temporal but rather are purely material. Such connections have, of course, been realised by historical forces, but are not exhausted by the fortuitousness of the latter. The significance, the dignity and the substance of justice, religion or knowledge lie completely beyond the question concerning the manner in which they were historically realised. (Simmel, 1978:54)

Of interest here is the undermining of the argument by its literary presentation. The excerpt proclaims, at beginning and end, a discontinuity, a complete difference between a philosophy and a history of money. The literary means of presentation rests on a familiar "not . . . but . . . " contrast structure. It is so filled with it, however, as to disturb confidence in the adequacy of logical contrast to decode the message and therefore the meaning of the message itself.

A minor coding disturbance occurs in negotiating sentences 2 and 3. In ordinary language, preconditions and origins belong equivalently to the same paradigm; here they are separated out to contrast philosophy with history. This turning of a normal equivalence into a difference is made all the harder by the fact that the list of preconditions includes "mental states" and "social relations," as well as "logical structures." The empirical cast of the first two preconditions frustrates any move to distinguish preconditions (studied by philosophy) from origins (studied by history) in terms of the Kantian distinction between a priori knowledge and empirical knowledge. The equivalences made by the list also confound the initially strong contrast, repeated in the first sentence here, between philosophy and science. "Mental states" and "social relations" are both objects of scientific study, embedded in empirical, contingent, historical conditions, yet the list equates them with "the logical structure of reality and values" in a supposed contrast of philosophy (examining preconditions) with science. The scientific connotations of the "philosophy" list confound the reader's attempt to follow the instruction to see strong separateness from science. As if to renew the attempt, the theme of separateness is turned shortly after into a dramatic proclamation: "Not a single line of these investigations [*The Philosophy of Money*] is meant to be a statement about economics [the economic science of money]." The philosophy of a phenomenon is presented as something that can be written separately from its science, at a lower (analytic) and upper (synthetic) boundary with it, yet not be about that science.

The largest jolt to seeing discontinuity in the "not . . . but" contrasts, forcing the adequacy of that normal reading strategy into question, is administered in sentence 4 of the extract. The philosophy of a phenomenon is said often to rest on conceptual, psychological, or ethical connections "that are not temporal but rather are purely material." It is the last word which is contextually unexpected and disruptive. Instead of supplying a conventional philosophical contrast to temporal, like essential, necessary, a priori, the sentence confronts us with a word (material) conventionally associated with temporality (as in body-soul, matter-spirit contrasts). The effect is amplified by the inclusion of "psychological" in "purely material" connections, negating the normal mental-material opposition.

To sum up, the use of "material" to complete a not-but contrast with "temporal" uncomfortably confounds conventional expectations and lets in terms usually equated with temporality. The sentence requires us rethink "material," its semiotic value, such that it is transformed from an antonym of essential, necessary, and so forth, into a synonym, and from a synonym of "temporal" into an antonym. Whatever the results of this enforced realignment of semiotic values, involving a reconstruction of conventional discursive meaning space, the viability of the philosophy versus history (and science) division has been compromised and the interpretive adequacy of binary decoding through mutually exclusive opposites made questionable.

Of course disturbance or disruption of prior plausibility structures and interpretive codes is only an experience of negation. For writing to be defensibly dialectical, rather than dismissible as merely confusing, muddled, or capricious, it must be shown to move us in a positive direction. In Simmel's case, though this is not yet the appropriate place to attempt a textual demonstration, the direction is toward truth to the integrity and flux of life against the fragmentation and fixity of rational understanding. I would note, as one marker of the company of texts to which Simmel's writing belongs, that he was often referred to as "the German Bergson" and that in America William James took up Bergson's doctrine that life has characteristics opposite to those of rational discourse. One of Simmel's favorite students, Georg Lukács, was highly responsive to the doctrine—"nothing is ever completely fulfilled in life, nothing ever quite ends. . . . Everything flows, everything merges into another thing" (quoted in Simmel, 1978:19)—and sensed this in Simmel:

> Simmel's importance for sociology—I am thinking here primarily of his *Philosophy of Money*—lies in the fact that he drives the analysis of determinations so far and crowns it with such sensitivity as has never been carried out before him and yet, at the same time, he makes evident with inimitable precision the sudden changes in the determinations, their autonomous limitations, their halting before that which they cannot determine. (quoted in Simmel, 1978:16)

Here I would stress again that a dialectical writer is not necessarily a dialectical philosopher, nor vice versa. A dialectical schema may well be propounded in nondialectical writing or dialectical writing used against a dialectical schema. A famous example of the latter, again providing a marker of the company to which Simmel's text work belongs, is Kierkegaard's critique of Hegel. What Kierkegaard finds revulsive in Hegel is abstraction from existence: the reduction of its openness and so the actuality of choice to system formulas, the "metaphysical assassination of ethics" (Thulstrup, 1980:278), the absorption of existential either/or contradiction—"the key to heaven,"—into speculative both-and-neither synthesis, "the way to hell" (Bretall, 1946:19). Yet this was no simple relationship of rejection; Kierkegaard strangely admired Hegal. Bretall (1946:191) recalls his observation that if Hegel had only appended a footnote to his systematic edifice saying that it was only a "thought-experiment," he would have been the greatest of thinkers. As it is, Hegel's pretensions make him "merely comic." Again, Thulstrup (1967:94) cites a journal entry for 1837, where Kierkegaard sympathizes with great philosophers who have suffered popularization: Kant first, and now Hegel "the one of all modern philosophers, who by his difficult style surely most commands silence." That this is a positive valuation is attested by Kierkegaard's choice of the pseudonym Johannes de Silentio to convey the highest, the religious form of life in *Fear and Trembling: A Dialectical Lyric* (1843).

The stylistic affinity between Hegel and his close critic is that both wrote dialectically: both composed that kind of reading experience, though with different devices and specific effects. Michael Moran (1970) has characterized Hegel's style in a way that fully displays the type of writing and in specific terms identical to those used of Simmel.

Simmel has been called guest, wanderer, stranger, marginal, ambivalent, paradoxical, excessive, and noncomformist (Levine, 1971:x;

Frisby, 1981:7; Coser, 1965:29–39; Novak, 1976). These are imprints made against ground-rule norms of scholarly presentation and discipline specialization. Simmel's stylistic offences, in summary review, are:

1. A presentation method requiring a phenomenon to be rotated through multiple facets, representing areas of knowledge too diverse for a single person to claim expertise in all of them or therefore that particular insurance for the results. The reading relationship is not secured, nor is it fettered by the imprimatur of expert authority. One is reminded of an entry in Kierkegaard's diary (1851): "Without authority, to draw attention to the phenomenon of religion and of Christianity—that is the description which applies to the whole of my literary activity. From the start I stated . . . that I had no authority; I prefer to consider myself as the *reader* of my writings rather than as the *author* of them" (quoted by Diem, 1965:84–5). Bracketing the special reference to religion and Christianity, this applies also to Simmel's literary activity. The suspension of hierarchical authorial privilege, of normatively conferred authority to speak, can be taken as a necessary feature of dialectical writing: writing that shifts the locus of meaning from authorial dictate to interaction with the reader.

2. A jettisoning of footnotes, supportive references, and so on, that effaces conventional indicators of membership in a tradition and community. This is for Simmel a means of suspending normative authorial authority.

3. A methodological cultivation of paradox contrary to the rules of logic which empiricism and the philosophy of science make binding on rational discourse. The most elementary level of empirical measurement is nominal classification based on internally homogeneous and mutually exclusive categories. Simmel's elementary supposition is that phenomena are compounds of conceptual opposites.

4. A fragmentary, analogical, nonlinear organization of materials around flexible themes, as opposed to the norm of cumulative, linear, demonstrative organization around firm propositions.

5. A preferred form of literary expression, the essay, which belongs to art, not science. Its "political" implications and relevance for dialectical writing are brought out well in O'Neill's study of Montaigne's textwork:

> The essay is, then, an experiment in the community of truth, and
> not a packaging of knowledge ruled by definitions and operations.
> The essay is a political instrument inasmuch as it liberates the writer

and reader from the domination of conventional standards of clarity and communication. The essay is a basic expression of literary initiative, authority, style and gratuity accomplished against the limits of received language. (O'Neill, 1982:9)

Moran describes Hegel's accomplishment as the fashioning of a literary style which reversed "certain internationally accepted canons" (1970:577) —derived from the beginnings of modern rationalism in the seventeenth century (Bacon, Descartes, Locke) and its extension in the Enlightenment (Leibniz, Hume, Kant)—making it possible, within philosophy, to write and think in a radically different way. Its direction is exactly that of Simmel's writing: willfully paradoxical, nonlinear, and reflexively labyrinthine. Hegel's style, like Simmel's, informed his lectures as well as his writing, yielding similar responses of bewilderment, outrage, bedazzlement, and fascination. G. H. Hotha, who attended Hegel's lectures in the late 1820s, reports that they did not advance in definitional, propositional steps, but "kept turning with similar words again and again round the same point . . . slowly and carefully, by apparently insignificant intermediate steps, a thought had been made to limit itself so as to show its one-sidedness. It had been broken up into distinctions and entangled in contradictions" (Moran, 1970:577–78). Always, however, to make a higher unity of the starting thought, not to engage in schoolboy paradoxes for their own sake.

In Hegel, as in Kierkegaard, in Bergson, and in Simmel, there is an express disjunction between the limits of normal propositional forms of discourse and the structure of concrete reality, between the logic of referential, rational language and the (anti) logic of life. As Lukács said of Simmel, Hegel drives propositional and definitional limitations to the point where they halt before that which they cannot determine.

Moran offers as an example a passage where Hegel is defining reality. After advancing several propositional predicates, Hegel concludes with a deconstructive paradox: "Only in this movement in itself, which is also perfect rest, does the Idea, Life, Spirit, dwell." (quoted in Moran, 1970:578.) Comparable passages, using conventional discursive formats to confound conventional understanding, abound in Simmel. An example, which with redoubled aptness is about marginality, occurs at the beginning of an essay on the transcendent character of life: "Man's position in the world is defined by the fact that in every dimension of his being and his behavior he stands at every moment *between two boundaries*. . . . By virtue of the fact that we *have* boundaries everywhere and always, so accordingly we *are* boundaries" (Simmel, 1971:353; italics in original).

The passage states a "fact" from which a logical connector ("so accordingly") leads to an inference which by conventional usage is at odds with its premise. An equation has been made, through logical syntax, which exceeds logical sense. In such ways does dialectical writing move to convey the transcendent character of concrete reality—of life—relative to concept.

Moran comments that Hegel's writing is not descriptively, but linguistically, referential, which is to say in Jakobson's terms (table 2) metalingual, because its terms of reference fold back upon themselves and their coding conventions rather than extending straight out into extralinguistic observables. Indirect support for my association of Simmel with the language crisis marking the advent of modernism appears in Moran's further observation that one of the key articulators of the crisis, Mallarmé, was spellbound by Hegel's reflexive incantations and their eclipse of plain language and delusive common sense. This encourages me to conclude that dialectical writing is not just an analytic type but a historical style running parallel to, and entwined with, plain, clear rational discourse. The line runs back from Derrida, through carriers of the language crisis, to Kierkegaard, Hegel, and if Moran's genealogy is accepted, German mystical writers like Meister Eckhart and Jacob Böhme. It is a stylistic lineage to which Simmel's writing belongs, even if only marginally.

Reflexive and Deconstructive Writing

Reflexive writing is writing that thematizes its constitutive code(s), for example, its generic conventions, not, however, by theorizing them but in performance. As we have seen, modernism is defined precisely by this characteristic. Distinctively modernist, for example, is Pirandello's mirror play, *Each in His Own Way,* where the "real" audience faces a scripted audience, and where actors placed in the auditorium insist that they are the real characters being wrongly represented by actors on stage. Also modernist are reflexive novels like Nabakov's *Pale Fire,* D. M. Thomas's *White Hotel,* and C. Scott's *Antichthon.* Modernism delights in parody, and parodies are reflexive performances of generic conventions.

Deconstructive writing I will define narrowly as a form of reflexive writing identified by a particular code it folds back along. The code includes what Moran refers to as the canons of empiricism and rationalism, a code translated into syntactic rules and carried into mainstream sociological method by the philosophy of (social) science, an idealized reconstruction of natural science inquiry intended to methodologically guide social inquiry. To name the entire form of thought to which this, for our purpose, especially pertinent code belongs, I will borrow from Derrida (1976) the term logocentrism.

Systems of thought—ways of knowing the world—are ruled by domain assumptions whose writ runs throughout a cognitive community. The history of such communities reveals an honorable line of enfants terribles who stand at the edge of the crowd and cry that the emperor has no clothes. With logocentrism, Derrida gives the cry in reverse: there is no emperor, nothing, inside the clothes. I have recorded it already in discussing the anxiety of ontological emptiness (chapter 3), but its meaning needs closer understanding. We must ask first, what does deconstructive writing deconstruct? It is not analytically adequate, for our purpose, to answer in the usual manner of Derridaian literary critics: "The deconstruction, rather, annihilates the ground on which the building stands by showing that the text has already annihilated that ground, knowingly or unknowingly. Deconstruction is not a dismantling of the structure of a text but a demonstration that it has already dismantled itself" (Miller, 1976:341).

Not only is the attribution of dismantling power to a text open to the charge of reification, and the reduction of the reader to an innocent bystander disingenuous, but this kind of formulation vaguely conflates deconstructive writing with any reflexive negation whatsoever and could even be taken to apply to merely inept or grammatically incoherent writing. Many student essays undecidably defy determinate meaning and collapse themselves into textual ruins, but one would not want to call them deconstructive writing, unless for satirical effect. It is to avoid such problems and to sharpen concepts that I conceive reflexive writing to be an emergent organization of reading responses in which generic coding conventions, whatever they may be, are made performatively salient; and I conceive deconstruction as a particular variant in which (*a*) the coding conventions are those of logocentrism, and (*b*) they are made not merely salient but performatively inoperable. I say inoperable, rather than impossible, to retain the dialectical notion of something being negated yet not abandoned. In other words, reading does not just grind to a halt and start again on a different foundation; it reworks the foundation. I take this to be the force of Derrida's observation that not a single destructive proposition can be pronounced outside the form and logic of what it seeks to contest (1978:280).

What then is logocentrism? I will reduce it, logocentrically, to the nutshell form of three basic tenets: (1) within experienced reality there is something—essence, being, absolute presence—to which (2) phonetic writing has privileged access over other forms; because (3) it represents the spoken word which in turn represents the mental imprint of reality itself. There is a chain of representation linked to ontological mimesis in which reality, the signified, has an immediate relation to the spoken word and a mediated one with written signs. Logocentrism presupposes the possibility of bringing them into alignment so that a mimesis of reality can be achieved in truthful words. Writing in this hierarchy is only, at best, an accurate recording instrument of words: a faithful servant of language. Timothy Reiss, characterizing what he calls the analytico-referential model of discourse, says, "Its exemplary formal statement is *cogito-ergo-sum* (reason–semiotic mediating system–world)," where three orders, rational, linguistic, and real, are brought into a coincident identity called truth (Reiss, 1982:31).

Logocentrism, whose classic scholarly expression is metaphysics, has ruled large areas of thought in Western culture from Ancient Greece until modern times. Now its foundation is deconstructively revealed as irremediable absence—infinite deferment of the signified—rather than absolute presence. The entirely conventional, ontologically arbitrary nature of all, including phonetic, signifiers has come to awareness. Far from writing being a subordinate convenience of language, language is only one form of "writing" (in the broad sense of semiotic coding, the possibility of inscription). The semiotic inside of language has folded back and around to become also an outside. The word (logos) has turned out to be only a sign; the signified only a "differance" (Derrida's neologism) between signs.

Derrida claims no personal role in deconstruction; he attributes it to intellectual and technological developments. For example, the practical efficacy, demonstrated in science, of "unreal" mathematical symbols and the attendant devalorization of words in relation to truth; the discovery and positive valuation of nonphonetic notation systems by anthropologists and historians of writing; the cybernetic concept and invention of information-processing systems; and the demonstrated coding of biochemical messages in organic materials.

I would add that while Derrida describes historically a special relation between logocentrism and metaphysics, this does not justify the argument made by Rorty that since metaphysics is a spent genre of largely historical interest, deconstruction has no important work to perform (1984). The code has been transmitted to other discourses (I

112   THE STYLE AND TEXT WORK OF SIMMEL

have mentioned the philosophy of science as an important one) and to multifarious institutional practices sanctioned by them: social research methods, applied social science, policy analysis, factual reportage, and the entire apparatus of rational, bureaucratic administration (see, for example, Foucault, 1977; 1980). The same social phenomena to which critical theory is a response also give deconstructive writing work to do.

Further clarification is called for by a divergence between Derrida's insistence that deconstruction is already a movement of language within logocentric structures—a preoccupying presence "inhabiting them *in a certain way,* because one always inhabits, and all the more when one does not suspect it" (1976:24)—and the typical view of expositors (for example, Rorty 1984; Leitch, 1980; Culler, 1982) that deconstruction is a method, a critical strategy, a militant program applied to texts from the outside. (Marxian theorists are used to similar difficulties over the place of Marx's work in the demise of capitalism.) The problem could be patched over by distinguishing, in ideal-type fashion, between texts that manifestly enact their own deconstruction by making such moves an obligatory part of reading response, and those which, because the moves are latent and hidden, must be supplemented by deconstructive commentary. However, this would still leave a question my account must address: What is the nature of the relationship between logocentric and deconstructive writing?

In the case of Simmel's writing—and here I accept Rorty's stricture that the "big esoteric problem" of the "onto-theological tradition" needs to be replaced by "lots of little pragmatic questions" (Rorty, 1984:3)—the most appropriate answer lies in Miller's essay "Critic as Host" (in Bloom et al., 1979:217–53). Departing from the title, Miller makes great play with the relationship of parasite to host.

Characteristically, Miller moves through an etymological restoration of lateral meanings. The root "para" connotes simultaneous proximity and distance:

> Something simultaneously this side of a boundary line, threshold, or margin, and also beyond it, equivalent in status and also second-ary or subsidiary, submissive as of guest to host. . . . A thing in "para," moreover, is not only simultaneously on both sides of the boundary line between inside and outside. It is also the boundary itself . . . allowing the outside in, making the inside out, dividing them and joining them. (Miller, 1979:219)

In the same passage, Miller describes words with "para," including, of course, paradoxical, as refusing settlement in a sentence. He compares them to "a slightly alien guest" inside a linguistic family circle. One can see this in the circle that includes parasite and host. The sense of opposition between them is readily confounded. In original Greek usage, a parasite was a welcome guest to share food (*sitos*); the words guest and host go back to a common root.

Simmel might on several grounds be accounted a theorist of the "para." His reception epithets prominently include guest, marginal, wanderer, and stranger; he used paradox as a literary method of theorizing; also, of course, he famously thematized marginality in "The Stranger." (Simmel, 1971: chap. 10.) Yet, as was shown in the passage discussed previously on man being a boundary between boundaries, the characterization has to be justified by the style, not the content. To illustrate once more, consider the opening paragraph of "The Stranger":

> If wandering, considered as a state of detachment from every given point in space, is the conceptual opposite of attachment to any point, then the sociological form of the "stranger" presents the synthesis, as it were, of both these properties. (This is another indication that spatial relations not only are determining conditions of relationships among men, but are also symbolic of those relationships.) The stranger will thus not be considered here in the usual sense of the term, as the wanderer who comes today and goes tomorrow, but rather as the man who comes today and stays tomorrow—the potential wanderer, so to speak, who although he has gone no further, has not quite got over the freedom of coming and going. He is fixed within a certain spatial circle—or within a group whose boundaries are analogous to spatial boundaries—but his position within it is fundamentally affected by the fact that he does not belong in it initially and that he brings qualities into it that are not, and cannot be indigenous to it. (Simmel, 1971:143)

The topic is broached by a sentence having the conventional structure of a logical connection: if, on the one hand, *X,* then, on the other hand, Y. It turns out, however, to carry an alogical juxtaposition of wandering X with the stranger Y, whereby the former is characterized by the presence of detachment and the absence of its opposite, while the latter is paradoxically characterized by the presence of both. By no stretch of reasoning can this be read as a logical connection, even though the syntactic structure requests it. This is followed by a statement (which Miller would delight to note is parenthetic), inviting itself to be read as a generalization of which the first sentence is "another indication." Again, the rational structure invoked is impossibly overburdened. The first sentence simply cannot be read as an indication of any empirical generalization and certainly not that given in the rest of the statement.

The third sentence not only defies the logical linkage to its predecessor signified by "thus," it supplements the opening term "wandering" in such a way as to nullify the original definition. This does not result in mere muddle, because the supplementary phrase "potential wanderer" can be recognized as a paraphrase of "stranger." Admittedly, this means accepting the strange idea of a wanderer fixed in social, perhaps physical, space, but at least some internal sense of analogical coherence has begun to appear in the ruined place of conventional coherence: from within a group the stranger is to the wanderer as the actual is to the potential.

In conclusion, an important point to retain for the case study to follow is that a parasitic binding of deconstructive to logocentric writing can be achieved in different ways. One way, closely analyzed by Althusser and Balibar (1970), is exemplified by Marx's deconstructive embrace of the concepts of political economy, especially (in the crucial first volume of *Capital*), its labor theory of value. His procedure is a discursive cultivation, in its own terms, of the founding concepts of political economy: commodity, labor, use value, exchange value, surplus value. Following Althusser and Balibar's reconstruction, the procedure is conducted on two premises: first, that the concepts are abstractions from a real material base which they represent only in gaps and blanks; second, these absences are not remediable oversights but are essential to the coherence of the system of thought, to its internal rationality.

Marx's most subversive move is to reiteratively apply the labor theory of value to the value of labor. This shows that (*a*) the theory only makes sense by accepting that labor is not only a commodity but a socially situated power of production grounded in flesh-and-blood people; (*b*) in terms of political economy's system of concepts, labor is an excessive phenomenon, because it alone of all commodities has an economic value in excess of the value of labor time needed to produce it; this is the only real surplus value; and (*c*) bringing the latent notions of labor power and its workaday production of a value surplus to its true wage value into political economy destroys a thought system whose coherence depends on formulaic enclosures of labor in the abstract. Marx reveals from within a concept it must but cannot contain.

A totally different strategy of deconstruction is displayed in Kierkegaard's text work. There multiple, pseudonymous authors are used to enact successively subversive shifts through aesthetic, ethical, and religious ways of being in the world.

Kierkegaard's method of what he called "indirect communication" is designed to be self-involving in the sense of enforcing responsibility and choice on the reader (the first of these being Kierkegaard himself). Louis MacKey (1971:248) quotes Kierkegaard to the effect that he needed "polynymity" in order to convey possibilities of relationship to existence that would be free of the judgments and biasing colorations that a single consistent authorial voice cannot help but communicate. His dialectical writing aspires to keep itself open: "Every human activity is diffracted immediately into a host of relativities, for the literary presentation of which Kierkegaard's device of multiple interlocking pseudonyms was the happiest available instrument" (MacKey, 1971:255).

A mark of Kierkegaard's determination to avoid interpretive closure appears in a journal entry from near the end of his life called "A Sad Reflection." Using terms identical to those of Simmel reflecting near death on his work, Kierkegaard says, "I shall leave behind me, intellectually speaking, a capital by no means insignificant" (Kierkegaard, 1946:432). He fears that his wealth will pass only to a decisive interpreter, the Professor, then adds an oddly deconstructive note, odd because it hits home yet is impossible to heed. It is a defensive gesture which, especially coming from a polyonymous author who has abdicated authority over the reader, dismantles itself: "And even if the 'Professor' should chance to read this, it will not give him pause, will not cause his conscience to smite him; no, this too will be made the subject of a lecture. And again this observation, if the Professor should chance to read it, will not give him pause; no, this too will be made the subject of a lecture." Here, surely, is writing that is simultaneously reflexive, deconstructive, and dialectical.

Given the different literary devices through which deconstruction can be woven into logocentric writing, we must ask of Simmel's text work in *The Philosophy of Money* what devices are paramount. Also, and relatedly, we must try to identify particular structures, particular coding rules of logocentrism to which Simmel deconstructively adheres, and not be content to talk vaguely of the logocentric tradition in general.

THE STYLE AND TEXT WORK OF SIMMEL

5   A Textual Analysis of
The Philosophy of Money

A distinction was made in chapter 3 between two meanings of the word "about" in the primitive reading question, What is it about? One, the normal meaning, is thematic content; the other denotes a dynamic principle forming lexical and syntactic materials into a text. The concept of text work directs attention to the latter meaning, but in the spirit of complementing rather than abandoning the former. Accordingly, my presentation of a textual analysis of *The Philosophy of Money* begins with thematic contents and from these departs toward compositional dynamics.

What the Book Is About

The question of the content of *The Philosophy of Money* will be approached through two sets of summary statements: those of external readers and those of the first, the internal reader, Simmel, given in the preface to the book.

Readers' Summaries

Even in 1981, eighty-one years after its first publication, Donald Levine could reasonably claim that *The Philosophy of Money* "must surely rank among the greatest unread works in the entire literature of the social sciences" (in Rhea, 1981:73). Of course, "unread" is not to be taken literally. It refers to the fact that prior to the complete English translation by Frisby and Bottomore in 1978, only isolated fragments were available and these were largely unregarded. However, there exist several German-language commentaries which Frisby (1984:93–111) has conveniently drawn into an overview of the content. The content includes the following: the attitudes and values of capitalism; the effects of the institutionalization of money on individual cognition, feeling, and motivation; its effects on social, legal, and economic institutions; the relativistic ethos carried by money; exchange as a form of sociation; money as the reification of social exchange; the relationship of a money economy to social differentiation and individual freedom; the role of money in lengthening and sustaining calculative means-ends chains of action; the role of money in turning all ends into relative means; cynicism and the blasé attitude as styles of life nurtured by a money culture; the detachment, atomization, and privatization of the individual; the reconstruction of collective life around voluntary associations of free individuals; the leveling of qualitative unique value by quantitative monetary valuation; intellectualization and formal rationalization as correlates of monetary calculation; the growing disproportion between objective culture and subjective cultivation, accumulated culture, and active participation; and estrangements of consumer from commodity, worker from means of production, and worker from work.

There would, I think, be high agreement on thematic content but much less in characterizing the treatment of materials. Frisby and Bottomore, in their valuable introduction to the 1978 translation, suggest that the diversity of intentions embraced by the book, including a sociology of money, a theory of modern culture, a philosophical revision of the concept of value, and a metaphysical representation of the nature of life, helps explain the variability of contemporary accounts of its plan and purpose. Their documentation of variability includes the following items (references are given in Simmel, 1978:1–49).

Gustav Schmoller, an economist, saw the real purpose of the book as an analysis of the social and human effects of the money economy. He compared Simmel's "sociological-philosophical" treatment of money to Durkheim's similar treatment of the division of labor. Schmoller astutely anticipated readers' problems but made of them only pejorative satire instead of a possible clue to the significance of the text: "The more immature, the more uneducated the reader is, the more easily and often will he put the book aside, shaking his head, and say that he does not understand it, that it is too refined for me, too artificial, *that he does not know what to do with it*" (Simmel, 1978:9; italics in original).

The philosopher Karl Joël also thought that the book would resist ready understanding, because its apparent subject, money, was only a symbol—an image—of its real one: the infinite reciprocity that links every part of life with every other part. Kracauer, another friendly reader, took a very similar view: "His observations, however, result neither from an economic nor a historical standpoint but grow out of the purely philosophical intention to reveal the interwoven nature of the assembled parts of the diversity of the world . . . a comprehensive picture of the interconnectedness and entanglement of phenomena" (Simmel, 1978:7).

I would add that, from the standpoint of literary methods, the interest is in how interconnectedness is exemplified: how the intention is transacted in the composition of reading responses. When Kracauer

118   THE STYLE AND TEXT WORK OF SIMMEL

calls Simmel's work "not merely a practically operating but also a theoretically grounded relativism" (Simmel, 1978:7), I would reverse the order of emphasis and take "practically operating relativism" to refer to a certain practice of writing. This direction of inquiry is given extra significance by Simmel's letter to Herman Keyserling in 1908, which depicts his earlier work as a search for "a new concept of determination" to prevent modern consciousness of historical mutability and relativity from degenerating into mere scepticism and a nihilistic "loosening of all determinations" (Frisby, 1981:135). He intended a practice of relativism that would transcend the merely negative content of relativist ideas. In literary practice that would mean the accomplishment of what I have called dialectical writing.

Rudolf Goldscheid interpreted *The Philosophy of Money* as "a very interesting correlate to Marx's *Capital*" which could not have been written without that precedent text and constitutes "a supplementation of Marx's life work" (Simmel, 1978:11). The effective significance of Simmel's supplement is, however, dangerously ambivalent and warrants careful assessment. This is a task for subsequent discussion, but it can be said in advance that Goldscheid's concept of an innocent filling out of Marx is no more adequate to describe the relationship than the view proposed by Conrad Schmidt, a socialist economist, that *The Philosophy of Money* is a would-be competitor to Marx's theory of money and value in capitalist society.

Simmel's Summary Preface

Simmel's summary preface is a well-considered statement. Simmel repeated it, with only a minor addendum, in the second edition (1907), implying its endorsement as a declaration of intent. It covers only four pages and concentrates on two tasks: establishing the methodological coherence of the book in the face of admitted diversity of contents and warranting its strong division into two parts, the analytical and the synthetic.

The opening paragraph claims an irreducible validity for philosophical inquiry and firmly locates the text in that domain. The location of the domain itself, however, is less than firm. It exists at the two boundaries of every exact science where its thought stops short and ceases to be exact: (1) reflection on the nature of reality and the preconditions for knowing it; and (2) reflection on the totality of existence, the comprehensive whole making interpretive sense of particular knowledge. The split domain of philosophy is thus below and above the ground of exact science rather than on the same plane. Its definition is dualistic (corresponding to Simmel's division of analytical and synthetic), marginal, and relative to exact science. Its inexactness is compounded by the assertion that in its analytical aspect, philosophy has a goal, to think without preconditions, "which is located in infinity" (Simmel, 1978:53).

The Philosophy of Money then is reflection at either boundary of the economic science of money; as such it might be said to be about economics, with the proviso, dramatized by Simmel, that not a single line belongs to economics. Economics serves the role of halted reflection, absent guest, around which philosophical inquiry forms, spinning toward an infinite goal:

> Just as the very standpoint of a single science . . . never exhausts the totality of reality—so the fact that two people exchange their products is by no means simply an economic fact. Such a fact— that is, one whose content would be exhausted in the image that economics presents of it—does not exist. . . . Even when it is considered to be an economic fact, it does not reach the end of a cul-de-sac; rather, in this guise it becomes the object of philosophical study, which examines its pre-conditions in non-economic concepts and facts and its consequences for non-economic values and relationships. (Simmel, 1978:55)

If we glance now from what Simmel says to what the writing does, the above passage displays three compositional features characteristic of the entire preface. First, and this recalls my earlier analysis of the second paragraph in the preface, a normal form of rational discourse is used to subvert a normal set of thought—a prior plausibility structure—by conveying a discordant message: a message which, to be accepted, must undermine the validity of either the plausibility structure or, at a deeper coding level, the discursive form itself. In paragraph 2, the normal form is a contrastive "not . . . but" opposition; here, in paragraph 4, it is the subject-predicate structure of a proposition. The subject of the second sentence is "a [scientific] fact," here exemplified by an elementary observation statement about economic exchange; its predicate is "does not exist." This is discordant with the normal meaning of "fact," and the entire message disrupts the usual associations of science with hard, solid facts of reality and the opposite association of philosophy with abstract, airy speculation. Scientific exactness, it seems, is purchased by dealing with facts artificially refined from reality. In this light, the meaning of the opening paragraph must be renegotiated; philosophical inquiry is not residual to exact science—a marginal pursuit—but a means of restoring its methods and results to reality. The parasite guest becomes host.

The subversion of normal meanings and the enforced renegotiation of previous understandings of the text indicate another of its compositional features—one that provides a valuable indicator of what the whole book, the transactive work of the book, is about. Running throughout the preface is a rhythm of declaration and unsettlement, discursive statement and reflexive undoing. Reinforcing it is a third feature: the insertion, typically at the ends of paragraphs, of formulaic summaries serving to normalize the author: to normalize, that is, in terms of generic conventions of scholarly writing. In the above extract, the function is served by a closing programmatic definition of philosophical study. In both paragraphs preceding it, the function is served by a programmatic clarification of the organization of the inquiry. For example, in paragraph 3:

> This combination of the money principle with the developments and valuations of inner life stand just as far behind the economic science of money as the problem area of the first part of the book stood before it. The one part seeks to make the essence of money intelligible from the conditions and connections of life in general; conversely, the other part seeks to make the essence and organization of the latter intelligible from the effectiveness of money. (Simmel, 1978:54)

One might not be sure how this will be implemented, but at least the symmetry of the formula makes the plan seem clear. The assuring formula is shortly disturbed, however (in paragraph 5), by an opening sentence which so drastically devalues its keystone word, "money," that the organizing topic of the book is now left a vacuum to be filled anew: "In this problem-complex [as an object of philosophical study], money is simply a means, a material, an example" (Simmel, 1978:55).

But a means to, an example of, what? The paragraph offers a series of answers which between them exceed any definite identification or substantive naming of the object of inquiry:

> the presentation of relations that exist between the most superficial, "realistic" and fortuitous phenomena and the most idealized powers of existence, the most profound currents of individual life and history . . .
>
> to derive from the surface level of economic affairs a guideline that leads to the ultimate values and things of importance in all that is human . . .

salvation [of individual phenomena, especially those of practical existence] from isolation and lack of spirituality . . .

finding in each of life's details the totality of its meaning. (Simmel, 1978:55)

The listed extracts display a clear concern to save mundane phenomena from their isolated, self-evident "reality" by placing them, in a hermeneutic circle of cosmic proportions: the totality of existence. However, the list offers an easier refilling of the object of inquiry than the paragraph itself. When money is called simply a means and example, are we to take it that money is one of life's details, one of those phenomena needing salvation, or that money itself, in practical life exemplifies such salvation and thus offers an analogue of philosophical reflection, an exemplar in practice of what must be grasped in thought? The central sentences of the paragraph push the reader toward the analogue interpretation, while at the same time their deconstructive composition suspends certainty and defers a final decision:

Here the achievement of such salvation will be exemplified in only a single instance, but in one which, like money, not merely reveals the indifference of purely economic techniques but rather is, as it were, indifference itself, in that its entire significance does not lie in itself but rather in its transformation into other values. But since the opposition between what is most superficial and insubstantial and the inner substance of life reaches a peak here, there must be the most effective reconciliation if this particular fact not only permeates, actively and passively, the entire range of the intellectual world but also manifests itself as the symbol of the essential forms of movement within this world. (Simmel, 1978:55)

(*Note:* Having battled several times through these sentences and failed to achieve security, I suspected the effect might only be a translation artifact, but personal correspondence with the translator, David Frisby, convinced me this is not the case.)

I take the closing phrase, "the symbol of the essential forms of movement within this world," to be a strong warrant for the analogue interpretation, assuming that it is money that is being referred to in the sentence: that the pronoun "here" in the opening phrase does indeed stand for "money." The matter would be clear except that the first sentence does not refer simply to money, but an instance like money, holding open the possibility that there is at least one other instance of moneylike salvation from isolation. Subsequently, I will argue that this other instance, the never-named but constantly represented and effec-

THE STYLE AND TEXT WORK OF SIMMEL

tive working subject of the book, is language: more precisely, semiotic representation. However, there is one more summary statement to be drawn from the preface, and one so revealing of Simmel that it deserves an extended commentary.

Supplementing Historical Materialism

Rudolf Goldscheid, cited previously, read *The Philosophy of Money* as an unparalleled supplementation of Marx's life work. It is time to see what, in Simmel's writing practice, this might mean.

The penultimate paragraph begins with a supposed restatement of what has gone before which is unexpected, indeed startling:

> Methodologically, this basic intention can be expressed in the following manner. The attempt is made to construct a new storey beneath historical materialism such that the explanatory value of the incorporation of economic life into the causes of intellectual culture is preserved, while these economic forms themselves are recognized as the result of more profound valuations and currents of psychological or even metaphysical pre-conditions. (Simmel, 1978:56)

Given that the methodological distinctiveness of historical materialism lies precisely in debunking metaphysical or similar "profound" causes and relegating them to the status of epiphenomena, reflexes, and superstructures, the end of the passage sounds more like an ironic subversion than a simple extension. The three ensuing sentences reinforce the suspicion that historical materialism is being turned back onto its Hegelian head. Even more unsettling, they project an endless twist between material and ideal explanatory factors that undermines the very idea of causal determination:

> For the practice of cognition this must develop in infinite reciprocity. Every interpretation of an ideal structure by means of an economic structure must lead to the demand that the latter in turn be understood from more ideal depths, while for these depths themselves the general economic base has to be sought, and so on indefinitely. In such an alternation and entanglement of the conceptually opposed principles of cognition, the unity of things, which seems intangible to our cognition but none the less establishes its coherence, becomes practical and vital for us. (Simmel, 1978:56)

Simmel's "new storey," far from shoring up historical materialism, would draw it and its negative principle, idealism, into an endless spiral of reciprocal entanglement. It is clear, moreover, that a method premised on indeterminacy, and one which makes contradiction in thought an essential complement of unity in things, cannot be reconciled with causal explanation in any form, be it materialist, idealist, mono-, multi- or anything else. The method denies the regulative ideal of causal thinking: to arrive at an account of the factors which between them are necessary and sufficient to explain a phenomenon. As has frequently been pointed out, "explain" derives from the Latin *explanare*, "to flatten out." Eric Partridge (1966:499–500), tracing the origins of the root word, "plain," says: "the basic idea is that of 'flat' . . . whence that of 'easy to see or determine' (hence 'easy to build upon'): this fact illuminates the identity of *plane* or *plain* with *plat* or, in the Germanic mode, *flat*."

Simmel's proposed method is a dialectical negation of flatness, plainness, and explanation, just as at the literary level the opening metaphor of an architectural story (in England, the story of a house is commonly called a flat) is successively turned into an incompatible image of infinite depth. These mutually reinforcing movements of methodological message and literary composition against plain, horizontal thinking, occurring near the end of the preface, are found also at the beginning. The preface opens, it will be recalled, with a topographic image of philosophy being a boundary of exact science and therefore a coexistent area on a single plane. As we have seen, the relationship is far more complicated than the metaphor of spatial extension allows for, and again, at the literary level, involves loading one term (philosophy) with images of incommensurability. Its goal is "located in infinity," it orients to the "totality of life." The first paragraph closes with an analogy between the irreducible gulf separating philosophy from science and that separating the visual arts from a "mechanical reproduction" of images. Subsequently, Simmel's concept and literary practice of philosophy turn out to be as disturbingly orthogonal to exact science as they are to historical materialism.

The discursive incompatibility of Simmel's method with historical materialism has been remarked by Lieber (cited in Simmel, 1978:47, n. 141). He understands Simmel to ground the validity of philosophical inquiry about social life in a distinction between historical, time-bound occurrences and essential forms removed from history, giving rise to "an ahistorical social philosophy or social ontology" (quoted in Simmel, 1978:31). However, our interest lies in the possibility that the dehistoricization of social life noted by Lieber is not merely a content or implication of Simmel's thought but an effect carried by his writing style.

An essential lead here is provided by a receptive epithet noted in chapter 4, which I passed by then with scant attention: fragmentary. Simmel's fragmentary style is documented and made an interpretive topic by Axelrod (1977). However, while his idea of Simmelian style as dialectical method coincides with mine, he makes little use of it except to celebrate Simmel's nonconformity to norms of systematic rationality in social scientific writing. What we seek is analytic demonstration; an explicit literary connection between fragmentary style and historical materialism which will bring out the deconstructive complicity between them.

The connection we require is provided by Walter Benjamin's writing. The introduction of his name is by no means arbitrary. Commentaries by Frisby (1981) and Habermas (1983:34–38) provide good warrants. Frisby depicts Simmel as a "sociological impressionist" preserving an aesthetic distance from the phenomena he so sensitively retrieves, in part by conceiving them, especially the most fleeting and least noticed, sub specie aeternitatis. This, appended to the term *Momentbilder,* "snapshots," was the title given to seven contributions— Frisby calls them "parables" (Frisby 1981:102)—made by Simmel to the avant garde journal *Jugend* between 1900 and 1903. The title is, for Frisby, itself a revealing snapshot of Simmel's working method. To enlarge it, he borrows Benjamin's image of the city stroller, the flâneur, used by Benjamin (1973; 1978:146–52) to convey the poet Baudelaire's way of looking at the city scenes of nineteenth-century Paris. Frisby would say of Simmel what Benjamin says of Baudelaire: for example, that the flâneur is an ever-watchful, unidentified observer, an avid collector of things and experiences that arouse interest, disinterestedly interested in details of existence. The flâneur perfectly matches Kierkegaard's characterization of an aesthete. George Bedell (1972), summarizing Kierkegaard, highlights two characteristics which are specifically relevant to Simmel's relation to historical materialism: "the aesthete always lives in a state of possibility" (Bedell, 1972:101), and "because of his lack of commitment to the concrete, the aesthete also finds the category of time to be an anomalous and uncomfortable dimension of existence" (Bedell, 1972:103). Some qualification is called for. As a dimension of human existence, that is, of experience, time is not a given universal constant, but a variable mode of perception constituted in a cultural matrix and carried in definite forms of language: myth, epic poetry, the narrative novel, medieval chronicle, modern historiography, and so on (see, for example, Canary and Kozicki, 1978). Thus, it is not time as such, the category, which can be found anomalous, but only ever a version encoded in certain conventions of language or genres of writing.

Returning now to Benjamin, his notes on Baudelaire contain an observation crucial for our search: "Baudelaire's genius, which is fed on melancholy [perhaps the melancholy of remembering what has been missed, the virtual in the actual], is an allegorical genius . . . the gaze of the allegorist that falls on the city is estranged. It is the gaze of the *flâneur*. . . . The flâneur is still on the threshold, of the city as of the bourgeois class." (Benjamin, 1978:156).

The passage names a literary genre, allegory, through which Benjamin injects not only estranged, marginal reflection, but also fragmentary style, into historical materialism. The connection is made explicit in a paper by Higonnet et al. (1984) showing how Benjamin's fragmentary style is dictated by his concept of the task of historical materialism:

> The technique of fragmentation inheres in Benjamin's "Theses on the Philosophy of History," written in 1940. For Benjamin, the historical materialist must consider the past "only as an image" which "flashes up at a moment of danger." He must blast such moments free from the oppressive continuities and empty homogeneity of organicist historicism. Tradition and the process of reception threaten to overpower us in a surrender to conformism. . . . Fragmentation, the technique of materialist history, is also the technique of allegory. . . .
>
> Allegory is the chosen genre of the materialist historian who seeks the saving cracks, the luminous chips of time. Benjamin's non-Marxist, poetic method mirrors a Marxist vision of history: "Allegories are, in the realm of thoughts, what ruins are in the realm of things." (Higonnet et al. 1984:393–94)

Clearly this, the gaze of the flâneur-allegorist, cuts across the mutually fixed stares of proponents and opponents. It disrupts equally historical materialism's self-concept as an exact science and the obverse view that it is a form of "organicist historicism," reducing change, via ideological formulas, to "empty homogeneity." Perhaps the former must be abandoned in order not to succumb to the latter.

No doubt Benjamin's proposal is disruptive and strange. He was even by the revisionist standards of the Frankfurt School a marginal adherent to Marxism (see Adorno, 1973; Habermas, 1983:149–59). But it is not idiosyncratic; it has roots and grounds. Since I wish to argue that Simmel's working relation to historical materialism and the meaning of his intent to insert a new story beneath it is close to Benjamin's disruptive allegorism, it is important to establish what those roots and grounds are and how Simmel shares them.

Starting abstractly, the formal definition of the literary genre allegory, drawn from canonical medieval texts, rests on the idea of a coherent spiritual or abstract message represented in a precisely detailed narrative of concrete events and mundane actors. The conjunction of spiritual "tenor" with a materially specific "vehicle" places allegory near symbolism; it differs, however, in being less open to creative interpretation (because of the prior coherence of the doctrine and the literal precision of the narrative) and in more obviously declaring itself to be only a way of speaking otherwise (the word derives from Greek roots, *allos*, "other," and *agoreuin*, "to speak"). J. Hillis Miller observes the difference in almost Marxian terms: "What seems specific to allegory is a larger degree of manifest incompatibility between the tenor and the vehicle than we tend to expect in symbol, where the 'material' base and the spiritual meaning are thrown together, as the name suggests, with some implications of overlapping, consubstantiality, or participation" (in Bloomfield, 1982:357).

Miller sees in allegory a manifest divide of sign from signified, a "structure of incongruous allusion," which gives it a powerful deconstructive force when applied to referential texts claiming to contain or proportionally represent reality. In other words, when such texts are allegorized—read as allegories instead of reality representations—a radical unsettlement can be achieved. One might, for example, point to Marx's critique of commodity fetishism at the end of the first chapter of *Capital*. The political economists, articulating the collective consciousness of capitalism, represented commodities as material containers of a certain amount of objective value determining their exchange relations. Marx allegorizes their account by showing "actual" commodities to be only expressions of a commodity form of value, itself socially fashioned and historically contingent, not objective. Their account is shown up as a "structure of incongruous allusion." Appropriately, the section (4) begins with an allegorical story of a table that became a commodity and, upside down, spun from its wooden brain grotesque ideas about its origin and value.

If we expand our view of historical materialism to include the critique of political economy, the critique of Hegel's upside-down, inside-out dialectic, the formulaic substructure-superstructure explanatory schema, and a redemptive vision of historical class conflict, it becomes clear that historical materialism is awkwardly related to allegory. Marx's critiques can be read as examples of an allegorizing technique of fragmentation directed against unitary schemata claiming to take the measure of concrete reality; examples that someone like Benjamin might well want to follow. On the other hand, the growth of historical materialism into a unitary schema means that it too could become a mode of allegory production misrepresenting itself as literal truth and thus liable to the same kind of critique.

At this point, we must pause to make some necessary conceptual distinctions. Maureen Quilligan (1979) makes an essential distinction between *allegory,* referring to a definite genre of writing, and definite rules of reader response, and *allegoresis,* meaning an allegorical interpretation of something written in another genre. She reminds us that allegoresis began as written commentary on oral epic poems. We must remind ourselves, in addition, that allegoresis, like any form of marginal commentary, can function either as an enlivening disturbance of conventional reading responses or a confirming settlement of them; she would confine it to the latter. Conversely, I would resist her claim, shared by Miller, de Man and other modern celebrants of allegory (see Bloomfield, 1981; Greenblatt, 1981), that this is an inherently reflexive form of language which compels dialectical revision and interpretive renewal from its own resources:

> Allegory engenders an unsettling and intersubjective self-consciousness within the reader's attitudes toward himself as an interpreter of the fiction, beyond the looking glass, but not on the story side of it. Ultimately readers are forced to reflect on how they have read the action, but in reflecting on this operation they are forced to realize as well that the choices they have made about the text also reflect the kinds of choices they make in life. (Quilligan, 1979:253)

The encomium is not necessarily deserved. Allegory can easily become a routinized decoding exercise, a reinforcement of know-how for those already in the know. Taking one of Quilligan's examples, a suitably sophisticated reader would readily recognize the armor of the young knight at the opening of Spenser's *Fairie Queen* as the armor of God in Ephesians 6:11–17 and take it from there. By the same token, a reader inured in historical materialism could decipher allegories of class conflict all life long without once disturbing the "presumptuous sense that he already knows how to interpret" (Quilligan, 1979:227).

To summarize: we must analytically separate allegory, a generic method of composition, from allegoresis, a method of interpretive commentary. Thus Benjamin's previously cited aphorism that allegories are to thought what ruins are to things should be taken to refer to allegoresis, of a certain kind. The distinction I have made between writing that confirms and writing that unsettles the interpretive certitude of a reader applies both to allegory and allegoresis. To some extent, this is a local distinction depending on the reading situation, the particular competences of the reader, and so on, but there are texts that maintain a capacity to unsettle diverse readers across long periods: the classic texts of sociological theory are of this kind.

Historical materialism combines at least three methods of allegoresis. First, it allegorizes religious, philosophical, legal, artistic, and other superstructural contents by making them incongruous allusions to forces and relations of material production. The disruptive potential of the procedure is enhanced by its unusual application of the allegorical code. The usual opposition between "spiritual" tenor and "materialist" vehicle is reversed, the tenor now being materialist. Moreover, the coherence of the tenor is seen as masked and concealed by the vehicle rather than just encoded in it. The vehicle systematically conceals its message, just as, for Freud, the manifest dream content conceals (yet reveals in concealing) deep dream thoughts. The materialist allegoresis is thus revelatory rather than just exegetical.

Second, historical materialism allegorizes descriptive details of history, especially the least-regarded facts of least-regarded people, by making them tell a story of the eventual realization of full human identity through the most dehumanized of classes, the proletariat, and the most mundane of dynamics, economic production. Following a usage suggested by Schor (1984), I would call this a transformation of descriptive into *diegetic* detail, meaning a prosaic object or event which serves as a narrative catalyst. Associated with this—but worth separating because it is directly connected to Benjamin's method of allegory and can also turn back critically on historical materialism—is the wrenching loose of details from a prior narrative structure, a breaking of interpretive frame, so that they take on a new significance. This is Benjamin's technique of fragmentation. He applies it on behalf of historical materialism against orthodox history and "organicist historicism," yet to the extent that historical materialism becomes an historicist orthodoxy or mechanically repeated allegory, the technique becomes a double-edged sword. Benjamin makes it an excessive technique because he grounds it in a concept of history that exceeds all interpretive isms, systems, or formulas. His article "Theses on the Philosophy of History" conveys this in a tempestuous vision of the angel of history:

> His face is turned toward the past. Where we perceive a chain of events, he sees one single catastrophe which keeps piling wreckage on wreckage and hurls it in front of his feet. The angel would like to stay, awaken the dead, and make whole what has been smashed. But a storm is blowing from paradise; it has got caught in his wings with such violence that the angel can no longer close them. The storm irresistibly propels him into the future to which his back is turned, while the pile of debris before him grows skyward. This storm is what we call progress. (Benjamin, 1969:257–58)

Habermas (1983:137) usefully notes that for Benjamin the catastrophe is that "everything just keeps on going" in a seamless, seemingly endless continuum of happening, passing away, and receding. Benjamin calls it the permanence of the unbearable, by which I take him to mean the unbearableness of sheer actuality unredeemed by value—the same condition provoking Simmel's demand that individual phenomena be given effective, not just abstract, merely postulated "salvation from isolation and lack of spirituality, even from repulsiveness" (1978:55).

For Benjamin, the piled wreckage of history contains retrievable marks of an original need for goodness, justice, and truth that transcends temporality. He calls such marks (more exactly, the significatory force in them), "the presence of the now." The first priority is to disrupt the continuum—the appearance—of history, recovering the standpoint of the angel of history, so as to prospect for redemptive value in its fragments, "rescuing" them from the past. Benjamin speaks of this directly in an essay on Eduard Fuchs. Fuchs was an historical materialist and for Benjamin an exemplary collector of "art" passed over in art history:

> Any dialectical representation of history is paid for by renouncing the contemplativeness which characterises historicism. The historical materialist must abandon the epic element in history. For him history becomes the object of a construct which is not located in empty time but is constituted in a specific epoch. . . . The historical materialist explodes the epoch out of its reified "historical continuity," and thereby lifts life out of this epoch . . . historical materialism presents a given experience with the past, an experience which stands unique. The replacement of the epic element by the constructive element proves to be the condition for this experi-

ence. The immense forces which remain captive in historicism's "once upon a time" are freed in this experience. To bring about the consolidation of experience with history, which is original for every present, is the task of historical materialism. It is directed towards a consciousness of the present which explodes the continuum of history. (in Arato and Gebhardt, 1978:227)

Critical reflection excavates the ruins of history left by materialist allegoresis in order to retrieve their life value, which is always that of a present time, now. It is a rescuing mission with redemptive, indeed messianic overtones. The overtones, the apocryphal vision of history—the idea of allegorical interpretation as the key to truth—belong to an old, often subterranean tradition of thought linking Marx, Simmel, and Benjamin that we must now consider.

Habermas (1983:67–68) notes the capacity of Marx to arouse in appropriate readers the strains of a tradition extending back to medieval cabalism. Directly relevant for us is the fact that the texts and authors gathered together in what Habermas calls the heritage of Jewish mysticism confirm the existence of a company of texts around *The Philosophy of Money* which is crucial for understanding what is at work in it:

> The fantasy of Jewish scholars in general was sparked by the power of money—Marx, especially the young Marx, was an example of this. . . . In Simmel, however, one also finds the other typically Jewish interest besides the sociological: the interest in a philosophy of nature inspired by mysticism. His diary includes this: . . . "treat not only each human but also each thing as if it were an end in itself that would result in a cosmic ethics." (Habermas, 1983:37)

Further in the same passage, Habermas refers to a "golden vein of speculations on the ages of the world" that leads from the mystical writer Jacob Böhme to, among others, the Tübingen seminarians, the most prominent of whom was Hegel. There is then a heritage connecting Böhme, Hegel, Simmel, and Benjamin; however, our interest is not simply that it is a shared intellectual tradition but that it forms a communality of style. Here I would recall Moran's (1970) observation that Hegel had a significant, particularly linguistic relation to the German mystical writers Eckhart and Böhme. Their language is said to suspend logical sequence, narrative continuity, and the like, so as to release the significatory power of words in themselves. Its self-canceling paradoxes, for example, jar words loose from conventionally appointed routines: "they work through the structural 'shock' of mutually incompatible juxtapositions" (Moran, 1970:578).

Comparable in effect is Benjamin's literary execution of his plan to fragment continuity and induce "dialectics at a standstill" (Higonnet and Higonnet, 1984:395):

> His own style . . . derives from the "lightening bolts" of his para- bolic fragments, disruptions, and silences . . . Benjamin uses syntactic and semantic gaps as spaces to breathe and think. . . . Each setion of Benjamin's analysis [in "Paris, Capital of the Nine- teenth Century"] begins with a quotation. The notebooks declare his intentions. He will let "the rags, garbage" of the past "come into their own." . . . "The work must develop the art of quoting without quotation marks to the highest point. Its theory is most closely linked to that of montage." "For a piece of the past to be touched by the present, there must be no continuity between them." (Higonnet and Higonnet, 1984:393)

Peter Demetz (in Benjamin, 1978:xxxix) specifies the idea of syntac- tic spaces in grammatical terms. Benjamin's writing displays a remark- ably high proportion of paratactic to hypotactic constructions. Paratac- tic means an arrangement of propositions without connectives—a montage syntax—while hypotactic means propositions linked sequen- tially and in dependent clauses. Hypotactic syntax is the mainstay of normal scholarly exposition, logical argument, and scientific demon- stration: the grammatical backbone of logocentric discourse. Paratactic syntax, along with paradox and other estranging devices, belongs to a form of disruptive writing hosted by logocentric discourse: a form also that being reflexive disperses itself and resists definite settlement: "Ben- jamin belongs to those authors on whom it is not possible to gain a purchase, whose work is destined for disparate effective histories; we encounter these authors only in the sudden flash of relevance with which a thought achieves dominance for brief seconds of history" (Habermas, 1983:130).

As with Benjamin, so it is with Simmel, writing "snapshots *sub specie aeternitatis*" and anticipating on his deathbed the diaspora of his ideas, like money, he said, to whoever would take them. In Simmel, as in Benjamin, there is a textual binding, enacted through style more than theme, of Jewish mysticism with empiricist, rationalist, historicist dis- course. Because these are major forms of logocentrism, the outcome may be properly called deconstructive writing. And since this de- constructive binding to a host code of language is one of the elements working in *The Philosophy of Money*, it is also in that sense what the text is about.

In summary, I would call Simmel, like Benjamin, a disruptive allegorist of empirical, rational, historicist discourse on social life. However, it is necessary to be careful about the scope of the judgment, and to stress differences as well as similarities between Simmel's literary practice and that of Benjamin.

To begin with, there is no claim that Simmel's writing contains allegories in any exact sense of that literary genre. He does, however, practice allegoresis considered as a distinct method of interpretation. His commentaries on society and culture display several of the same characteristics as those identified with allegorical writing in Quilligan's (1979) discussion.

Allegoresis relies upon an interpretive apparatus of vertically organized levels of meaning, whereby an initial surface meaning is successively reconstructed and radically deepened in being conducted through them. A medieval prototype is Dante, who said that *The Divine Comedy* was organized like the Bible into four levels of meaning: the literal level of real events; what such events signify about the relation of God to humanity; the implications for our inner, moral condition; and what this tells us about the possibility of elevation to a higher sphere of being. Reading onto other levels is, of course, common to most interpretation; specific to allegoresis, however, is the overtly spiritual, cosmic, or "religious" nature of the ultimate level towards which meaning is guided. In Simmel's sociological theorizing the levels are: (*a*) surface details taken from familiar interpretive frames; (*b*) readily recognizable (for members) forms of social life like exchange, conflict, and sociability, and also typical actors and situations such as the stranger, the miser, and the adventure; (*c*) underlying forms of sociation, these being paradoxical transforms of the readily recognizable forms and types, showing them to be unities of opposite principles; and (*d*) the ultimate level, the totality of life.

Benjamin, clinging to his commitment to historical materialism, differs from Simmel in that he looks to a chiliastic vision of history rather than a transcendent vision of life to provide the ultimate level of interpretation. It is this difference which allows Simmel the possibility of interpretively escaping all chronological schemata, Marxian or otherwise, and inserting another level beneath historical materialism. His is an ahistorical, synchronic allegoresis, announced in the intention to find in each of life's details the totality of its meaning. Characteristically, however, and reinforcing the impression of subversive reflexivity in Simmel, he placed even this ultimate concept in a historical series and thus relativized it. Frisby (1981:27–28) quotes a letter written by Simmel to his friend Keyserling in 1911, where he refers to every major intellectual epoch being defined by a central interpretive concept: "for the Greeks the concept of Being, for Christendom that of God, in the 17th and 18th centuries that of Nature, in the 19th that of society and now that of 'Life' appears to have entered in this position." Simmel wants to say that the word "life" denotes a transcendent presence that necessarily exceeds any attempt to name it, indeed a presence marked only in excess of language and thought, as a border surrounding them:

> Since life is the antithesis of form, and since that which is somehow formed can be conceptually described, the concept of life cannot be freed from logical imprecision. The essence of life would be denied if one tried to form an exhaustive conceptual definition. In order for conscious life to be fully self-conscious, it would have to do without concepts altogether, for conceptualization inevitably brings in the reign of forms; yet concepts are essential to self-consciousness. The fact that the possibilities of expression are so limited by the essence of life does not diminish its momentum as an idea. (Simmel, 1971:392)

Simmel's allegoresis of life's details depends upon showing in performance—in text work—the limits of language. This is why we find in his writing signs both of a concept of language based upon ontological fullness, or absolute presence, and a modernist consciousness of the ontological emptiness of language. His writing is on either side of the advent of cultural modernism. This too is what *The Philosophy of Money* is about, a clue to be followed up shortly.

Two other relevant features of Simmel's style are associated by Quilligan (1979) with allegory, not allegoresis; but if it is accepted that interpretive unsettlement and settlement cross-cut the distinction (instead, as she insists, of defining it), then we can take what she attributes to allegory alone as applying also to allegoresis whenever it serves to unsettle and renew interpretation. Both features have been discussed previously so only a brief commentary is called for.

First Simmel follows allegorical practice in choosing the most mundane facts of experience to reflect the ultimate truth and spiritual meaning of existence. His writing enacts incongruous equations between "trivial" and important, quotidian and cosmic, considerations, leading him to be called frivolous by those who could not swallow such disproportion. There is in Simmel an allegorical sublimation of ordinary things into diegetic and telling details. It could be said of his style what Schor (1984:707) says of Balzac's method of composition (which is reflexively allegorized in his novel *Le Curé de Tours*): "the prosaic quality of the diegetic details will be overcome by their insertion in a framework which ensures their transcendence."

Second, Simmel's style, as we have seen, rests upon semantic paradoxes and syntactic deviations which force attention to the verbal surface of the text, requiring a reading attitude of conscious deciphering rather than routine message retrieval. Admittedly in allegory it is the motive to find continuity of narrative rather than coherence of argument which is textually obstructed, and by unfitting details and polysemous words rather than by problematic completions of logical formulations, but the effect on the reader attributed by Quilligan to allegory belongs also, at his best, to Simmel:

> All his [reader's] intellectual efforts at constructing a coherent meaning for the text, faithfully following its exfoliations that never proceed by a neat series of cause and effect, attending to the text's tortuous verbal complexities . . . all these efforts do not result in a controlled display of objective meaning . . . they result instead in a weighty self-consciousness not merely at the end of the narrative but at each stage of the reading experience where the text constantly invites and then exposes the reader's imposition of meaning. (Quilligan, 1979:253)

To conclude my discussion of Simmel's preface, I can say, with Simmel, that *The Philosophy of Money* is methodologically about historical materialism, but this cannot be said simply. His seemingly modest gesture of support for its method, adding a new story beneath it, turns out to entail an endless substitution of material detail for ideal meaning, a truly "dangerous supplement" (Derrida, 1976:141) directing inquiry to a completion which exceeds our linguistic and cognitive capacities for completion:

> So viewed, life has two mutually complementary definitions. It is *more-life*, and it is *more-than-life*. The "more" does not arrive by accident to augment a life already stable in its quantity, but life is the movement which at every moment draws something into itself—for each of its parts, even when these are comparatively pitiful—in order to transform it into its life. . . . From its center, life stretches out toward the absolute of life, as it were, and becomes in this direction more-life; but it stretches out toward nothingness as well. (Simmel, 1971:369)

Simmel's account of the necessary movement of life towards excess, exorbitance, and nothingness is semantically close to the view of language developed by Saussure's deconstructionist heirs. Simmel himself names money rather than language as the mundane analogue of life's movements, but since money is a familiar analogue of language and Simmel accords it a semiotic significance, the three terms life, money, and language must be considered interchangeable in his treatment.

What the Title Tells

What *The Philosophy of Money* is about can be further specified from the title of the book, if the title is connected with its proper intertexts. A proper intertext is one without which a target text cannot be fully read. When Goldscheid says: "*The Philosophy of Money* could undoubtedly not have been written if it had not been preceded by Marx's *Capital*" (in Simmel, 1978:11), he is in effect claiming *Capital* as an intertext. The possibility or impossibility of a book having been written is, however, too speculative to be a satisfactory criterion. Our preferred criterion, necessity for a full reading, is admittedly loose but has the advantage of being open to experiential testing: the test of interpretation and response in disciplinary communities. This I take to be the sense of Barthes's claim that a text is not an object, the book one holds, but a "methodological field." He describes it also, and in terms very close to my Cooleyean concept of text work, as a force of production: "The text 'works,' at each moment and from whatever side one takes it. Even when written (fixed), it does not stop working, maintaining a process of production. The text works what? Language." (Barthes, 1981:36).

That is, language in the pure Saussurean sense of combinative possibility and potentially infinite sign play, which achieves only a provisional stability in local conventions of speech and writing, including the codifications of reader response we call genres. It is the recombinative possibilities of pure language, an inherently unfettered system of signification, which "work" a text and allow interpretive work to be done on it. The working rhythm of language is deconstruction-reconstruction, and a text is a field, actively a force-field, of its operation. Barthes is now able to define intertextuality as one of the operations of the field:

> One of the paths of this deconstruction-reconstruction is to permute texts, scraps of texts that have existed or exist around and finally within the text being considered: any text is an intertext; other texts are present in it, at varying levels, in more or less recognisable forms: the texts of the previous and surrounding culture. Any text is a new tissue of past citations. Bits of codes, formulae,

rhythmic models, fragments of social languages, etc. pass into the text and are redistributed within it . . . the condition of any text whatsoever, cannot, of course, be reduced to a problem of sources or influences; the intertext is a general field of anonymous for-mulae whose origin can scarcely ever be located; of unconscious or automatic quotations given without quotation-marks. (Barthes, 1981:39)

I would add to this that the deconstructive-reconstructive rhythm of language can be weak or it can be strong in a piece of writing. Where it is strong, as we have seen in Benjamin and Simmel, both of whom composed advertent intertexts by Barthes's definition, one is justified in collecting works together under some such heading as deconstructive or dialectical writing (the latter indicating a compensatory stress on reconstruction), and speaking of a community of texts identified by the sheer strength of textuality at work in the writing. Starting from the hypothesis that Simmel belongs to that community, my concern is to show how he belongs, the textual companions closest to his work, and his particular composition of deconstruction-reconstruction effects.

I would add also to Barthes that interpretation reads text fragments, and so on, retroactively into target texts; therefore the relevant range of intertexts cannot be chronologically confined to "past citations," "pre-vious culture," and the original context of writing. A text becomes such—achieves its status of a productive field, a redistribution of lan-guage—in being read, not in being written, and reading cannot help but be presently located.

Returning to Simmel's title, it is crucial to try to read fully the term "money" so as to appreciate the significance of its being joined with "philosophy" (not with psychology or sociology, as it might have been) and to confirm our understanding of why money should be a topic of such evident drawing power for Simmel's way of theorizing. To this end, *Capital* is indeed an indispensable intertext; not, however, for its technical analysis of the capitalist monetary system but for its renewal of familiar analogies between money and language, coins and words, and the echoing problematic of the source of the value of money.

Rossi-Landi usefully reminds us of the extensive circulation of mon-etary analogies:

Horace spoke of the "coinage of words"; Francis Bacon of the "money of intellectual things and of words as "tokens in use and accepted for the concepts, as money for values"; Hegel spoke of logic as the money of thought . . . Ryle understands *parole* as commerce which employs *langue* as monetary capital. Bruno Leoni has drawn a parallel not only between language and money in general, but also between production, exchange, and falsification of monies and words. The various passages in which de Saussure compares the value of signs to economic value are well known. (Rossi-Landi, 1980:360)

Saussure makes his comparisons in the context of arguing that the linguistic value of a word depends entirely on its location in a set of words, not on correspondence to a preexisting concept, and reinforcing this purely relational definition, that value is not to be confused with signification. The former is a relationship of relative difference from other terms in an associative (paradigmatic) set; the latter a relationship between signifier and signified, the evocation of an idea or concept by a sound image. Thus the French *mouton* and English "sheep" may have the same signification—translators exchange them freely—yet the English word is differentiated from a close term, "mutton," which is lacking in French. The combinative possibilities of the English word are consequently not the same as those of its French equivalent; its linguistic value is not the same. This is why literal translation between languages is impossible even though translatory exchanges are universal.

In monetary terms, the signification of a five-dollar bill is whatever dissimilar things—for example, bread—it can be exchanged for. Its value, however, depends on its differential relation to other terms in a sign system: for example, other notes and coins. One can see what Saussure meant by making the subtlety of the distinction between signification and value the cause of their common confusion. What must be made clear, he insists, is that the value of a signifier is determined entirely within its own domain, not by any external reality: "Signs function, then, not through their intrinsic value but through their relative position . . . it is not the metal in a piece of money that fixes its value." "Language is a form and not a substance . . . all our incorrect ways of naming things that pertain to language stem from the involuntary supposition that the linguistic phenomenon must have substance" (Saussure, [1916] 1959:118, 122).

Given that linguistic values are determined in associative sets, which are synchronic entities analytically removed from actual, situated usage, from time and history, it follows that there must be a radical separation within linguistics between the study of linguistic values and the study of social languages in historical time. Linguistics is not alone; the same duality has been forced upon economics, and also because it studies values. There the division is between "political economy" (concerned with general principles and universal laws) and economic history. Saussure equates his proposed semiotic science with political economy: "Here as in political economy we are confronted with the notion of *value;* both sciences are concerned with *a system for equating things of different orders*—labor and wages in one and a signified and signifier in the other" (Saussure, [1916] 1959:79; italics in original).

He goes on to claim that any inquiry concerned with values must as a matter of practical, even absolute, necessity align its subject matter along two cross-cutting but analytically independent coordinates: "the axis of simultaneities, which stands for the relations of coexisting things and from which the intervention of time is excluded; and the axis of successions, on which only one thing can be considered at a time but upon which are located all the things on the first axis together with their changes" (Saussure, [1916] 1959:80). Placing this alongside the previously quoted observation of an "involuntary supposition" that language must have a substantive, not merely relational and formal, character, Saussure is saying that to study value, linguistic or otherwise, is to enter a discursive realm circumscribed by two constitutive problems: the dissociation of value from substance, and the separation of synchronous, system-state value from historical, situated, experienced value—combinative possibility from realized performances. I will call this the problematic of value studies. If Saussure is correct, it should be operative in Marx's *Capital* and Simmel's *Philosophy of Money*.

Although *Capital* is a critique of political economy, Marx works closely with its formulas and reflects both features of the semiotic frame of inquiry which Saussure assigns to it. The dissociation of value from substance (and the constant problem of seeing it) is discussed, for example, in a section titled "Coin and Symbol of Value" (Marx, 1954:125–30); also in "The Fetishism of Commodities and the Secret Thereof" (76–87), to which Simmel was so strongly drawn.

The former section discusses the function of money as the "circulating medium" of commodities. Prices are the "money-names of commodities" (Marx, 1954:125). Marx describes an evolution of money from substantive sign to functional symbol, in the course of which value becomes completely independent of substance. The most common substance is a precious metal like gold. Coins begin as certain amounts of the substance with the weight stamped on them. In circulation— in exchange—they become worn by usage and lighter than their face value: "Name and substance, nominal weight and real weight, begin their process of separation" (Marx, 1954:126). To serve the function of circulating medium it is the name that matters. At first this was half recognized by setting limits of weight loss below which coins were no longer legal tender. It was fully recognized when the exchange function was vested entirely in the name, which could now be written on anything, turning money into the purely symbolic function it actually was from the beginning. At this stage money achieves in plain view the status of mediator, relative measure, and signifier: "Its functional existence absorbs, so to say, its material existence" (Marx, 1954:129).

However, not everything is plain to participants in the circulation of commodities. In money's circulatory function, the money name is only a transient moment—a substitutory phase—in the chain of commodity exchange. Yet such is the persistence—the current necessity—of substantialist thinking that the "transient apparition" (Marx, 1954:129) is read by participants as standing for an objective value lodged in the commodity itself. It is this condition of substantialist misperception that Marx calls commodity fetishism: "in it the social character of men's labour appears to them as an objective character stamped upon the product of that labour" (Marx, 1954:77). Participants in commodity exchange can read the money names, but cannot interpret them, because the social context of their coinage and provenance is hidden to them. This is true even of scientific readers—the political economists— who, while correctly interpreting money names as representing (beyond local supply-and-demand ratios) the relative amount of labor time needed to produce a commodity, understand that amount to be an objective character of commodities, as natural as their size and weight, not a sign of the peculiar conditions of production in capitalist society which make it possible not only to claim validly that labor is reduced in commodities to something homogeneous, variable only in quantity, but to perceive that unproblematically as a natural fact. Marx would restore a sociohistorical dimension not only to political economy's subject matter but also to its way of knowing, relativizing both to historical modes of production. Here we encounter the second element of the Saussurean problematic of values: the separation of synchronic—purely structural—from diachronic inquiry.

Clearly Marx's relation to political economy and its ahistorical, timeless formulations represents the obverse of Saussure's position. The separation demanded by Saussure as a methodological necessity for any science of values is for Marx a basis of critique. Not that the difference is total: Marx's modes of production are total structures articulated conceptually along "the axis of simultaneity" prior to being

THE STYLE AND TEXT WORK OF SIMMEL

placed along "the axis of succession" as complete structural transformations (revolutions). However, in his critique of political economy, indeed as its critique, Marx accords it the status of ideological knowledge, possessing only an unreflected "social validity" (Marx, 1954:80), precisely because it is confined to the synchronic dimension of abstract, timeless formulations and cannot see the historical constitution either of its subject matter, which it takes to be in nature, or of its own forms of thought and way of knowing. It cannot do so because abstraction from history is a premise built into its mode of cognition and inseparable from it.

To this I would add that the previous representation of commodity fetishism as a reading problem—a hermeneutic distortion—is not an unmotivated metaphor. It is warranted by the terms of Marx's diagnosis and reinforced in the famous description of how a critical resolution is to proceed: "Value, therefore, does not stalk about with a label describing what it is. It is value, rather, that converts every product into a social hieroglyphic. Later on, we try to decipher the hieroglyphic, to get behind the secret of our own social products; for to stamp an object of utility as a value, is just as much a social product as language" (Marx, 1954:79).

Enough has been said of Marx to support the interpretive hypothesis I would apply to Simmel through his book title: whenever money is treated philosophically, which is to say theoretically, analytically, and analogically, it brings into play the entire problematic of values identified for us by Saussure. *Capital* is a proper intertext of *The Philosophy of Money* because it provides thematic fragments to initiate the play and a methodological motivation to carry it on.

Finally, it should be observed that when money is made a philosophical topic it cannot be examined with objective security or kept at the distance of an object, because it brings into discourse the possibilities and conditions of representation, hence of language, and in principle the linguistic self-formation of discourse itself. All of which means that for philosophically committed discourse, money is by its nature a reflexive topic. We might see here a significance in the fact that the germ of Simmel's book was a paper called "Psychology of Money" (published in 1889). A psychological (or sociological or any other scientific) treatment might better hope to objectify money and deflect its reflexive potential to disturb discourse than would a philosophical one. The reason, pointing to our next topic, is suggested by Derrida's apocryphal definition of a philosophical text: "Even if there is never a pure signified, there are different relationships to that which, from the signifier, *is presented* as the irreducible stratum of the signified. For example, the philosophical text, although it is in fact always written, includes, precisely as its philosophical specificity, the project of effacing itself in the face of the signified content which it transports and in general teaches" (Derrida, 1976:160; italics in original).

Derrida is attributing to philosophy, as that which makes a text "philosophy" in its reading, the logocentric project of a complete, hence self-effacing representation of being, or some such concept of absolute presence, in language. Deconstruction haunts the project because writing begins in separation from presence, a divide from "that other that can be neither excluded nor recuperated" (Spivak, 1981: 382). It is a structural necessity imposed on writing, because in language "there are only differences without positive terms" (Saussure, [1916] 1959:120); language "works in the borderland where the elements of sound and thought combine" (p. 113), but in a combination producing only form detached from substance. At the borderland of the philosophical aspiration to enclose absolute presence is, then, linguistically dictated absence. Derrida refers, perhaps melodramatically, to an "abyss of presence" (1976:163) traced out by the movement of writing in its endless substitution and infinite multiplication of signifiers. The deconstructive impossibility of complete representation is nowhere more striking than in philosophy, because complete representation is its formative goal. In a general sense all writing contains this deconstructive contradiction, but it is foundationally vital to philosophical texts.

As I have argued before, while all writing can be seen as deconstructive and can be brought out as such by that kind of commentary, it is analytically worthwhile to reserve the term for a specific form of writing: that which, in performance, brings the impossibility of logocentric representation to the reading surface. Simmel, it has been suggested, writes in this way. At the same time his prefatory dedication to disclosing the totality of life commits him completely to the logocentric project. Again, then, we are drawn to the conclusion that Simmel's text work is an unusually strong working of antithetical principles of language: logocentric representation and deconstructive textuality. It is unusually strong because it combines the following: a totally philosophical aim, a topic that is analogically entwined with questions of language, and a style of writing that reflects a subterranean and subversive way with words.

What the Text Does

Speech palled
On them and they turned to the silence
Of their equations. But God listened to them
As to a spider spinning its web
From its entrails, the mind swinging to and fro over an abysm
Of blankness. They are speaking to me still,
He decided, in the geometry I delight in, in the figures
That beget more figures. I will answer
Them as of old with the infinity
I feed on.

(From R. S. Thomas, "Dialectic")

God is one of several figures through which Simmel's text evokes, settles, and renews what I spoke of in chapter 3 as an immanent anxiety of writing: the anxiety of ontological emptiness. I can be more specific. The text oscillates between obverse images of ontological emptiness and fullness. (See appendix 1 for a rough charting of their incidence.) These are typically occasioned by observations on the nature of money, but through the analogical association of monetary with linguistic exchange and value, they trigger a corresponding oscillation between concepts of language. The association is not arbitrarily read into Simmel, he several times introduces it himself. For example:

> As a visible object, money is the substance that embodies abstract economic value, in a similar fashion to the sound of words which is an acoustic-physiological occurrence but has significance for us only through the representation that it bears or symbolises. (Simmel, 1978:120)

> In some respects, money may be compared to language, which also lends itself to the most divergent directions of thought and feeling. Money belongs to those forces whose peculiarity lies in a lack of peculiarity, but which, none the less, may colour life very differently because their mere formal, functional and quantitative nature is confronted with qualitatively determined contents and directions of life, and induces them to generate qualitatively new formations. (Simmel, 1978:470)

Paramount among the "forces" that indifferently quantify life are of course mathematical sign systems; Simmel's inclusion of money and language in this company reinforces the contention that he is interested in money as a semiotic phenomenon. I do not say that Simmel's interest in money is exclusively semiotic, only that much of the text is informed by it, and the book needs to be read in this way, among others. Let me advance a definite interpretive argument. Though the topic of money, Simmel's text conducts a tense interplay between three forms of language. These are also three concepts of language, but they have been realized culturally in more than intellectual ways. For the sake of taking stock they can be called the primitive, the representative, and the semiotic forms. In the first, language and reality are one; in the second, reality parallels and anchors language; in the third, language is on its own. In the first, language is ontologically suffused; in the second, ontologically fastened; in the third, ontologically empty. They are dynamically related in Simmel's text work. There the first serves to defend against the third, and both work to subvert the second (the regular language of empiricological discourse). It is the third form which prevails in the reading experience, even though Simmel's philosophy would recommend the first.

The sections to follow will review the literary methods through which these relationships between antithetical forms of language are played out, beginning with the third—the semiotic form—and proceeding to its counteraction by the first. Simmel's subversion of the second form will be made a special topic in the final section of the chapter.

The Semiotic Form of Language

In accordance with previous discussions, this form can be detected through metaphors and metonyms of certain themes: the suspension of sign systems in an ontological void, the substantive arbitrariness of signifiers, and the illimitable run of meaning along significatory chains. Since I would like to show that such figures recur throughout the text, not just in isolated corners (see also appendix 1), I will review them on a chapter-by-chapter basis. The translation divides the chapters into short sections, using subheadings in Simmel's annotated table of contents, and I have numbered these to help map the text.

A metaphor of semiotic insecurity occurs in the explanation of primitive man's distaste for exchange relations (chapter 1, section 12). In part it arises from a fear of surrendering to a substitutive movement unanchored by absolute value: "he is always afraid of being cheated in exchange, in the absence of any objective and general standards of value" (Simmel, 1978:97). The fear is metonymically continuous with John Locke's empiricist repudiation of all figurative and nonliteral words as "perfect cheats," cited in chapter 1. Locke, of course, was concerned to save science from uncertainty; Simmel, however, uses science itself as a further figure of it (sections 14 and 15).

Whereas the "first tendency of thought" (Simmel, 1978:102) construes an orderly world through concepts of "the substance and the absolute," later thought, most strongly expressed in modern science, posits "a ceaseless development" (p. 103), an incessant transformation, in terms of purely quantitative, hence relative, differentiation. Simmel asks how such a series of cognitions "is not to be suspended in the air," and responds that "it must have somewhere an ultimate basis, a supreme authority, which provides legitimation to other members of the series without needing legitimation itself" (p. 103). This is, of course, a retreat to a metaphysical stronghold, but the apparent relaxation of semiotic tension is immediately canceled by the observation that the ultimate basis can never be known: "yet we shall never know what this absolute knowledge is." In cognitive practice, then, the discovery of truth is endlessly postponed: "Cognition is thus a free-floating process, whose elements determine their position reciprocally, in the same way as masses of matter do by means of weight. Truth then is a relative concept like weight. It is then perfectly acceptable that our image of the world 'floats in the air,' since the world itself does so. This is not an accidental coincidence of words but an allusion to a basic connection" (Simmel, 1978:106).

The last sentence is of extra interest because it is not, like the rest, a statement of semiotic awareness, but an indirect reflection of its tensions expressed as a denial of accidental coincidence in words. I would call it a symptom rather than an indicator of semiotic awareness.

The unattainability of ultimate validation is turned by Simmel into a principle of penultimacy: "to avoid dogmatic thought, we have to treat each position at which we arrive as if it were the penultimate one" (Simmel, 1978:104). The principle expresses the semiotic concept that the meaning of a sign only emerges in relation to another sign, its interpretant, and that another sign is always possible. Deferment along a series is an inescapable feature of signification because proximal difference is the source of linguistic value.

Section 16 in chapter 1 is packed with references to infinite articulation, a correlate in semiotics of the concept that meaning is made by difference, where another difference is always in prospect. The following are typical:

> The fact that what we perceive as absolute is nevertheless relative
> can only be resolved by admitting that the absolute signifies a road

> stretching to infinity whose direction is still marked out no matter how great the distance we cover. (Simmel, 1978: 111–12).

> Ultimate comprehension is transferred to infinity, since every point in one series [the past] refers to the other series [the present] for its understanding. (p. 112)

> Knowledge follows a course of infinite regress, of infinite continuity, of boundlessness, which is yet limited at any particular moment. (p. 115)

The remaining chapters can be reviewed along the same lines.

Chapter 2 conducts an examination of the relation between monetary substance and monetary value which closely parallels Saussure's contention that the substantive side of language, that is, its sounds and referential contents, is entirely subordinate to its formal side and must be analytically set aside in order to grasp linguistic value: "Whether we take the signified or the signifier, language has neither ideas nor sounds that existed before the linguistic system, but only conceptual and phonic differences that have issued from the system. The idea or phonic substance that a sign contains is of less importance than the other signs that surround it" (Saussure, [1916] 1959:120).

Homologously, as money becomes historically pared down to its essence, monetary value is revealed to lie neither in the particulars it can buy nor in the metals and so on of which it is made. This is the theme of Simmel's chapter on "The Value of Money as a Substance." Civilization shows a tendency to "more and more extensive experiments with representatives and symbols that have virtually no relation to what they represent" (Simmel, 1978:151). Money is a crucial expression of this tendency. Simmel is careful, however, not to exchange "the dogma of the intrinsic value of money" (p. 152) for the opposite dogma, that it is valueless. The task is to conceptualize monetary value apart from substance, which is to say in purely formal or functional terms: "Thus, money is involved in the general development which in every domain of life and in every sense strives to dissolve substance into free-floating processes." "Money, whatever represents it, does not *have* a function, but *is* a function" (Simmel, 1978:168, 169; italics in original).

So, almost identically, does Saussure say that in language substantive combinations of sound and thought produce only a form, not a substance ([1916] 1959:113, 122). His discussion of the functional, positional, "incorporeal" value of the linguistic signifier includes a specific comparison to money: "it is not the metal in a piece of money that fixes its value. . . . Its value will vary according to the amount stamped upon it and according to its use inside or outside a political boundary" (p. 118).

For Saussure, phonic and visual substances are only materials which language puts to use. Simmel is forced by his critique of the idea of intrinsic value toward this purely functional, that is, semiotic concept of value tokens, but spends the major part chapter 2, sections 25–37, resisting the final step. Logically, he admits, the money function needs only numbers and is moving toward the status of "a pure symbol of economic value" (Simmel, 1978:157). However, there are practical reasons why this cannot be reached—why the function must remain fastened, however lightly, to something of substantive value. At first these seem to be entirely technical: "money cannot cast off a residue of material value, not exactly for inherent reasons, but on account of certain shortcomings of economic technique" (p. 158). For example, it is said that the price of a given commodity adequately represents its exchange value only if the ratio of the money amount to the total money supply is approximately the same as the ratio of the commodity to the total quantity of commodities. Since this is at best an intuitive, inexact calculation, economic actors need "the support and complementation" of an "intrinsic material value" attached to money (like a precious metal) if they are to assess proportions with any certainty.

Simmel's talk of a limiting uncertainty is given a psychological turn when he locates the calculation of ratios in "the subconscious of economic subjects" (Simmel, 1978:159). For us it has a semiological resonance, because at issue here, as in language aspiring to truth, is the interpretation and acceptance of value tokens at face value. A recurring anxiety of language is to ensure proper ratios between words (as in rules of logic and the translation of concepts into observation terms) and true ratios between words and the world: in short, to ensure rational discourse. The semiotic suspension of substantive limits and externally conferred values opens up arational prospects of infinite articulation and indeterminate valuation. Simmel comes to express this in talk of monetary misuse, calculative anarchy, and inflationary emptying of value. As the discussion proceeds, it multiplies images of deregulation and expands the reasons necessitating a material supplementation of symbolic values from economic practicalities to features of human nature and exigencies of social reality. I take the scope of the discussion to be an index of the strength of the concern at work in the text.

Misuse arises from the temptation to print more paper money to pay government debts: "paper money can escape the dangers of misuse by arbitrary inflation only if it is tied to a metal value established by law or by the economy" (Simmel, 1978:160). Interestingly, in the light of Saussure's derivation of linguistic values from impersonal systems of signs, Simmel insists (p. 159) that "no human power" could guarantee the value of mere token money. Only the systems of law and economy can do so, and by tying the token to a material substance.

In a later twist of the argument, Simmel accepts that the material substance itself is open to arbitrary fluctuations that may disturb the stability of value. Perfect stability, he says, is like perfect love. Ideally it would have no carnal supplement, but in human practice the sensual bond is indispensible: "Thus, although money with no intrinsic value would be the best means of exchange in an ideal social order, until that point is reached the most satisfactory form of money may be that which is bound to a material substance" (Simmel, 1978:191).

Again, we see Simmel's text move to the very edge of a semiotic concept of value, only to fashion a figurative barrier, or retreat, out of metaphysical concepts.

The movement towards a semiotic formulation is renewed in his chapter 3 through the topic of ends and means. Money is characterized as an absolutely indifferent and formally perfect means of exchange, capable of integrating any series of purposes whatsoever. This is because it is utterly impartial, "not influenced by any determination from a different series," and teleologically empty, a pure instrument that "has no purpose of its own" (Simmel, 1948:211). The functional perfection of money carries with it a fateful bias towards disproportion and imbalance in human conduct; money so thoroughly encodes all ends that it, a teleological void, is readily taken to be an ultimate purpose. The result is to radically extend a tendency already at work in human conduct through the exercise of calculative reason: the relativization of ends as further means in an endless shifting forward of volition. The tendency is described exactly as a search for complete meaning or natural stopping places along chains of sign differences:

> Where does the limit to our search lie? If the teleological sequence does not terminate in the last consciously conceived link, then does that not open up the way to its continuation to the infinite? . . . every point arrived at is actually experienced as only a transitional stage to a definitive one. . . . Out of the endless series of possible volitions, self-developing actions and satisfactions, we almost arbitrarily designate one moment as the ultimate end. . . . At this point of extreme tension between the relativity of our endeavours and the absoluteness of the idea of a final purpose, money again becomes significant . . . money symbolises the established

fact that the values for which we strive and which we experience are ultimately revealed to be means and temporary entities. (Simmel, 1978:235–36)

At the individual level, the mistaking of money for purpose is dramatized in exorbitant expenditure of the signifier (extravagance) and unlimited hoarding (avarice). The former supposes intrinsic value to lie in the signifieds of money, the latter in the signifiers themselves. Avarice therefore represents a more complete and helpless capture in the play of signification: "Instead of seeking out the enjoyment of real entities, it searches for the intangible, which extends to the infinite and has no external or internal reasons for its restriction" (Simmel, 1978:249).

The themes of calculative deferment, endless series, unanchored desire, and insatiable proliferation are repeated, with heightened rhetorical effect, in chapter 6. This, the last chapter, closing the "synthetic" half of the monograph, amplifies in sociological terms the topics shaped from philosophical considerations in chapter 3, the last of the "analytical" half. The topical complementarity between the chapters makes it fruitful to read them in conjunction.

Chapter 6 begins with the relation of monetary valuation to the exercise of will and intellect. Will refers to two kinds of actions: the subcalculative fastening of value to some part of reality, making an essentially unpredictable (Saussure would say unmotivated) connection between those mutually independent categories of experience, and the subsequent transfer of will to other contents of reality construed as means to the initial purpose. Intellect, like money, assembles means into series attached to purpose. The strength of intellectuality in a way of life is directly proportional to the length of such series. Money allows qualitatively diverse lines of value conduct to be merged into correlated series, tending towards a single continuous chain: "Since money itself is an omnipresent means, the various elements of our existence are thus placed in an all-embracing teleological nexus in which no element is either the first or the last" (Simmel, 1978:431).

The constructed world of value comes increasingly to resemble a single calculative enterprise, attached by fewer and fewer points of cathectic will to the parallel realm of existence, thus becoming an autonomous calculus of value. The subjective coloration of such a style of life is strongly portrayed in a section (121) titled "The pre-eminence of technology":

The lack of something definite at the centre of the soul impels us to search for momentary satisfaction in ever-new stimulations, sensations and external activities. Thus it is that we become entangled in the instability and helplessness that manifests itself as the tumult of the metropolis, as the mania for travelling. . . . Money stands in a series with all the means and tools of culture, which slide in front of the inner and final ends and ultimately cover them up and displace them. Money is most important in illustrating the senselessness and the consequences of the teleological dislocation, partly because of the passion with which it is craved for, and partly because of its own emptiness and merely transitional character. (Simmel, 1978:484–85)

The ontological emptiness of money, being nothing except in further substitution, and the compulsion for more which its very emptiness feeds are major themes in chapters 4 and 5. The former seeks to name conditions of personal freedom. Among them is taking possession of objects that mean something to us: making objects responsive to ourselves. Because money represents so many possible objects, and because it is so completely obedient to our commands, we cannot help but treat it as meaningful; yet by virtue of the emptiness which is the secret of its infinite capacity to represent and subserve, money in possession also lacks meaning:

Money is both the most responsive and, because of its complete emptiness, the most irresponsive object . . . an object can mean something to us only by being something substantial in itself. . . . Money means more to us than any other object of possession because it obeys us without reservation—and it means less to us because it lacks any content that might be appropriated beyond the mere form of possession. (Simmel, 1978:235)

The incessant, insistent "slide" of money in front of substantial objects has a dual effect, discussed at length in chapter 5: deferring the significance of substantial objects in shifting meaning to that which formally represents them and absorbing the individual interpretant into a system of signification where his autonomy can find no substantial purchase. To the extent that things are purchasable they cease to give purchase to the individual quest for meaning:

The levelling effect of the money equivalent becomes quite evident as soon as one compares a beautiful and original but purchasable object with another equally significant one which is not purchasable. We feel from the outset that this latter object possesses a reserve, an independence, a right to be exclusively evaluated according to the objective ideal—in short, it possesses a distinction that the other object cannot attain. (Simmel, 1978:393)

Anything exchangeable has its distinction eroded. Easy exchange is associated with qualitative devaluation: for example, "well-worn phrases" or clichés, that can be exchanged "without further ado" because they are trivial and become trivial because they can be exchanged so unresistingly. Prostitution illustrates the same point. Here, however, Simmel posits something like a need for substantial meaning which is expressed in substitutory and fantastic love objects: "Because the prostitute has to endure a terrible void . . . she searches for a substitute relationship in which at least some other qualities of the partner are involved" (Simmel, 1978:379).

The prostitute, like the restless modern individual, the compelled traveler seeking meaning in difference, and the speaker imbued with semiotic awareness, suffers from something like ontological pathos: a longing to have significance conferred by the possession of an inherently significant object; a longing for relief from further movement along a chain of signifiers where there is no meaning except in the movement. There is a distinctly modern sensibility that satisfaction is always just over the horizon, but that "the core and meaning of life always slips through one's hands," giving rise to a yearning for a "new and more perceptible significance of things" (Simmel, 1978:404).

The idea of insatiable movement arising from the erosion of values and of the deregulation of conduct by "teleological dislocation" is a familiar one in sociological theory. It is caught in the concept of anomie, appropriated by Durkheim from French conservatism. There, however, it is a remediable dysfunction of social institutions. I wish to take advantage of Simmel's proximity to linguistic formulations of the idea and his conspicuous way of letting language play, to draw it towards the event we have seen brought to scientific thought by Saussure and later registered and ambiguously celebrated by Derrida and deconstructionism: the advent of semiotic consciousness. The passages I have cited are rich in semantic concomitants of the event, in word-for-word echoes of crucial terms.

We return now from openings of semiotic theorizing in Simmel's working of the topic of money to closures composed of metaphysical commitments to absolute presence and figures of undifferentiated unity.

Rhetorical Closures on Semiotic Insecurity

At the outset, in the very first section, a semiotic chord is struck in the pronouncement of a radical separation between "reality," a naturalistic category of experience, and "value," a judgmental category whereby significance—qualitative difference—is inserted in the seamless "indifferent necessity" of the real:

> Our whole life . . . acquires meaning and significance only from the fact that the mechanical unfolding elements of reality possess an infinite variety of values beyond their objective substance. At any moment when our mind is not simply a passive mirror or reality— which perhaps never happens, since even objective perception can arise only from valuation—we live in a world of values which arranges the contents of reality in an autonomous order. (Simmel, 1978:60)

Autonomous valuation is homologous to semiotic signification. It creates meaning apart from objective substance and ontological limitation, yielding the problem of authentication and finding "visibly appointed stopping-places" (Henry James, cited in Miller, 1980:118).

The semiotic chord is swiftly muted, however, (though only for the time being) by the mobilization of a strong figure of absolute presence and transcendent meaning, the unitary soul: "Reality and value are, as it were, two different languages by which the logically related contents of the world, valid in their ideal unity, are made comprehensible to the unitary soul, or the languages in which the soul can express the pure image of these contents which lies beyond their differentiation and opposition" (Simmel, 1978:62). The section ends with the suggestion there are no linguistic terms in which the soul can express the unity it knows "unless it be in religious symbols" (p. 62), the most comprehensive of which is God.

Simmel's theological rhetoric of ultimate meaning might be thought far removed from the utterly mundane phenomenon of money. However, money in itself, the pure form impurely embodied in actual currencies, turns out in the text to be so complete a measure of value as to take on the attributes of universal convertibility, indifferent necessity, and disregard for differences assigned initially by Simmel to reality. Money, purely speaking, is a language of value which encodes the grammar of reality. In this fusion money becomes comparable to God, and later in the text, by an entirely typical curving of conventional opposites to a point of identity, the two are equated:

> In reality, money in its psychological form, as the absolute means and thus as the unifying point of innumerable sequences of purposes, possesses a significant relationship to the notion of God. . . .
> The essence of the notion of God is that all diversities and contradictions in the world achieve a unity in him, that he is—according

to a beautiful formulation of Nicolas de Cusa—the *coincidentia oppositorum*. . . . In so far as money becomes the absolutely commensurate expression and equivalent of all values, it rises to abstract heights way above the whole broad diversity of objects; it becomes the centre in which the most opposed, the most estranged and the most distant things find their common denominator and come into contact with one another. (Simmel, 1978:236)

Simmel calls the basis of his equation psychological, but the term is inadequate to cover the scope of his statement. Certainly (in sentences omitted here), it refers to subjective feelings, but much more to the structure of consciousness, thus belonging to phenomenology more than psychology, and also to the public structuring of diverse purposes, which is either sociological (compare Parsons, 1969, on exchange media) or sociolinguistic (compare Burke, 1962:94–113, on money as a syntactic substitute for God in our grammar of motives). Our interest, however, is in the rhetorical function of the topos, God, in Simmel's text work—its working of language. Our methodological problem is not to exegetically elaborate the statement but reasonably and warrantably to take it to document a primitive form of language obversely entwined with the semiotic concept articulated by Saussure.

An indirect warrant is provided by one of Saussure's inheritors, Derrida, who has been several times introduced as a companion of Simmel. The context is Derrida's claim (made also against Saussure) that writing, far from being only a secondary representation of spoken words, a signifier of the signifier of a thought, is, now that we can properly understand it, a primitive possibility of making and sensing differences, manifested now electronically in cybernetics, that includes language, spoken and written. A difference that makes a difference is called a trace, and since its meaning always awaits the unfolding of a sequence, Derrida condenses the ideas of difference and deferment in a useful neologism, "differance": "The trace is the differance which opens appearance and signification . . . the trace is not more ideal than real, not more intelligible than sensible . . . and no concept of metaphysics can describe it" (Derrida, 1976:65). Semiotic awareness, promoted by linguistic science, literary theory, and electronic technology, erodes the long-standing ontological anchors of language: "all the strongholds, all the out-of-bounds shelters that watched over the field of language" (p. 7). In a passage describing attempts to preserve privileged signifieds from semiotic erosion, Derrida describes the significance of God in terms almost identical to those of Simmel and more than that offers an exact description of what is going on in Simmel's text:

> All dualisms, all theories of the immortality of the soul or of the spirit, as well as monisms, spiritualist or materialist, dialectical or vulgar, are the unique theme of a metaphysics whose entire history was compelled to strive toward the reduction of the trace. The subordination of the trace to the full presence summed up in the logos, the humbling of writing beneath a speech dreaming its plenitude, such are the gestures required by an onto-theology determining the archeological and eschatological meaning of being as presence, as parousia, as life without difference: another name for death, historical metonymy where God's name holds death in check. That is why, if this movement begins its era in the form of Platonism, it ends in infinitist metaphysics. Only infinite being can reduce the difference in presence. In that sense, the name of God, at least as it is pronounced within classical rationalism, is the name of indifference itself. Only a positive infinity can lift the trace, "sublimate" it. . . . We must not therefore speak of a "theological prejudice," functioning sporadically when it is a question of the plenitude of the logos; the logos as the sublimation of the trace is theological. (Derrida, 1976:71)

The use to which Simmel puts the idea of God places him in an "onto-theology" central to Western philosophy. In the passages I have cited he pronounces the name of God as the name for sublime indifference and speaks it "within classical rationalism." Here, and in all his other invocations of absolute presence, Simmel is recalling intertexts of the movement from Platonism to "infinitist metaphysics" that would fasten language to being and sublimate the humble making of "difference." Yet his writing does more; it mixes sublimation with the release of semiotic insecurity—the undoing of metaphysical safety nets of language—by way both of figurative imaging of semiosis and the performative deconstruction of certain linguistic patterns of logical discourse. Simmel's writing advances the semiotic anxiety "his" philosophy would halt. When Simmel pronounces the name of God it is with a foreign accent.

Rhetorically related to God in Simmel's text work are the concepts of the rudimentary ego and undifferentiated consciousness. Whereas "God" comprehends the separation of value from reality, these concepts comprehend and make evident the separation of subject from object which is the root of valuation. They provide figurative means to endow valuation, which includes all signification—all language—with an extralinguistic core or origin: securing it in a sub- and prevaluative structure of existence from which it can be seen to emerge. Valuation can then be represented in developmental, historical, and evolutionary terms, locating it, as Saussure would say, on the axis of successions instead of simultaneities, and inhibiting a semiotic presentation of the "language" of value. For example, undifferentiated consciousness is assigned, in accordance with standard diachronic formulas, to children, primitives, and ancient society:

> Mental life begins with an undifferentiated state in which the Ego and its objects are not yet distinguished. (Simmel, 1978:63)

> Antiquity was much closer than were later periods to the stage of indifference in which the contents of the world were conceived as such, without being apportioned between subject and object. (P. 64)

> The primary state is a complete unity, an unbroken indifference which is completely removed from the opposition of the personal and objective sides of life. . . . Both the child and primitive man immediately conceive of the psychological forms of the transitory moment, the fantasy, and the subjective impression as reality. The word and the object, the symbol and what it represents, the name and the person are identical, as has been shown by innumerable ethnological findings and by child psychology. (P. 301)

Images of fusion between words and objects, signifiers and signifieds, are incompatible with the semiotic isolation of signifiers and their perception as an autonomous system of purely internal differences, displacements, and exchanges. However, representations of an original bonding of language with reality cannot provide a sufficient closure on semiotic insecurity, because the securing location is ascribed to a past moment, left far behind. Consequently, other rhetorical devices are called for to renew the defence.

One such device is to hyperbolize art as a fusion of subject with object, and signifier with signified, making art a sophisticated return of a primal condition. Moments of intense aesthetic enjoyment efface the difference between subject and object in which deferred possession and therefore conscious valuation originate. In such moments of "unbroken unity" (Simmel, 1978:66), the art object is directly experienced as inherently significant: "the content of the feeling is, as it were, absorbed by the object and confronts the subject as something which has autonomous significance, which is inherent in the object" (p. 73). Like all rhetorical devices, this one is not only a conceptual conceit but also a literary artifact made of word fragments. Among these are key terms of semiotic theorizing: unnecessary, arbitrary, unreal, infinite signification. Take, for example, Simmel's depiction of the hermeneutic circle: a perfect figure of absolute presence. Semiotic terms are woven into the depiction, thus becoming part of Simmel's textual defense against the anxiety they carry. In his account, an artist begins with a free selection of elements which in isolation are outside the categories of truth or falsehood and may be "fantastic, arbitrary and unreal" (p. 109). Only as a form or pattern begins to appear do the elements acquire necessity and truth: "So long as the elaboration is harmonious and consistent, the whole will produce an impression of 'inner truth,' whether or not an individual part corresponds to outward reality and satisfies the claim to 'truth' in the ordinary and substantial sense" (Simmel, 1978:109).

The unity of a work of art confers truth and necessity upon the elements entering it independently of substantial certification. The unity is therefore that of a self-enclosed circle rather than a linear series parallel to reality. This places the art work in a group of strange entities which Simmel names with an oxymoron: the "concrete infinity" (Simmel, 1978:118). Others are Spinoza's *substantia sive Deus,* a universal substance from which single objects are differentiated, thus "defined," by relation to other things around them; the Marxian mode of production with its "relativistic dissolution of things into relations and processes" (p. 118); society—"society is the universal which is concretely alive" (p. 101); money—called the "unmoved mover" (p. 171), "the unconditional *terminus a quo* to everything, as well as the unconditional *terminus ad quem* from everywhere" (p. 223), and "symbol in the empirical world of the inconceivable unity of being, out of which the world, in all its breadth, diversity, energy and reality flows" (p. 497); and—would we not have to say—language?

The circle is an apt figure for such entities because it too possesses "an immanent infinity" and, unlike other lines which return to their beginning, does so in a purely internal way where every point is determined by "the interplay of all parts" (Simmel, 1978:119). As Derrida (1976:71) puts it, only "a positive infinity" can draw the sheer trace of "differance," into an absolute pattern, turning the indefinite line or spiral of semiotic inscription into an ontological entity.

The remaining defensive devices refer to the unitary presence of an absolute interpretant of meaning rather than an absolute unity of being. They are still, however, representations of an entity that combines concrete, positive existence with absolute metaphysical presence (a status which Habermas [1974:8–10, 14–15] has with a hint of desperation called "quasi-transcendental").

As we have seen, the opening section evokes a more than personal interpretant of meaning in the theological figure of a "unitary soul." This is shortly exchanged for a philosophical figure, that of the transcendental ego, in the context of establishing the provenance of value as a third term formed, like love and desire, in the separation of object from subject. Since Simmel, in accordance with his entire style of thought, construes the formative structures of life to be concrete infinities or generalia that are real, all three components of valuation, for him a basic process of forming a value-ordered, value-relevant world, are construed in this way:

> This value, which we conceive as being independent of its recognition, is a metaphysical category, and as such it stands as far beyond the dualism of subject and object as immediate enjoyment stands below it. The latter is a concrete unity to which the differentiating categories have not yet been applied; the former is an abstract or ideal unity in whose self-subsistent meaning the dualism has again disappeared, just as the contrast between the empirical Ego and the empirical non-Ego disappears in the all-comprehending system of consciousness that Fichte calls the Ego. (Simmel, 1978:68–69)

The transcendental ego, whose role in the grasp of independent objects is elaborated in phrases that make it a close textual cousin of Kant's "transcendental unity of apperception" (Kant, 1929:76–90), is endowed with volitional as well as cognitive capacity. Will gives us a power to break through the substitutive shuttle of representation and exchange and fasten ourselves to life, the ultimate signified in Simmel's philosophical writing. A concentrated account of this heroic power occurs in chapter 3 (section 46), in a discussion of final purposes, which elsewhere (p. 431) are called "the turning points of life." In my interpretation, "they" (the words in which they are represented) are metaphysical fastening points through which language, in Simmel's text, works to bind itself to a world beyond:

> The creation of a final purpose is, under all circumstances, possible only by a spontaneous act of the will, whereas the relative value of a means can only be adjudged by way of theoretical knowledge. . . . The notion that we are free with regard to the first step but slaves with regard to the second is nowhere more applicable than in the teleological sphere . . . the final authority of our will is independent of all rational logical foundation. (Simmel, 1978:229)

Just as in philosophical writing (according to Derrida) metaphysical absolutes impart ontological significance to intermediate definitions and arguments, so in life (according to Simmel) the spontaneous act of will imbues elected elements with an intrinsic value which spreads to contiguous elements:

> Precisely because the sense of value has nothing to do with the structure of things but possesses its impassable realm beyond them, valuation does not strictly adhere to its logical boundaries but evolves liberally beyond the objectively justified relations to things. There is something irrational in the fact that the relatively high points of our mental life tinge the contiguous moments that do not have those qualities, but this reveals the whole happy wealth of the soul which wants to live out its interest in the once-sensitive significant elements . . . even according to the full measure of its inner resonance to things, without anxiously asking for the legitimate reason for their sharing this value. (Simmel, 1978:228)

The defensive role of absolute presence and intrinsic value against semiotic anxiety here comes very close to the surface of the text.

Power to make contact with existence beyond cognition and language is not the only transcendent attribute of the transcendental ego. It is in itself incommensurable and invaluable. Thus the inner interpretant of value escapes relative value and the perpetual motion of exchange; it is the still point of the turning world of signification by "differance," the ultimate basis for the intuition of irreplaceable value in events, objects, and others: "The two poles between which *all* values stand are: at one extreme, the absolute individual value whose significance does not lie in any general quantity of value that could also be represented by any other object, and whose position in our value system could not be filled by any other object; at the other extreme, that which is clearly interchangeable" (Simmel, 1978:124).

Belonging to the first pole is the metaphysical concept of absolute distinction, and to the second the semiotic concept of relational difference. The second concept is held in check by the first: "Distinction represents a quite unique combination of senses of differences that are based upon and yet reject any comparison at all" (Simmel, 1978;390). The "absolutely incommensurable personality" (p. 406), the inner aspect of the transcendental ego, is the opposite pole to money, "the absolutely commensurable entity" (p. 406). Between them the practical world of comparison, measurement, and exchange, which is also the world of rational discourse, spins along.

Simmel's metaphysical conceits look toward a form of language more than just rationally fastened to the world—one indistinguishably fused with it. The full form is allegorically presented in Simmel's account of primitive money and the development of substantively valuable items into purely functional money tokens (chapters 2 and 5). To draw out the characteristics of the form and its antagonism to the representative form (the form of rationalism, empiricism, and science), it is helpful to place Simmel's account in the context of Michel Foucault's linguistic excavation of past knowledge codes.

Foucault (1970: chap. 2) analyzes a code where things are words and world is text. The chapter heading, "Prose of the World," is from Hegel. The code is identified as an anciently derived, pre-Enlightment way of knowing the world:

> In its raw, historical sixteenth-century being, language is not an arbitrary system; it has been set down in the world and forms a part of it, both because things themselves hide and manifest their own enigma like a language and because words offer themselves to men as things to be deciphered. The great metaphor of the book that one opens, that one pores over and reads in order to know nature, is merely the reverse and visible side of another transference, and a much deeper one, which forces language to reside in the world, among the plants, the herbs, the stones, and the animals. (Foucault, 1970:35)

> [Commentary] calls into being, below the existing discourse, another discourse that is more fundamental and, as it were, "more primal," which it sets itself the task of restoring. There can be no commentary unless, below the language one is reading and deciphering, there runs the sovereignty of an original Text. And it is this text which, by providing a foundation for the commentary, offers its ultimate revelation as the promised reward of commentary. The necessary proliferation of the exegesis is therefore measured, ideally limited, and yet ceaselessly animated, by this silent dominion. . . . One speaks upon the basis of a writing that is part of the fabric of the world; one speaks about it to infinity, and each of its signs becomes in turn written matter for further discourse; but each of these stages of discourse is addressed to that primal written word whose return it simultaneously promises and postpones. (Foucault, 1970:41)

We can join Foucault's description of the prerationalist knowledge code with Benjamin's theory of language and correlate the joint set with Simmel's treatment of money.

Habermas (1983:146) asserts that Benjamin adhered throughout his work to a "mimetic theory of language." We might hesitate to accept a label that seems so severely to separate Benjamin from a semiotic theory; he did, after all, refer only to a mimetic element in language which needs a certain kind of bearer to become evident, and that bearer is "the semiotic element" (Benjamin, 1978:335). However, it is true that he regarded nature and language as a seamless web, resemblance as a feature of natural creation, and the linguistic faculty of producing and seeing resemblances (Benjamin calls it the mimetic faculty) the extension of a primordial power in nature. The important point is that Benjamin's is an ontologically suffused concept of language which, like the prerationalist code identified by Foucault, is structured by the idea of resemblance. The following quotation from Foucault, describing the prerationalist code, could as well be taken to describe Benjamin's position on language: "The nature of things, their coexistence, the way in which they are linked together and communicate is nothing other than their resemblance. And that resemblance is only visible in the network of signs [Benjamin says "the semiotic element"] that crosses the world from one end to the other." (Foucault, 1970:29).

Compare this (and the passages previously cited) to Benjamin's essay "On Language as Such and on the Language of Man" (Benjamin, 1978:314–32) which, it can be added, reveals traces of the heritage of Jewish mysticism in its exegesis of the book of Genesis. Verbal communication is taken to be only a case of human language, which speaks in robes, ceremonies, technical artifacts, and so forth, while human language in turn is only a completion of something in nature: communicative linkage. The existence of language is coextensive "with absolutely everything" (p. 314), including all events and things in animate and inanimate nature. There is a great chain of linguistic being, an interrupted flow of communication, running from the dumb, unspoken "word" in the language of things, through the sonic and written "prattle" (the word is taken from Kierkegaard) of the human language of knowledge, to the ultimate language of all creation, that of God. The movement from one form of language to another, a movement permitted and enforced by the internal differentiation traced parabolically to the Fall, is a translatory search for equivalents to meanings already possessed but not in themselves enough—a substitutory movement towards value that promises to fill a gap or want. This is not, however, an endless glide or infinite spin into emptiness, but an ascent towards full revelation of a textually composed world. Translation from the language of things to that of mankind is an advance because the naming the nameless adds knowledge to nature. Beyond this, however, is the authorial presence of the creative word of God which guarantees the possible validity of human translation, allowing it to reach towards a grasp of "the world as such in an undivided whole" (p. 330): "All higher language is a translation of the lower, until in ultimate clarity the word of God unfolds, which is the unity of movement made up of language" (Benjamin, 1978:332). In Foucault's terms, below commentary there is the sovereignty of an original text woven into the fabric of the world that ceaselessly animates and corrigibly constrains the movement of language towards knowledge. Consequently in this form language cannot be an arbitrary system, which supports my argument that it functions in Simmel's text to hold in check the anxieties of the semiotic form.

Simmel makes equations between primitive valuation and thought, characterizing both as mimetic processes confined to recognizing and reproducing sensuous resemblances between things. Primitive thought can no more surrender itself to substantively empty intermediate propositions in chains of reasoning than primitive valuation can surrender itself to substantively valueless money mediation in chains of exchange (see, for example, pp. 142–43, 150–51, of *The Philosophy of Money*). To see value in valueless tokens, as in logical symbols, requires "growing intellectuality" (p. 142), or in Benjamin's terms (1978:335), the extension of the mimetic faculty to nonsensuous correspondences and similarities.

As an example of truly primitive valuation, Simmel (1978:144–45) cites the natives of New Britain, who use strings of cowry shells for money and demand a length equal to that of the commodity, say a fish, for payment. More highly developed, though still tied to substantive mimesis, are old coins stamped with a symbol of the commodity for which they may be exchanged, and the common practice in primitive economies of selecting large, heavy objects as money units to make their value mimetically evident. The originary bias toward concrete, literal valuation was still evident in medieval Europe (the locale of Foucault's account of the prerationalist mode of cognition). Whereas money in its full development is nothing but a symbol of relative value between things, medieval thinking still included it among those things, regarding value as something internal to objects, and therefore objective: requiring of the seller a "just price" in which the objective value of the commodity would equal the objective value of the money units. Simmel comments that this concept of value, appropriate to a barter economy, "corresponds with the substantial-absolutistic world view of the age" (p. 126), adding that the same "error of substantialist interpretation" finds later expression in the individualistic doctrine of human rights, which thinks them to be inherent attributes of the substantial person instead of relational attributes established by a system of norms. The comment is, of course, easily extendable to language and the conception that meaning inheres in individual words or sentences instead of arising from relational differences in systems of signs. This is not an imposed interpretation; it is authorized by the section immediately following that on medieval money—the last section of the first chapter—where Simmel states what I take to be the guiding thesis of the entire book, and incidentally makes further sense of the cryptic prefatory statement that the book is not about money as such, but money as a philosophical exemplar:

> The philosophical significance of money is that it represents within the practical world the most certain image and the clearest embodiment of the formula of all being, according to which things receive their meaning through each other, and have their being determined by their mutual relations. It is a basic fact of mental life that we symbolise the relations among among various elements of our existence by particular objects; these are themselves substantial entities, but their significance for us is only as the visible representatives of a relationship. . . . Thus a wedding ring, but also every letter, every pledge, every official uniform, is a symbol or representative of a moral or intellectual, a legal or political relationship. . . . The telegraph wires that connect countries, no less than the military weapons that express their dissension, are such substances; they have almost no significance for the single individual, but only with reference to the relations between men and between human groups that are crystallised in them. (Simmel, 1978:129)

The passage further demonstrates the presence of something close to semiotic thinking in Simmel. But my immediate task is to show, in his philosophical working of the significance of money, the currency of a form of valuation his discussion assigns to ancient times. My problem is to demonstrate that this primitive mode of thought, attached to a primitive concept of language, is present in his work other than as an historical topic.

Foucault raises the problem in a seemingly decisive act of closure on the prerationalist mode of cognition: "There is nothing now, either in our knowledge or in our reflection, that still recalls even the memory of that being [of language]" (Foucault, 1970:43).

But this declaration of absolute discontinuity cannot be taken literally in a discourse which analytically represents that bygone being—still less in one declaring itself (in the subtitle) to be an "archeology" of knowledge, where by definition everything pre- must also be sub- and therefore potentially present. Foucault admits as much in the very next sentence, with an exception to his judgment very much relevant to my entire interpretation of Simmel's text work: "Nothing, except perhaps literature," meaning specifically modern literature, "from Hölderlin to Mallarmé and on to Antonin Artaud"; a form of writing that in separating itself from all political, ethical, and other discourses has brought language towards a purely semiotic realisation where it grows "with no point of departure, no end, and no promise" (Foucault, 1970:44). Relevance for my interpretation of Simmel lies in Foucault's observation, in the same location, that this ontologically released, semiotic form of language is "finding its way back from the representative or signifying function of language to this raw being that has been forgotten since the sixteenth century."

Foucault's observation allows us to retake our bearings. There are images, arguments, and precepts in *The Philosophy of Money* which hark back to an ancient unity of language and reality. It is implied in Simmel's entire philosophical strategy (evident also in Hegel and Benjamin) of reproducing from division an original state of unitary being. Simmel, like Benjamin, uses the Biblical image of paradise to depict a situation "in which subject and object, desire and satisfaction are not yet divided," a situation which has been destined "to disintegrate, but also to attain a new reconciliation" (Simmel, 1978:75). My interpretive argument, however, is that whatever Simmel recommends by precept and proposition (and let us recall that he recommends a rigorous science of society as well) is undercut and unraveled by his style. This is how his text turns between three forms of language in such a way as to recommend the semiotic form, not by precept (ontological emptiness is thematized in chapter 6 of *The Philosophy of Money* as a critique of the modern form of life), but by example. Full understanding of Simmel depends upon combining what the text does with what it says. For example, his metaphysical figures of original unity are presented with a hyperbolic exaggeration that prevents our taking them literally and instigates rational distancing in us. Also, the representation of ontologically full signs of value through an account of primitive money means, in textual effect, that this model of language is being addressed in a distinctly modern voice through distinctively modern writing, which is to say, at a distance. Above all, however, is Simmel's deconstructive cleaving to countersemiotic forms of language in the course of presenting them. This will be shown briefly in his presentation of metaphysical conceits and at more length in his strenuous employment of logical oppositions. The latter will be given extensive treatment because it looms so large in Simmel's text work. We will proceed in that order.

Let us consider just one passage presenting a metaphysical conceit. Simmel is discussing bribery, a cheating form of exchange—a cheating of exchange itself—because a value we are is exchanged for a value that we only possess:

> Certainly both concepts are interrelated; for all the contents of our existence present themselves to us as possession of that purely formal, insubstantial centre that we experience as our centrifugal Ego and as the owning subject, in contrast to the objects owned in terms of qualities, interests and emotions. On the other hand, possessions are, as we saw, an extension of our sphere of influence, a power of disposal over objects which thereby enters into the circle of our Ego. The Ego, our desires and feelings, continues to live in the objects we own. On the one hand, the innermost core of the Ego—inasmuch as it is a single definite capacity—is located outside the centre as an objective ownership belonging to its central point; on the other, even the most extraneous factors, if they are true possessions, rest within the Ego. In owning the objects, the Ego becomes competent to deal with them and without any one of them it would change into something else. Looked at logically and psychologically, it would therefore be arbitrary to draw a dividing line between being and owning. If we none the less consider it to be objectively justified, then this is because being and owning, in terms of the distinction between them, are not theoretical objective concepts, but value concepts. If we designate our being as being different from our owning, we attribute a certain kind of value and standard of value to our contents of life. If one interprets those that lie close to the enigmatic centre of the Ego as our being and the more remote ones as our owning, then their arrangement in this series—excluding, of course any sharp demarcation—is only produced through the diversity of feelings of value that accompanies both of them. (Simmel, 1978:389)

The passage reduces the interpretant ego, the worldly expression of the "unitary soul," the "ideal unity" (both previously cited), and "unity of spirit" (p. 455) to something "insubstantial" and "enigmatic" that makes a mockery of the word "center" applied to it. The literary enactment of the reduction is worth a short review, albeit digressively, because it repeats methods already observed in analyzing the preface and the opening paragraph of "The Stranger," thus reinforcing the claim that they are features of a definite style of text work intrinsic to Simmel's theorizing.

The opening reference to a conceptual relationship waiting to be clarified is a standard formula of rational discourse and cues the reader into that interpretive frame. The remainder of the sentence, however, puts clarification on hold and tenses the frame by contrasting owner- ship of objects with possession of something, the ego, which in being called purely formal and insubstantial defies the very notion of posses- sion, as well as the accompanying notion of a center.

The standard frame is cued again in the second sentence by the phrase "on the other hand": the second half of a routine formula for organizing a judicious weighing of arguments in credit-debit terms. Two circumstances undermine the cue: the first half of the formula (on the one hand) is nowhere to be found in the preceding context, while the next but one sentence repeats the formula completely. The dis- mayingly unbalanced sequence is thus "on the other hand," "on the one hand," "on the other hand," with one hand missing. As if to ensure that the reading posture of judicious weighing and discursive accountancy remains off balance, the sentence structured by the full formula is inter- nally loaded with contradictions in terms. We have an innermost core located outside the center, yet belonging to the center, and extraneous factors located within. Moreover, a parenthetic insertion casts further doubt on whether a center can be said to exist at all.

The pattern of inviting and confounding the rational frame of in- terpretation—which we might here call a monetary method of reading, since a form of double-entry accounting is involved—persists through the rest of the passage. Pursuing the question of a conceptual difference between being and owning (which is crucial for Simmel's critique of modern life), the semiotic concession is made that to draw a line be- tween them would be arbitrary. It is then seemingly withdrawn by the introduction of a supplementary distinction between objective con- cepts and value concepts, but as this is left ungrounded and unex- plained, readerly unsettlement is not resolved. The last sentence leaves everything in suspension by attempting to draw a distinction between being and owning in terms that cannot work: namely, closeness and distance in relation to the innermost core of the ego. Since, however, the existence of any such center has already been made undecidable—a textual fact recalled in the word "enigmatic"—the spatial notion of distance is rendered inoperative; since, moreover, a parenthetic denial of firm demarcation is inserted, the reader is left suspended in a discursive void: suspended, yet not, one feels, cheated or deprived of meaning, only of a bottom line. Whether or not this is regarded as a self-evident fault depends on whether or not the frame that has been deconstructed is regarded as the only way to read and therefore write social theory. The elucidation of other possibilities is precisely the value that I have attributed to the study of classical works and their exemplary worth.

As a final commentary on the passage, taking it back to the main theme of the analysis so far, it is interesting, and surely more than coincidental, that Simmel occasions unsettlement here, as in the preface, through playing with spatial images of conceptual relationships—center and periphery, nearness and distance, inside and outside—that are serious bases of classical, logocentric, rational discourse. Derrida (1976:30–65) dwells especially on the last opposition (subtitling one section "The Outside is the Inside") in bringing out the impossibility of grasping the graphic sign—the differentiating trace of writing—in classical terms of inner-outer, essence-appearance, original-image, reality-representation, which even the semiotic pioneer Saussure relied upon. The foundational necessity of such imagery for logocentric discourse was sensed long ago by Jeremy Bentham in his shamefully ignored theory of linguistic fictions. Distinguishing the rhetorical fictions of poets, orators, and lawyers from the indispensable fictions of rational discourse about reality, calling the latter "inferential real entities" and according them a higher reality value than sensory impressions of corporeal substances, he comments reflexively: "Of nothing that has place, or passes, in our minds can we give any account, any otherwise than by speaking of it as if it were a portion of space, with portions of matter, some of them at rest, others moving in it" (Bentham, 1962:199).

Assuming this to be a valid generalization about the form of writing in which social theory is composed and must be composed to achieve generic recognizability, it follows that any strong effect of deconstruction there would have to include an unraveling of spatial constructs. This provides a further specification of deconstructive writing and allows me to claim again that the continuity noted here between Simmel and Derrida is more than coincidental.

The Deconstruction of Dichotomies

We move finally to a linguistic activity of the text which provides a response to the task set at the end of chapter 4: this being to specify the particular codes of logocentric discourse to which Simmel's work deconstructively adheres. We have seen the erosion in use of logical accounting formulas such as "if . . . then," "on the one hand . . . on the other hand," but overwhelmingly the activity of the text is to evoke and confound basic dichotomies of philosophical discourse (including socio-ethical offspins), eroding the "either . . . or" coding rule which dichotomization is based upon. A complete list of the dichotomies evoked in the text, roughly classified by intellectual field to show the scope of the activity, and with section number locations, is given in appendix 2. The procedure will be to review the activity, demonstrate its deconstructive importance by showing the crucial place of the "either . . . or" formula in the structure of rational discourse, and bring out its interpretive significance for understanding Simmel's work. The last will involve using the activity to identify a working community of texts: other texts for which the deconstruction of ontological-epistemological-ethical dichotomies is also a working necessity.

The purpose of the review is to establish as a pervading fact of the text—of the reading experience it composes—a movement to dissolve either-or thinking. This could be done by piling up more and more instances to show that for Simmel opposites are facets of unitary phenomena; that any positive term of a "biad" (a neologism I borrow from Condren [1985:87] to describe dichotomies that overlay logical either-or exclusiveness with appraisive either-or choice) turns into its negative if taken far enough; that the real interest of phenomena—the interest of the real—lies in margins, boundaries, or separations that link. For example, Simmel finds the interest of money in being a pure function evolving from material substance, yet needing still a trace of materiality; in being a means so pure that it achieves the significance of an absolute end; in being a neutral ground where irreplaceable qualitative value is transmuted into replaceable quantitative value; and in being a separation that links, as in separating modern people from nature it has thereby created a desire for nature, forming "a link between the two at the very same time it separates them" (Simmel, 1978:479). All this could be demonstrated by further instancing, but it would be largely redundant because the conclusion it would reach is already included in Simmel's text as a self-commentary. It would be like straining to fasten a description on someone which he already applies to himself. It is true that a technical analysis of linguistic mechanisms of biadic deconstruction would demand direct and exhaustive textual excavation, but I am not attempting that here. Simmel's self-commentaries are enough for our purpose, since even if analysis revealed the performance to be technically inadequate or ineffective, the attempt would still be an active fact of the text.

A direct commentary appears in Simmel's account of the enigmatic unity of the person, composed between social isolation and integration, individuation and socialization. The account gives rise to reflections on the necessary falseness of logical thought, necessary in the dialectical sense of a falseness that must be gone through to move thought towards a truer condition:

> It seems as if our life employs or consists of a unified basic function which we are unable to grasp in its unity . . . the singular entity in its separateness makes an absolute claim on us and the unity that comprehends everything singular makes the same demand, so that a contradiction emerges from which life often suffers. This contradiction becomes a logical contradiction since both elements presuppose each other in their existence: neither would have any objective meaning or intellectual interest if the other did not stand in opposition to it. Thus the peculiar difficulty arises—as with many other contrasted pairs—that something unconditioned is conditioned by another unconditioned item which in turn depends on the former. (Simmel, 1978:111)

Thought seeks through either-or contrasts to comprehend both-and-neither unities which are glimpsed, negatively, in the struggle and failure of contrasts to hold firm. In theoretical and practical reason alike we can only back into the unity of being through rebuff of unavoidably one-sided concepts and actions: unavoidable because that is the way of rational judgment and practical decision:

> In practice, we can only cope with the variety of elements and tendencies that make up life by allowing our behaviour, in every context and at every period of time, to be governed by a uniform and one-sided principle. But in this way the diversity of reality catches up with us again and again. . . . If the practical world is formed in such a way that our will is focussed upon eternity and only attains the world of reality by being deflected and rebuffed, then here too the structure of practical life has predetermined the theoretical structure. On innumerable occasions, our concepts of things are made so unalloyed and absolute that they do not reflect experience, and only their qualification and modification by opposing concepts can give them empirical form. However, these concepts are not for that reason thoroughly bad; it is precisely through this unique procedure of exaggeration followed by retraction in the formation of concepts and maxims, that a view of the

world which is in conformity with our understanding emerges. The one formula through which our mind establishes a relation with the oneness of things, which is not directly accessible, by supplementing and reproducing it, is in practice as well as in theory a primary too-much, too-high, too-pure. (Simmel, 1978:167)

Another expression of the incommensurability of logical thought with unitary being is that the former operates on the principle of clear, discontinuous division, while the latter is a continuum. Between phenomena there are indeterminate differences, "even a mixture of concepts which, according to their actual meaning, exclude one another" (Simmel, 1978:448). Such is the case, for example, with freedom for subjective development and self-cultivation under conditions of advanced social organization. Money, as pure exchange function, promotes a completely depersonalized organization of power, a subordination to norms of calculative rationality instead of other individuals, a removal of individuals from objective conditions of production and control that would seem logically antagonistic to subjectivity and freedom. But in actuality the dissociation of the individual from all elements of personal subordination, the placing, as it were, of organizational operations on automatic control, leaves subjectivity and functional organization free to develop independently, undisturbed by each other: "Thus, money would bring about one of those frequent developments in which the importance of one factor turns into its opposite as soon as it has unfolded a basic, consistent and all-pervasive effectiveness out of its original limited efficiency" (Simmel, 1978: 337).

Money serves to transform social life into a perfectly functional system of relative, interchangeable, equivalent values standing apart from all that is absolute, incommensurable, and a value for itself. Institutionally it works to turn society into a substantively unlimited exchange system: an image of itself.

At the "end" of the book (Simmel recommended to his friend Keyserling that he begin with the last chapter), money is portrayed as a fittingly strange symbol, as well as an agent, of the relational character of everything existent. It is at once an economic good, a tangible item, "the most ephemeral thing in the external-practical world" (Simmel, 1978:511), and an incessant transcendence of every tangible, particular thing: "it lives in continuous self-alienation from any given point and thus forms the counterpart and direct negation of all being in itself . . . it stands as the point of indifference and balance between all other phenomena of the world" (p. 511). Clearly, money is a phenomenon that transcends either-or classification; Simmel demonstrates this in repeated applications of standard dichotomies which, far from pinning down the phenomenon, are set spinning by it. Determinate dichotomization, which is the bedrock of the most basic form of measurement—nominal categorization—can grasp concrete things in isolation and metaphysical entities in abstraction, both of which allow thought to "perform the play of the world according to purely arithmetical relations" (p. 279), but it cannot grasp money. By the same token, however, it cannot grasp "the formula of all being" (p. 129) that money represents: the contextual conferment of "real" value by relational placement. It hardly needs repeating that versions of this formula underlie modern theories of semiotic signification and textual meaning.

We turn now to the place of the either-or cast of thought in the structure of rational discourse. It needs to be located in a whole cluster of logical-linguistic principles centered on the principle of identity (whose other side is the prohibitory principle of contradiction). These are summarized, for convenience, in table 3.

Aristotle, at the dawn of logocentism, made the law of identity the natural starting point of reasoning towards truth; Leibnitz, at the onset of modern rationalism, confirmed and elaborated it (see, for documentation, Ishiguro, 1972). In modern times, Dummett (1973, 1978) has reworked the logical notion of truth into a semantic theory of meaning, hoping thereby to disentangle controversies and provide a basis for selectively abandoning and retaining elements of the cluster. For example, he seeks to preserve the law of excluded third in his theory of rational meaning, while giving up the bivalence principle associated with the law of excluded middle. I have no wish to follow Dummett into these very fine distinctions; his relevance for our purpose lies in the use he makes of the bivalence principle to separate epistemological realists from antirealists. In his contrast, realism is the belief that for any statement there are extralinguistic states of the world rendering either it or its negation true. It follows that the realist is constrained to accept the law of excluded middle and its semantic counterpart the principle of bivalence. The antirealist relativizes truth to knowing what counts as evidence for a statement to be true, accepting that what counts depends upon prevailing and contingent methods of assembling and evaluating evidence, and that for any given statement a determinate truth value may never be assigned. He is constrained to suspend the law of excluded middle and the principle of bivalence in order to make room for the

TABLE 3   Dichotomous Principles of
Reasoning

Logical Principles	Semantic Expression
Law of Identity	No statement is both true and false.
Law of Excluded Middle	Every statement is either true or false (called the bivalence principle).
Law of Excluded Third	A statement can only be true or false; there is no third truth value of equal status to truth and falsity.

embedded, situated, constructed, and temporal character of knowledge and truth.

By Dummett's criterion, Simmel's conscious deconstruction of bivalence places him with the antirealists. David Gorman (1983:54), in a helpful review of Dummett's work, notes that Nietzsche, Benjamin, and Foucault prominently, though differently, represent antirealism, affording further suggestions on textual companions of Simmel. Of these Nietzsche deserves further mention for the sake of his critique of the law of identity and contradiction in sections 515–22 of *The Will to Power* (1967).

Nietzsche reveals his antirealist credentials in statements stressing that knowledge is constructed within linguistic, anthropologically grounded, and pragmatic courses of action: "Rational thought is interpretation according to a scheme that we cannot throw off" (1967: 283). Aristotle's law of identity and contradiction, the most certain of all principles of reasoning, cannot be taken as an assertion about being, because that would imply a prior and certain knowledge of being, which we do not have. Consequently, it can be taken only as a normative instruction not to ascribe contradictory attributes to things, because our distinctive human will and capacity is to master the world, its sensory multiplicity, through determinate classification. Logic is not an imperative to know the true, but "to posit and arrange a world that shall be called true by us . . . a means and measure for us to *create* reality, the concept 'reality,' for ourselves" (Nietzsche, 1967:279). The laws of logic are, then, norms tied to the pragmatic anthropological task of fashioning effective rules of conduct. The principle of identity reflects a need to delimit sensory flux, the temporal flow of sensations, the world as an endless becoming, by positing internally coherent entities that stay the same even amid change. Classical logic endorses being against becoming and constructs a fictitious world for the sake of rational mastery. Of course the effectiveness of serious make-believe depends upon reflexive innocence. Nietzsche says that modern nihilism is a dawning awareness that the world we rationally inhabit is after all only one we have constructed (1967: section 12). The category of "being," and its associates "unity" and "aim," through which value has been read into the structure of the world (in Simmel's terms, through which a language of value has been imposed on reality), no longer binds us, leaving a world that looks valueless. Absolute being dissolves into relative becoming. This is the context which makes sense of Simmel's declaration to Rickert, concerning *The Philosophy of Money,* that he could maintain his relativism only if it were capable of solving all the problems of absolutist thought (cited in Frisby, 1981:113). I take him to mean that it would have to be a positive, vital relativism capable of restoring value, including truth value, to the world. For this it would be necessary to make "becoming" rather than "being" the directional focus of philosophy. Money, a "direct negation of all being in itself," enveloping every substantial thing in a fluid totality of relative and interchangeable value, provides the perfect practical exemplar through which to articulate a relativistic and, in Dummett's terms, "anti-realist" world view. (In *The Philosophy of Money,* the most explicit and sustained promotion of relativism over absolutism is in the section covering pages 108–19.)

To confirm the insight gained from Dummett that any form of antirealist epistemology, which is to say any form making reality and truth float irremediably upon contingent methods of constructing them, entails an abandonment of bivalence. I would recall the claim made earlier that William James, in taking up Bergson's doctrine of the essential excess of life over logical divisions, placed himself in textual company with Simmel. The aspiration linking them is to fashion a philosophy true to life: that is, to its processual, emergent, creative, holistic character.

James, more eloquently and disputatiously than Simmel, is explicit on the shortcomings of formally rational, logically ruled discourse:

> When we conceptualize, we cut out and fix, and exclude everything but what we have fixed. A concept means a that-and-no-other . . . whereas in the real concrete sensible flux of life experiences compenetrate each other. . . . Past and future, for example, conceptually separated by the cut to which we give the name of present, and defined as being the opposite sides of that cut, are to

some extent, however brief, co-present with each other through-out experience. The literally present moment is a purely verbal supposition, not a position; the only present ever realized concretely being the "passing moment" in which the dying rearward of time and its dawning future forever mix their lights. . . . For conceptual logic, the same is nothing but the same, and all sames with a third thing are the same with each other. Not so in concrete experience. . . . The whole process of life is due to life's violation of our logical axioms. (James, 1967:574–75)

Given the impossible disjunction between reality and logical language, what is the philosopher or philosophically sensitive theorist of life to do? Stop talking? Yet to do even that, to make cessation signify meaningful silence, there would have to be an ongoing discourse that was conspicuously broken off. Lukács, in a comment quoted previously, saw Simmel's importance to the theorization of social life as lying precisely in his strenuous cultivation of conceptual determinations, pulling them this way and that until they (in practice, the decoding strategies of the reader) are halted by that which finally resists determination. The value of Simmel's writing does not, like James's, lie in the rhetorical strength of its protest on behalf of life, but in its capacity to bring the reading experience to border areas where concepts, no longer able to go further forward in an inferential line, begin to fold back upon themselves. The programmatic espousal of a philosophy true to life given by James is consistent with, but different from, the composition of an experienced excess of meaning over logical concepts achieved by Simmel's writing style.

I could, of course, go further in bringing out Simmel's strategic commitments on philosophical issues. It might, for example, be relevant to point out that whereas Simmel is by Dummett's criterion an epistemological antirealist, he is by Charles Peirce's equally cogent test for separating conceptual realists from nominalists a conceptual realist, albeit of a special and distinctly modern kind. Peirce (1958:80), defining the real as that which exists regardless of what any particular mind may happen to think of it, formulates a decisive test question: Are universals, that is types and classes of phenomena, held to be real? Thus a sceptical empiricist believing only in the reality of sensory experience, and regarding universals as nothing but cognitive conveniences, must give the nominalist answer, no, to the question. Simmel, it is true, criticized the reification of abstract nouns, for example, organicist treatments of society as a substantive entity. Frisby (1981:53) cites an essay published two years before *The Philosophy of Money* where Simmel condemns conceptual realism as mysticism. The context, however, makes it clear that he is referring to hypostatization "that makes human concepts into autonomous and substantive essences." His own theory of social forms, based on the premise that every social phenomenon has two elements "which in reality are inseparable," a content given by individual impulsions to action and a form "through which, or in the shape of which, that content attains social reality" (Simmel, 1971:24), and also his theory that the reality of money lies in its being a function, not in being a substance that has one (Simmel, 1978:169), unquestionably provide a positive, realist answer to Peirce's question. The reality of universals for Simmel is not, however, that of material substances or metaphysical essences, but the distinctively modern reality of Kantian categories of possible experience, grammatical structures of possible utterances, linguistic syntagms, sign systems, genres: in short, the reality of constitutive codes.

As I say, we could go further along these lines, but all I want to do is establish a methodological principle for the textual study of sociological theory. This principle is that strategic commitments on philosophical options like epistemological realism (and they are unavoidable whether stated or not) carry with them textual entailments. Conversely, a given method of composition will be consistent with certain options, tending to rule them into reading experience, and inconsistent with others, tending to rule them out, again regardless of stated intent. My claim about Simmel's method of composition is that it works against the general set of options called logocentrism associated with classical rationalist-empiricist discourse.

To return to my opening theme, every theoretical perspective in sociology entails appropriate literary methods of enactment. My purpose is to begin thinking about them through particular cases: identifying methods, bringing out the strategic commitments they mutually entail, and preparing in this way to move towards normative evaluation of better and worse methods of writing sociological theory. The ensuing case study of Max Weber will have the same aim.

Summary of Results in Part 2

Applying questions and concepts developed in Part 1 to the work of Georg Simmel, the following results were obtained:

1. The reception history of Simmel's work is marked by repeated words and phrases which can be called receptive epithets. They are regarded as reading imprints of Simmel's style of composition. The epithets fall into three sets according to internal family resemblances.

Each set is shown to contain a nodal epithet of particular informative value. They are multi-faceted, modern, and marginal. A search is conducted for the literary methods of which these are imprints.

2. Pursuing the epithets associated with "marginal," I characterize Simmel's writing as simultaneously dialectical, reflexive, and deconstructive. Dialectical writing is defined by a certain type of reading experience where a transactive engagement and nullification of normal decoding strategies and interpretive routines leads toward a higher-level reordering of interpretation. Reflexive writing is any which thematizes its own constitutive codes, making its composition part of its referential content. Deconstructive writing is any which reflexively thematizes and thus renders problematic a particular interpretive code: the classical canons of rationalist-empiricist discourse which, following Derrida, I call logocentrism.

3. To analyze the text work of Simmel's *The Philosophy of Money*, I advanced the principle, following earlier leads, that text work is always a working of language: its realized forms, possibilities, and internal tensions. Specified to the selection, treatment, and rhetorical deployment of topics in the text at hand, the principle yields the conclusion that three historically realized possibilities of language are working the text:

(*a*) The semiotic possibility that meaning is only difference in a system of signs, leaving language fraught with characteristic tensions of ontological emptiness.

(*b*) The representational (logocentric) possibility that written words represent spoken words which represent impresses of reality on the mind, leaving language ontologically anchored as required by rationalist-empiricist discourse.

(*c*) The ancient possibility that the whole of creation is textually structured so that language is ontologically suffused and provides direct access, through analogies and resemblances, to knowledge of the world. This possibility is shown to correspond to the pre-Enlightenment knowledge code identified by Foucault (1970), and also to what Habermas (1983) calls the heritage of Jewish mysticism; a lineage which connects Simmel to, among others, Hegel and Benjamin.

The presence of the three forms, in varying relations of deconstruction and defence, is revealed in Simmel's account of the significance of money as a semiological phenomenon, a rational measuring device, and an analogue of the structure of existence. The three possibilities of language working the text are projected into its quasi-linguistic subject matter: money.

4. The identification of Walter Benjamin as a textual companion allows Simmel's analogical method of exposition to be associated with the literary genre of allegory, Benjamin's stated method of theorizing history and social life. I do not claim that Simmel wrote allegories, but that he practiced a method of commentary corresponding to what literary critics call allegoresis. This is shown, through the case of historical materialism (named by Simmel as the methodological base of *The Philosophy of Money*), to be deconstructively related to standard narrative and causal forms of explanation.

5. Within the general cognitive-linguistic code of logocentrism, it is shown that *The Philosophy of Money* is especially active in deconstructing the related core principles of identity, contradiction, and bivalence.

Part Three: Weberian Writing

and the Spirit of Casuistry

6 The Casuistic Tradition and Max Weber

Chapters 6 and 7 are guided by a single interpretive hypothesis which will, I believe, draw us toward the special exemplary value of Weber's method of theorizing. The hypothesis is that Weber's method of theoretical composition—its strategic commitments and their literary means of performance—belongs to a definite intellectual tradition and associated genre of writing identifiable under the term casuistry. I say "identifiable under," rather than "identified by," because the label has come to cover much that is of no exemplary value, except perhaps negatively: all that has given casuistry a bad name. The hypothesis appeals then to a positive concept of casuistry as a method of theorizing worth preserving in sociology. However, since the concept has no standing in sociological discussion, it cannot assure the pertinence of the hypothesis for sociological interests. Consequently, I feel obliged to issue some promissory notes in anticipation of the findings.

The interpretive hypothesis bears instructively upon at least four interests that inform commentary on Weber's work and are consequential for debate on the proper practice of sociology:

1. The relationship between Weber's scholarly work and his philosophy of life. Especially the meaning of his self-denying principle of "value-free" social science in relation to his self-embracing "ethic of responsibility." The demands of the ethic are eloquently conveyed in the public lecture, "Politics as a Vocation," given the year after the end of the First World War. They are conveyed no less by the occasion and Weber's response to it than by the prescriptions of the lecture itself. Against a background of national crisis and the exciting spectacle of the Russian Revolution, and addressing students fired with idealistic hopes of building a new world, Weber administers the rhetorical equivalent of a cold shower. The political pathway to authentic selfhood passes through ethical choices made soberly, in "an attitude of detachment" (Weber, 1978a:212) and with maximum awareness of consequences. The supreme values here are realistic appraisal and open-eyed choice, without the comfort of ideological fervor, doctrinaire certainty, or dogmatic selective perception. The heroic connotations of forcing oneself to a realistically responsible choice are multiplied throughout the lecture and make clear the indispensable role of value-free (one might

better say value-suspended) analysis for practicing the ethics of responsibility: "What matters is the disciplined dispassionateness with which one looks at the realities of life, and the capacity to endure them and inwardly to cope with them" (Weber, 1978a:233). What I will want to argue is that the casuistic tradition includes intellectual strategies and literary tactics for combining relentless analysis with situated choice to achieve something like a heroic ethics of responsibility: one which, it should be added, is as hostile to utilitarian or hedonistic ethics of accommodation, adjustment, and happiness as to ideological ethics of absolute ends. (See, for example, Weber's diatribe against all ethics of accommodation: Weber, 1978a:383–88.)

2. The awkwardness, aridity, some would say the unreadability of much of Weber's sociological writing, especially that which is most strongly theoretical, such as the first part of his magnum opus, *Economy and Society*. Reinhard Bendix, introducing his particularly fine exposition of Weber's work, comments with a degree of puzzled irritation on the interpretive difficulties posed by Weber's style:

> Not all misinterpretations are due to a reliance on translations, however. The plain fact is that Weber's work is difficult to understand. Whatever may be said in justification of long sentences and scholarly qualifications is not enough to explain the characteristic "style" of Weber's sociological writings, which tend to bury the main points of the argument in a jungle of statements that require detailed analysis, or in long analyses of special topics that are not clearly related to either the preceding or the ensuing materials. Weber undertook several interdependent lines of investigation simultaneously and put all his research notes into the final text without making their relative importance explicit. (Bendix, 1960:xxi)

Along the same lines, Karl Löwith, comparing Weber and Marx, observes in both a passion to comprehend, to assimilate, and to master which overwhelms ordinary discrimination between great and small events, major and minor thinkers, relevant and irrelevant materials. Both had gifts of demagogic arousal and lucid exposition, "yet both have also written almost unreadable works, whose lines of thought seem often to peter out, being overburdened with supportive material and footnotes. With extravagant and remorseless care, Weber follows up the theories of obscure contemporary mediocrities. . . . Both Marx and Weber pile scientific acerbity and personal animus upon seeming trivialities; short articles grow into unfinished books. Thus the question arises: what is the vital impulse behind such vehemence, which is aimed equally at an everyday legal case, an academic appointment, or a book review—or at the future of Germany?" (Löwith, [1932] 1982:21, 22).

The observations of Bendix and Löwith are to be welcomed in that they elevate to an explicit problem what is typically passed by in the literature with only casual curiosity, if it is mentioned at all. However, while Löwith does try to answer his question of the "vital impulse" underlying Weber's stylistic excesses, the idea of a totalizing vocation to save human dignity is hardly convincing, and in any case, does not respond to the level of textual facts calling for explanation. An adequate response would have to be at the same level and couched in terms of cognitive-literary style and genre. The general situation we find around the issue of Weber's writing style is an interpretive vacuum with no methodological guidance for filling it. As one might expect, arbitrary glosses have flourished in these conditions. Bendix's complaints imply something like overcommitment to scholarly caution, want of self-editing, carelessness, haste, and inadequate organization of work. Paul Lazarsfeld (1972:93–95) advances a psychological gloss to the effect that Weber, for reasons having to do with the domestic tensions and inner conflicts that resulted in his nervous breakdown, needed to erect a barrier between himself and the emotional realities of human behavior; this he did in part through scholarly distancing and a "pseudo-logical terminology," a shielding labyrinth of formal definitions. Leo Strauss resorts to positing a character flaw—childishness—to account for Weber's stylistic practice of placing ethically significant terms like class situation and revolution in quotation marks: "To put the terms designating such things in quotation marks is a childish trick which enables one to talk of important subjects while denying the principles without which there cannot be important subjects—a trick which is meant to allow one to combine the advantages of common sense with the denial of common sense" (Strauss, 1963:434).

The methodological principles advanced in part 1 of this study forbid me to allow personal attributes of the author to account for features of textual composition. At most they are indirect clues or indicators of phenomena demanding literary analysis and explanation. By locating Weber and his method of composition in a literary tradition of casuistry, I will show otherwise merely puzzling and irritating features of his style to have a coherent meaning and positive significance: something completely lost in personalized glosses of them as childish trickery, neurotic anxiety, lack of editorial discipline, and the like. These result either in slanderous discrediting or at best in making allowances for regrettable excesses, inexplicable aberrations, and minor, because only stylistic, blemishes. The casuistic hypothesis, in contrast, makes Weber's style an intrinsic, indispensable feature of his mode of theorizing instead of an excrescent growth on a beautiful body of thought.

3. A major thematic interest in Weberian commentary is the meaning and significance of the ideal-type method. This is a vexatiously elusive topic, as the sheer volume and indeterminacy of the literature devoted to it testifies. A crucial reason, I believe, is that the method serves three distinct functions which have not been adequately separated or therefore integrated even in Weber's own self-commentaries. At this stage it is enough simply to name the functions; they are the explanatory, the interpretive, and the critical. Now the mere existence of multiple and inadequately explicated functions would in itself provide ample room for commentators to talk sincerely and at great length past one another. Here, however, there is an additional complication. The functions have tended over the history of sociological theory to become separated out into distinct and competing theoretical perspectives. Contemporary chroniclers have come, rather grandiloquently and misleadingly, to call them paradigms. At any event, this differentiation means that commentators on Weber are talking from different places and lack a common sphere of discourse sufficient to hear one another clearly. A possible advance would be to say that the ideal-type method took shape initially to mediate tensions between the opposing claims of scientific nomothetic explanation and hermeneutic idiographic interpretation, and adding in critical theory, its context of understanding still lies between conflicting perspectives. In between is where its meaning and significance are to be found. This seems to me valid as far as it goes, but it must be acknowledged that no-man's-land lacks positive satisfactions, except perhaps for masochistic heroes who want to see how much they can stand. It is more fruitful, viable, and hence valid to locate the three functions of the ideal-type method in a coherent mode of theoretical discourse: casuistry. In this context one can make procedural sense of the entire method, including its literary means of composition. I will be more specific. The explanatory, interpretive, and critical functions of the ideal-type method are performed in Weber's work through varying combinations of three facets of casuistic composition: denominative (definitional), indicative (establishing relevant factual conditions of action), and ethical (advisory and normative application to a choice). To avoid unnecessary misunderstanding, I would emphasize that there is no one-to-one correspondence between the three functions of the method and the three facets of casuistry; the former are textually performed through combinations of the latter. Also, in Weber's scholarly

182

work, disciplined by the principle of value neutrality, one would not expect the ethical aspect to appear directly, even though it is the ultimate point of the procedure as a whole. My argument here will be that ethical casuistry is present in Weber's text work as something approached and strenuously withheld; moreover, withheld by means of denominative and indicative casuistry. This will be a major theme of chapter 7.

4. Associated with the previous interest is a more particular one in the potential of Weber's sociology for undertaking social critique. Historically it has taken polemical shape in the negative reception of Weber by neo-Marxian critical theory. Herbert Marcuse (1968) provides adequate documentation. He argues that Weber's value-free methodology allows obligations to be imposed on sociology from the outside, allows normative debate to run parallel and undisturbed by social science, and in its operation promotes the rule of formal rationality, thus mirroring and legitimating the self-concealing ideology of industrial capitalism:

> It is precisely Max Weber's analysis of industrial capitalism, however, which shows that the concept of scientific neutrality, or better, impotence, vis-à-vis the Ought cannot be maintained: pure value-free philosophical-sociological concept formation becomes, *through its own process,* value criticism. Inversely, the pure value-free scientific concepts reveal the valuation that is contained in them: they become the critique of the given, in the light of what the given does to men (and things). The Ought shows itself in the Is: the indefatigable effort of thinking makes it appear. In *Economy and Society,* that work of Max Weber which is most free from values and where the method of formal definitions, classifications, and typologies celebrates true orgies, formalism attains the incisiveness of content. This authentic concretion is the result of Weber's mastery of an immense material, of scholarship that seems unimaginable today, of knowledge that can afford to abstract because it can distinguish the essential from the inessential and reality from appearance. With its abstract concepts, formal theory reaches the goal at which a positivistic, pseudoempirical sociology hostile to theory aims in vain: the real definition of reality. The concept of industrial capitalism thus becomes concrete in the formal theory of *rationality* and of *domination* which are the two fundamental themes of *Economy and Society.* (Marcuse, 1968:202–3)

For Marcuse, Weber's work has the same dubious significance accorded by Marx to political economy: it reveals with symptomatic validity the operation and rationalistic self-masking of capitalist-bourgeois consciousness, including its intrinsic depravity. Weber shows the transformation of formal into capitalist rationality, seeming to allow a critique to begin, but aborts the possibility by accepting the development of capitalist rationality, which is humanly irrational if truly seen, as an inevitable march of reason itself: "But then the critique stops, accepts the allegedly inexorable, and turns into apologetics—worse, into the denunciation of the possible alternative, that is, of a qualitatively different historical rationality" (Marcuse, 1968:208). Marcuse is referring here to what he has previously called Weber's spiteful denunciation of socialism.

Against his view, and it is widely shared among critical theorists, I will argue that a far-from-negligible critical function is served in Weberian theory by the application of denominative and indicative casuistry to value-laden terms through which decisions on social action are unavoidably conducted. The procedure, properly cultivated, induces a critical reflexivity in social discourse which is essential to prevent any strong vocabulary of action, including neo-Marxian critique itself, from degenerating into an apologia for a predesigned social plan.

In summary, then, the promise of locating Weber's work in the casuistic tradition is to represent familiar interpretive issues in a new light and rethink more challengingly Weber's distinctiveness and the exemplary significance of his practice of sociological theory.

From Weber to Casuistry: A Trail of Evidence

The interpretive hypothesis guiding the analysis emerged from a casual observation in reading *Economy and Society*. Weber occasionally uses the terms "casuistry" and "casuistic" neutrally, that is, descriptively, and even with positive connotations. For example:

> We will not deal here with any detailed "casuistry" and terminology. However, we will distinguish two types of economic action. (Weber, 1978b:339)

> It is not our intention here to produce the further casuistic distinctions and specialization of concepts which would be required for a strictly economic theory of the city. (P. 1217)

The idea of casuistry as somehow necessary to adequate theorizing is more explicitly stated by him in a referee's letter urging rejection of an article submitted by a Freudian for publication in the *Archiv für Sozialwissenschaft und Sozialpolitik,* jointly edited by Weber, Jaffé, and Sombert. The letter notes conceptual difficulties in applying Freud's theories. Not only have they undergone internal development so that their final form is still not certain, but important concepts have become so loosely used by others as to lose all precise meaning. More disturbing, they are as a result available for the illicit imposition of ethical judgments under the guise of science. Thus, while Freud's theories contain a possible value for interpreting cultural phenomena, it cannot be realized without increased terminological rigor:

> An essential precondition would be the creation of an *exact casuistics* of a scope and a certainty which, despite all assertions to the contrary, does not exist today . . . instead of this kind of work, which is of necessity specifically *specialist* in character, we see Freud's followers, especially Dr. X, spending their time partly in metaphysical speculation, and partly (what is worse) on a question which, from the point of view of exact science, is a childish one, namely, "Can one eat it?"—that is, cannot one construct a practical "world view" from it? That is certainly no crime: *every* new scientific or technological discovery has had the consequence that the discoverer, whether of meat extract or the loftiest abstractions of natural science, has believed himself to have a mission to discover new values or to reform ethics—just as, for instance the inventors of colour photography thought they were called to be reformers of painting. But I can see no need for the nappies of this seemingly inescapable baby stage of science to be washed in our "*Archiv.*" (Weber, 1978a:384; italics in original)

I have quoted this passage at length less for its devastating satire than its indication of the serious offices casuistry is called upon to perform in the service of mature science and adult ethics. It requires little imagination to enter the new science of sociology into the account and hear names other than Freud among the scientific inventors lending themselves to reformative missions: Comte and Marx spring to mind. Read in this way the passage clarifies Weber's reluctant self-location as a sociologist, as expressed, for example, in a letter to a colleague, Robert Leifmann, written in the last year of his life: "If I am now a sociologist . . . I am so essentially in order to put an end to the use of collective concepts, a use which still haunts us" (cited in Frisby, 1976:xlii). It also helps to make sense of his stubborn determination to develop an exact sociological casuistics, in spite of knowing that it was intolerably tedious for students and would make people shake their heads with puzzlement (see Marianne Weber, [1926] 1975:676). However, these are matters for later discussion; I must return to the trail of evidence.

My initially mild curiosity about Weber's departure from the conventionally religious (and typically derogatory) use of the term casuistry gave way to active interest when, reading for another purpose, I came across a comment by Lazarsfeld that opened my eyes to its possible compositional significance. Reviewing Weber's painstaking decomposition of social structures and processes into a standard terminology of social action, the purpose of which is in turn to interpret the cultural significance of social structures and processes in historical contexts, Lazarsfeld observes: "At first glance the circular character of this 'casuistic' (Weber himself uses this legal expression) is surprising" (Lazarsfeld, 1972:86). The parenthetical insertion made me realize belatedly that Weber was not just using a word whose meaning could be recovered by consulting a lexicon, but was expressing a tradition of thought whose meaning could only be recovered by textual analysis. Lazarsfeld suggests that the tradition was encoded in German legal science, to which Weber was exposed through his education and professional training in law. It seemed possible, moreover, that if casuistry had legal and religious expressions, it might have others. In short, I began to think of the possible existence of a company of texts linked by common purposive commitments, cognitive strategies, and literary methods of enactment, to which Weber's mode of theorizing might belong: one indeed which if it existed would be indispensable for reading Weber adequately. Accordingly, I decided to see if anything like a coherent casuistic tradition had been identified in literary criticism. This turned out to be so. Starr (1971) and Slights (1981) provide textually detailed accounts sufficient to fashion a compositional model of casuistic discourse, one capable of serving as an interpretive testing ground for the style of an author. Before describing it, however, I should complete the trail of circumstantial evidence leading to the hypothesis that Weber's writing transacts a casuistic mode of social theorizing.

Starr's topic is the style of Daniel Defoe's novels. It struck me, however, in reading his prefatory sketch of Defoe's casuistic writing methods, that the name Weber could validly be substituted as the subject of almost every statement. The impression of a more than coincidental affinity between them was greatly reinforced by the information that Defoe wrote within a specific tradition of casuistry associated with seventeenth-century Protestantism. This tradition, expressed in sermons, tracts, diaries, letters, essays, and the like, is a central element of the same Protestant ethic which Weber regarded as the interpretive key to modern society and to which, as Mitzman's (1970) study makes clear, Weber was drawn by more than scholarly interests. He recognized in it a vital part of his own identity. I would add only that Starr includes among the prime exemplars of Protestant casuistry Richard Baxter, the same Baxter who at the end of Weber's *The Protestant Ethic and the Spirit of Capitalism* (1958) inspires the powerful "iron cage" denouncement of modern materialism and formal rationality. It is a passage which brings into especially sharp focus an internal tension between relentlessly thorough factual assessment and action informed by ethical integrity, the deliberate cultivation of which to maximum intensity is, I will argue, a generative feature of casuistic discourse and Weberian social theory alike. If this sounds premature, let me say only that Baxter's name places Weber in the textual vicinity of a definite casuistic tradition.

A Compositional Model of Casuistic Discourse

Slights (1981) raises a pertinent preliminary question for a model of casuistic discourse: Can casuistry properly be called a literary genre? Taking English Protestant casuistry as her prototype, she observes that while displaying typical syntactic structures and rhetorical strategies, it did not develop literary rules sufficiently strong to constitute a genre, perhaps because it was primarily an oral vehicle (for settling cases of conscience) to which writing was only an adjunct. Consequently she adopts the looser term "literary paradigm," proposed by Isabel MacCaffrey to describe a commonality between perhaps generically diverse works, where a certain kind of thematic concern dictates certain structural characteristics. MacCaffrey gives the "pastoral paradigm" as an example. The evasive value of the term for moderating title disputes is clear. I would argue, however, that its higher value is to push those claiming the existence of a genre to show that the stronger, more definite, hence superior term is warranted. For example, Alpers (1982) struggles to show that pastoral is after all a genre and not just a loose collection of resemblances. Similarly, I would be willing to accept that casuistry is a literary paradigm only as a concession of defeat; I want to show that it is a genre. To this end I would stress Slights's point that "the formal and conceptual characteristics of casuistry constitute a distinct way of understanding experience" (1981:xiv), adding that as literature it is tied to a distinct composition of reading experiences through certain methods of writing. Casuistry is a generative code reproducing itself and its distinct way of understanding in particular writings. Also, being a genre it contains generative principles that give it form. A genre is more than a convenient collection term; it is a local bounded area of the life of language, a configuration of certain possibilities and tensions. These generative principles will be identified subsequently.

The Encyclopaedia Britannica (11th edition) defines "casuistry" as applied morality, "the art of bringing general moral principles to bear on particular actions" and proceeds to make a crucial distinction between two concepts of morality involving two types of application. I will call them *formal casuistry* and *situated casuistry,* looking to the latter for whatever might be of positive exemplary value for sociology, and treating the former as the negative face of casuistry, although a generatively indispensable negative.

Morality may consist of objectified law operating through institutional authority and logical inference or of inward disposition operating through conscience, common sense, and moral sentiments. The former gives rise to what the article calls sacred book casuistry, associated especially with Judaism and Islam, which is contrasted with Greek casuistry, where there were no sacred books and no manuals laying down rules of conduct; where, also, there was a distaste for formulaic laws of morality, "unvarying rules of petrified action," and a preference for flexible adaptation according to particular circumstances and the practical exigencies of real life. English Protestant casuistry, like Weber's, belongs to the Greek or situated type. Weber's concern to break the hold of collective reifications in sociological theory, his resistance to all doctrinal isms, master principles, and "world-formulae" (see Roth, in Weber, 1978b:xxxv), his aversion to the bureaucratic petrification of conduct and the modern rule of formal rationality (for example, Weber, 1978b:1400–1403), his rejection of all save an ethics of responsibility—all follow the same pattern of opposition as situated casuistics.

Here a caution is needed regarding the positive and negative connotations of casuistry. I have proposed that insofar as it has any exemplary value for sociological theorizing, this will be in situated rather than in formal casuistics. There is no implication, however, that the formalization of applied morality is necessarily bad; it can be shown historically, as Weber has done, to have advanced equality, justice, and other such values. Nor is situated casuistics necessarily good; it can result in accretions of particularistic rules as alien to the operation of conscience, common sense, and moral sentiment as is formalized law. Weber himself alerts us to this point in his sociology of law (chapter 8 of *Economy and Society*) when contrasting typical possibilities of applied law. His discussion also helps clarify the sense of my distinction between formal and situated casuistics.

The organization of legal practice tends always toward formalism, a rationalization of procedures for receiving and processing the facts of the case so as to make them properly legal facts; but this can take two distinct directions: logical formalism, relying upon logical analysis of the meaning of evidence plus abstract rules and definitions to establish legally relevant factuality, and concrete formalism, relying upon extrinsic, sense-data characteristics such as "the utterance of certain words, the execution of a signature, or the performance of a certain symbolic act with a fixed meaning" (Weber, 1978b:657). Weber observes of the latter, and in terms close to literary analysis, that it can develop parallel to or independently of "logical sublimation": "Highly comprehensive schemes of legal casuistry have grown up upon the basis of a merely paratactic association, that is, of the analogy of extrinsic elements" (Weber, 1978b:655). Removed from logical organization, such paratactic accretions of rules and definitions cannot subordinate cases to abstract legal propositions from which decisions may be derived. Weber says that they exhaust themselves in casuistry. Elsewhere he introduces historical approximations under the term formalistic casuistry. This must be understood, however, as a degeneration of situated casuistics losing itself in particularity, not the opposite possibility of its being absorbed in formal casuistry where particularity—thus casuistry itself—is emptied into abstract propositions and logical derivations.

For example, English legal practice, compared to continental practice, is said to be closer to concrete formalism. Historically this is associated with the fact that in England preference was given to legal training as learning a craft by apprenticeship and practical experience rather than becoming qualified through the study of legal theory and legal science:

> This kind of legal training naturally produced a formalistic treatment of the law, bound by precedent and analogies drawn from precedent. Not only was systematic and comprehensive treatment of the whole body of the law prevented by the craftlike specialization of the lawyers, but legal practice did not aim at all at a rational system but rather at a practically useful scheme of contracts and actions, oriented towards the interests of clients in typically recurrent situations. (Weber, 1978b:787)

Thus far the passage reads much like a description of exemplary situated casuistry, but it proceeds to bring out the degenerate implications anticipated in the phrase "formalistic treatment," and in terms provocatively close to discussions of sociological method and critiques of atheoretical empiricism:

> The upshot was the emergence of what had been called in Roman law "cautelary jurisprudence," as well as of such practical devices as procedural fictions which facilitated the disposition of new situations upon the pattern of previous instances. From such practices and attitudes no rational system of law could emerge, nor even a rationalization of the law as such, because the concepts thus formed are constructed in relation to concrete events of everyday life, are distinguished from each other by external criteria, and extended in their scope, as new needs arise, by means of the techniques just mentioned. They are not "general concepts" which would be formed by abstraction from concreteness or by logical interpretation of meaning or by generalization and subsumption; nor were these concepts apt to be used in syllogistically applicable norms. In the purely empirical conduct of legal practice and legal training one always moves from the particular to the particular but never tries to move from the particular to general propositions in order to be able subsequently to deduce from them the norms for new particular cases. This reasoning is tied to the word, the word which is turned around and around, interpreted, and stretched in order to adapt it to varying needs, and, to the extent that one has to go beyond, recourse is had to "analogies" or "technical fictions." (Weber, 1978b:787)

I have quoted the passage at length because it so delicately reflects the fine line between nomothetic generalization and idiographic case study, and their divergent methods of concept formation and application, which Weber attempted to draw in recommending the ideal-type method (for a detailed account of his theory of concept formation, see Burger, 1976). An ideal type is explicitly a "technical fiction" assembled for some pragmatic task of interpreting new particular cases in the light of past ones. However, the purpose is to move from particulars to generalities and back again, resisting confinement to the level of particulars, where discursive movement can amount to nothing better than verbal stretching through metaphor and analogy: a kind of paratactic poetics of the particular. English legal practice, of course, only distantly and faintly represents such a possibility, and in contrast to relatively scientific continental practice. Closer to it in Weber's account are theocratic (versus secular) legal practice and Ancient Roman (versus Greek) ethical practice of religion. Both contrasts, more obviously the latter, bring us back to the Encyclopaedia Britannica distinction between formalized and flexible casuistics.

In theocracies, legal training is oriented to sacred laws fixed by an oral or literary tradition and tends toward a "purely theoretical casuistry" (Weber, 1978b:789) governed more by the needs of scholarly intellectualism than the practical needs of social actors. Insofar as theocratic legal practice does enter mundane social life, it does so as a formalistic casuistry "in the special sense that it must maintain, through reinterpretation, the practical applicability of the traditional, unchangeable norms to changing needs" (Weber, 1978b:790). Weber observes subsequently (p. 814) that patrimonial and authoritarian secular regimes of justice are more flexible in their casuistic mediation between tradition and new circumstances than theocracies, because they are less tied by sacred words. Ancient Rome was not a theocracy, but compared to Greece its citizens were more closely ruled by casuistic calculations. The religious Roman "surrounded his entire daily life and his every act with the casuistry of a sacred law. . . . The characteristic distinction of the Roman way of life was its ceaseless cultivation of a practical, rational casuistry of sacred law, the development of a sort of cautelary sacred jurisprudence and the tendency to treat these matters to a certain extent as lawyers' problems" (Weber, 1978b:408, 409). Cautelary jurisprudence refers to the employment of legal counselors to write directions and formulate etiquette about the correct administration of sacred or other laws. In Roman religious life there was considerable conceptual analysis of the precise jurisdictions of the numerous deities and a finely divided fixed schema of admissable actions with reference to them.

Weber's discussions of concrete formalism and formalistic casuistry help define, like dark edges around a shape, the meaning of situated casuistry. Sharper definition along the same lines is provided by two nineteenth-century English writers sensitive to the tradition, George Eliot and Thomas De Quincey. Eliot, speaking through a character in *The Mill on the Floss,* brings out the significance of casuistry for making general rules true to the situated exigencies of individual life:

> The casuists have become a by-word of reproach, but their perverted spirit of minute discrimination was the shadow of a truth to which eyes and hearts are too often fatally sealed: the truth, that moral judgments must remain false and hollow, unless they are checked and enlightened by a perpetual reference to the special circumstances that mark the individual lot. (Cited in Starr, 1971:iv)

To "moral judgments" a casuistic sociologist would want to add generalizations, typologies, and lawlike propositions. All sociology biased towards qualitative, interpretive, case-study approaches shares something of the casuistic spirit, a point appearing more clearly in De Quincey: "After it [morality] has multiplied its rules to any possible point of circumstantiality—there will always continue to arise cases without end, in the shifting combinations of human action, about which a question will remain whether they do or not fall under any of these rules. . . . The name, the word, Casuistry, may be avoided, but the thing cannot; nor *is* it evaded in our daily conversations" (Cited in Slights, 1981:4).

Nor has sociology, despite its founding impulse towards scientism, been able to evade it. From the casuistic standpoint, the aspiration of nomothetic sociology to subsume social life under universally valid laws must appear as overwhelming hubris. Again, Weber's sociology of law provides a representative anecdote. After the French Revolution, Napoleon aspired to create a completely rational civil code, one which would enable the legal system to operate almost automatically in the manner of a calculus or "a technically rational machine" (Weber, 1978b:811). Behind this one hears the intent of Jeremy Bentham, whose considerable influence on continental law is noted by Weber, to produce logically rigorous codes of law, written in exact standardized vocabularies, whereby the need for interpretation by lawyers, judges, or other specialized exegetes would be eliminated, because every law would speak for itself and say the same thing to every reader. In short, the text of the law would be the standard of the law. Weber claims that the Code Civil, taking its place alongside Anglo-Saxon and Roman common law as the third of the world's great systems of law, has approximated this entirely scientistic ideal. Immediately relevant for our purpose is his claim that through doing so it has completely eliminated casuistry (p. 865).

Returning all this to the crucial distinction made previously, I would say that formal casuistry belongs to an active historical tendency towards logical formalism that moves to eliminate situated casuistry, which I take to be the authentic core of casuistry itself; consequently it represents internally the negative principle of casuistry. However, dialecticians have taught us that every living entity is indispensably tensed by its own negation. Situated casuistry, therefore, needs its negative, in the course of its performance, as a compositional presence, to remain lively and avoid degeneration into quibbling elaboration. In terms of sociological practice, the interpretive examination of particular, local, historical cases needs to be tensed by the contrary pull toward absorption in universally valid categories and generalizations to escape degeneration into endlessly elaborative description. This is surely what underlies Weber's strenuous methodological mediations between concrete historical interpretation and nomothetic explanation and his insistence that sociological accounts be "adequate" at the level of both meaning and causality. I do not wish to equate interpretive sociology (however that is understood) with casuistic discourse, even though Weber, who fastened the former label to himself, offers an exemplary model of casuistry: to do so would be an abortive conflation of terms. But I do say that interpretive (qualitative, case-study) sociology reflects something worth preserving of the casuistic tradition in its opposition to logical formalism and its cultivation of sensitivity to particular circumstances and the individual lot.

Stylistic Characteristics of Casuistry

Slights (1981:13) tells us that a casuistic examination begins with a "doubtful action" and problematical considerations. I should add that the action to be resolved is trebly doubtful: there is doubt over the proper naming of alternative actions (denominative doubt), the factual assessment of consequences (indicative doubt), and what action should be chosen (ethical doubt). They correspond to the three facets of casuistry identified previously.

Two major forms of settling doubt can be distinguished in the tradition. First, "probabilism," associated with Jesuitry and condemned by English Protestants for encouraging a cynical manipulation of the faculty of practical reason (the joint exercise of conscience, common sense, and moral sentiment). Its principle is that any action can be chosen as long as it is probable that a given moral rule sanctions it. Second, "probabiliorism," the method of Protestant case divinity, recommends that the action be chosen which is most strongly reasonable to the conscience of the actor after a scrupulous and exhaustive weighing of circumstances and options. It is the second which interests us in connection with Weber's exemplary practice of sociological theory. Slights's (1981:15) quotations from Jeremy Taylor's account of the method (Taylor was a seventeenth-century Protestant casuist) are worth repeating at this point. Taylor observes that the effect of the procedure is to yield an accumulation of probabilities making "a milky and a white path, visible enough to walk securely," rather than a logical demonstration of correctness. The experience of accumulation is crucial here. Small stars in isolation are useless for guidance, but if they are placed together in a constellation, mariners can steer by them even though the light is less than that of the sun or moon.

Two related compositional features emerge here. The value of casuistic examination lies less in the conclusion arrived at than in the experiences (denominative, indicative, and ethical) accumulated along the way; there is a priority of way or method over end result. Also, the result is not to end doubt but to restructure it sufficiently to go further. Thus, Taylor does not offer his figurative mariners any guarantees; he says only that "very regularly they enter into the haven" and always travel "with trepidation." A stylistic hallmark of casuistry is to cultivate doubt in the course of seeking a way through it, and as part of the way through.

Slights (1981) indicates the priority of way over end in the title of her second chapter, "Method as Form." Starr states the point directly. Summarizing the exploration of conscience conducted by the fictitious narrator "H.F." in Defoe's *A Journal of the Plague Year,* he says: "It is noteworthy that this 'advice' or 'direction' extends only to the decision-making process, not to the substance of the eventual choice: the narrator suggests a 'method' for discovering one's duty rather than laying down the duty itself" (Starr, 1971:61).

Additionally noteworthy is Starr's placement of key words in quotation marks, an imitation of the same casuistic device which Leo Strauss saw in Weber's work as only a "childish trick." Placing it in the context of generic performance, we can now see that it belongs to a constitutive function of casuistry: the cultivation of denominative, indicative, and ethical doubt. One of the many havens in which conscientious thought finds relief from work is the taken-for-granted meaning of ordinary words. Quotation marks in casuistic discourse bracket ordinary usage and open normally sealed words for possible examination. They are a hesitation device, along with many others. Starr notes also the profusion of qualifications and disclaimers in H.F.s journal: "I dare not affirm that; but this I must own". . . . "This I believe was in part true, tho' I do not affirm it: But it is not at all unlikely, seeing . . ." (Starr, 1971:55–56, n. 7). The associated sentence structure is one of intricately branching development, as if thought were feeling its way forward and growing in reaction to encountered obstacles, deflections, and openings: "The sentence structure conveys a sense of deliberation-in-progress, of groping uncertainly towards a difficult decision" (Starr, 1971:51).

Casuistic discourse is by no means lacking in logical constructions, but they are fashioned into stochastic networks of reasoning rather than demonstrations or proofs: "the process is *in*clusive, not *con*clusive" (Starr, 1971:52).

Branching qualifications and stochastic exploration of what is probably the case are related by Starr to another hallmark of casuistry: the establishment of an authority to speak on the basis of disclaiming any privileged, institutional access to truth: a dialogical, Socratic authority of principled doubt and scrupulous assessment. For example, the casuistic narrator H.F. is an anonymous saddler for whom medical or theological expertise is disclaimed, yet Defoe projects him as an authority on the thorny, real-life issue of whether in the face of the plague one should prudently flee the city or trust in God's will and see it through, superior to the physicians and divines whose opinions on the subject were currently in print. Casuistry disclaims the preemptive authority of great names, expert qualifications, dogmas, churches, parties, and the like for the sake of initiating an exercise of individual reason and conscience. H.F. cannot prescribe a decision, only recommend and exemplify a mode of deliberating. The same feature is noted in Defoe's "manuals of conduct," such as *Religious Courtship* and *The Family Instructor*, where ethical dilemmas were investigated through stories and dialogues:

> Cases of conscience are thus explored in a stochastic, not a peremptory manner. The family discussions in *Religious Courtship* represent an extension of the same device, with the members of the group given more specific and distinct identities, and their views more fully articulated and qualified in the give-and-take of dialogue. Defoe himself may finally be "The Family Instructor," but he is careful to keep from delivering the instruction ex cathedra, or even from above. Rather he is fond of making it move in the opposite direction. (Starr, 1971:37)

The self-tutoring efficacy of casuistic writing requires the authorial position to be vacated by the performative writer so that the reader is compelled to fill it.

The refusal of ex cathedra authority is related to the episodic, fragmentary, disjointed nature of casuistic writing. Gunther Roth's judgement of Weber, that he "never wrote a well-wrought book" (in Weber, 1978b:cvii), just like the observation following it that Weber overqualified his sentences with terms such as "perhaps," "more or less," "frequently but not always," needs to be grasped as a statement about the casuistic genre, not about personal stylistic mannerisms. Weber, like Defoe or anyone in this compositional code, must not simply avoid but enactively discredit "a transcendental scheme of things" (Starr, 1971:viii). It is another of those havens where the conscientious exercise of practical reason ceases. The exercise of that faculty is the dynamic principle of casuistry, and it demands the authentic representation of conflicting, or merely different, world views from the standpoint of the actors themselves. This is, of course, precisely the aim of interpretive sociology announced by Weber (for example, Weber, 1978b:4–15; Weber, 1975:125–91). The same pattern is also evident in his incredibly patient reconstructions of the positions of contemporary scholars, no matter what their reputational standing, in his methodological writings. Often, as Starr observes of Defoe's fictional narrator H.F. (1971:67) in his scrutiny of "old women's" thoughts about the meaning of the plague, Weber will begin a reconstruction with ironical distancing, then work himself so thoroughly into the other's position that his own becomes ambivalent. It is the scholarly equivalent of "going native" in ethnographic fieldwork. I previously cited Karl Löwith's wonderment at the "extravagant and remorseless care" with which Weber reconstructed the ideas of "obscure contemporary mediocrities." Again, however, this must be grasped as an expression of the casuistic genre, not as an idiosyncratic mannerism or a personal failing, if it is to be understood.

Other standpoints of action include values and emotions, as well as goals, means, and circumstances; consequently casuistic discourse entails the cultivation of empathy as well as rational understanding. More definitely, its method requires cultivation of empathy with valuations and emotions on all sides of given dilemmas and problematic courses of action, necessarily including ones which are alien or disagreeable to the reader. Starr says that one of the most striking features of Defoe's fictional works is the way they draw the reader into an understanding of actions which by moral convention are obviously wrong: the ragged pickpocket's stealing in *Colonel Jack* and the multiple crimes of Moll Flanders. This is not done by critically attacking moral conventions, by overwhelming them with emotive evocations of suffering, or by deterministically overriding the possibility of choice, but through an almost forensic reconstruction of intentions, goals, and feelings in a context of particular circumstances such that the reader, in spite of moral considerations always kept in mind, is led to think that if he had been in that position he might have behaved the same way. It would be too vague and generally unspecific to say simply that casuistry entails the cultivation of empathy and sympathetic understanding. It does so (*a*) to supplement rational observational understanding of situation, ends, means, options, consequences, and limiting circumstances: and (*b*) as part of a strategy to enforce responsible choice and optimally exercise the faculty of practical reason.

Responsible choice means choice unforced by the power of rhetorical persuasion. Hence the cautiously supplementary use of empathy, the predominantly objective, logical tone of address, and the preference observed by Slights (1981:40) for "relatively plain and unadorned" language in casuistic discourse. Moreover, responsible choice requires that all relevant considerations be included, however minute and subtle, making for intricate elaboration and saturated coverage of topics. Slights says of the Protestant casuistic tradition: "All this produces a dense prose style that carries forward a closely reasoned argument. Numbered sections and subdivisions outline the argument and create the sense of a systematic and exhaustive treatment" (Slights, 1981:54). It is the conjunction of such a style with acute ethical dilemmas and bitterly contested public issues that gives casuistry its distinctively strained tone of dispassionate distance.

A final compositional characteristic to be noted derives from the strategic commitment of casuistry to the faculty of practical reason. Since ethical responsibility refers inescapably to individuals making choices in the face of contradictory pulls and circumstantial pressures, casuistic discourse must posit the individual actor as the focal unit of analysis and a high degree of voluntarism and autonomy in making decisions. In short, casuistic discourse posits methodological individualism. There is no need to document the doctrine or relate its technicalities (see, for example, Lukes, 1968). Two quotes from Weber sufficiently indicate its meaning:

> Social collectivities, such as states, associations, business corporations . . . for the subjective interpretation of action in sociological work . . . must be treated as *solely* the resultants and modes of organization of the particular acts of individual persons, since these alone can be treated as agents in a course of subjectively understandable action.

> It is a tremendous misunderstanding to think that an "individualistic" *method* should involve what is in any conceivable sense an individualistic system of values. . . . Even a socialistic economy would have to be understood sociologically in exactly the same kind of "individualistic" terms; that is, in terms of the action of individuals, the types of officials found in it. . . . The real empirical sociological investigation begins with the question: What motives determine and lead the individual members and participants in this

socialistic community to behave in such a way that the community came into being in the first place and that it continues to exist? Any form of functional analysis which proceeds from the whole to the parts can accomplish only a preliminary preparation for this investigation. . . . (Weber, 1978b:13, 18; italics in original)

In summary, the stylistic characteristics are as follows:

1. Initiation by ethical doubt and guidance toward an ethically and rationally responsible decision

2. Instructional guidance on method or way rather than on the right decision

3. Systematic cultivation of denominative, indicative, and ethical doubt in and as the method

4. Accumulations of denominative, factual, and ethical probabilities of correctness, rather than decisive demonstrations and proofs

5. A systematic suspension and bracketing of normal meanings and conventional terms of social discourse

6. A stochastic growth of argumentation to form an intricate, branching network of qualifications, disclaimers, and scrupulously balanced assessments

7. A systematic avoidance of dogmatic or rhetorical closures of the reasoning process and a resistance to institutional, preemptive authority to know what is true and right

8. Avoidance of transcendental schemes or universal formulas to carry the burden of examination, resulting in a typically episodic, fragmentary presentation of materials

9. The authentic representation of different cognitive, evaluative, and affective standpoints on given issues, including rational reconstructions supplemented by empathic understanding of actions

10. Exhaustive coverage of relevant considerations, goals, motives, values, circumstances, and so on, typically involving a proliferation of sections, subsections, and subordinate divisions

11. Methodological individualism and the attribution of high voluntarism and autonomy to individual agents of conduct

The Generative Tensions of Casuistic Discourse

Explanatory accounts of social actions contain two virtual tensions which are jointly necessary to generate a casuistic mode of discourse: (1) fidelity to the concrete and particular versus optimal, valid generalization; (2) ethical efficacy versus objective assessment, or in Weber's terms, value relevance versus value neutrality. The tensions become sufficient to generate casuistic discourse when (1) they are made explicit orienting features in the composition of accounts, and (2) when the accounting bias is towards truth to the particular (rather than truth about the general) and towards ethical efficacy. One must emphasize always a resisted tendency towards one pole against the pull of the other, never a one-way surrender, because casuistry flourishes near equipoise and equipollence; methodological certainty on either dimension is incompatible with it.

In one respect sociology is a promising field for casuistry, being informed by keen methodological awareness of the two tensions. However, its intellectual and institutional struggles for internal coherence and external recognition have made for strong choices between camps, with tensions regarded as stigmatic failings to be overcome by doctrinal warfare or comprehensive synthesis, rather than as forming a possible place of theorizing close to the demands of practical reason. Thus, on the dimension of particular versus general truth, the latter, via quantitative methods, has been made a symbol of scientific respectability and an identification of difference from history, ethnography, journalism, and the like. On the other dimension, generative tension has been dissipated in the "paradigmatic" separation of scientific from activist or "critical" sociology. I am talking about loss of cognitive, compositional tension built into the structure of theorizing and into the literary structure of its performative texts, not of polemics between individuals or groups. Of that kind of tension there is more than enough. The conclusion I would draw here is that the casuistic mode of discourse, while discernible in many areas of applied morality (one finds it to varying degrees in courtrooms, in problem-oriented television talk shows, in how-to-live advisory manuals, and, as De Quincey observed, in daily talk about problems of life), is in sociology systematically deprived of the conditions needed to generate it. This why Weber's example is so distinctive, troublesome, and difficult to grasp within the discipline, and so worthwhile.

The two generative tensions are prominently marked in accounts of Protestant casuistry and its literary derivatives. Starr observes of John Dunton's *Athenian Mercury:* "An interest in the concrete and particular case goes hand in hand with a concern for its wider implications of conscience" (Starr, 1971:23). Immediate dilemmas are referred systematically to a theoretical context, but always to illuminate the former. Similarly, Slights concludes:

> While professing the uniqueness of each case, the casuist must also try to create a model resolution that will apply to the problems of many men. This attempt to universalize while preaching particu-

larity leads to a proliferation of exceptions and qualifications that can try the patience of even the most sympathetic reader.

[The casuist] is distinctive in his constant acknowledgment of the distance between generalized rules of conduct and the actuality of a single mind operating morally in a particular situation. (Slights, 1981:63, 66)

The constitutive tension between ethical efficacy and objective observation is so obviously built into the casuistic programme of scrupulously weighing circumstances to reach a moral decision that no further documentation is needed. I would, however, with Weber in mind, note Martin Price's comment that Defoe's characters "live in a moral twilight," while the author himself seems most at home "in an ethical no-man's-land," the very place where "casuistry flourishes" (cited in Starr, 1971:vii).

In conclusion, the application of the model of casuistic discourse must make due allowance for the distinctive tasks of sociology. This is especially so with achieving ethical efficacy. A sociological casuistry, like any other form of the genre, would have to be ethically effective through the internal operation of its deliberations, the exemplary effect of a certain conduct of analysis; here the operation of a definite scholarly practice in social science. This excludes effectuation through extensions of or departures from scholarly practice; for example, social engineering, social reform, social movements, political causes, and moral rhetoric. Also, since the proper tasks of sociology do not include saving souls, easing consciences, or initiating moral self-tutelage on personal dilemmas, the question must be asked: What shape might ethical efficacy take in sociological casuistry? I will attempt to extract an answer from the examination of Weber's practice of sociology in chapter 7. At this point, however, a preliminary response can be obtained from the negatively instructive example of Charles Cooley's sociology.

Picking up what was said of Cooley in chapter 3, and relating it to the compositional model developed here, there are several respects in which he might be thought close to casuistry. We recall the concept of tentative process and its "working," represented in Cooley's description of the stochastic, branching growth of a vine along his garden fence; his programmatic application of tentative process to truthful thinking and writing; his espousal of an interpretive sociology utilizing introspection and sympathetic understanding, his resistance to systematizing, and his championing of the case method against quantitative abstraction from particularity. For example, in an essay titled "The Life-Study Method as Applied to Rural Social Research" (in Cooley,

1930), there is a criticism of "extensive abstract observation, commonly known as the method of statistics" (p. 332) because it obliterates particularity in averages, scales, and graphs. Its defect is "always remaining abstract and schematic, never grasping life in its organic reality. It has numerical precision (which is by no means the same as truth to fact) but does not attempt the descriptive precision which may be obtained by the skillful use of language, supplemented, perhaps, by photography, phonography, and other mechanical devices" (p. 332). Cooley wants sociology to reproduce whole patterns or prints of social life (see also "Case Study of Small Institutions as a Method of Research," in Cooley, 1930), a task for which abstractive measurement is inherently unsuited. Realistic novels offer greater truth to social life than statistical studies:

> The basis of reality for our knowledge of men is in sympathetic or dramatic perceptions; without these we are all in the air. . . . The novelist gives us something human, dramatic, real; colored, no doubt by his temperament and point of view, but far nearer the truth than any numerical description. He is a behaviorist who portrays people in action and shows minds and bodies functioning together in organic process. We cannot wholly scorn his method if we hope to put across sociology as a science of life. (Cooley, 1930:333)

Cooley's methodological statements might well be placed in a casuistic manifesto for sociology, yet it could not be said with any conviction that his own writings approximate the genre. In terms of my compositional model, this is because it lacks one of the generative tensions necessary for casuistry to form: there is no internally tensed striving towards an ethical effect in Cooley's sociology. I do not mean that Cooley the man lacked moral and political concerns. As Coser (1978:306) reminds us, Cooley considered himself a member of the Progressive movement, which was part of the highly moralistic matrix of early American sociology. However, Coser adds that his reforming zeal is not "salient on the surface" of his work. In itself this would not prevent Cooley's work from being casuistic; indeed, commitment to scholarly integrity requires of sociological casuistry that it does not preach reform or arouse moral passions. What is required, however, and what the surface of Cooley's work, his text work, lacks, is a strenuous containment of moral passion and ethical intention by and within a rationally ruled discourse. Going further, if ethical import is not to be added to the work but is contained in and by it, then it can only come from the subject matter, the materials presented. The subject matter itself must be imbued with value significance, moreover, a specifically sociological one.

Slights (1981:65) says of the casuistic prototype: "The attempt to construct in prose an example of a difficult moral decision involves the casuist at once in intrinsically interesting and important material." That is to say, casuistry begins with a reader, endowed with capacities for rational assessment and moral decision (the faculty of practical reason), for whom certain materials cannot help but be significant because they represent events and actions that test and exercise the faculty. Naturally, these will vary in substance between times and places. More immediately relevant for us, however, is the consideration that since total individual identity is divided into distinct facets, corresponding to different spheres or modes of experience, casuistry can take different forms according to which facet of identity is being addressed. Thus classical casuistry addresses the individual as a moral person seeking a right path through dilemmas. Sociological casuistry addresses the individual as a social member, cultural being, and product of history. Max Weber, in a crucial document written in his last year, characterizes himself and his intended reader in exactly this mode: "A product of modern European civilization, studying any problem of universal history, is bound to ask himself to what combination of circumstances the fact should be attributed that in Western civilization, and in Western civilization only, cultural phenomena have appeared which (as we like to think) lie in a line of development having universal significance and value" (Weber, 1958:13). In the same vein is an oft-quoted passage which takes on new significance in the light of the casuistic hypothesis: "The cultural problems which move men form themselves ever anew and in different colors, and the boundaries of that area in the infinite stream of concrete events which acquires meaning and significance for us, i.e. which becomes an 'historical individual,' are constantly subject to change. The intellectual contexts from which it is viewed and scientifically analyzed shift" (Weber, 1949:84).

For Weber, the task of sociology is to scientifically analyze materials whose intrinsic importance derives from their association with cultural problems that form part of the consciousness of living in a particular historical location. As Guenther Roth remarks of part 1 of *Economy and Society,* which "Weber liked to call his *Kategorienlehre* or casuistry" (Weber, 1978b:C), it "builds a sociological scaffolding for raising some of the big questions about the origins and directions of the modern world." (Weber, 1978b:xxxv).

We do not have to accept Weber's particular locational terms "Western civilization" and "universal history," but some such collective horizon of signification is necessary for a distinctively sociological casuistry to occur. The exercise of practical reason upon the big questions of one's time, indispensable for the maturation of the sociohistorical facets of individual identity, depends upon materials imbued with just that particular kind of significance. Cooley's interpretive sociology, typically microscopic, introspective, domestic, and ahistorical, lacks such materials. Consequently it cannot achieve the specific form of ethical efficacy required of sociological casuistry. The same observation would apply to a sociology whose materials are selected for their significance as instances, examples, and tests of nomothetic theory, and at the other extreme, one which attends idiographically to the particularity of actors, groups, places, and times for their own sake, as if the concrete was a value in itself.

I am now able to state an important addition to my compositional model, referring to the particular demands of sociology. A necessary condition for sociological casuistry to form is that materials for discussion be selected within the horizon of a collective historical consciousness of significant issues. The negative corollary is that predominance by any other selection frame will prevent sociological casuistry from occurring. The two major alternative frames in Weber's methodological environment were nomothetic theory construction and the idiographic reconstruction of concrete phenomena; the former tended in sociology to degenerate into abstract system mongering, the latter into historicist antiquarianism and sheer saturation with detail. If, as I propose, Weber's compositional method is inwardly formed by the generative tensions of casuistry, his tortuous attempts to locate sociology between the nomothetic and idiographic concepts of knowledge, bound up in the ideal-type method, would cease to appear as only a knot inviting still more exegetical teasing and cutting; they would make sense as the operation of a method in its own right: the borderland method of casuistry. Discussion of this interpretation will be continued in chapter 7. Meanwhile, I would like to give it stronger face validity and prepare the ground a little more by showing that the casuistic method of discourse was practiced in an area closer to Weber: legal science.

Radbruch and the Logic of Legal Science

Radbruch is methodologically, textually, and biographically close to Weber. Radbruch and Weber both articulate possibilities of knowledge through a neo-Kantian philosophical vocabulary, looking especially to Rickert as a methodological mentor; each references the other with approving respect, and their careers at Heidelberg overlapped from 1904 to 1914. Radbruch's work, like Weber's, bears strong imprints of the generative tensions and resultant mode of inquiry defining the casuistic tradition. Apart from helping to specify further the meaning of the tradition in nontheological areas, here the sociocultural sciences, the discussion is intended to show that there existed around Weber an extensive methodological field conducive to casuistic discourse.

My discussion is confined to a monograph by Radbruch on legal philosophy and the logic of legal science, first published in 1914 and revised, though not significantly changed, in 1932. The revised version is translated in Wilks, 1950:47–224. The only claim I wish to make is that the monograph exactly reflects the spirit of casuistry and in its account of the logic of legal science provides a prospectus and rationale for casuistic sociology that is continuous with Weber's logic of the cultural sciences. I will not try to argue, although it might be possible, that Radbruch's writing style, his literary working method, is casuistic. This is a task reserved for the subsequent analysis of Weber.

In the preface, Radbruch calls his position relativism. It affirms that where ethical, moral, and political disagreements are concerned nothing but partisan views are possible, and a partisan view can neither be demonstrated nor refuted; it escapes definitive logico-empirical judgment. Radbruch's relativism displays the same rejection of absolutely valid, transcendental schemes of judgment and prescribed decisions also necessary for casuistry to begin. Furthermore, like casuistry, the possibility of reasoned judgment is not abandoned, only limited to a situated emergence of agreements worked up from considerations of intent, circumstance, and the interpreted application of general rules. Since no "standpoint above the parties" is acknowledged, the only standpoints of reasoned argument available are those of adverse views, implying the discursive necessity of recovering and entering the views of others in full awareness that one might thereby be changed. This position corresponds closely, of course, to the demands of Weber's ethics of responsibility and the procedure of interpretive sociology; in this context it is significant that Radbruch refers to Weber as an "outstanding representative of relativism," and as a "great ethical personality" (Radbruch, 1950:56), because he had the courage to renounce a scientific or any other transcendental establishment of right decisions but not reasoned decision itself. The reason for the praise is entirely characteristic of the casuistic spirit.

On its own, Radbruch's advocacy of relativism could easily be heard and forgotten as another plea for tolerance and understanding. What gives it more lasting value is that it is tied to a working method and a distinctive logic of inquiry. He presents them in an account of legal science and its role in relation to the philosophy and practice of law. I will review the account in terms of the two generative tensions of casuistic discourse and point to compositional correlates in passing.

The title of Radbruch's opening section, "Reality and Value," names the two poles defining one of the generative tensions; the argument itself locates legal science between them, in company with all the sociocultural sciences. Beginning with the neo-Kantian postulate of raw experience, where value is directly perceived in things, events, and actions as their intrinsic attributes, Radbruch describes four attitudes in which this unreflective commingling of reality and value can be broken and reflection, inquiry, and knowledge take shape: (1) a conscious suspension of evaluation in a "value-blind attitude," yielding a realm of thought objects called nature, the methodical application of which is the essence of natural science; (2) a "deliberately evaluating attitude," whose systematic cultivation produces normative thought and the discipline enunciating general rules of goodness (ethical philosophy), beauty (aesthetic philosophy), and truth (logic); (3) a "value-relating attitude" which is "the methodical attitude of the cultural sciences" (Radbruch, 1950:50); (4) an attitude of incorporating reality into values, the attitude of religious faith, born of "the unbearableness of the contrast between reality and value" (p. 51). Radbruch expresses the relation between the four forms of thought in a most intriguing way. The cognitive realms of nature and the ideal are two isolations which the "the never-to-be-completed bridge of culture and the ever instantaneously accomplished flight of religion" (p. 51) seek to span. The idea of cultural science and religious faith as belonging to alternative spanning devices between the real and the ideal, with faith implying flight from the mundane world rather than working in and with it, lends extra significance to the peroration of Weber's public lecture, "Science as a Vocation," where after relentlessly urging the inability of science to tell us what should be done, he advises those who cannot bear the value-blind ethos of the times to return silently but without shame to the open arms of the old churches. Meanwhile, for those who can stand it, there is the never-to-be-completed work of culture, cultivation, and cultural science. Cultural science responds then to a religious, one might say existential, problematic; it is a vocational call to exercise the faculty of practical reason, to depart from the value-blind side of the gap in life towards the normatively ideal without abandoning the way of work for that of faith. This also, though departing from the opposite side and using different materials, is the design of Protestant casuistry.

The in-between character of legal science is underlined by Radbruch's observation that, like any cultural science, its objects of study emerge within a constitutive field of human values. The quiddity of law, conferring the status of a legal fact on whatever embodies and conveys it, resides in the value, the anthropologically rooted disposition, called justice. The facticity of law, like that of any cultural phenomenon, consists of value-approximating, -deviating, -implementing, -failing meanings; it is a value-created form of reality and therefore does not exist in the value-blind attitude: "Law can be understood only within the framework of the value-relating attitude. Law is a cultural phenomenon, that is, a fact related to value. The concept of law can be determined only as something given, the meaning of which is to realize the idea of law. Law may be unjust, but it is law only because its meaning is to be just" (Radbruch, 1950:52).

Legal science, like every cultural science, fashions knowledge from a value-given reality, a "concept" of its domain, which on the one hand cannot be made to coincide with a natural science concept arrived at in value blindness, even though the scientific aspiration to empirical adequacy constantly draws it back in that direction, and on the other, is drawn towards the value source, the "idea" of its domain, without ever, in scientific integrity, being able to complete that trajectory. It follows that every cultural, including social, science is self-constitutively tensed in two directions—negatively, against natural science value-blindness, and positively, towards normative value deliberation—and cannot abandon either pole without losing coherence. Radbruch conducts a critique of Stammler, on of the most influential legal scholars of the time and the object of a comparable critique by Weber in 1906 (see Weber, 1977; also Weber, 1978b:325–33) on the grounds that his dualistic separation between "is" and "ought," giving rise to an empirical science of law strictly divided from legal philosophy, obliterates the value-constituted nature of legal reality: "The mere antithesis of Is and Ought, of reality and value, is not enough . . . a place must be saved for the relation to values, that is, between nature and ideal, a place for culture. The idea of law is value, but the law is a reality related to value, a cultural phenomenon. This marks the transition from a dualism to a triadism of approaches" (Radbruch, 1950:69–70).

The in-between character of legal science on the value dimension is confirmed and is extended to the generalizing-individualizing dimension essential to casuistry by Radbruch's specification of its logic. I will pursue this in some detail for the sake of the light it casts on Weber's methodological position.

The idea of law (and again one must hear this as true of any normative source of cultural reality) is not a pure, static ideality. It contains elements in addition to its core value—justice—giving rise to antinomies which allow and compel the idea of law to work itself out into the practical accommodations "for the living-together of human beings" (Radbruch, 1950:76) that legal science grasps as the concept of law. There are two other ideal elements: expediency and legal certainty. With casuistic discourse in mind, the outstanding feature of the elements is that they involve opposite cognitive tendencies toward uniform truth and fidelity to circumstances, that is, the circumstances of particularly situated actors pursuing purposes. Whereas justice, with its absolute demand for equal treatment, and legal certainty, with its absolute demand for unequivocal classification, both take thought towards total generalization, "expediency is bound to individualize as far as possible" (Radbruch, 1950:109), simply because it is the principle of adaptation to purpose. Thus even the idea of law, its normative frame of reference, contains a relativist orientation to the particular, and this element becomes all the more pronounced in the social implementation of law. Here the scope of universally valid concepts is drastically limited. Pursuing Kant's critique of the pretensions of pure reason in relation to natural law theory, Radbruch observes: "Consequently, we may indeed grant that there is universal validity in the *question* concerning the 'natural,' that is, the right law; but to any of the answers to it we may concede validity only for a given state of society, for a definite time and a definite people. Only the category of right, just law, but none of its applications, is universally valid" (Radbruch, 1950:60). Subsequntly (p. 150), Radbruch says of legal science what Weber (1949:84) says of all cultural science, that it must be rewritten in every age to retain validity. This does not mean starting completely anew, as if there were no commensurability, but it means at least refusing anything like an inductively or deductively assembled "table of categories" with which to order data, or a "symmetrical schedule" of a priori concepts, because such concepts unfold only against the fullness of facts "and these unfoldings can no more be exhaustively enumerated in advance than can the facts with which the concept will be confronted" (Radbruch, 1950:78). Weber too refused all schemes for ruling inquiry in advance with systems of concepts; as will be argued subsequently, this was not the intended purpose of the typological distinctions assembled in part 1 of *Economy and Society,* even if they have this effect. I would note here just how deeply different an architechtonic theorist like Talcott Parsons is from Weber, in spite of any demonstrable continuity at the level of particular concepts. Location of Weber's writing in the casuistic tradition makes it clear that Parsons's systematic theorizing does not develop or carry forward Weber's work but compositionally negates it. They are exemplary opposites.

Radbruch's rationale for legal science includes the biases as well as the tensions necessary for casuistic discourse to form. He says it is "an interpretive cultural science. As such it is characterized by three features: it is an understanding, individualizing, and value-relating science" (Radbruch, 1950:149). The third feature has already been discussed, and I have no special comment on the first except that Radbruch, like Weber (see on this point Munch, 1975), distinguishes the empathic understanding of subjective meaning from the rational, or one might say grammatical understanding of objective meaning. The initial task of legal science is to interpret the objective meaning of legal rules, an idea illustrated by references to the objective meaning of a move in a game of chess or an utterance in a language. The point is that the wrestling between objective meaning and subjective interpretation, central to the casuistic tradition, was built into neo-Kantianism through its reception of hermeneutics. One need only recall, for example, Dilthey's reception of Schleiermacher's distinction between the grammatical interpretation and psychological interpretation of texts (see Dilthey, 1976:253–60). In chapter 7, I will argue that one function of Weber's ideal-type method is to draw out the objective meanings of religious ethics, cultural codes, and the like so as to prepare for a "grammatical" examination of social actions complementary to subjective understanding and capable of articulating culturological pressures on conduct.

Radbruch calls legal science, by virtue of its cultural nature, an individualizing science. This has two meanings, one pointing toward the casuistic concern for the particular, the other to its compositional orientation to the acting, deciding individual. On the first point, Radbruch says that although legal science moves to comprehend the entire legal order of a society, and in that sense moves towards systematization, its aim "is not to advance beyond the peculiarity of the particular (say German or French) legal system to rules common to all legal orders, but rather to understand these legal orders in their individuality" (Radbruch, 1950:150). This means that the interest of each legal case examined is not as an instance of a general process of type, but inheres in the course and resolution of the case itself. The interest of the legal (as cultural) scientist "unlike that of the natural scientist, is not in making a generalization but rather in a summarization of many individual statements by way of an economy of thought" (p. 150). In the same spirit, while legal science aims to reconstruct a "collective will" conferring an objective meaning beyond subjective, local variation on legal rules, it is understood to be only a heuristic construct within a hermeneutic circle, not an actual entity, and provisional, not finished:

> To the extent, however, that interpretation is practical, creative, productive, transscientific, it is determined in each case by the changing requirements of the law. Therefore, the legislative will, which it aims at and results in determining, is not fixed by interpretation as a definite content for all times but remains able to respond with new meaning to new legal requirements and questions under the conditions of changing times; it must be understood not as a single act of the will, which once called the law into being, but as the changeable permanent will that keeps the law in existence. (Radbruch, 1950:142)

The second meaning of being an individualizing science is that legal science is addressed to the exercise of individual reason and conscience; to taking decisions surrounded in doubt and ensuring that doubt is kept stretched to the full, never displaced into procedural resolution by a mechanism or relieved by formulaic certainty. The address to reason is evident in Radbruch's observation that legal science does not stop at collecting and ordering legal evaluations pertaining to justice and equity (the justice of the individual case), nor even with exploring the intended meanings of the individuals issuing them, which is but a starting point; the further aim is to establish the objective meaning of an evaluation, that which the individual according to that starting point "should have intended in causal and logical consistency" (Radbruch, 1950:56). In short, legal science entails an ideal-type construction of the rational meaning inherent in actual legal evaluations that can be set against meanings arising from other sources—emotion, custom, situational contingencies, and the like—to promote an interpretive cultivation of the sense of law. Subsequently Radbruch contrasts the requirements of such cultivation with dutiful obedience to the dictates of conscience:

> The sense of law, quite different from conscience, presupposes an active intellect. We are told of our duty in a particular case by our conscience without having first had to become conscious of the general maxim on which it is based. Of our right, on the contrary,

we become conscious only by recalling the general norm from which it flows. For the moral norm applies to men in isolation, the legal precept to men in relation to one another; and whereas the moral duty demands of one recognition regardless of whether it claims validity for others in the same situation, a right, by its very concept, I may attribute to myself only if I am ready to concede it to others in the same situation. Without such generalization, claims can be raised only through a feeling of arbitrariness and not through a feeling of right. So the sense of law requires a nimble mind that is able to shift from the specific to the general and back from the general to the specific. (Radbruch, 1950:135)

It is, of course, exactly such nimble mental shifting against the background of conscience that is the method and purpose of casuistic discourse in the Protestant tradition. In both cases, however, the intention is not to elude conscience by clever quibbling but to use rational consciousness to make its exercise more strenuous, more responsible to situation and circumstance. Radbruch emphasizes that a legal philosophy founded on legal science can bring different concepts of law into clear, explicit focus but cannot relieve the individual of choosing between them: "It is limited to presenting to him exhaustively the possibilities of decision, but it leaves his decision itself to the resolution he draws from the depths of his personality—by no means, then, to his pleasure, but rather to his conscience" (Radbruch, 1950:57).

The concept of law operant in a collectivity always reflects a certain combination of the three elements making up the idea of law—justice, expediency, and legal certainty—but no inherent hierarchy of priority can be established between them; consequently "in case of conflict there is no decision between them but by the individual conscience" (Radbruch, 1950:118).

Putting together these references to the "practical, creative, productive" role of interpretive legal science, its active enlistment of reason to exercise conscience, and the attribution of like functions to neighboring disciplines, the conclusion is justified that the concept of cultural science developed in the domain of neo-Kantian philosophy was shaped by a self-educative and self-testing purpose close to that of Protestant casuistry. When Radbruch describes in the man of law, the producer and enactor of legal science, a dualistic conflict between ethical commandment, brooking no compromise, and the accommodating voice of legal reason, he sketches a version of the ideal reader intended by a casuistic text in the Protestant tradition and in stylistic terms that could have come straight from its pages:

Let us for a moment hark to their dialogue: Says conscience: "Whosoever smite thee on thy right cheek, turn to him the other also; and if one man will sue thee at the law and take away thy coat, let him have thy cloak also." But the sense of law replies: "Do not let your right be trampled underfoot by others. He who makes himself a worm cannot afterwards complain of being trampled upon" (Kant). Resumes conscience: "But I say unto you that ye resist not evil." But the sense of law insists: "I'd rather be a dog, than a man if I am to be trodden upon" (Kleist). And again conscience: "Love your enemies, bless them that curse you." And against this the sense of law: "The fight for one's right is a command of moral self-preservation" (Jhering). "Blessed are the peacemakers," says conscience, but the sense of law rejoins: "He who feels the law on his side must act roughly; a polite law won't mean anything" (Goethe). This does not silence conscience; only we cannot continue to listen to their unending dialogue, loath as we are to leave the last word with one or the other party. (Radbruch, 1950:133–34)

Interestingly for our argument, when Radbruch traces the dialogue into artistic thematizations of the suppressed rights of life, and pagan vitality against the oppression of Christian conscience, he refers to Ibsen's explorations of the contradiction as a "dramatized ethical casuistry" (p. 134), offering us a reassuring sign that we are on the right track.

Returning to the question of educative purpose, Radbruch indirectly raises it, and in a way directly relevant to our concern for the literary methods of sociological theory. He argues that law, to meet the demand of legal certainty, which is an aspect of its founding idea, develops a language suitable for inscription in codes, constitutions, and law books—the paper equivalents of stone tablets—and in doing so renounces educative intent: "The language of the law is frigid, renouncing any emotional tone; it is blunt, renouncing any argumentation; it is concise, renouncing any intention to teach. Thus there comes into existence a lapidary style of self-imposed poverty" (Radbruch, 1950:138).

Clearly this is part of the sense of law, but such a language cannot achieve adaptation to circumstances or equity, the experienced justice of the individual case. This requires persuasion and passion, because "passion alone is able to fill the abstract thought of justice with the effective fire of individual life" (Radbruch, 1950:135). Legal science in its active aspect must combine "generalizing intellectualism," or logical persuasion, with "individualizing passion"; consequently "the adequate form of expression of legal controversy is rhetoric, the essence of which is to endow the general with the obviousness and effectiveness of the particular" (p. 138).

Now it would not be difficult to appropriate Radbruch's comments for a literary critique of sociological theorizing. Indeed this direction has been taken by many critics of quantitative sociology, one or two of whom are cited in my opening chapter, who from a standpoint of artistic and/or historical sensitivity to the particular, condemn its frigid, blunt, qualitatively impoverished, and unedifying style, linking this to the mistaken ideal of articulating universally valid and certain laws of conduct. Comparable also with Radbruch is the countervailing appeal of some such critics to a rhetorical form of sociology (see, for example, Burke, 1954, 1966; Weaver, 1970; Brown, 1977; Edmondson, 1984). My position, as I argued at the outset, is that the development of forms of sociological theorizing must (*a*) proceed from analysis of the constitutive tasks of sociology within the human sciences as a whole; (*b*) build from exemplary possibilities preserved in its tradition; and (*c*) treat forms as working procedures and compositional activities, not as counters for use in ideological language games like battling schools, defining paradigms, and synthesizing the field. Ruled out by these requirements are merely imitative importations from other areas, which is all a general recommendation to adopt a rhetorical method might come to; turning abruptly away from the scientific aspirations of the discipline, as if something essential to a tradition could be simply rejected; and defining alternative forms by way of obverse switching: qualitative for quantitative, humanist for scientific, and so on.

I would not then want to use Radbruch to fashion a stick, "rhetorical method," with which to beat "scientific sociology," a straw man which must by now be a dead horse. However, his demand that legal science be educatively rich in argumentation, coupled with further observations on the constitutive ground of the cultural sciences and some ideas from Eduard Spranger, opens a promising line of speculation on what a casuistic understanding of the purpose of sociology might amount to.

Radbruch says repeatedly that the reality of law, like that of all cultural phenomena, is of a "peculiar kind," because it comes into being at the conjunction of the existent and the ideal, the empirical and the transcendent, "positivity and normativity" (Radbruch, 1950:76). The law is composed of empirically observable evaluations and demands negotiation between particular actors, yet their recognizably legal quality derives from the immanent yet transcendent ideal of justice. Also of this kind are "conscience, the cultural phenomenon related to the moral idea; taste, that related to the aesthetic idea; and reason, that related to the logical idea" (p. 76). The justifying purpose, or good, of legal science is to cultivate a sense of law optimally responsive to its ideality and positivity. Comparably, we could say that the good of traditional casuistry is to cultivate a sense of moral duty, that of aesthetics to cultivate a sense of the beautiful, and so on for the senses arising in this peculiar kind of reality. The human sciences could then be located in this general task of cultivation and their good defined by the particular value senses they grow from and tend.

This way of defining the constitutive field of the human sciences is exactly that proposed by Gadamer (1975:10–19). In a wonderfully economical account of the career of the concept of culture (*Bildung*) in German philosophy, he states explicitly that this is the element in which the human sciences move and from which, without admitting it, they draw their life. Most relevant of all for us are the connotations of the concept which require the cultural sciences to be understood as actively self-cultivating sciences. These begin to appear in Kant's idea of duties to oneself that include developing one's talents and capacities, but it is Hegel who decisively develops the concept. He speaks of "*Sichbilden* ('educating or cultivating oneself')" (p. 11) as a Kantian duty, but transcends any merely personal notion of developing aptitudes; he assigns to cultivation an anthropological significance in the formation of human identity. It is part of a self-generating, -finding, -incorporative process to which work also belongs.

Human nature includes a capacity for rational reflection on meaning that alienates it from what is merely given and immediate; humankind needs to be able to see significance in the particular and promote it to the universal. Human consciousness and action thus move to turn mere immediacy, including inner immediacy of unconsidered desire and egoistic want, as well as external exigencies of time, space, and materiality, into significant objects and forms. Hegel says that the working consciousness (practical Bildung), in forming meaningful objects and experiences for others, also forms itself. He points as a strong example (and reminding us of Protestant and Weberian calls to live one's life as a vocation), to professional work:

> Practical Bildung is seen in one's filling one's profession wholly, in all its aspects. But this includes overcoming the element in it that is alien to the particularity that is oneself, and making it wholly one's own. Thus to give oneself to the universality of a profession is at

the same time "to know how to limit oneself, i.e. to make one's profession wholly one's concern. Then it is no longer a limitation." (Gadamer, 1975:14)

Self-cultivation in the normal sense of becoming a cultured person, to the extent that it is contemplative, (as in cultivating knowledge, taste, tact, a sense of beauty, a sense of history, and so on), belongs to "theoretical Bildung." However, it is still defined by the formulas of promotion to the universal (the complete, the ideal), and return to oneself; hence it is continuous with "practical Bildung." Together they entail the cultivation of a prospectively complete, completely human identity in each particular person. This then might be taken as the constitutive field or anthropological ground of the cultural sciences.

Since the Hegelian formulation, even with Gadamer's expositional help, might seem metaphysically distant from workaday science, it is helpful to recall that something of this tradition found its way into child psychology and education theory: most strongly in what came to be called the Würzburg group, beginning around 1910, and especially in the work of Karl and Charlotte Bühler on mental development and maturation. (Here I am following the account of the group given in Lazarsfeld, 1972:56–82.) Lazarsfeld points out that the German word *geistig,* rendered as "mental" in the 1930 translation of Karl Bühler's *The Mental Development of the Child* (first published in 1921), connotes everything characteristic of the mature human being: "The mature human being is characterized by creative activity on physical and social objects" (Lazarsfeld, 1972:61).

Charlotte Bühler's subsequent work on maturation in children and adolescents explicitly includes culture in the object areas of creative activity. Her theory also stresses the themes of transcendence and vocational dedication found in Hegel:

> The adolescent has the first glimpses of the notion of devoting his life to an objective transcending his own individual existence. What was the further development of this goal striving? Charlotte Bühler introduces the concept of "self-determination" meaning the striving toward a selected goal, implying the individual's intent to dedicate himself and his feeling that he is meant to accomplish certain specific things, a feeling which in the case of some people assumes even the conviction of being destined to a certain role or development. (Lazarsfeld, 1972:62)

Within this framework it is possible to see a clear consonance between the cultural sciences, collectively concerned with the cultivation and maturation of human identity, and the aim of classical casuistry to cultivate conscience, the moral side of human identity. Moreover, the multiple sensibilities involved, senses of law, beauty, history, and so on, can be associated with various sides of human identity, and can allow the cultural sciences to be distinguished according to which sides they cultivate. Radbruch implies as much in his adoption of Eduard Spranger's theory of human nature to define the man of law, the cultivational object of legal science.

Spranger, following the action analysis tradition in German human science (see Lazarsfeld, 1972:82–101), identifies human "forms of life" which gather over historical time around basic values and exist in individuals as "structures of the mind." He labels the forms of life in terms close to sides of human identity: theoretical man, economic man, aesthetic man, social man, political man, and religious man. The man of law, responsive to the compound demands of justice, social expediency, and legal certainty, combines social, political, and theoretical elements of identity, and it is their emergent organization into a coherent configuration that legal science works to achieve. The adequacy of Spranger's particular analysis of the components of human identity is not important here; the point is that the identification of primary anthropological values and corresponding forms of life and aspects of identity provides a rationale for the division of the cultural sciences and for the specific cultivational task of sociology within it. I will not speculate on what might be the value service to which defines social reality (applying Radbruch's formula that law is the reality the meaning of which is to serve justice), or the specific educative aim of sociological casuistry. I will instead, in chapter 7, analyze the shape it took in Weber's sociology and treat this as exemplary.

In summary, it has been shown that there existed in the methodological field where Weber's work took shape a structural configuration of tensions and biases (in the sense of weighted directions) that corresponds in all important respects to the casuistic tradition of discourse identified in Protestant case divinity. By a structural configuration, I mean to imply that the elements tend to be found together and that when they are they give rise to typical compositional features at the level of writing style and reading experiences: features summarized previously in the model of casuistic discourse derived from the work of Starr and Slights. These claims must now be demonstrated in Max Weber's sociological writings.

7   The Casuistic Character
of Weber's Sociology

Weber's methodological essays (Weber, 1949, 1975, 1977) leave no doubt that his concept of sociological inquiry is completely and comprehensively informed by the same tensions I have identified as the generative matrix of casuistic discourse. They are couched in terms and structured by debates reflecting the same neo-Kantian divisions between individualizing and generalizing, and value-blind versus value-related forms of inquiry we have witnessed in Radbruch. Weber's reception of neo-Kantianism and his participation in the so-called *Methodenstreit* of the day are already well documented (Burger, 1976; Hekman, 1983; Huff, 1984) and need no detailed demonstration here. I will, however, briefly describe the presence of the tensions in his program for the sake of being clear about the functions of the ideal-type method in relation to them: not in simply mediating opposite positions, and certainly not in relaxing the tensions, but in retaining them with just the tolerance and directional bias required for casuistry to form. For my purpose, it is important to be clear about these functions at the programmatic level, because the argument to be made is that they are performed at page level by casuistic writing methods: more specifically, by methods corresponding to the denominative, indicative, and ethical facets of casuistry.

The Programmatic Base of Weberian Casuistry

In Weber's program, apart from the main tensions between (1) the cognitive aim of universally valid abstraction from particularity and idiographic grasp of it, and (2) value-free and value-grounded inquiry, there is a third tension between causal explanation from without and interpretive understanding from within that gathers in elements of both of the others. With respect to containing these tensions and keeping inquiry pointed toward the individualizing, value-grounded, interpretive poles of inquiry, the functions of the ideal-type method are, respectively: (1) comparative recognition of pattern in particularity; (2) critically purging, while retaining, value-laden concepts from social life; and (3) promoting interpretive explanation (Weber uses the term meaningful causality). This is the form of explanation specifically suited to casuistic sociology.

To consolidate this account of the programmatic base of Weber's casuistic text work, I will introduce evidence from the methodological writings bearing upon the tensions in and the functions of the ideal-type method in building them into a course of inquiry.

Pattern Recognition and Interpretive Explanation

A tensely balanced discussion of the claims of truth to concrete reality against abstraction appears in the 1904 essay "'Objectivity' in Social Sciences and Social Policy" (Weber, 1949). The discussion begins with a clear statement of direction: "The type of social science in which we are interested is an *empirical science* of *concrete reality*. Our aim is the *understanding* of the *characteristic uniqueness* of the reality in which we move" (Weber, 1949:72; italics added). In the first sentence, I have emphasized the terms "empirical science" and "concrete reality" both to bring out the strain imposed on normal understandings of them (normally read within the empiricist natural science tradition) by the supplementary gloss in the second sentence, and the further strain imposed by a subsequent assertion that concrete reality, whether physical or cultural, cannot be deduced from general laws relating factors abstracted from reality. Whatever the social science announced here might be, it is not a nomothetic pursuit of universally valid laws; correspondingly, it turns its back on the positivist ideal, associated especially with Comte, of rationally ruling social reality through scientific prediction and control.

To explicate the idea of concrete reality and its irreducibility to the status of essentially nothing but an instancing of abstract categories and an unfolding of abstract laws, Weber finds it instructive to include the cultural sciences among pursuits of "astronomical" knowledge. The description neatly confounds the simple division made in neo-Kantianism between physical and psychical sciences: the natural sciences studying external, spatiotemporal reality, the cultural sciences inner, subjective reality. The result also of course is to deny that the "understanding" aimed for by social science consists only of empathetic insight, intuitive grasp, and other kinds of intersubjective affinity. Astronomical knowledge involves rational or objective understanding also. It is addressed to particular "configurations" of phenomena, the components of which even if law governed in analytic isolation, come together in patterns not deducible from those laws. An essay on Karl Knies, published in 1905 (in Weber, 1975) cites "the physiological hunches of a stock breeder," the "economic estimates of labor negotiator" and "weather forecasting" (p. 121) as examples of configurational understanding. More generally, any scientific address to an individual configuration—biological, geographical, meteorological, or whatever—would only draw on nomothetic principles to provide limiting possibilities and probabilities within a total interpretive apparatus being applied to concrete, hence recalcitrant, reality, not to achieve certain calculation from necessary truths. Recalling the provisional, probabilistic cast of casuistic discourse, it can be said that sociocultural science is limited to making probabilistic judgments, but this is dictated by its aim of understanding individual configurations, not by the special psychical nature of its subject matter.

In another essay of the same period, "Critical Studies in the Logic of the Cultural Sciences" (Weber, 1949), there is an examination of the probabilistic assessment procedure of historical science. Beginning with a concrete reality such as the unification of Germany under Prussia, there would be a causal assessment of how and why it took shape and whether or not the alteration of particular events, say Bismark's declaration of war against Austria in 1866, might have made it turn out otherwise. The logic of inquiry would not be basically different from other pursuits of astronomical knowledge (including, I would add, casuistic inquiry into causally and morally adequate lines of conduct). It should be stressed, however, for the sake of understanding the role of ideal types in configurational explanation, that causality has a different meaning in knowledge of the concrete than in nomological knowledge. Again the 1905 essay an Knies provides useful elaboration:

> The form in which the category of causality is employed by the various disciplines is quite different. . . . Its complete, one might say "fully developed" sense includes two sorts of components. On the one hand, the idea of an "*effect,*" the idea of a dynamic bond— as it might be put—between phenomena qualitatively different from one another. On the other hand, the idea of subordination to "*rules.*" The "effect," the substantive content of the category of causality, invariably loses its meaning and disappears wherever, in the interest of quantified abstraction, the mathematical equation is established as the expression of purely spatial causal relations. . . . The only meaning the category of causality can retain under these conditions is that of a generalization about the temporal sequence of movements. And even such a generalization can have meaning only as an expression of the metamorphosis of an *equivalence* which is essentially timeless. On the other hand, the idea of a "*generalisation*" disappears from the category of causality as soon as we consider the absolute qualitative uniqueness of the temporal cos-

mic process and the qualitative *uniqueness* of every spatio-temporal aspect of that process. . . .

Those empirical disciplines which employ the category of causality and investigate the *qualities* of reality—history and every "science of culture" of any sort belong to this group of disciplines—invariably employ the category in its full meaning. (Weber, 1975:195, 196)

The crucial evidence for my thesis here is the closing statement that every science of culture employs the category of causality in its full sense, that is to say, it incorporates both the components described even though they are in pure form antithetical. This is why elsewhere Weber insistently uses a dualistic formula to characterize the aim of sociocultural science: it seeks adequacy on the level of meaning, where the "dynamic bonds" within and between qualitative configurations are grasped (for example, the Protestant ethic and capitalism); and causal adequacy, where probable correlation and repetition is displayed (see Weber, 1978b:12, for a typical formulation). However, the achievement of explanatory adequacy is less easily achieved in individualizing sciences than the formula might suggest. If the object of explanation is addressed as a singular configuration rather than a repeatable phenomenon, then the task of establishing causes changes significantly. For example, in both cases causal reasoning takes the form of asking, What if X were changed or missing? But whereas the nomological scientist can extract or change X, either physically or through statistical equivalents, the individualizing scientist can only engage in thought experiments, aided by probabilistic references to comparable patterns in analogous situations. A major purpose of ideal-type constructions— whether of purely rational conduct given ends and means, or of culturological fictions like the Hindu mystic and sociological fictions like the medieval city—is to discipline and sharpen these thought processes. Also involved, however—returning to the level of meaning—is the overriding aim of cultural science to render intelligible the value-conferred significance of the configuration being explained: "knowledge of the *cultural significance of concrete historical events and patterns* is exclusively and solely the final end which, among other means, concept-construction and the criticism of constructs also seek to serve" (Weber, 1949:111).

The design and employment of concepts for cultural science is, Weber argues, a special task precisely because of the value-constituted nature of its phenomena and the cognitive interest in understanding their relevance for the historical and collective dimensions of our identity. The interest cannot, he argues, be satisfied by the nomological employment of concepts as abstractive collection devices; it calls for concepts capable of bringing a salient configuration—say the capitalistic mode of production—into a clear structural focus which will draw out its qualitative particularity and historical significance. Included here is a grasp of origins and possible lines of future development. Weber formulates the difference of individualizing from nomological concept design as one between genetic and generic concepts. As always, he does so in such a way as to retain rather than resolve the tension between them: making resistant engagement with generic concepts and wary use of genetic ones another work site of sociocultural science, and from our perspective, another compulsion towards casuistic discourse.

If genetic and generic concepts are seen as options, there seems little doubt that for Weber the former are the kind more appropriate for cultural science; yet, as will be shown, the preference is hedged around with such studied equivocation that the cultural scientist can no more in this than other aspects of his craft settle comfortably into a clear choice. Consider, for example, Weber's strictures against "naturalist prejudices" in cultural science. He inveighs particularly against "the naturalistic prejudice that the goal of the social sciences must be the reduction of reality to 'laws'" (Weber, 1949:101). In this kind of science, the goal of grasping the individuality of phenomena in their historical significance cannot be achieved by "the subsumption of the event under some general rubric as a representative case" (Weber, 1949:78). Here the aim of concept construction is to make explicit "not the class or average character but rather the unique individual character of cultural phenomena" (p. 101). By the same token, concept design and employment depends on the cultural setting and historical horizon of problems for study; consequently the concepts of cultural science can have only relative, circumstantial, and transient validity: "the relationship between concept and reality in the cultural sciences involves the transitoriness of all such syntheses. . . . Nothing can be more suspect than the construction and application of clear-cut concepts" (pp. 105, 106).

There is no question here of an eventual turning of genetic into generic concepts as cultural science progresses; the very aspiration "to order its data into a system of concepts, the content of which is to be acquired and slowly perfected through the observation of empirical regularities" (Weber, 1949:106) is a distortive, undermining ideal to be resisted. It is as inappropriate to cultural science as, for Protestant casuists, invariant, general, completed rules of morality are for the cultivation of conscience. Small wonder that Weber was dismayed when *The Protestant Ethic and the Spirit of Capitalism* was read, even with praise, as the nomological presentation of a causal link between two generic concepts: "these two cultural components were at the time not related to one another in terms of a 'lawful' dependency, such that where X (ascetic Protestantism) is, there must by Y (capitalist spirit) without exception—in view of the causal intricacies of historically complex phenomena, this must be accepted *a priori*" (Bendix and Roth, 1971:310). The essay was for him an interpretive explication of the capitalist ethos, a "concrete" individual phenomenon, achieved by locating it in a historical constellation: the value elements and worldly derivatives of ascetic Protestantism. It is a "grammatical" and historical interpretation of dynamic bonds forming a singular pattern. For such a task, which is that of interpretive sociology as a whole, genetic rather than generic concepts are required. Whereas the scientific function of a generic concept is to identify an abstract (and abstractive) property allowing diverse objects or events to be combined in some kind of average type, that of a genetic concept is to decompose historical wholes into constituent elements, to reconstruct intellectually the internal structure of the whole, and to prepare for historical explanation of its occurrence. Using Weber's example (Weber, 1949:90), the term "sect," instead of being employed generically to classify organizations according to a common denominator, might be employed genetically to collate elements considered essential to "the sectarian spirit," forming an interpretive apparatus through which both to recognize what is sectarian in designated organizations, including diverse patterns of approximation, and to guide historical accounts of emergence and change. With this in mind, Weber's magnum opus, *Economy and Society,* must be approached as a summary presentation and application of the genetic concepts considered adequate by Weber to analyze the problems set by his culture and time: a vast interpretive apparatus with no claim to universal validity. To the extent that it might have a permanent value, it would be in its way of theorizing, not as a nomologically conceived content verified by subsequent research. Indeed, it is a further mark of Weberian resistance to a generalizing kind of science that ideal-type concepts are not liable to empirical validation: they do not have that kind of relation to reality:

> It follows that every interpretive scheme is not *only*—as has been claimed—a "hypothesis" analogous to the hypothetical "laws" of the natural sciences. They can *function* as hypotheses when the

interpretation of concrete processes is employed for heuristic purposes. However, in contrast to hypotheses in the natural sciences,
to establish in a concrete case that an interpretation is *not* valid is
irrelevant to the question of the theoretical value of the interpretive
scheme. (Weber, 1975:186)

The cognitive value of an ideal-type construct lies as much in diver-
gences from it as correspondences to it; the decisive consideration is
clarification of pattern in concrete reality through applying to it a perfectly consistent blueprint of conduct drawn up purely from cultural
codes and their inferred psychological correlates (not observed empirical correlations which belong to the concrete reality to be assessed).
Consequently: "Theoretical differentiation (*Kasuistik*) is possible in
sociology only in terms of ideal or pure types. . . . The more sharply
and precisely the ideal type has been constructed, thus the more abstract
and unrealistic in this sense it is, the better it is able to perform its
functions in formulating terminology, classifications and hypotheses"
(Weber, 1978b:20, 21).

The direction of Weber's program away from generic concept use is
clear, but he will not let us rest with the conclusion that generic concepts are to be avoided and genetic concepts wholeheartedly embraced
in cultural science. One consideration is that the naturalist prejudices
endemic to cultural science explanation include the mistaking of genetic
concepts for real forces. Weber warns:

> Nothing, however, is more dangerous than the confusion of theory
> and history stemming from naturalist prejudices. This confusion
> expresses itself firstly in the belief that the "true" content and the
> essence of historical reality is portrayed in such theoretical con-
> structs or secondly, in the use of these constructs as a procrustean
> bed into which history is to be forced or thirdly, in the hypostatiza-
> tion of such "ideas" as real "forces" and as a "true" reality which
> operates behind the passage of events and which works itself out in
> history. (Weber, 1949:94)

I take the second item to refer to a tyranny of generic concepts, as
discussed above, and the first and third to the illicit employment of
genetic concepts. This part of the warning is repeated with more specific focus in the essay on Roscher (Weber, 1975), as an attack on the
"Hegelian emanatism" found in Roscher and other members of the
"historical school" of economics. The direction of the attack is in itself
evidence of Weber's in-between location, since the Methodenstreit of

the time, the historical school was opposed to abstractive nomological economics (the "classical school"), and would, on this ground alone, have been expected to enlist Weber's sympathy. However, he takes Roscher to task for his Hegelian and romanticist imagining of vital forces—*Volk* psychologies—incarnating themselves in collective behaviors, social institutions, and national political economies: "the metaphysical Volk-soul manifested in all these phenomena is conceived as a constant which always remains identical with itself" (Weber, 1975:75). Interestingly, since these developmental processes occur in fixed stages, like organic phenomena, the historicist school is led back towards the same error found in its extreme nomological opponents: treating conceptual reconstructions as if they were actual forces with causal efficacy and making them—the universal patterns they describe—the reality of which particulars are only component manifestations. In the "Objectivity" essay, Weber comments on the unique value of Marx's concepts when used as heuristic ideal-type devices for assessing analytic pattern in concrete reality, and similarly on "their perniciousness, as soon as they are thought of as empirically valid or as real (i.e. truly metaphysical) 'effective forces,' 'tendencies,' etc." (Weber, 1949:103). When constructs are integrated into a genetic classification unfolding with the necessity of a universal law, the result is as damaging to knowledge as the aspiration to integrate hypotheses "until a final 'completed' and hence deductive science emerges" (Weber, 1949:106).

Weber's loosely advertised nominalism amounts to no more than a resistance to the concretization of constructs so as to stick to the task of understanding concrete reality; it is apparent, however, from his endorsement of genetic concepts (that way of designing and employing concepts) that the conventional nominalist-realist division is incapable of grasping Weber's position, although its inability to do so is illuminating.

This brings us to a second consideration regarding Weber's studied equivocation between genetic and generic concept use. Generic concepts are accepted in his program (part 1 of *Economy and Society* is a compendium of classificatory definitions), provided that they are subordinated to the task of constructing genetic ideal types for use in particular inquiries, which means, in turn, total theoretic subordination to significant cultural problems, individual cases, and circumstantial particularity. While it may be true that "in the cultural sciences, knowledge of the general or the universal is never valuable in itself" (Weber,

1949:80), this is not to say that it is of no instrumental value. Weber expresses the point in a passage whose stochastically branching style as well as methodological message are in the casuistic tradition:

> Class or generic concepts—ideal typical generic concepts—ideas in the sense of thought—patterns which actually exist in the minds of human beings—ideal types of such ideas—ideals which govern human beings—ideal types of such ideals . . . *theoretical* constructs using empirical data illustratively—*historical* investigations which utilize theoretical concepts as ideal limiting cases . . . they are pure mental constructs, the relationships of which to the empirical reality of the immediately given is problematical in every individual case. (Weber, 1949:103)

One cannot imagine Weber, in the work style of Durkheim, finding it beneficial to formulate tutelary rules of method. In fact, he denigrated methodological writings of this kind as a pestilence within the discipline which his own interventions were meant to contain, and denied that "methodological/epistemological reflection is a necessary condition for fruitful scientific research" (cited by Oakes in Weber, 1977:11). At best, methodological discussions might discredit false ways of inquiry and recall for practitioners that case engagement with materials to grasp their particularity and significance is the only way to cultivate what they need: good judgment and a trained eye.

Ethical Intent and Intension in Weberian Sociology

It has been shown that Weber's program, true to the casuistic spirit of being most at home "where many contradictions whir" (Goethe), stretches sociology equivocally along one dimension of casuistic discourse and in the direction necessary for casuistry to form. Now the same will be shown for the second generative dimension; the pull between value-free assessment and ethical self-cultivation. I will describe what might be called the critical or purgative function of ideal-type construction and use the occasion to begin introducing samples of Weber's compositional movements through the denominative, indicative, and ethical dimensions of casuistic discourse. Justification for making the ethical dimension the primary opening to textual analysis receives justification from my model of casuistic discourse. According to the model, fully responsible ethical decision is the starting point and destination of all, including sociological, casuistry—its source, direction and axis of movement—while denominative refinement and indicative deliberation are implementive dimensions.

The Separation of "Ought" from "Is"·

       Textbooks commonly associate Weber with the ideal of a value-free social science divorced from normative inquiry, and there is some truth to this. The essay on "'Objectivity' in Social Science" (Weber, 1949), even though its crucial first word is shrouded in doubt marks, opens with a criticism of the sociocultural sciences for having failed to incorporate themselves around "the *logical* distinction between 'existential knowledge,' i.e. knowledge of what 'is' and 'normative knowledge,' i.e. knowledge of what 'should be'" (Weber, 1949:51; italics added): for example, historicist "laws" of history and sociological "laws" of evolution which trade on equations between the natural, the immutable, and the normatively binding to collapse the two kinds of knowledge. The message is amplified in another essay in the 1949 volume: "The Meaning of 'Ethical Neutrality' in Sociology and Economics," and in his deeply felt attacks on the conflation of scientific with normative authority by professorial preachers and ideologues in academic clothing (Weber, 1946:133–56; Weber, 1978a:69–98). What the message amounts to is that questions of what best to do cannot be answered by logical deductions from existential knowledge. Seemingly, the logical separation of "ought" from "is" would entail the exclusion of the former from social science, cut the Gordian knot of their unfortunate entanglement, and dissolve the tension between them. This indeed has been the meaning conferred and taken by modern scientific sociology. It is not, however, the only interpretation possible. The logical separation of factual judgments from practical evaluations does not require their discursive segregation, any more than the recognition by Protestant casuists of an inherent gap between general moral rules and individual conduct in concrete circumstances required exclusion of the former from their case examinations. In fact, it is the ineluctable presence of the gap in their writtings that transforms them from abstract pronouncements and extrinsic formulas to human documents with self-educative value. Upon closer inspection, this also is the role of the logical is-ought separation in Weber's work: it is to found a certain kind of deliberation, not warrant a division of intellectual labor.

      Consider, for example, the fact that Weber always speaks of building social science around or upon the logical divide, never on its existential side alone. Nor, given his acceptance of the principle, shared with Radbruch and Rickert, that the subject matter of social science is value constituted, could he possibly have advocated a clean split:

Empirical reality only becomes "culture" to us because and insofar as we relate it to value ideas. (Weber, 1949:76)

The problems posed in the empirical disciplines are, of course, to be answered in a "value-free" way. They are not "evaluative problems." But in the field of our disciplines they are influenced by the relationship of reality "to" values. For the meaning of the expression "value relevance" I must refer to my own earlier discussions and above all the well-known works of Heinrich Rickert. (Weber, 1978a:87)

From the principle of a value-constituted subject matter it follows that the sociocultural scientist needs to be value sensitive: "anyone who wants to achieve anything in art history, in however purely empirical a vein, must also have the capacity to 'understand' artistic activity, and this is of course inconceivable if he does not also have the capacity for aesthetic judgment, or in other words the *ability* to evaluate" (Weber, 1978a:98). The exercise of normative knowledge is then indispensible to cultural science. The construction and application of ideal types in sociology must involve value empathy, which is a self-involving experience, not just a technical procedure. Sociocultural science cannot help but be a value-relevant activity for those who engage in it, whether as researchers or readers. Weber's nearest reader, his wife Marianne, understood this perfectly:

Besides, empirical research does not of itself supply any uniform principle in accordance with which culturally significant components of reality could be given a definite, scientifically compelling arrangement. Rather it always leads only to a multiplicity of ultimate ideas of value and forces of life— "gods"—which vie with one another for the domination of existence. . . . One day, when Weber was asked what his scholarship meant to him, he replied: "I want to see how much I can stand." What did he mean by that? Perhaps that he regarded it as his task to endure the antinomies of existence and, further, to exert to the utmost his freedom from illusions and yet to keep his ideals inviolate and preserve his ability to devote himself to them. (Marianne Weber, [1926] 1975:678)

All in all, a most apt description of what a casuistic sociology would seek to cultivate.

The Critical Function of Ideal-Type Construction

In the preceding quotation, Marianne Weber refers to Weber's struggle to devote himself to his ideals and suggests that his scholarly work was somehow intrinsic to it, not something separate.

Since all casuistry aims at self-education and is in that sense didactic, my interpretation is supported by recalling Weber's strongly didactic style of devotion to ideals. It is hardly going too far to say that he pursued, through his work, something like a collective pedagogy: a tuition of the collective consciousness of his generation, his nation, and of all fellow children of Western civilization. Certainly this is how he was seen by others. Gunther Roth (Bendix and Roth, 1971:6–33) reports that by age twenty-nine Weber had become a "generational spokesman." In 1893 he spoke to the Welfare Policies Association of the cultural tasks facing the post-Bismarkian generation of nation builders, and repeated some of these sentiments in his inaugural address at Freiburg two years later. The demands of "our responsibility before history," he said, could only be met through calm, ruthlessly illusion-free thought, and he called for social scientists to engage in a "tremendous effort in political education" (cited in Bendix and Roth, 1971:17). Weber himself set an example, speaking and writing for the Social Policy Association, the Evangelic-Social Congress, the Pan-German Association and workers' education classes, and, in 1896, co-founding the National-Social Association. Roth also cites a letter written in 1906 to the church historian Adolf von Harnack that is doubly fascinating in the light of our interpretive linkage of Weberian text work to Protestant casuistry: "That our nation never went through the school of hard asceticism, in no form whatever, is the source of all I hate about it and myself" (cited in Bendix and Roth, 1971:18).

The pedagogic task of social science then is belatedly to fashion through scholarly means an intellectual equivalent to the school of hard asceticism. I would endorse Mommsen's opinion that "his scholarly work was, to a substantial degree, intended to make it possible for personalities to live in the modern world without giving themselves up to irrational faiths, myths or prophecies" (Mommsen, 1974:111), and agree also that Weber's didactic impulse extends beyond his generation to include, in the most familiar of Weberian themes, all those who must make a home among the organizational structures created by Western formal rationality.

Within this tremendous labor of education, which is also one of the cultivation of critical self-reflection in the collective consciousness of individuals, ideal-type construction plays a small but significant role, and one which looms large for sociological theory. Again, Marianne Weber sensitively registers what has been a relatively underplayed aspect of Weber's method and helps us make sense of some otherwise puzzling facts: that he began working on the terminological schema (the denominative casuistry) comprising part 1 of *Economy and Society,* after completing the substantive monographs on law, religion, and domination making up the main second part, as if someone would erect a scaffolding around a finished building; that he spent much of the precious final two years of his life rewriting and remolding the schema, even though he knew "people are going to shake their heads" and it "would at first not only be hard to understand but would also strike people as strange" (Marianne Weber, [1926] 1975:676), an anticipation borne out by the usually devoted students abandoning his classes in droves. What makes sense of this tedious and seemingly gratuitous labor is Marianne Weber's suggestion that the schema was more than an instrumental preparation for the analysis of materials; it was a critical reflection on key categories of social thought, political discourse, and policy making: a purgative appropriation of central concepts in the collective consciousness—meaning the public language—of his society. An enterprise in its own way comparable to Marx's critical appropriation of the categories of political economy—the scientific expression of the collective consciousness of capitalist society—in *Capital,* but a casuistic compared to a dialectical performance of critique:

> Simple, self-evident, and even banal as this may seem, the appropriate reconstitution of generally known concepts was in the nature of a *logical revolution.* In particular, Weber's definitions relating to political and legal sociology seemed so odd to jurisprudence and his definitions in the area of the sociology of religion struck the theologians as so strange that at first they presumably did not have much use for them. The deliberate elimination of all their customary overtones of value gives to concepts . . . an entirely new and purely logical meaning, a meaning that is, of course, strangely cold and devoid of pathos. And even though Weber rejects any claim to their exclusive validity, they nevertheless are uncomfortable for the accustomed thinking and feeling, for their very existence brings the extrascientific components of the other, equivalent intellectual systems into focus, thereby showing which of their aspects were not logically compelling and could not be forced on anyone. Besides, it is possible that with many people the inevitable by-product of this logical disenchantment of historical structures will be another evaluation. (Marianne Weber, 1975:679–80).

Obviously the procedure intends to carry out the programmatic aim of purging normative elements from social concepts to leave them indicatively pure; but the last sentence suggests that logical defamiliarization, discomfort, and disenchantment of social concepts can have its own value significance (she specifies it as realism), reinforcing the claim that this is social critique, not merely a preparation for inquiry. Furthermore, the extrascientific elements of concepts are not simply purged away like waste matter, but brought into focus. That is to say, they are retained at a tense distance from the reconstituted concepts; not always, even typically, in the surface content of the writing, but between the words and at the margins for readers accustomed to them in other contexts.

If we recall from the famous typology of social action that both purely customary and purely affectual actions lie "very close to the borderline of what can justifiably be called meaningfully oriented action" (Weber, 1978b:25), which is, for Weber, the definition of social action, then the ethical intent of his social science can be understood as resistance to the unreflective determination of social decisions by value habits and emotions built into public language: resistance, that is, to the determination of conduct by ideological and rhetorical language use, for the sake of making conduct optimally responsible and fully social. If, also, we accept Richard Rorty's definition of edifying thinkers as those whose aim is "to help their readers, or society as a whole, break free from outworn vocabularies and attitudes" (Rorty, 1980:12), then Weber's denominative-indicative casuistry may be said to have an edifying intent.

Did Weber authorially intend all this? The methodological essays contain evidence that he did. For example, the "Objectivity" essay, written to state the aims of a journal cofounded by Weber, says openly "the express purpose of the *Archiv* ever since its establishment has been the education of judgment about practical problems—and in the very modest way in which such a goal can be furthered by private scholars— the criticism of practical social policy" (Weber, 1949:50). The education of judgment means exercising it by strenuous movement between "existential" and "normative" knowledge, which is precisely the movement of casuistic discourse. Weber warns that "an attitude of moral indifference has no connection with scientific 'objectivity'" (p. 60).

Towards the end of the same essay, explicit reference is made to the role of language critique in educating judgment about practical problems: "The greatest advances in the sphere of the social sciences are substantively tied up with the shift in practical cultural problems and take the guise of a critique of concept construction" (Weber, 1949:106).

Weber goes on to link valid judgment with conceptual analysis, which "always endangers the security of the reader's orientation, and often that of the author himself concerning the content and scope of his judgments" (Weber, 1949:107). He describes the neglect of conceptual critique as a sociopolitical danger, adding, "collective concepts taken from everyday life have particularly unwholesome effects" (p. 108).

There is more to be found, however, than supportive snippets. In the essay, "The Meaning of 'Ethical Neutrality,'" Weber describes what is in effect a protocol of value analysis; it combines denominative analysis (critical concept construction) and indicative investigation to serve the casuistic aim of optimally responsible individual decisions about practical problems.

Weber's Casuistic Protocol of Value Analysis

Weber asks in the "Objectivity" essay, What is the purpose of a scientific critique of ideals and value judgments? The answer is entirely in accordance with the casuistic tradition: to lead the individual through all relevant considerations to the threshold of a decision, then withdraw. It is educatively vital that inquiry should not try to go beyond that point: "To apply the results of this analysis in the making of a decision, however, is not a task which science can undertake; it is rather the task of the acting, willing person: he weighs and chooses from among the values involved according to his own conscience and his personal view of the world. . . . The act of choice itself is his own responsibility" (Weber, 1949:53).

An incident in Weber's biography suggests that he lived as well as worked in a casuistic attitude. Marianne Weber quotes a letter concerning a young theologian, Herr Voigt, who had been brought into the family circle by the mother to counsel her problem son, Karl. She describes Weber's precocious ability to empathize with standpoints far removed from his own and says of the letter, it "reflects, above all, his respectful solicitude for a developing, struggling human being. His feeling of responsibility toward a younger man prohibited him from impugning a faith for which he was unable to substitute anything better. He avoided forcing his own value judgments upon him and was equally careful not to put the other man in a position where he would have to commit himself prematurely. His later scholarly attitude seemed prefigured in the fact that he wished only to help the other man attain greater clarity about the various possibilities of thinking and believing, thus guiding him to the point where he could make a choice of his own" (Marianne Weber, [1926] 1975:152–53).

Weber's protocol translates such guidance into definite scholarly procedures and literary methods. To bring out their casuistic character, I will juxtapose them with an outstanding example of Protestant case casuistry summarized by Camille Slights (1981): Robert Sanderson's examination of whether or not a person of royalist sympathies could with good conscience take the oath of allegiance to a kingless commonwealth demanded by Oliver Cromwell's government after the Civil War.

I will use Weber's own words, at length, to describe the protocol, because the passage will serve additionally to exhibit his casuistic writing methods. It is from the essay on ethical neutrality in sociology, and gives an itemized account of the functions of value analysis:

(*a*) The elaboration and explication of the ultimate, internally "consistent" value-axioms, from which the divergent attitudes are derived. People are often in error, not only about their opponent's evaluations, but also about their own. This procedure is essentially an operation that begins with concrete particular evaluations and analyzes their meanings and then moves to the more general level of irreducible evaluations. It does not use the techniques of an empirical discipline and it produces no new knowledge of facts. Its "validity" is similar to that of logic.

(*b*) The deduction of "implications" (for those accepting certain value-judgements) which follow from certain irreducible value-axioms, when the practical evaluation of factual situations is based on these axioms alone. This deduction depends on the one hand, on logic, and on the other, on empirical observations for the completest possible casuistic analysis of all such empirical situations as are in principle subject to practical evaluation.

(*c*) The determination of the factual consequences which the realization of a certain practical evaluation must have: (1) in consequence of being bound to certain indispensable means, (2) in consequence of the inevitability of certain, not directly desired repercussions. These purely empirical observations may lead us to the conclusion that (*a*) it is absolutely impossible to realize the object of the preference, even in a remotely approximate way, because no means of carrying it out can be discovered; (*b*) the more or less considerable improbability of its complete or even approximate realization, either for the same reason or because of the probable appearance of undesired repercussions which might directly or indirectly render the realization undesirable; (*c*) the necessity of taking into account such means or such repercussions as the proponent of the practical postulate in question did not consider, so that his evaluation of end, means, and repercussions becomes a new problem for him. Finally: (*d*) the uncovering of new axioms (and the postulates to be drawn from them) which the proponent of a practical postulate did not take into consideration. Since he was unaware of the axioms, he did not formulate an attitude toward them although the execution of his own postulate conflicts with the others either (1) in principle or (2) as a result of the practical consequences, (i.e. logically or actually). In (1) it is a matter in further discussion of problems of type (*a*); in (2), of type (*c*). (Weber, 1949:20–21)

A constitutive feature of casuistic writing (and we note the appearance of that term in part [*b*] of the protocol) is the systematic splitting, spreading, and involution of the reading process through what might be called hedging devices. These include quotation marks around normal words (for example, "validity," "implications"); parenthetical insertions; a profusive use of qualifying clauses and subordinate exceptions in statements; and branching subdivisions that eventually circle back upon themselves. *Chambers Twentieth-Century Dictionary* (1972) says that a hedge is figuratively a barrier and to hedge is "to enclose with a hedge: to obstruct: to surround: to guard: to protect oneself from loss on, by compensatory actions, e.g. bets on the other side." As an intransitive verb it means "to shuffle, as in argument: to be shifty." In these definitions we find the roots of familiar objections to casuistry—evasive, quibbling, inconclusive—as well as clues to its critical value in the face of either commonsensical or nomological certainty of judgment. The "education of judgment" to which Weberian social science aspired meant the incessant exercise of judgment, not substantive tuition on correctness of thought.

Weber's protocol is almost exactly illustrated in Robert Sanderson's discussion of the loyalty oath issue (see Slights, 1981:43–59). Sanderson is replying to a plea for advice from a rector in Gloucester, who says that refusing the oath, as his royalist conscience instructs, might endanger his church living and threaten his family with poverty. He wants to remain true to the Rule of Faith, meaning faith to the king as the only lawful sovereign, yet fears for consequences harmful to those for whom he feels moral and personal responsibility. He wants to know whether taking the loyalty oath (called the Oath of Engagement) would in fact be a repudiation of the Rule of Faith; if so he will obey his conscience, refuse the oath and take the consequences. However, he is unsure whether this oath might not really be only a promise and therefore not so binding; also whether the wording of the oath, if it is truly one, might not be open to different interpretations, one of them compatible with the Rule of Faith. It reads: I do declare and promise that I will be true and faithful to the Commonwealth of England as it is now established without a King or House of Lords.

Sanderson's prefatory remarks seem decisive: there is no moral difference between an oath and a promise (Sanderson thus closes off a pathway to quibbling casuistry opened up by the rector); keeping an oath is an absolute value axiom because it is "done in the sight of God"; therefore, if a man believes in the Rule of Faith, and if the meaning of the oath is to repudiate it, then he would sin by taking it. Everything then depends upon the meaning of the oath; this is where the doubt must be focused and resolved.

In part 1 of his examination, Sanderson takes up the notion of political allegiance and clarifies the moral components—justice, legality, civil order, and the like—entering into it. This corresponds to function (a) in Weber's protocol, the explication of ultimate value axioms contained in a practical evaluation: moral component analysis. Part 2 (the division is Sanderson's own) turns to the meaning of the oath and introduces factual considerations—for example, that some men who were close to the king have taken the oath—to argue that its implications for royalists are at least open to question. The relevant function in Weber's protocol is (b), the deduction of implications, in the light of logic and observation, from ultimate value axioms. This is continued in part 3 where Sanderson analyzes the presuppositions and implications of oath taking in general, such as an honest intent to comply with the terms as understood in common, normal language use. Parts 4 and 5 turn from the logical to the empirical side of function (b) through examining the meanings of the particular words in the Oath of Engagement. He seeks out ambiguities in it: Does "commonwealth" refer to just this particular government, this regime, or to the English nation? Does the last phrase "as it is now established," etc., mean that lack of a king is only a temporary, contingent feature of the commonwealth, or is it intended to be a defining feature? Does "true and faithful" refer possibly to the Rule of Faith to the lawful sovereign, to the kind of faith owed by any loyal citizen to his country, or perhaps to the kind of promise given by prisoners to captors not to attempt escape? Depending on how these ambiguities are resolved, three readings are possible within the authority of normal language use:

1. A promise of permanent allegiance to the present regime

2. A promise to do what every loyal citizen should to preserve civic order and the safety of his country

3. A promise to be a good citizen for the present, on the under-

standing that one's ultimate allegiance is to the lawful sovereign of the Commonwealth

Sanderson scrupulously weighs the plausibility of each one and advances empirical observations to assume that the publicly intended meaning was the third one: many known royalists have taken the oath; some members of the government have endorsed that reading; the wording could have been made stronger and more binding; the lenient phrase "without a King" is used instead of "against a King"; it is empirically verifiable that disputed governments usually try to conciliate disaffected subjects rather than provoke them by forcing them to act against their conscience; moreover, since this government has proved itself pragmatically rational in other respects, it is all the more likely to be following the general rule of conciliation.

Finally, in part 6, Sanderson moves to the act of signing the oath— to the circumstances of the signatory, his intentions, and the probable repercussions: function (*c*) in Weber's protocol. It is worth quoting Sanderson's conclusion, if such it can be called, for the closeness of its stochastic, branching format and the lessons it would impart to Weberian social science:

> That if any man, after a serious desire and moral endeavour of informing himself as rightly and impartially as he can, what are the duties and obligations of his Allegiance on the one side, and what is most probably the meaning intended by the words of the Engagement on the other side, shall find himself well satisfied in this persuasion, that the performance in the mean time of what is required by the Engagement, so understood as he apprehendeth it ought to be, is no way contrary (for anything he can discern for the present) to his bounden Allegiance, so long as he is under a force, as that he cannot exercise it; and likewise, that whensoever that force is removed from him, or he from under it, as that he hath power to act according to his Allegiance, the Obligation of the Engagement of itself determineth and expireth; and out of these considerations, rather than suffer extreme prejudice in his person, estate, or necessary relations, shall subscribe the Engagement; since his own heart condemneth him not, neither will I. (In Slights, 1981:59)

The examination has conducted its intended reader, the doubt-ridden actor, through exactly those considerations of value commitment, motive, meaning, circumstance, and consequence occasioning the doubt in the first place, sharpening and elaborating the perplexities through an involuted network of denominative, indicative, and ethical deliberation, to bring him at the end squarely back to the necessity of a personal decision. Sanderson himself is aware that he has only turned the reader into a traveler and brought him back to his point of departure, not given definite advice. But this is the virtue he claims for his examination; procedural, not definitive: "If I should allow it [signing the Oath] in any case lawful, what ill would certainly be made thereof by multitudes of people . . . to swallow it whole without chewing, that is, resting themselves upon the general determination of the lawfulness to take it hand over head, without due consideration either of the true meaning of it or of other requisite cautions and circumstances" (In Slights, 1981:50).

The equivalent ill in social science would be the abstraction of research conclusions from the social circumstances of data collection and the methodological circumstances of analysis and argumentation. The equivalent in the practical application of social science would be to turn empirical propositions imbued by testing with lawfulness into formulaic solutions of problems, as in social engineering and other positivist programs of rational intervention.

For Weber, the purpose of sustaining an attitude of "ethical neutrality" in social science is to ensure, as in Sanderson's procedure "a serious desire and moral endeavour" of informing oneself, in preparation for an ultimate exercise of responsible judgment. In both cases "each new fact may necessitate the re-adjustment of the relations between end and indispensable means, between desired goals and unavoidable consequences. But whether this re-adjustment *should* take place and what *should* be the practical conclusions to be drawn therefrom . . . can not be answered by any science whatsoever" (Weber, 1949:23). Weber is clear that science cannot exercise a legislative or adjudicative role. He satirizes procedures for rationalizing practical decisions (in effect, automating them) by "weighing them off against one another in a cameralistic fashion or like modern Chinese administrative memoranda" (Weber, 1949:24). The hedging of judgment from formally rational mechanisms of decision, turning it away from that especially tempting way of shuffling off responsibility, is central to the educative function of casuistic sociology.

Casuistic Text Work in Economy and Society

I will analyze two sections of *Economy and Society:* chapter 5 of part 2, "Ethnic Groups," and segments of chapter 2 of part 1, "Sociological Categories of Economic Action." The first to comment further on the educative function of sociological casuistry; the second, to help identify necessary conditions for sustaining vitality in this form of discourse, absence of which results in its degeneration.

Ethnicity, Race, and Nation

One way in which sociological casuistry might hope to exercise a self-educative, that is, socially self-reflexive, effect is suggested (though no more than that; one could not say demonstrated) by Weber's discussion of race, ethnicity, and nation (Weber, 1978b:385–98, 921–26). The three concepts, apart from being semiotically close in modern political discourse, have in common the property of being highly charged with moral emotion. They are terms linked by association and usage to strong passions and deep moral sentiments. If a writer given to purple prose were to say that these words are written in modern history with letters of blood, one could resist the hyperbole, but not fail to understand the meaning.

Borrowing the concept cathexis from psychoanalysis, such highly charged words can be called cathectic terms of social life (which we think of as life arising in and through language). The educative intent of sociological casuistry takes particular shape here as a scholarly cooling of cathectic terms, a decathexis, such that emotional investment is dispersed, withdrawn, or disinvested. As Slights (1981:54) observes, the characteristic tone of casuistry, even when formulating "a bitterly debated contemporary problem," is "the calm, unruffled voice of the academician."

It follows of course that an educative effect of this kind can only be achieved in readers for whom given terms are emotionally charged and who can thus supply what is needed for the effect to work: the anticipated pleasures of moral judgment and emotional expression—the pleasures of dogmatic, ideological, oratorical, and hortatory writing which it is the ascetic concern of casuistry to deny. Its educative effect is achieved through experiences of blocked anticipation and voided pleasure, where a desired reading is negated by a textually constrained one: through reading in a double or split attitude across which a reflexive arc is generated.

We can be sure that Weber's scholarly writing about race, ethnicity, and national identity came from one side of a split attitude, and that he could presume at the time fitting readers to complete the reflexive arc. Mommsen (1974: chap. 2, "The Champion of Nationalist Power Politics and Imperialism") observes: "Even the most superficial inspection of Weber's various political writings was after all bound to reveal not only his criticism of Wilhelmian Germany and his advocacy of a parliamentary system, but also his passionate, even violent nationalism" (p. 24). Marianne Weber's biography provides ample supporting evidence in addition to the political writings. For example, his early excursions into survey research on behalf of the Social Policy Association in 1891 and 1893 were motivated by a concern to find ways to "weld small farmers to the soil of the fatherland," so that Polish peasants would not be tempted to move into borderlands left empty by German out-migration; his Inaugural Lecture at Freiburg in 1895, referring back to the same problem in the context of economic policy as a whole and stressing that "the power interests of the nation are, wherever they are in question, the ultimate decisive interests that must be served by that nation's economic policy" (Marianne Weber, [1926] 1975:218); the letter to his sister Lili on the occasion of her husband's death in the first weeks of World War I, saying "this war really is great and wonderful beyond all expectations"; and a comparable one to his mother on the death of his younger brother Karl: "He had a beautiful death in the only place where it is worthy of a human being to be at the moment." It is difficult to dispute Mommsen's conclusion that "Weber was, as much as most of his contemporaries, subjected to the overriding influences of an age dominated by the ideology of nationalism" (Mommsen: 1974:25), except it should be added that the influences did not override his vocation of science.

As to a fitting readership, on the scholarly front I have already referred to the historical school of economics and its belief that the language, law, polity, and culture of each people are emanations of a quasi-biological *Volksgeist*, or "Volk-soul." Beyond this was a more popular and contentious literature, represented by Houston Chamberlain's *Die Grundlagen des neunzehnten Jahrhunderts* (1900), presenting a neo-Darwinian theory of blood-based racial superiority and inferiority and claiming for the German nation a special greatness due to the predominance in it of Teutonic stock. Martindale (1981: 169) tells us that the Kaiser read it aloud to his sons and had it distributed to army officers and "displayed in all libraries and bookshops in Germany." Such ideas also began circulating in university courses.

Weber was as passionately negative about the idea of race as he was positive about the nation. He inveighed against Treitschke's anti-Semitic lectures, against "zoological nationalism" (Bendix and Roth, 1971:25, 53), and at the first meeting of the German Sociological Association, in 1910, called it "a scientific crime" to circumvent sociological investigation by "the uncritical use of completely unclarified racial hypotheses" (Weber, 1978b:398, n. 1). The strength of Weber's feelings about race and nation, together with his involvement in the value-charged ideas and happenings of the time, form part of the context of awareness ideally needed for his dispassionate discussion to achieve a reflexive, educative effect. For the ideally fitting reader, the blank margins of the text would be teeming with heated words and events, and their overt absence would be felt as a disturbing gap requiring interpretive work to fill. Mommsen correctly observes that "it is not easy to reconcile the record of Max Weber's actual attitude to nationalism and power politics with his theoretical findings on the same issues" (Mommsen, 1974:36), but can make no more of it than their being "two sides of the same coin" (p. 25), related as motivation is to research selection. We make of it a clue to how Weber's denominative and indicative casuistry can achieve for fitting readers a critical effect. The qualification is essential because to the extent one is not a fitting reader (perhaps because the concerning concepts have grown old and stale) the effect will not appear. Here we can make a crucial point about the entire mode of theorizing represented by Weber's work (regardless of how one labels it). This way of cultivating critical reflexivity in social life is bound to particular historical and cultural experiences; practical effectiveness therefore is relative to particular conditions of readership. It does not proceed as if there were formulas with an intrinsic power to reform consciousness or universally valid laws through which to gain a secure leverage on social reality; such reaching for invariant effectiveness belongs to either magic or applied natural science. It maintains a purely relative and relational notion of practical relevance: one which is of course entirely consistent with the neo-Kantian postulate of a value-constituted subject matter in the cultural sciences and its corollary that such sciences must be constantly rewritten: "there are sciences to which eternal youth is granted . . . all those to which the eternally onword flowing stream of culture perpetually brings new problems. At the very heart of their task lies not only the transiency of all ideal types but also at the same time the inevitability of new ones. . . . The relationship between concept and reality in the cultural sciences involves the transitoriness of all such syntheses" (Weber, 1949:104–5).

Weber takes up the topics of race, ethnicity, and nationality, in that order, in the course of establishing the primary bases of group organization. The thrust of the argument is that biological characteristics are entirely subordinate to social forces and historical contingencies in the formation and separation of groups. They may enter into retroactive myths of origin, legitimating ideologies of superiority and the like, but "they are not positively group-forming" (Weber, 1978b:392). The discursive effect intended by the argument is to undermine the rational authority of its focal concepts: race, ethnic group, and nation. This can be seen by summarizing its progression.

The opening topic is racially based attraction and antipathy. It quickly introduces evidence on the abhorrence of intermarriage between whites and Negroes, from both sides, in the United States, then moves decisively to squash a racial interpretation of it: "but this development began only with the Emancipation and resulted from the Negroes' demand for equal civil rights. Hence this abhorrence on the part of the whites is socially determined by the previously sketched tendency toward the monopolization of social power and honor, a tendency which in this case happens to be linked to race" (p. 386). The reasoning is repeated through other evidence, such as the less negative implications of admixtures of "Indian blood" compared to "Negro blood," leading to the conclusion of this section: "Mere anthropological differences account for little, except in cases of extreme esthetic antipathy" (Weber, 1978b:387). These core messages are further elaborated in Weber's section 2, on belief in common ethnicity, with regard to a broad range of social relationships. It is admitted that racial physical characteristics often enter into senses of sameness and difference, but denied that they have any special status or necessity. For example, "the more or less easy emergence of social circles in the broadest sense of the word may be linked to the most superficial features of historically accidental habits just as much as to inherited racial characteristics" (p. 387); any and all differences "regardless of whether they are biologically inherited or culturally transmitted" (p. 388) are liable to be built into conscious group identities, but their status always is that of signifiers which have real world efficacy conferred on them through usage (especially in monopolistic competitions for wealth, status, and power) and shared experience; none has ontological force.

As the core messages are repeated with cumulative insistence and strength, the coherence and credibility of referring to racial groups and ethnic groups is undermined. The effect is reinforced by the subtitle of Weber's section 3: "The Disutility of the Notion of 'Ethnic Group'" (p. 393). The section itself ends with a crucial clarification of discursive intent that displays the critical objective of the chapter as a whole: "The concept of the "ethnic" group, which dissolves if we define our terms exactly, corresponds in this regard to one of the most vexing, since emotionally charged concepts: the *nation,* as soon as we attempt a sociological definition. (Weber, 1978b:395)

I take this to be a direct expression of the critical project of sociological casuistry: the withdrawal of rationally preemptive affect and effect from cathected concepts of social discourse. Weber pursues it in the remaining section (4) of the chapter and in the segment on the nation in chapter 9 (Political Communities). Two quotations, one from each location, both casuistically styled, will provide sufficient illustration:

> Time and again we find that the concept "nation" directs us to political power. Hence the concept seems to refer—if it refers at all to a uniform phenomenon—to a specific kind of pathos which is linked to the idea of a powerful political community of people who share a common language, or religion, or common customs, or political memories. (Weber, 1978b:397–98).

> If the concept of "nation" can in any way be defined unambiguously, it certainly cannot be stated in terms of empirical qualities common to those who count as members of the nation. In the sense of those using the term at a given time, the concept undoubtedly means, above all, that it is *proper* to expect from certain groups a specific sentiment of solidarity in the face of other groups. Thus the concept belongs in the sphere of values. Yet there is no agreement on how these groups should be delimited or about what concerted action should result from such solidarity. (Weber, 1978b:922)

For the reader who has undergone the destabilizing effects of Weber's treatment of the concept "nation," the central phrase of the second passage—"the concept undoubtedly means"—cannot but strike him with a consuming doubt which any surviving hope of a definitive statement would only serve to intensify. His interpretive situation is that of the concerned reader of Sanderson's examination of the Oath of Engagement upon reaching the "concluding" statement of advice, or indeed that of any negotiator of a casuistic discourse.

Moving down now from the level of genre to that of style, we can specify some of the literary methods through which the educative effect is performed in Weber:

1. Suspension of the indicative certainty of key terms through use of quotation marks and verbal equivalents that draw attention to the conventional character of indication. The effect is to add reflexive echoes, such as "so-called," "they choose to call," "we choose to call," to the pronunciation of certain words. The device needs no further documentation, but its significance in estranging ordinary language use and making it an opaque object of reflection needs to be brought out. Marianne Weber, speaking of *Economy and Society,* comments:

> The language of the entire work, particularly of the theory of concepts, is very different from that of his other writings. . . . Arranged by numbers and letters, sentence follows upon sentence, blow upon blow, as it were. The definitions are expressed pithily according to a peculiar formula: Sociology shall mean . . . , Social action shall mean . . . Organization shall mean . . . , Domination shall mean . . . These imperatives, however, are not a claim to the validity of the new constructs outside the framework of this special sociology; on the contrary, their meaning is this: "In *my* theory of concepts this shall be the meaning, this is what *I* shall call these structures for certain methodological purposes, and only the scholarly yield shall justify my procedure; let other sociologies and, above all, other disciplines proceed differently for their scholarly purposes." (Marianne Weber, [1926] 1975:676–77)

Putting key terms in quotation marks is not then, as Leo Strauss would have it, a childish trick by Weber to avoid responsible discourse, but part of a procedure to conspicuously conventionalize normal usage so that in the reading process we are kept aware this is, like all language use, only a way of world making and consequently that the responsibility for world making rests with us, members of language communities. The potential for critical distancing in Weber's casuistic style can be gauged from this contrast made by an anthropologist between our culture and that of a preliterate society, the Wintu:

> [Among the Wintu there is a] recurring . . . attitude of humility and respect toward reality, toward nature and society. I cannot find an adequate English term to apply to a habit of thought that is so alien to our culture. We are aggressive toward reality. We say, This is bread; we do not say, as the Wintu, *I call this bread* or *I feel* or *taste* or *see it to be bread.* The Wintu never says starkly *this is;* if he speaks of reality that is not within his own restricting experience, he does not affirm it, he only implies it. If he speaks of his experience he does not express it as categorically true. (Dorothy Lee, 1959:129; cited in Brown, 1977:24)

Perhaps Weber would have felt at home among the Wintu; in any case, while there may be no English term to adequately describe "a habit of thought that is so alien to our culture," casuistic comes close enough for our purpose. I would note also, with a view to the critical potential of casuistic sociology, that the aggressive certitude brought to critical light by contrast with the Wintu is precisely the positivist stance toward reality, in thought and practice, which the Frankfurt School and neo-Marxian critical theory have made a prime object of attack. However, we must return to the summary of Weber's literary methods.

2. Metonymic shifting of a cathectic term to substitute words with little or no emotional charge; renaming with a cooling effect. For example, chapter 5 opens by renaming race "race identity" and formally defining it as "common inherited and inheritable traits that actually derive from common descent." Subsequently the section renames "race identity" as "persons with anthropological similarities" (Weber, 1978b:385), "anthropological types" (p. 386), and in the last sentence of the section, "mere anthropological differences" (p. 387). Metonymic reduction is a literary counterpart of the procedures called formal and operational definition in theory construction manuals, though its significance there is different from that in a casuistic framework because the informing purpose is different.

3. Metonymic extensions of indicative and denominative doubt from a target term to associated terms familiar in social discourse. Thus Weber, having undermined the referential integrity of the terms "race" and "ethnicity," draws others into his casuistic net:

> The content of joint activities that are possible on an ethnic basis remains indefinite. There is a corresponding ambiguity of concepts denoting ethnically determined action, that means, determined by the belief in blood relationship. Such concepts are *Völkerschaft*, *Stamm* (tribe), *Volk* (people), each of which is ordinarily used in the sense of an ethnic subdivision of the following one (although the first two may be used in reversed order). (Weber, 1978b:392–93)

4. The measured allowance into the text, always between strong acts of containment or discrediting, of emotively charged connotations of target terms. One might regard it as a controlled restoration of cathexis, a representation of that which calls for the casuistic discourse and provides for the possibility of its being educative. Following a generic rule, it incorporates cathectic intertexts, or tokens of them, into itself: for example, the abhorrence of sexual relations between whites and blacks (Weber, 1978b:386), the notion of being a chosen people (p. 391), and the existence of racial smell and "Negro odor" (p. 392). In each case, the topic is made an occasion to reinforce the dominant movement of the discussion: the deconstructive turning of supposedly natural affinities and differences into ones that are social, conventional, and contingent. Thus "the 'Negro odor,' of which so many fables are told" (p. 386) is made a weak and only imaginary factor in comparison with

the rancid smell of butter given off by Scythian women whose custom it was to oil their hair with it.

5. Ironic inversion of the normal significance of cathectic terms. Whereas race, ethnicity, and nation normally connote natural, deep-rooted phenomena, Weber's discussion equates them with phenomena that are artificial and superficial. Also, the cognitive weakness revealed in their dissolution contrasts ironically with their rhetorical power in social discourse. A special case of ironic inversion displayed extensively by Weber is the representation of supposedly deep natural causes as contingent ideological effects. Given the literary trope involved one might call this a synecdochical reversal of normal signification.

Richard Brown (1977:172) says that "to render something ironic is to take it from its conventional context and place it in an opposite one," in this way promoting critical self-awareness. Against a reading context of "zoological nationalism," Volk-soul romanticism, and neo-Darwinian racial theories, Weber's explication of national, ethnic, and racial groups as contingent formations involving such diversity as to lack referential coherence is a sustained exercise in ironic inversion and interpretive dissonance.

The overall movement of the discussion to turn (seemingly) natural into (actually) artificial phenomena has already been described; the following quotation shows the movement in literary performance. In reading it one must recall that Weber has already associated tribe, Stamm, with Volk as one of its conventional subdivisions, and tribal consciousness with Volk consciousness:

> The tribe is clearly delimited when it is a subdivision of a polity, which, in fact, often establishes it. In this case, the artificial origin is revealed by the round numbers in which tribes usually appear, for example, the previously mentioned division of the people of Israel into twelve tribes, the three Doric *phylai* and the various *phylai* of the other Hellenes. When a political community was newly established or reorganized, the population was newly divided. Hence the tribe is here a political artifact, even though it soon adopts the whole symbolism of blood-relationship and particularly a tribal cult. Even today it is not rare that political artifacts develop a sense of affinity akin to that of blood relationship. Very schematic constructs such as those states of the United States that were made into squares according to their latitude have a strong sense of identity; it is also not rare that families travel from New York to Richmond to make an expected child a "Virginian." (Weber, 1978b:393)

Weber's use of images drawn from the blatently artificial realm of mathematics ("round" numbers, cartographic "squares"), nicely points the irony of blood-bond groups being originally divisions of political convenience. The passage also, of course, illustrates synecdochical reversal of a conventionally presumed cause-and-effect relation. Instead of being an ineluctable causal force in history and society, blood affinity is only an ideological effect of circumstantial contiguity, the causal efficacy of which is limited to that of any other subjective beliefs:

> The sharp demarcations of areas wherein ethnically relevant customs predominate, which were not conditioned either by political or economic or religious factors, usually came into existence by way of migration or expansion, when groups of people that had previously lived in complete or partial isolation from each other and became accommodated to heterogeneous conditions of existence came to live side by side. As a result, the obvious contrast usually evokes on both sides, the idea of blood disaffinity (*Blutsfremdheit*), regardless of the objective state of affairs.

> We shall call "ethnic groups" those human groups that entertain a subjective belief in their common descent because of similarities of physical type or of customs or both, or because of memories of colonization and migration; this belief must be important for the propogation of group formation; conversely, it does not matter whether or not an objective blood relationship exists. (Weber, 1978b:392, 389)

The reduction of blood affinity and disaffinity to a produced subjective belief turns a supposedly primary phenomenon into a secondary one, in time and in importance. Moreover, the mere heterogeneity of its possible causes suggests that this "deep" wellspring of history and society, so imbued with value significance, is, truly speaking, nothing special, indeed, superficial. Weber several times conjoins blood affinity and disaffinity with superficial phenomena in a relationship of belittling equality. For example:

> Apart from the community of language, which may or may not coincide with objective, or subjectively believed consanguinity, and apart from religious belief, which is also independent of consanguinity, the ethnic differences that remain are, on the one hand, esthetically conspicuous differences of the physical appearance (as mentioned before) and, on the other hand and of equal weight, the perceptible differences in the conduct of everyday life. Of special importance are precisely those items which may otherwise seem to be of small social relevance, since when ethnic differentiation is

concerned it is always the conspicuous differences that come into play.

> Ethnic repulsion may take hold of all conceivable differences among the notions of propriety and transform them into "ethnic conventions" . . . conventionalization (a term expounded else-where) may take hold of such things as a hairdo or style of beard and the like. (Weber, 1978b:390, 391)

In summary, it can be said that chapter 5 of *Economy and Society* conducts a concentrated containment, belittlement, and undermining of powerful cathectic concepts taken from the social context, using literary methods like parenthetic suspension of ordinary usage, metonymic emptying, and ironic inversion. Of course such methods are not specific to casuistic discourse. Richard Brown (1977: chap. 5; 1983), for example, argues convincingly that irony is latent in all theorization of social life because it characteristically suspends the adequacy of members' knowledge, considers conventional opposites as actual unities, seeks unintended or antithetical consequences of actors' intentions, and defamiliarizes the familiar to make it examinable. This is true, but I would claim that casuistic theorizing brings certain compositional devices, including ironic inversion, to center stage because they are especially congenial for its work: the working of its constitutive tensions and self-educative aim. It should be remembered that casuistry itself, sociological or otherwise, is a strategic (in literary terms, generic) concept and must be defined at that level; there are no genre-specific methods here or elsewhere in literature. If Weber's theorizing in *Economy and Society* is to be called casuistic, this must be taken to refer to the overall movement of the text within the meaning frame of his scholarly program, not to a particular class of literary devices. Every mode of theorizing selectively prefers certain textual materials and methods over others, but there are no definitive ties. To complete this observation, it needs to be added that the strategic (generic) level also places negative constraints on the tactical (textual) level. For example, because casuistry generically works to cultivate respect for circumstances, wariness of accepted definitions, and humility in the face of contingent reality, its working methods are always in an ascetic direction: towards disciplining and limiting the play of words. This is why ironic inversion of cathectic concepts is congenial to casuistic discourse. Conversely, however, casuistry is no more capable than irony of animating or (following LaCapra, 1983: chap. 9), "carnivalizing" the language of social life; it rules out exuberant and excessive kinds of text work.

The distinction between strategic and tactical, regulative and implementive, levels obviously has implications for interpreting evidence on the generic identity of a text. In the present case, the chapter I have analyzed does not offer strong examples of casuistic word work. Typical imprints are there but not notably marked. It does not contain good compositional evidence for the casuistic hypothesis such as one finds elsewhere in *Economy and Society*, especially in part 1. However, I still take it as confirmatory evidence, because it so clearly displays the compositional strategy of the genre. Apart from the educative intent already documented, there is the fact that Weber pauses four times in his brief discussion to indicate what a full sociological treatment of the topics would require and each time gives directives toward an extensive denominative refinement, which is to say, a more complete casuistic schema:

> A specialized sociological study of ethnicity would have to make a finer distinction between these concepts than we have done for our limited purposes. (Weber, 1978b:390)
>
> All in all, the notion of "ethnically" determined social action subsumes phenomena that a rigorous sociological analysis—as we do not attempt it here—would have to distinguish carefully. . . . It is certain that in this process, the collective term "ethnic" would be abandoned, for it is unsuitable for a really rigorous analysis. (pp. 394–95)
>
> The classification could easily be enlarged, as every rigorous sociological investigation would have to do. It turns out that feelings of identity subsumed under the term "national" are not uniform but may derive from diverse sources. (p. 397)
>
> In the face of this value concept of the "idea of the nation," which empirically is entirely ambiguous, a sociological typology would have to analyze all the individual kinds of sentiments of group membership and solidarity in their genetic conditions and in their consequences for the social action of the participants. This cannot be attempted here. (p. 925)

I take all this to be evidence that Weber's idea of sociological theorizing and its bearing upon the analysis of value-significant phenomena is appropriately grasped by calling it casuistic.

In the remaining section, I will examine a textually rich sample of casuistic composition in Weber and use it to draw extendable conclusions about the conditions under which sociological casuistry tends toward degeneracy.

Degenerate Casuistry in Economy and Society

My proposal to treat canonical texts like *Economy and Society* as exemplary modes of theorizing does not imply uncritical approval of everything in them. To the contrary, an exemplary model once explicated serves as a regulative ideal against which to see shortcomings even in the particular writings from which they have been drawn. What after all—thinking of literary analysis—is the point of locating a text or a body of work in a genre, if not to be able to hold it accountable to the best possibilities of its kind? In this section, the most heavily casuistic part of Weber's summation of his scholarship will be held accountable to the best possibilities of casuistry—which I have argued is its intrinsic genre—and there found wanting. In drawing implications for sociological theorizing I assume that authentic casuistry has positive value as a form of discourse on social life, and degenerate casuistry a negative value. On this assumption, degeneracy of the genre necessarily implies degeneracy as sociological discourse; it then becomes socially bad language about society.

The subtext to be analyzed is chapter 2 in part 1 of *Economy and Society,* titled "Sociological Categories of Economic Action." It can appropriately be called monumental, not only to indicate its size (143 pages) and densely packed content, but also to recall its legalistic format and Radbruch's comment: "The language of law is frigid, renouncing any emotional tone; it is blunt, renouncing any argumentation; it is concise, renouncing any intention to teach. Thus there comes into existence a *lapidary style of self-imposed poverty*" (in Wilks, 1950:138). In this comment lie important clues to the seeds of degeneracy in Weber's theory of categories. Further clues appear in Guenther Roth's apologetics for part 1. Roth, the coeditor of *Economy and Society,* admits "it is certainly true that the definitions are not 'readable,'" but excuses the fault on the grounds that "Part One is really a reference text" (in Weber, 1978b:cl), and only meant to accompany part 2 as a special dictionary of correct usage. One must doubt that this interpretation is entirely adequate. It would be curious to have a glossary, in itself not readable, placed deliberately in front of the text to be read and therefore something which must be read in advance. Reference texts are something made available as accompanying aids when needed, not compulsory preparations. Moreover, it is not literally true to say that part 1 is not readable in its own right; English language students of social science have been reading it as a self-contained text since the Henderson and Parsons translation, *The Theory of Social and Economic Organisation,* in

1947. What is interesting here is that Roth, in spite of such obvious objections, can plausibly insist on the reference text interpretation as the best one possible. Clearly it has something of that quality to it, and one could cite Weber's own apologetics, as he addresses the laboring reader, for support:

> For only the facts of the economic situation provide the flesh and blood for a genuine explanation of also that process of development relevant for sociological theory. What can be done here is only to supply a scaffolding adequate to provide the analysis with relatively unambiguous and definite concepts. It is obvious not only that no attempt is made here to do justice to the historical aspect of economic development, but also that the typology of the genetic sequence of possible forms is neglected. The present aim is only to develop a schematic system of classification. (Weber, 1978b:116)

> This whole discussion in such an abstract form has been introduced only in order to make an approximately correct formulation of problems possible. (p. 201)

Suppose then we accept both that part 1 has a reference text quality and that readers are expected to read it entirely and as a whole in advance of the more substantive materials in part 2. The point I would make is that to isolate concepts from situated circumstances of usage and abstractly regulate their meaning in advance is against the spirit of authentic casuistry. As Slights (1981) and Starr (1971) have made clear for us, respect for circumstantial usage is precisely one of its hallmarks. In terms of the compositional model developed previously, abstract regulation in advance of usage undermines one of the constitutive tensions of casuistry, which is to work from individual situations to abstract concepts and back again, so that the individual lot, the particular circumstance, is the point both of departure and return. Weber's procedure here violates that requirement of authentic casuistry. Thus scientistic appropriations of part 1 in formal theories of social action (most comprehensively by Talcott Parsons) are, in this view, completions of its degenerative casuistry.

Roth makes another observation giving a clue to the degeneracy in Weber's theory of categories. Speaking of chapter 2, he says:

> The chapter on the sociological categories of economic action is remarkable for its length, the same as chs. I and III together. It is likely that Weber wanted to compensate for the relatively brief economic casuistry of Part Two. However, the many pages of seemingly dry definitions and comments owe some of their

length—and hidden fervor—to Weber's political involvement with the problems of postwar economic and political reconstruction in the wake of the Empire's collapse and in the face of the victor's harsh demands at Versailles. The chapter also reflects the phenomenon of the wartime "state-socialist" economy and the syndicalist and socialist proposals for economic reconstruction. (In Weber, 1978b:ciii).

Like the chapter on race, ethnicity, and nation, this one was written in a context teeming with emotive events, morally charged issues, and cathectic words associated with them. What is even more remarkable about chapter 2 than its length is the thoroughness with which that writing-reading context is contained, to the point of exclusion. One would not even be able to guess from it that the writer was a personally involved practical actor, an emotionally engaged intellectual seen by many as a possible leader of his country in a turbulent political scene. Roth speaks of a "hidden fervor" in the casuistry; I will speak of an inhibition of critical desire. This idea could be pursued psychobiographically, along the lines of Mitzman (1970). I will confine discussion to textual evidence.

The relevance of an inhibition of critical intent to casuistic degeneracy is readily brought out through my compositional model of the genre. Critical inhibition undermines the second constitutive tension of casuistic discourse: its working from practical value decisions to logical-empirical assessment and back again. The compositional principle involved here is the joint necessity of all three dimensions of casuistic discourse—denominative, indicative, and ethical—to its integrity and therefore vitality. Given the specification of the ethical dimension as the directive axis of movement, the principle amounts almost to a self-evident truth: a text detached from the purpose of its intrinsic genre will to the extent of its detachment tend towards degeneracy. In the case at hand, its movement will in effect be reduced to a casuistic circling in two dimensions, denominative and indicative. I will show this to be the tendency of chapter 2. More particularly, I will trace the contours of the writing around ethically charged topics, showing how they are closed off instead of opened to reflection, and attempt through close description to build an analysis of the textual dynamics of casuistic degeneracy which would have extendable critical relevance.

Section 9 is a good place to begin the examination. Its title ("Formal and Substantive Rationality of Economic Action") and opening paragraph identify a distinction capturing many issues between proponents and opponents of capitalism: that between allowing economic action to be governed by quantitative calculation and market mechanisms, and governing economic action with reference to collective values of some kind. The critical potential of the distinction is evident, given the long history of rationality as a criterion value in Western civilization; but Weber, having introduced the potentiality, moves quickly to contain it: "The terminology suggested above is thought of merely as a means of securing greater consistency in the use of the word 'rational' in this field. It is actually only a more precise form of the meanings which are continually recurring in the discussion of 'nationalization' and of the economic calculus in money and kind (Weber, 1978b:85)." Then, as if to more securely hedge the concept of substantive rationality, which might so easily be held against the formal rationality of contemporary society, he insists that it is "full of ambiguities," since it can cover any value content whatsoever, egalitarian or feudalist, pacifist or militaristic, hedonistic or moralistic, and ends the section with a casuistic dispersal of the opening contrast: "There is no question in this discussion of attempting value judgements in this field, but only of determining and delimiting what is to be called 'formal.' In this context the concept 'substantive' is itself in a certain sense 'formal'; that is, it is an abstract generic concept." (Weber, 1978b:86).

Nonetheless, the field—the field of discourse that is the other side of the text—regularly pushes up topics charged with value judgments that the writing must negotiate. There are forty-one numbered sections in the chapter, seventeen of which (sections 4, 9, 11–14, 16, 19, 20, 22, 23, 25, 26, 30, 36, 41) contain clear surface expressions of value-charged issues, that is, explicit declarations and/or the insertion of cathectic intertexts (which may be phrases and isolated terms, as well as propositions). The ten-paged section 11, titled "The Concept and Types of Profit-Making: The Role of Capital," is one of the most densely packed with inhibited issues. It contains (in a double sense) four issues.

First, the creation of consumer wants, hence effective demand, by producers. The issue is introduced as a qualification of the axiom in economic theory that the wants of the marginal consumer regulate the flow and direction of production: "In actual fact, given the actual distribution of power, this is only true in a limited sense for the modern situation. To a large degree, even though the consumer has to be in a position to buy, his wants are 'awakened' and 'directed' by the entrepreneur" (Weber, 1978b:92). But having introduced a "hot" topic from Marxian critiques of capitalist ideology, Weber (the text) immediately closes it off by switching without comment to another; both belong to an open-ended unpackaging of the concept of capital accounting, the "form of monetary accounting which is peculiar to rational economic profit-making" (p. 91); and the effect, underwritten by the listing format of the whole part 1, is to construe the significance of the topic, or any entered and left in this way, as that of assembling a series to explicate a definition. In other words, its latent intertextual significance is deflected and subordinated to one that is purely internal, or intratextual; a readable opening to social discourse is turned inwards to serve the development of a precise, comprehensive denominative list. The topical formulation is left hanging as the list moves on; nothing is made of it. This method of containment, involving a radical interiorization of significance through subordination to a listing program, is illustrated again at the end of section 11, when the same topic is reintroduced in even stronger terms. Weber speaks here of the "aggressive advertising policies" through which capitalistic enterprises make wants appear and disappear (pp. 99–100). Again, however, it is simply terminated and left hanging, this time followed by a new section and new orienting concept; so again its significance is reduced to the internal one of being point 5 in a summary list of denominative considerations.

A second charged issue enters the section as next topic in line to the first appearance of the want-creation issue. It includes a cathectic intertext that Weber himself places in italics: "Capital accounting in its formally most rational shape thus presupposes the *battle of man against man*" (Weber, 1978b:93). The italics positively invite a discussion of conflict as a structural imperative of "rational" profit making. Instead the next sentence sets the serial assembly line in motion again: "And this in turn involves a further very specific condition." Interestingly for our purposes, however, the further condition only increases the value pressure in the text by making a claim with such deep implications that it cries for discussion: "No economic system can directly translate subjective 'feelings of need' into effective demand, that is, into demand which needs to be taken into account and satisfied through the production of goods. . . . This is true of consumption in every kind of economic system, including a communist one" (p. 93). Here the paragraph breaks off, but the string of value-cathected topics is not abandoned. Instead the next paragraph returns to the diverted topic of the battle of man against man and channels it into a fourth issue, the shaping of economic demand by power position, that runs back to the other three. Production depends on profitability, but "it is possible to produce profitably only for those consumers who, in these terms, have sufficient income"

(p. 93). Income sufficient, that is, not only to purchase a commodity but to effectively bid for its production in competition with other consumers making other bids: "it is only demand made effective though the possession of purchasing power which is and can be satisfied. . . . Profitability is indeed *formally* a rational category, but for that very reason it is indifferent with respect to *substantive* postulates unless these can make themselves felt in the market in the form of sufficient purchasing power" (p. 94). At this point there is an accumulation of charged topics pressing for release in argument, in debate, in critique, in vindication. Instead Weber caps them with a paragraph of pure denominative casuistry that bears no discursive relationship to what has gone before and makes sense only as part of a lexical elaboration of the term "capital accounting": " 'Capital goods,' as distinguished from mere possessions or parts of wealth of a budgeting unit are all such goods as are . . . 'Capital interest,' as distinct from various other possible kinds of interest on loans is: 1) . . . ; 2) . . ." (p. 94).

I will not attempt an exhaustive catalogue of value-charged topics in chapter 2. Suffice it to say that they are typically coded through the antinomy of formal against substantive rationality (for example, rational imperatives governing expropriation of workers from the means of production; the meaning of a rational organization of work, a rational division of labor, a rational occupation), and on each appearance immediately hedged, cooled out, diverted, dispersed, or capped, so that an argument does not form. Further discussion is selectively confined to bringing out the methods of this containment procedure.

Section 19 discusses the appropriation and expropriation of economic advantages, taking up terms cathected by Marxian critiques of capitalist society. The continuation of the first paragraph reads: "Objects of appropriation may be: the opportunities of disposing of, and obtaining a return from, human labor services (*Leistungsverwerkungschancen*); the material means of production;[36] and the opportunities for profit from managerial functions.[37] (On the sociological concept of appropriation, see above, chap. 1, sec. 10)." There are four hedges around the topic, four redirections of attention here: parenthetical inclusion of an original German term, suggesting that full meaning has not been retrieved in translation; two footnote references suggesting that more needs to be read to grasp the annotated phrases; and the parenthetical direction back to an earlier discussion. Of these, the last is the most consequential. The obedient reader who goes to the section indicated is hit with the full force of Weber's denominative casuistry. There, open social relationships are distinguished from ones which are closed. Closure may be determined by tradition, feeling, value rationality, or calculative rationality. Rational closure is probable where a relationship offers opportunities to satisfy, either absolutely or instrumentally, material or ideal interests. Satisfaction may be either through cooperative action or a compromise of interests. A closed relationship may allocate its advantages (*a*) through competitive struggle, (*b*) through rationing and regulation, or (*c*) through more or less permanent, more or less inalienable appropriation. Appropriated advantages will be called rights. Advantages may be for the benefit of the group, which may be either communal or associative in character, or for an individual. And so it goes on. Weber pauses once in the section to explain to the toiling reader that "the apparently gratuitous tediousness involved in the elaborate definition of the above concepts" reflects the fact that "we often neglect to think out clearly what seems to be obvious, because it is intuitively familiar" (Weber, 1978b:44). This can be read as a pointer to the educative task of authentic casuistry as discussed previously, yet here it only underlines the absence of a condition absolutely essential for casuistry to sustain its authenticity and avoid degeneracy: the rooting of discussion in concrete phenomena relevant to the resolution of decisions or guidance of conduct surrounded by doubt. Casuistry in abstraction from situated doubt, formal, legalistic casuistry cannot help but be degenerate. In this instance, Weber, having glanced towards authentic casuistry, resumes the abstracted labor of a definitional spinning out of terms with no occasioned beginning and no apparent end, which could, it seems, go on until time, space, energy, and ink run out, or some equally arbitrary limit is met.

How different it must have been for the audiences at Weber's lectures on Marxian theory, given at Vienna in 1918 (the same time he was perfecting the *Kategorienlehre*), under the title "A Positive Critique of the Materialistic View of History":

> Weber usually lectured about the sociology of religion for two and a half hours without pause, until it became dark in the beautiful paneled room. He had not yet regained the customary lecturing style. What he offered instead was usually an enchanting artistic achievement. The overabundant material was perfectly organized, everything was vividly presented, and the most remote civilization—the Orient—was related to the Occident. He would invariably *present his ideas in such a way that the remote material suddenly threw new light on the current problems that were familiar to all*—for example, when he explained the religious ideas by which the Indian caste system produced an anti-revolutionary frame of

mind and then juxtaposed with it the antithetical religious background of modern European socialism. (Marianne Weber, [1926] 1975:605)

Internal referencing to previous definitions is common throughout part 1 of *Economy and Society*. It reflects and helps implement a degenerative tendency (degenerative, that is, for authentic casuistry) towards making the text its own context of sense: a movement towards internal signification and self-sufficient meaning that I would call *autocontextualization*. The listing format of the presentation whereby, as I observed above, there are topic exits and entries whose only interpretive sense is to carry on an internally initiated definitional project, contributes to the same effect. The text issues a stream of definitional instructions: "we will call," "is to be understood as," "will be said." The reader cannot ignore them or their dense, cumulative proliferation without ceasing to understand what is emerging. Periodically a backward reference is made, such as the one on appropriation, that functions like a checking question in a self-instructional teaching apparatus. Each new definition builds upon preceding ones, typically in sets. If the reader skips one, he will likely run against statements that cannot be grasped. Other than going around them and increasing the probability of subsequent incomprehension, his only option is to backtrack and become more firmly instructed in the casuistry. In appropriate use, tied to initiating problems and the situated explication of doubt, this procedure is basic to the educative action of a casuistic discourse, serving, in Weber's words "to make an approximately correct formulation of problems possible" (Weber, 1978b:201); "to think out clearly what seems to be obvious," but which is often neglected "because it is intuitively familiar" (p. 44). To the extent that denominative-indicative casuistry becomes autocontextualized and therefore isolated from such practical contexts of sense, contexts representing the engagement of practical reason with concrete circumstances, it loses generative tension; it becomes, in other words, degenerative, because it contravenes its intrinsic conditions of vitality. What should be a self-instructive discourse degenerates into an autoeducational apparatus where the apparatus itself, the task of mastering it, is primary. This is the case with part 1 of *Economy and Society*. Roth's defensive argument (1978b:CI) that part 2 supplies a context adequate to redeem part 1 is not acceptable. First, as he points out, it was written prior to part 1, was never conceptually integrated with it, and in fact contains its own denominative casuistry that is by no means the same as the later system of definitions. Secondly, even if, following Roth's further defense, Weber had lived to revise the second part in light of the new system, part 1 would still stand as a unitary section of the text demanding by virtue of its placement to be read first, in its own right, and would not, pace Roth, be readable as a lexical supplement. That Weber regarded it has having a value and purpose in its own right is suggested by the fact that he insisted on delivering the content as an independent lecture course (at Munich in 1919) and called it an instruction (*Lehre*) in sociological categories; the suggestion is confirmed by justificatory insertions in the text itself such as those quoted above. We are not then judging a dictionary or lexicon but a readable discourse with its own context of sense. Given that "own" means both actual and ideal, the degeneracy argument amounts to a claim that in part 1 the context of sense ideally intrinsic to its form of discourse is voided in the actual performance. Let me add a little more illustration of the performance, focusing again on its repressive containment of value-charged content.

Returning to appropriation-expropriation, the fourfold hedging observed in the first paragraph of section 19 is followed by the dominant containment procedure of part 1, a dispersal of the topic into elaboratively subdivided possibilities. Appropriated labor power may go (1) to an individual or an organization, or (2) be sold on a market. In either case, four possibilities arise. The first is "monopolitic appropriation." I will quote the elaboration as strongly typical of the dispersive procedure employed throughout:

> (*a*) Monopolistic appropriation of the opportunities for disposal of labor services by the individual worker himself: the case of "craft-organized free labor!" The appropriated rights may either be hereditary and alienable, in which case type (1) above is illustrated by the Indian village artisan and type (2) by certain medieval non-personal craft rights; or they may be strictly personal and inalienable, as under type (1) all "rights to an office;" or, finally, they may be hereditary, but inalienable, as under types (1) and (2) certain medieval, but above all Indian, craft rights, and medieval "offices" of the most diverse kind. In all these cases appropriation may be unconditional or subject to certain substantive conditions. (Weber, 1978b:126)

There are at least six and conceivably, from the last sentence, twelve possibilities to keep track of here, and this is only the first of four general possibilities of appropriation. The reader becomes preoccupied with keeping track; reading attention is saturated by the demands of the format. Following a way through the branching definitions is an experience comparable to that of a pedestrian following the winding streets of a strange city and becoming immersed in the task of mentally mapping the terrain.

In light of my contention that Weber (his text) is working here to contain a topic cathected by Marxism, it is worth asking whether and how the Marxian concept of alienated labor appears in Weber's account of appropriation. In the section under discussion, it appears, though barely recognizable, as the third general possibility of the appropriation of labor services, and is ushered in by a containing phrase so inhibitory that it appears not only to ironically invert the Marxian view of labor under capitalism but to threaten the very coherence of the classification to which it belongs: "(*c*) The third possibility is the absence of any sort of appropriation: formally 'free' labor, in this sense that the services of labor are the subject of a contractual relationship which is formally free on both sides" (Weber, 1978b:127–28). At this point definitional elaboration takes over again, supplemented by collation with a scholarly terminology suggested by the economist Bücher. Then the discussion moves on to the fourth possibility. There are reappearances of the issues behind the terms of the discussion in the remainder of the chapter, but always they are decisively contained and dispersed in the ways I am illustrating. When, for example, in section 24 it is stated in almost Marxian fashion that "appropriation by 'owners' or organized groups of them can only mean the expropriation of the workers from the means of production, not merely as individuals, but as a whole" (Weber, 1978b:130), the possible opening to discourse is quickly turned into an inventory of items that may be appropriated and ways they might be employed. There is a four-page elaboration of historical forms of appropriation in six extensively subdivided sections, in the course of which format dispersal is complemented by another major cooling device, belonging now to indicative, more than denominative, casuistry: the transfer of a currently "hot" topic to neutrally stated details and far-removed instances. The elaboration turns the topic of expropriation of the means of production into a tumble of scholarly references to ancient Carthaginian and Roman plantations, medieval mines and mills, the Egyptian, Greek, Byzantine, and Mohammedan *ergasterion,* Chinese porcelain manufactories, serf workshops in Russia, and so on. One can speak here of the casuistic modulation of a value-charged or emotive topic into something more neutral. It is identical to Harold Bloom's notion of limitation by metonymy: "a change of name, or substituting the external aspect of a thing for the thing itself, a displacement by contiguity that repeats what is displaced, but always with a lesser tone" (Bloom, 1975:98). As before I would stress that there is nothing degenerate in the device itself; it is essential to authentic casuistry and only becomes degenerate when isolated from the framework that gives it purpose. The same applies here as to denominative explication. Isolation leaves the devices to whir and spin without limit, except whatever is provided by the internal setting and emergent contingencies of classificatory agendas. In order to see how it could have been otherwise—how close this casuistry was to the context needed to redeem it—one need turn only to appendix 2 of *Economy and Society,* added by the editors, Roth and Wittich as a sample of Weber's extrascholarly writing. It is subtitled, with Marxian echoes, "A Contribution to the Political Critique of Officialdom and Party Politics." I will cite merely one statement, on appropriation:

> In contrast [with medieval society], the hierarchical dependence of the wage worker, the administrative and technical employee, the assistant in the academic institute as well as that of the civil servant and the soldier is due to the fact that in their case the means indispensable for the enterprise and for making a living are in the hands of the entrepreneur or the political ruler. The majority of the Russian soldiers, for example, did not want to continue the war [in 1917]. But they had no choice, for both the means of destruction and of maintenance were controlled by persons who used them to force the soldiers into the trenches, just as the capitalist owner of the means of production forces the workers into the factories and mines. (Weber, 1978b:1394)

This occurs as part of an argument—a contribution to a critique—and supplies the kind of context needed for authentic casuistry to do its educative work: the kind of context strenuously voided in part 1. Consider, to take a final example, one of the most challenging statements in chapter 2, or indeed the entire book. It occurs at the end of section 22: "The fact that the maximum of *formal* rationality in capital accounting is possible only where the workers are subjected to domination by entrepreneurs, is a further specific element of *substantive* irrationality in the modern economic order" (Weber, 1978b:138; italics in original).

The ensuing section is titled "The Expropriation of Workers from the Means of Production—(continued)," but there is no continuity of the critical argument latent in the preceding statement, only a continuation of denominative work for the sake of its completion and elaborative dispersal of the topic along lines already familiar to us. The same applies to the latently critical topics introduced in the remainder of the chapter: "the distribution of occupations in a market economy consists to a large extent of technically irrational specification of functions, rather than of rational specialization of functions" (Weber, 1978b:141); "the likelihood that people will be willing to work on *affectual* grounds is greater in the case of specification of functions than in that of specialization of functions" (p. 151); "in socialism, too, the individual will under these conditions ask first whether to him, personally, the rations allotted and the work assigned, as compared with other possibilities, appear to conform with his own interests . . . violent power struggles would be the normal result . . . in short, appropriation processes of all kinds and interest struggles would also then be the normal phenomena of life" (p. 203). However, I will halt the analysis here since no new containment, cooling, or hedging devices appear.

The Structure of Degenerate Casuistry

I call part 1 of *Economy and Society* degenerate as casuistry, not because it is casuistic. Its fault, reverting to an earlier distinction, is in being formal rather than situated casuistry. Instead of self-educatively elaborating significant issues through considerations of circumstance, probabilities of meaning, likely consequences, shared stocks of experience, and situated value analysis, part 1 elaborates definitions in branching clusters according to the dictates of a comprehensive listing format that cumulatively turns back upon itself to become its own rationale and context of sense. The fault of this is not that the text is hard to read, syntactically convoluted, and aesthetically ugly, but that its format rules out argumentation. I think of argumentation as a way of organizing statements to move someone by reasoning towards or away from value positions. In part 1, statements are organized predominantly in the combined form of a lexicon and a legislative document, where the legislation pertains to linguistic usage. The format rules in juxtapositions of definitions, illustrative interjections, and denominative arrays, but cannot then find room for indicative reasoning and critical argument. Its mode of address is no more like that than is a lexicon, legal contract, or administrative order. Indeed there is a structural homology between those kinds of writing and formal casuistry which identifies one source of discursive degeneracy in the latter. All of them project clear-cut, mandatory definitions in advance of practical usage: in advance, that is, of occasioned purpose, interactional adequacy, task at hand, and local or individual circumstance. Following the lead of Harold Garfinkel (1967), I would call this a breach of practical by formal rationality.

Garfinkel brings out the incompatibilities between the two forms of rationality in a table (Garfinkel, 1967:271). Two features of comparison are "Semantic clarity and distinctness," and "Clarity and distinctness 'for its own sake.'" Whereas formal rationality—the rationality of science, written law, and bureaucracy—rules in these features as ideal and operative standards, practical rationality requires their specific absence "either as stable properties or sanctionable ideals." Garfinkel (1967:270) adds a critical point here: "any attempts to stabilize these features or to compel adherence through socially systematic administration of rewards and punishments" are sufficient, in the context of actions governed by the presuppositions of everyday life, "to multiply the anomic features of interaction." A simple demonstration directly relevant for our discussion is provided by one of Garfinkel's "breaching experiments." Students were instructed to engage an acquaintance in ordinary conversation and insist that all remarks be clarified with logical precision and semantic clarity. The result in every case was to deregulate ordinary conversation and make it anomic. I would say that something of this kind occurs in part 1 of *Economy and Society,* accounting not only for complaints about its unreadability, but also the frequent tone of indignation accompanying them; indignation being a sure sign that a moral order has been breached. This may also be the source of satirical attacks against formally rational documents of social life under such headings as "legalese," "bureaucratese," and "sociologese" (for example, Eschholz et al., 1982; Runciman, 1965).

Formally rational writing imposes on social life (its situated rationality) the ideal of seeking to define decisively all relevant terms, allow for all conceivable possibilities, and leave virtually nothing to chance. Putting it another way, its regulative ideal is a system of classifications capable of taking the nominal measure of social action. This turns out not only to be a cognitively hopeless task, no matter how many articles, clauses, subclauses, qualifications, and addenda are spun out, but one which violates the foundations of social life. This is the root of the contradiction between practical and formal rationality. Garfinkel's studies show that social discourse relies for its coherence, indeed its specifically social character, on letting words pass without formally rational question. It is sanctionably expected that statements be allowed to depend for their meaning on utterer's identity, circumstance of utterance, previous statements, prospective statements, potential relationships, and so on:

> These properties of common understanding stand in contrast to the features they would have if we disregarded their temporally constituted character and treated them instead as precoded entries on a memory drum, to be consulted as a definite set of alternative meanings from among which one was to select, under predecided conditions that specified in which of some set of alternative ways one was to understand the situation upon the occasion that the necessity for a decision arose. The latter properties are those of strict rational discourse. (Garfinkel, 1967:41)

In its reading effect, even though it is against the intent or informing tendency of Weberian cultural science, part 1 of Weber's *Economy and Society* becomes something like a memory drum. It needs to be stressed, however, that the fault in this cannot reasonably be ascribed to a breach of normal language use in everyday life, because we are dealing with a text that examines social life and which therefore merely as written theorization must breach the speech-constituted and temporally constituted character of what it examines. Unless the act of writing down social life is itself held to be wrong, sociological theory can reasonably be evaluated only in terms of how, and not because, it does so. The virtue I have found in situated casuistry, the intrinsic genre of Weberian sociology, is an attempt to transpose into written form the rationalities of everyday speech life. The fault I have found in *Economy and Society* is that it abandons, even inverts, its own generic virtue.

The immediate source of the fault, I have argued, is the detachment of the discourse from problems of decision and phenomena made concretely significant by them: a detachment made evident if this, the most strenuously scholarly of Weber's works, is juxtaposed with his political writings (for example, appendix 2 in the Roth and Wittich edition of *Economy and Society*). Behind this is a more basic source of casuistic degeneration which I have called in Weber an inhibition of critical desire. The term inhibition is meant to convey that in Weber's text work (I am not talking here of his personality, though that could be brought in), critically impassioned words are erased or overcome by a counterpassion, the ascetic calling of scholarship; they are not simply left out for the sake of objectivity. As Jameson (1973:52) observes: "Weber's *Wertfreiheit* was itself a passionate value judgement which has nothing in common with that positivistic and academic type of objectivity to which it has so often been assimilated by Weber's American interpreters." Jameson is describing one pole of a constitutive tension of casuistic discourse. The figure needed in writing performance to hold the tension in appropriate balance, that is, to compose and sustain it in reading experience, is an ethically involved yet rationally scrupulous interpreter-mediator-discussant. In authentic casuistry, the concerns, commitments, and considerations needed to exercise the faculty of practical reason are directed through the textual presence of such an author, and thereby to a correspondent reader. I could as before quote my selected authorities on the genre, Slights and Starr, but Weber himself, in his methodological writings, supplies a precise formulation of the requirement:

> To be sure, without the investigator's evaluative ideas, there would be no principle of selection of subject matter and no meaningful knowledge of the concrete reality. Just as without the investigator's convictions regarding the significance of particular cultural facts, every attempt to analyze concrete reality is absolutely meaningless, so the *direction* of his personal belief, the *refraction* of values in the prism of his mind, gives *direction* to his work. (Weber, 1949:82)

My reading of *Economy and Society*, especially part 1, is that the ascetic passion for value-free appraisal is so one-sidedly dominant that the required author is not effectively, which is to say textually and literarily, present. Borrowing Frederic Jameson's (1973) apt phrase, we may say that the author is effectively present in the work only as a "vanishing mediator," a self-marginalizing trace left around decathected topics, a containing movement around significant subjects, and one so severe that directive "refraction" is erased, leaving a kind of deregulated or anomic casuistry to twist inward upon itself. In a sense, these references to trace, margin, and circumscription are mere metaphorical conceits (currently valorized, it should be added, by Derrida's usage), but there is one place in *Economy and Society* where they attain an almost literal truth. The section on the nation in chapter 9 of part 2, which I referred to in previous analysis, ends with a phrase and an ellipsis. After referring to the "specifically predestined" role of intellectuals ("tentatively" so-called) in propagating the idea of a national identity, the text reads: "This happens when those cultural agents. . . ." Here the manuscript (being written, we must remind ourselves, by a cultural agent of German nationalism), breaks off. Not through illness or death (part 2 was written between 1910 and 1914), but for some other reason, perhaps self-censorship. What interests us here is the editorial comment inserted by Roth and Wittich: "The presentation breaks off here. Notes on the margin of the manuscript indicate that Weber intended to deal with the idea and development of the nation state throughout history. The following observations were found in the margin of the sheet" (Weber, 1978b:926).

In the margin of the manuscript we find signs of the author that authentic casuistry needs to be textually present. There are notes on the enhancement of cultural *prestige* by every victorious war: for example, Germany after 1871. This is an observable fact but "whether war *furthers* the 'development of culture' is another question, one which cannot be solved in a 'value neutral' way. It certainly does *not* do it in an *unambiguous* way (see Germany after 1871!)" (Weber, 1978b:926). Such an involved and involving question is, of course, exactly of the kind that animates authentic casuistry.

This is not an isolated example of self-marginalization in Weber. Roth (in Weber, 1978b:lix) cites a page of warnings about the paralysis of initiative by bureaucracy appended by Weber to his 1908 study "Agrarian Conditions in Antiquity" to display its contemporary relevance. It is, however, only appended (placed at the margin) and ends with a paradoxical cancellation gesture: "However, these perspectives do not belong here." Almost the same self-cancelling phrase appears at the end of the "iron cage" passage, the most widely circulated and consequential of any in Weber's work: "But this brings us to the world of judgements of value and faith, with which this purely historical discussion need not be burdened" (Weber, 1958:182). The force of "purely historical" here is "purely scholarly," and it is exercised with even sterner ascetic effect in the purely denominative casuistry of *Economy and Society*. There the involved mediator is completely withdrawn to the unwritten edges of the text. "He" (I am speaking here of a textual function) circumscribes a discursive work area through cathectic topics and relevant concepts but does not occupy it to get the work performed. This has to be done by supplementary interpretation where the presence of the author, the vanishing mediator, is restored. We can explain in this way why Weber's often insufferably tedious scholarship becomes infinitely interesting in secondary commentary on its meaning. In restoring the author there is a regeneration of latent possibilities, the possibilities I have argued of authentic casuistry, inhibited or suspended in the text themselves. Before we leave this point, it is interesting to record that Weber was not unaware of the functional power of denominative casuistry to contain desire. He observes it directly in chapter 3 of part 1 after talking of the narrowing of "the sexual sphere" by structures overlapping with domestic authority and imposing the first decisive limitations on it: "As blood relationships gain importance, incest transcends the house to include other relatives and becomes subject to casuistic regulation by the kin group" (Weber, 1978b:365).

Our concern, however, is with the casuistic regulation of critical desire, the critical cathexis lodged in particular topics and terms of social discourse, not metaleptic substitutes. I will close by recalling Marcuse's observation of the inhibitory consequences of Weber's formalism, quoted at the beginning of the case study. Marcuse outlines his own critical vision of capitalist society—the irrationality of anomic production, the destructive conquest of nature, the scientifically organized destruction of humankind, and the authorization of such irrationality as the unfolding of reason—then asks, "Did Max Weber foretell this development?" (Marcuse, 1968:207). Not explicitly; the development is implicit "in his conceptual scheme" but "implied at such a deep level that it appears as inexorable, final, and thereby, in turn (in the bad sense), rational" (p. 207). Weber gets as far as developing a value-free concept of capitalist rationality so pure that its real irrationality is made evident, but accepts this as historical fate rather than a contingency that can be changed by our decisions: "then the critique stops, accepts the allegedly inexorable, and turns into apologetics—worse, into the denunciation of the possible alternative, that is, of a qualitatively different historical rationality" (p. 208). Marcuse then appeals to Weber's professed class position—his bourgeois value commitments—to explain this inhibition of critique and its transformation into fatalistic apologetics.

There are interpretive shortcomings here that I will mention but not pursue. First, there is no textual evidence of an apologetics of capitalist rationality in Weber; indeed, as we have seen in his chapter 2, the opposition between formal and substantive rationality is replete with critical potential. The only evidence Marcuse can cite is Weber's denial that a socialist mode of production could do anything but extend the hold of formal rationality. However, this would entail a fatalistic acceptance of formal rationality only if socialism and capitalism were the only possibilities that Weber allows us to imagine. This, as Mueller (1982) shows, is not the case. A second flaw is Marcuse's appeal to an extratextual factor (bourgeois position) to directly explain textual features of Weber's work. It is an illicit and unmediated leap from one sphere or level of explanation to another which short-circuits the task of textual explanation and whatever might be gained from it. I would maintain that what we have gained, and what Marcuse misses, is the identification of a coherent mode of theorizing with its own concept and way of performing critical inquiry. In holding Weber accountable to a single allowable mode, and in conceiving critique entirely in terms of discursive content and not at all in terms of textual performance, Marcuse cannot possibly ask if there are other modes of theorizing and critique (other, in his case, than Marxian dialectics), nor can he direct critical attention to the textual, which is to say the performative, dimension of theory, in whatever mode. His claim that critique stops when we fail to conceive definite alternative possibilities in realistic fullness, is as valid for modes of theorizing as for modes of production. It is in this spirit of positive defence against the closure of possibilities to a single way that I regard it as valuable to develop alternative modes of theorizing from exemplary work, such as my development of a model of authentic casuistry from Weber's sociology, and to do so with explicit reference to the performative literary dimension. Literary methods are basic means and forces in the production of theory and no more to be ignored than material means and forces in the production of society.

Summary of Part 3

Over the course of chapters 6 and 7 it has been argued that Weber's methodological program, articulating his concept of cultural science, projects a form of theorizing which corresponds strategically and tactically, discursively and textually, to the tradition of casuistic case examination associated with seventeenth-century English Protestantism and its literary offshoots. A compositional model was extracted from these sources identifying two constitutive tensions which are jointly necessary and sufficient for a casuistic discourse to form and several literary methods typical of the genre. The textual dimension of casuistry is conceived as a literary genre corresponding to the discursive form.

The case study is guided by the interpretive hypothesis that casuistry is the inner form and intrinsic genre of Weberian sociology. The hypothesis is shown to have explanatory power in that it provides a coherent account of features of Weber's scholarly summation, *Economy and Society,* which have otherwise been noted in piecemeal fashion, often with puzzlement, and sometimes with irritation: its formalistic elaboration of definitions in branching networks; the apparent lack of an overall plan which would provide a rationale for topical sequencing within and between chapters (Roth points out that Weber never wrote a well-wrought book); the inconclusiveness of the substantive discussions; their failure to move decisively towards a definite conclusion

(*Economy and Society* does not conclude; it simply trails off); the proliferation of cautionary connectives and qualifiers—perhaps, but, yet—that yields entwining tangles of statements; the placement of so many ordinary terms in quotation marks; and the striking contrast between its stylistic defiance of straightforward reading and the lucid simplicity and eloquence of his extrascholarly writings and from all reports his spoken presentations. In addition, the hypothesis makes coherent sense of the ideal-type method by showing its functional relationship to the two constitutive tensions of casuistry identified in the model. In this way I have shown the procedural meaning and significance of the method in Weber's performance of theory, including in performance both discursive strategies (for example, value-free analysis) and literary style.

The casuistic hypothesis is also shown to have critical power. The concept of an intrinsic genre, in this case situated or authentic casuistry, points to internal, hence nonimposed, nonarbitrary standards of performance. It enables us to hold actual performances accountable to something virtually informing them and to speak of a degeneracy of form by performance. This is shown to apply to part 1 of *Economy and Society*. I endorse Marcuse's critical judgment that it is a real representation of the core element of modern society, formal rationality or reified reason, because it not only analyzes the phenomenon but in its style of thought and writing expresses it. Lukác's summary of Weber's analysis of the necessity of formally rational law in a formally rational economy can be read as a remarkably close description of the performative strategy of part 1: "There is a breach with . . . traditions tailored, subjectively, to the requirements of men in action, and, objectively, to those of the concrete matter in hand. There arises a rational systematization of all statutes regulating life, which represents, or at least tends toward a closed system applicable to all possible and imaginable cases" (Lukács, 1971:96).

Unlike Marcuse, however, I explain this tendency in part 1 as a textual phenomenon arising from specifiable breaches of the intrinsic genre of Weber's work, that is to say, as a performative degeneration, not, as he does, an intellectual reflex of Weber's bourgeois class location. My method of criticism focuses attention on the character and good of a mode of theorizing distorted or misrepresented in performance, not upon flaws in the performer to be attributed to psychological, sociological, ideological, or other extrinsic causes.

Looking outwards from the case study, I would say that the value of a literary approach to theory analysis is shown here in the retrieval of a form of discourse—situated casuistry—buried in Weber's writing and lost to sociological awareness, although it is latent in interpretive sociology, which is worth preserving. A casuistic sociology would not test hypotheses with a view to establishing lawlike generalizations; it would examine problems of social consciousness, of doubtful decision, through a scrupulously honest and precise protocol of value analysis oriented to making for oneself a fully responsible choice. The virtue of a casuistic text is in the way it operates, the characteristic experiences of clarification, doubt, and the sharpening of awareness it engenders, not in supplying conclusions and instructions. Ideological commitment is entirely alien to it, as is any kind of certitude or prescription. Its purpose is to merge formal into substantive rationality, dogma into decision, and exercise in its readers the faculty of practical reason. Its aim, as Weber said of social science, is to educate judgment. From this formulation it is evident that casuistry belongs to the problematic articulated by Kant's critiques of pure reason, practical reason, and judgment. A recent restatement of it, suggesting that conditions favorable to the form are developing in modern, or perhaps I should say postmodern, thought, is in the work of Jean-Francois Lyotard. David Carroll (1984), reviewing Lyotard's relation to Kant, observes that Lyotard finds attractive in the *Critique of Practical Reason* precisely what Hegel found unacceptable, "that obligation is not an object of knowledge and that the law can never be deduced" (p. 80). He goes on to say that for Lyotard there is a radical discontinuity between "phrases of obligation" and "phrases of knowledge," with no universal metalanguage to bridge the gap: "The question of the political for Lyotard will be that of how to deal with this abyss, how to link phrases across it" (p. 80). Casuistic discourse is one way to link phrases across it (the imagery is interestingly identical with that we saw used by Radbruch to define the work of cultural science), and one which studiously respects Lyotard's requirement that the temptation be resisted to collapse ethical legitimation and cognitive legitimation into one another.

Conclusion: The Judgment of Genres

The case studies have taken an analytic route towards an evaluative destination, guided by a simple principle: since language is the constitutive matrix of social life, the linguistic dimension of attempts to theorize it must be crucial to their value. Since, moreover, sociological theory is a written enterprise, its linguistic dimension is literary or, more exactly, textual. The second term is preferable, in spite of some currently trendy debauchment, because "literary" carries with it connotations of serious literature, great books, and aesthetically good style that are irrelevant to judging theory. Theory is a separate form of writing from literary artistry and cannot appropriately be held answerable to the standards of literature.

The particular route I have taken is to select canonical texts certified as "good" by usage, to analyze their literary methods of composition, their style, and their text work, and to project from them exemplary modes of theorizing. The result is to show what there is to be followed in classical good work such as that of Simmel and Weber, but in terms of compositional method rather than discursive content and empirical propositions. This is, of course, only an analytic distinction, but I would claim (as I argued in part 1) that the linguistic dimension of social theory is basic to the question of its truth or falsity to social life. There is more to its relation to social life than being an adjunct of empirical research; consequently it is not enough in critical appraisals to talk of explanatory power, empirical fertility, and predictive validity, nor to compare types of theory (functionalist, conflict, and so on) synthesized from conceptual and empirical contents. These common practices miss the linguistic medium which joins theory, subject, and subject matter into the peculiarly reflexive configuration called social science, and the literary dynamics of variations in that medium. The medium is not caught either in methodologically defined "paradigms" of inquiry (see, for example, Ritzer, 1980, 1981). The idea of multiple paradigms rightly stresses the constructed character of social reality in relation to our ways of knowing it, but its proponents typically construe the latter as abstract conceptual schemata lodged in minds somehow outside the social reality they cognitively shape, rather than as situated processes of hearing-speaking and reading-writing in which social reality is generated for communicants. It is this ethnomethodological character of social reality, here in the realm of the text, that I have tried to catch in analyzing theoretical works as compositions of reading experience: that is to say, performative textual constructions.

The critical implications of textual analysis lie in two directions: 1. immanent evaluation, where work is evaluated on its performance of a genre or mode of theorizing shown to be intrinsic to it; 2. generic evaluation, where genres or modes of theorizing are themselves critically evaluated in terms of some higher-order purpose or good belonging to theory in its own right.

Immanent Evaluation

Immanent evaluation is illustrated in my examination of degenerate casuistry in Weber. I would like to demonstrate it further with reference to Simmel. I claimed that a vital element of his mode of theorizing is the deconstruction of dichotomous reasoning, using the term deconstruction to indicate that the work is done by cultivating standard dichotomies to bursting point, not by direct argument against such reasoning. More particularly, the work is carried out in Simmel through an identifiable tradition of writing historically tangential to Western rationalism and strangely hosted by it. The tradition, stemming from Jewish mystical theology, runs also through Hegel, where its performative effects against dichotomous reasoning are supplemented by an explicit doctrine of the trichotomous (dialectical) constitution of being, hence of truthful thought.

Speaking on behalf of an authentic dialectics and, for me, the intrinsic genre of Simmel's theorizing, Kierkegaard objected to the speculative strength of Hegel's supplement, its subsumption of existence by logic, and its existent possibility by logical progression. He agreed, dialectically, that "the concept is a trichotomy" (cited by Wilde in Thulstrup, 1967:23), but added that reason, contrary to Hegelian pretence, remains always confined to either-or dichotomy. Concepts only escape that confinement through being drawn into the consciousness and conduct of individuals where they achieve real meaning through active working out. This is a third dimension through which reason can move beyond merely logical motions (beyond what, in analyzing Simmel, I called logocentrism). The problem for a dialectical writer, which I have taken Simmel to be, is how to break the frame of normal (here logocentric) reading so that our usual ratiocinative retrieval of propositional content turns into a reflexive activity that involves the self-understanding of the reader. Here the style of communication becomes crucially important.

Kierkegaard consciously sought to create reading experiences that would recreate in the reader particular forms of subjective life or ways of being in the world: the aesthetic, the ethical, and the religious. He called what he did "indirect communication." Indirect, first, because there is no step-by-step conveyance of content through inferential argument but a refraction of themes through analogies, images, allegories, and representative anecdotes. I noted the same procedures in Simmel's work, and Louis MacKey's observation about Kierkegaard that his writings "constitute demonstrations only in a world that is itself organized exemplaristically" (MacKey, 1971:257), would apply also to Simmel. Both require us to understand the coherence of the world as a "poetic" rather than a causal unity. (See Kenneth Burke, 1954, for a closely related account of that distinction.)

Kierkegaard's communication is indirect, second, because whereas direct communication is necessarily a univocal address from a clearly identified source, Kierkegaard uses multiple interlocking pseudonyms, and even when he addresses us under his proper name, we cannot be sure of his identity. A significant clue to the claimable good of his practice lies in the title of one of the few works he pointed to as his own responsibility: *Edifying Discourses*. The discourses themselves are homilies and not edifying in the sense of Kierkegaard at his playful, dialectical best, the sense described by Rorty: "Edifying discourse is supposed to be abnormal, to take us out of our old selves by the power of strangeness, to aid us in becoming new beings" (Rorty, 1980:360). "Great systematic philosophers are constructive and offer arguments. Great edifying philosophers are reactive and offer satires, parodies, aphorisms" (p. 369).

This sense of edifying discourse is found in Kierkegaard's *Philosophical Fragments or a Fragment of Philosophy*, whose very title contradicts the Hegelian equation of philosophy with system, and which closes with a satirical postscript responding to an imaginary book review by a German philosopher who had managed to distill a systematic doctrine from it. The same sense appears also in the *Concluding Unscientific Postscript*, where it emerges reactively from a critique of scientific thinking. Here an explicit equation is made between unscientific truth and indirect communication. In human life the most vital thing to be communicated is inwardness, the subjective quality of one's way of being in the world, but scientific thinking is "wholly indifferent to subjectivity, and hence also to inwardness and appropriation; its mode of discourse is therefore direct. . . . It can be understood directly and recited by rote. Objective thinking is hence conscious only of itself, and is not in the strict sense of the word a form of consciousness at all" (cited in MacKey, 1971:295).

Since inwardness, for Kierkegaard, is a solitary conjunction of subjectivity with ideality, or pure possibility (a conjunction we may recall also defining the individual for Simmel), "where sociality and fellowship is unthinkable" (MacKey, 1971:294), while communication is outward-reaching sociality, it follows that inwardness cannot be communicated directly. In terms of Jakobson's model (see table 2, chapter 4), the communicative act here must be poetic and reflexive rather than referential.

The structure of indirect communication is informed by the antinomies of inwardness-outwardness, isolation-sociality, and withdrawal-presence. Kierkegaard said he needed "polynymity" to evoke varieties of consciousness, because a single, consistent authorial voice would only reduce them to value judgements, to propositional content, to direct, directed, directive communication. It is necessary "to read solo the original text of the individual, human existence relationship" (cited in MacKey, 1971:248). Consequently there must be no directive author, only a catalytic conductor of discourse. Herman Diem (1965:42) cites Kierkegaard's statement that he regarded himself as the reader rather than author of "his" writings, adding that the aim of ironically cancelling the perspective of one invented author with another was to force the reader into a self-reflective freedom of understanding: "the reader can nowhere find any conclusion which Kierkegaard himself would guarantee" (p. 42).

A useful essay by Lars Bejerholm reports (Thulstrup, 1967:58) that Kierkegaard used the terms "reduplication" and "double-reflection" to describe the coexistence of deliverer and receiver in that which is understood. This feature of indirect communication is confirmed in the work of Derrida, the philosophically reflective craftsman of deconstructive writing in our own time. Spivak observes that much of his work "is on the double take," where "double" stands for the indefinite "mirror structure" of language (Spivak, 1984:19, 23); the undecidability of proper meaning, even proper names. The particular work she is discussing, *La carte postale*, reduplicatively takes in what is called the "scene of writing," meaning the textual marks of a writer's resistance to the necessity of being absent from written communication, his desire to "record the living act of a sole self" (p. 20), the desire which in Kierkegaard is the basis of indirect communication. In normal reading there is a desire only to possess the proper meaning of the words; consequently "the scene of writing is usually ignored and the argument is taken as the product of a self with a proper name. Writers and readers are thus accomplices in the ignoring of the scene of writing" (Spivak, 1984;20). We can now see more clearly the point of Kierkegaard's multiple, internally cancelling authorship and his refusal to be the proper-name source of "his" writings—"in the pseudonymous works there is not a single word which is mine" (cited by McKinnon, in Thulstrup, 1967:126). It is to breach the normal complicity of reader and writer which would make of writing nothing but the direct communication of a contained message.

Given the hypothesis argued in my case study of Simmel, that deconstructive writing is the intrinsic genre his work (at its best) exemplifies, I am now in a position to state two stylistic conditions under which the work will degenerate. It will degenerate whenever the writing allows the reader to settle into dichotomous reasoning, and second, where it invites itself to be read as systematic objective thinking, meaning nothing but the sum of contained conclusions. By way of example, both conditions can be shown to exist in sections 99–104 of *The Philosophy of Money* (my numbering), where a discussion of the labor theory of value is undertaken.

The discussion takes an orthodox scholarly form: the presentation, explication, and cross-examination of a theory. Simmel attributes the theory to socialism as its rationale for replacing ordinary currency with "labor money" in the good society, seeking to discredit the rationale because labor money "would be more threatening to the differentiation and personal creation of life's contents than money as it already exists" (Simmel, 1978:428), whatever its aspiration to recognize personal worth in the concrete existence of society. A scholarly frame is established at the outset by a minute examination of "a basically terminological issue" (p. 410): the distinction between labor and labor power in the labor theory of value. The point I wish to stress is that the frame is so strongly set and maintained throughout the discussion that one cannot follow it in any other reading posture, that is, except by way of complicity with the orthodox tutelary voice of a logical thinker directly communicating propositions to form arguments. I observed in the case study that Simmel characteristically plays upon conventional formulas of logical argumentation in the course of fast, multifaceted twists and turns of what is essentially an analogical, allegoristic, exemplaristic manner of presentation. Here, however, the writing becomes caught up completely in logical argumentation and therefore subject to its game rules. Relative to the intrinsic genre constituting the specific value of Simmel's work as a whole, this would have to be regarded as a lapse, a degeneracy, regardless of how well it was performed. The reflexive effect of his work depends upon its composing an indefinite mirror structure through oscillation between two authorial voices: logocentric reasoning and a tangential voice strange to it (a conjunction we saw registered in receptive epithets like evasive, secretive, relativistic, wanderer, stranger, and a man without qualities). Consequently, the mere fact of stilling the oscillation would be a degeneracy of the work. In this case, however, the problem is compounded by the fact that by the rules of the logocentric game it invokes, Simmel's discussion is poorly performed. In other words, we cannot say that Simmel switches competently from one mode of theorizing to another and simply focus on the fact of switching as the reading problem; rather there is an unsignaled turn into argumentation with a carry-over of stylistic features which become, in this mode of discourse, performative faults. Generic virtues of deconstruction become vices of scholarly argumentation.

Most damaging of all is the carry-over of the characteristic device of not giving quotations and references. Simmel takes up a theory whose provenance is crucial to its interpretation yet so problematic as to require the most careful explication, for which documented references would be indispensable. His presumed source, given textual clues like the claim (Simmel, 1978:413) to be aware of the difference between "present-day scientific socialism" and "mechanical-communist egalitarianism" and interested in the former and its grounding in "historical materialism," is Karl Marx's *Capital*. Marx, however, attributes the labor theory of value in its abstract form (the form exclusively discussed by Simmel) to the political economists, the scientific articulators of the capitalist mode of production, saying that they have discovered a valid law (for example, Marx, 1954:79) but have not grasped the historical conditions, realized in capitalist society, of its validity. That grasp, permitted by scientific socialism, is undertaken in Marx's "critique of political economy." The critique is, however, a sublation of the labor theory of value, neither its rejection nor, as Simmel thinks, its invention. Moreover, Marx (1954:97, n. 1) attributes the idea of labor money to Utopian socialists such as Robert Owen, and recalls his criticism elsewhere of its fantastic, unscientific character. We need not follow Marx's argument; the point is that his scientific socialism (*a*) only embraces the labor theory of value critically, and (*b*) rejects labor money as a fantasy of Utopian socialism. Certainly there is not for scientific socialism any entailment of labor money in the theory.

There is no intent here to second-guess Simmel, only to show the kinds of considerations present in the documents he is alluding to but not referencing or quoting and the unresolvable interpretive ambiguity that results. When, for example, we are told that the concept of labor money "arises in socialist plans" (Simmel, 1978:409), and "the socialist line of thought must none the less lead to labour money" (p. 412), we cannot determine the intended reference of "socialist" or the force of "must." Similarly, when the labor theory of value is criticized for reducing labor to "a very artificial abstraction" (p. 417) and leveling qualitative activities to homogeneous quantitative amounts, we wonder whether the author is aware that Marx, on behalf of socialism, saw this as a historically damning truth about capitalist society hidden in the labor theory of value. Since Simmel considers the quantitative leveling of labor by unit measurement to be a feature of socialist society, we must assume that he is not aware of the status of the labor theory of value in scientific socialism, any more than he is aware that the idea of labor money is separate from the theory, accepted only by Utopian socialists, and critically rejected as a scientific absurdity by Marx.

Returning to the court-room metaphor of cross-examination, the reader (the person constrained by the format to read for logical argumentation) is in the position of a juror listening to a badly briefed lawyer question a witness (labor money) about an accused (the "socialist" labor theory of value) who is not in fact known to the witness and has in any case been brought to court under a mistaken identity. The exchanges cannot be unambiguously interpreted as arguments for and against a case, because any shifts and uncertainties experienced can be attributed to misinformation, misunderstanding, and mistaken identity. Moreover, the interpretive obscurity of the proceedings cannot be transformed into a virtuous ambiguity by reconstruing them to be an ironic mock-up or reflexive double take of logical argumentation, because the reading frame is too firmly fixed to allow it. In terms of a distinction suggested by Roland Barthes, the writer function has in this segment of Simmel's text become dominant over the author function. Whereas "the writer" (that function of text work) seeks a direct conveyance of content undistracted by any other features of communication, "the author" (that function) "forbids himself two kinds of language . . . first, doctrine, since he converts despite himself, by his very project, every explanation into a spectacle: he is always an inductor of ambiguity; second, evidence, since he has consigned himself to language, the author cannot have a naive consciousness, cannot 'work up' a protest without his message finally bearing much more on the working-up than on the protest: by identifying with language, the author loses all claim to truth, for language is precisely that structure whose very goal (at least historically, since the Sophists), once it is no longer rigorously transitive, is to neutralize the true and the false" (Barthes, cited in Rabinow, 1985:2). Simmel's intrinsic genre, deconstructive writing, works at the boundary between writer and author, though from the side of the latter, and degeneracy occurs in the work whenever one function achieves dominance over the other. I believe it could be shown that Simmel's sociological writings are constantly liable to overbalance in one direction or the other, accounting for the extreme uncertainty of his reception into sociology, the polarization of opinions about the value of his work, and the fact that both positivistic and antipositivistic readers have been able to find value in it. However, when discourse becomes degenerate, in the sense of losing generic identity or integrity of any kind, then what Eco (1980) calls interpretive cooperation, whereby the actual reader negotiates the role of model reader implicit in a text, becomes impossible and value evaporates. Immanent criticism attends to the stylistic conditions under which generically specific theory values are composed and lost in particular writings.

Generic Evaluation

The prospect of making critical judgments between heterogeneous forms of theory without appealing to extratheoretic standards like research utility is not at all inviting. One feels already the baleful glare of unanswerable questions: Is one way of doing theory better than another? Is interpretive theory a better form of theory then critical theory, or is either better than positivist theory? Is Weberian casuistry, moving down to our preferred level of identification, a better way of theorizing than Simmelian deconstruction? Is *Economy and Society* a better work of theory than *The Philosophy of Money?*

A preliminary observation is that while such questions are as they stand unanswerable, or at least answerable only by assertion, they are readily brought into the sphere of reasonable evaluation by appending to each a phrase: for the purpose of X. The problem then shifts to a defensible identification of X. For us, given the distinction between autonomous and research theory pursued in chapter 1, this must be part of a regulative definition of what sociological theory is and does in its

274

own right; that is, in its own right as a linguistic feature of linguistically constituted social life, more specifically as a literary form of social life.

The problem with regulative definitions in grounding evaluative criteria has been strongly stated by the literary critic Stanley Fish (1980): such definitions are authoritative within interpretive communities but not between them. A defense of regulative definitions might be made in terms of the impossibly high price of extreme cognitive relativism, a price so high that a rational thinker could be heard only to pretend and not seriously to propose paying it. However, a more direct response, sufficient for our present concern, was anticipated in chapter 1. Let us for the sake of argument accept Fish's restriction of evaluative authority to interpretive communities; we must still, to make sense of the debatable location of historical individuals and particular works in relation to them, distinguish between actual communities, which are socially, institutionally existent groups, and virtual communities made up of the purposes, possibilities, and limitations of cultural forms of activity. It is my position that sociological theory (considered independently of research theory) is a cultural form of activity, one defined by reflective departure from and critical return to mundane social theorizing (including the semantic commonplaces, syntactic conventions, and sense-making formulas of particular institutional spheres, as well as the collective historical consciousness of a time), and that its emergent purposes, possibilities, and limitations constitute a virtual interpretive community within which comparative evaluations can be reasonably made: indeed which demands they be made.

Of course the regulative definition of an activity is too broad itself to be a value criterion; its office is to ground statements of purpose articulated with respect to the appraisal of particular works of theory. For example, a statement developed in appraising the theoretic value of Weber's work was that theory, meaning theory in literary performance, carries an educative purpose with respect to the exercise of practical reason and thereby the maturation of full human identity in the individual. If now a comparative appraisal of Weber's work with, say, Simmel's were to be attempted, it could use the statement of purpose to formulate a meeting place where their specific values could be brought together. The formulation would have to spell out the meaning of statement terms (here "the exercise of practical reason," "maturation," and "full human identity"), in whatever detail was sufficient. Also, its own terms should be correlative with stylistic characterizations of the work in question. Thus, taking the example a step further, Durkheim's (1961) model of moral education might be thought insufficiently detailed to provide performative criteria. Another candidate, Habermas's (1979) account of maturation toward autonomous ego identity, drawn from Kohlberg's theory of stages of moral consciousness, is performatively specified and in terms of communicative behavior, but the terms, taken from ego psychology and role theory, are very distant from stylistic analysis. More directly appropriate than either for comparatively evaluating the work of Simmel and Weber would be the concept of identity development informing Kierkegaard's polyonymous writings.

As indicated previously, Kierkegaard's authorial shifts were not an aimless transience by passages between stylistically communicated ways of being in the world, organized to edify the reader. In temporal order of publication the ways are aesthetic, ethical, and religious. The temporal order expresses a certain sense of maturational ascension in passing from one existential attitude to the next, and Kierkegaard does refer to them as stages on life's way, yet it would be wrong to think that they are set stages which one enters and leaves behind in growing older. Rather they are facets, one might say moments, of subjectively inhabiting a world given by history, culture, society, and nature. They can be variably formed, moved through many times and in different orders. The order of priority between them is therefore dialectical, showing the direction towards which reactive recognition of insufficiency moves the would-be total individual, and is neither chronological nor prescribed. In this sense only is the ethical attitude higher than the aesthetic, and the religious higher than both. To this picture must be added what Kierkegaard's close alias Johannes Climacus (the climber) refers to in the *Unscientific Postscript* as border areas between the three attitudes. Stylistically they can be thought of as performative transitions. Between the aesthetic attitude and the ethical attitude is irony, enacting a detachment or break from reality, a suspension of its validity: "it despises the actual and demands the ideal" (Kierkegaard, cited in Diem, 1965:43). Whereas aestheticism embraces the actuality of things as if they were self-sufficient, irony registers an emptiness in actuality and prepares for a reactive turn to the ideality of the ethical attitude. Between the ethical and religious attitudes is another transition area: humor. This is a sense of incongruity between ridiculously incommensurate things placed together: for example, the behavior of even the most ethical individual in the face of the demands of absolute goodness, or finite man in the gaze of infinity. The self-confident ethical person, an assured preacher, a sermonizer, an ideologue, lacks that sense of absurd disproportion and is thus vulnerable to it.

It is remarkable how many identity terms characterizing the aesthetic way of inhabiting the world, especially as viewed from the critically higher ground of the ethical, match receptive epithets fastened to Simmel's work (here we recall the discussion in chapter 4), and how many terms characterizing the ethical match epithets interpretively fastened to Weber. In the aesthetic way of being (here I am following the accounts of MacKey, 1971, and Bedell, 1972), the individual is an avid collector of experiences, a detached student of souls, an "experimental psychologist" roaming the world, someone drawn from one interesting thing to another who cannot in a real sense act because he lacks the commitments essential to make decisions of conduct. He has no firm identity, is an ambiguous equivocator, his life "wholly given over to preliminary runs" (Kierkegaard, cited in MacKey, 1971:40), disengaged from historical time, social issues, and political demands of the time (we recall here Simmel's comment that he could just as well have used imaginary as real examples to do his work), and forever dissolving himself in his own virtuosity: "For the aesthete, work, when it is not a sordid drudgery for subsistence, can only be understood as the unfettered and unproductive development of his talents, for which of course a fortune is required. For the ethical man a 'talent' is a 'call,' and his work is the activity of freedom by which he transforms a gift into a vocation." (MacKey, 1971:68).

The ethical person exercises prodigious effort to act responsibly in the mundane, historical world. Kierkegaard's religious author of *The Sickness unto Death*, Anti-Climacus, sees the heroism in the effort: "The Christian heroism (and perhaps it is rare to be seen) is to venture wholly to be oneself, as an individual man, this definite individual man, alone before the face of God, alone in this tremendous exertion and this tremendous responsibility" (cited in Bedell, 1972:140).

I have shown such heroic ethics of responsibility to be Weber's stated philosophy of life, the basis of his vocational dedication to scholarship, and the educative intent of his casuistic theorizing. Bedell adds a comment on the ethical attitude closely reminiscent of the intent of situated casuistry: "By choosing oneself, one establishes the unity between the universal and the particular and thereby overcomes the apparent relativity of the historical" (Bedell, 1972:146). Ethical choice, however, as stressed by "Judge William" in *Either/Or*, is not an application of dogma, or conformity to instruction, but working through concrete complexities to a decision.

The match between Kierkegaard's characterization of the ethical attitude and Weberian scholarship can be taken further, and in a way that begins to complicate the seemingly straight assignment of Simmel to the aesthetic sphere and Weber to the higher ground of the ethical. In this I return to the dialogical spirit of Kierkegaard's distinctions and away from the undoubted temptation to use them for nominal measurement. Judge William distinguishes positive from negative ethical conduct. A negative resolution of, say, a problematic desire is to refuse it; ascetic denial is an example. When scholarship is ascetically purified of desire and value commitment, it leads, as we observed in part 1 of *Economy and Society,* towards a hyperobjective contemplation of phenomena which is almost aesthetic in its formalistic inwardness and government by the scholarly imperative to artifactually complete an intellectual design. (Brown [1977] has usefully drawn together arguments for the aesthetic character of pure scholarship and science under the concept "cognitive aesthetics.") Judge William himself draws attention to the confluence: "The instant of deliberation is the momentary withdrawal from existence in which the ethical man surveys his possibilities and gathers his forces for a return via decisive choice and action. But the aesthete, striving to hold the moment fast in contemplation, make his whole life a withdrawal" (Kierkegaard, cited in MacKey, 1971:45).

The passage describes in its first sentence the dynamics of Weberian casuistry, while the second catches simultaneously both the source of degeneracy identified in Weber's work and a basic charge often brought against the work of Simmel. The commutative closeness of these two forms of theorizing appears further at the performative level of style. MacKey (paraphrasing Judge William's opinion of his young aesthetic friend "A"), says: "The aesthetic life is infinitely dialectical; but its infinity is spurious. Enthusiastically mediating one contradiction and thereby desperately generating another, A is never done and always lost" (MacKey, 1971:124).

The same might be said of Simmel's textual method of paradoxically undermining conventional oppositions, were it to be detached from a critical, ethical context of sense. Stylistically, an endless, abstractly motivated shift from one instance of deconstructive wordplay to another in an aesthetically pure version of Simmel's theorizing would not be very different from an abstractly motivated, aesthetically pure version of Weberian theorizing. The aesthetic condition of being lost in endless, internally generated contradictions is close to an ethical condition of being lost observed by a priest, a former classmate of Judge William, in *Either/Or.* Another paraphrase by MacKey brings out the comparison: "Kierkegaard's priest suggests that dogged persistence in an ethical way of life will bring a man to the point where he must either choose to acknowledge himself absolutely in the wrong or lose himself in a maze of casuistries" (MacKey, 1971:88).

Direct textual evidence could be provided to show that Simmelian and Weberian ways of theorizing are not confined to exclusive areas of the field circumscribed by Kierkegaard's categories, but criss-cross, interweave, and overlap across its surface. Both, for example, display border-zone irony concerning the real and an appreciation of incommensurable antinomies of existence (objective culture against subjective cultivation in Simmel; formal rationality against subjective rationality, and vocation against capability in Weber), though typically registering them, respectively, as tragedy and trial by ordeal, rather than in humor. However, enough has been said to establish my point that the aim of drawing diverse works into a single conceptual field like Kierkegaard's developmental schema is not to classify them but to appraise their value in a common purpose. The particular task I have suggested in response to the challenge of comparative evaluation is to find a schema capable of interpreting analytic descriptions of performative methods and reading effects into evaluative statements about educative (in the sense of self-educative or edifying) effects. The actual choice of an interpretive apparatus will of course be a craft decision dependent upon the materials and context of interpretation, but at least one requirement can be stated. The schema must contain, if only implicitly, an ultimate regulative ideal from whose standpoint it makes sense to speak of movement towards or away from awareness, insight, understanding, and the like. In Kierkegaard, the function is performed by the religious form of life. I would not like to be heard, however, as recommending this particular feature of his interpretive framework; it is problematic and probably unacceptable for evaluating sociological theory, not least because Kierkegaard's religious man is ultimately an asocial being who immolates himself in infinite totality and aspires to a condition formulated in utterly solipsistic terms. Kierkegaard (1939:103) spoke of himself as the author of a dialectical structure who "poetically died of longing for eternity, where uninterruptedly he would have nothing to do but to thank God." MacKey (1971:125) observes: "The characterization of the religious life, whatever special occasions elicit variety in its terms, is essentially the same edifying thing over and over again." Identical repetition is deadly not only for poetry but for irony, humor, and the social life of language. More appropriate beacons for sociological theory are idealizations of the ultimate human condition (developed most strongly, but by no means exclusively, in neo-Marxian critical theory), that stress autonomy and emancipation through society instead of beyond it. Most appropriate of all are idealizations expressing the good society in linguistic and communicative rather than merely political and economic terms.

Whatever interpretive schemata are used to appraise theoretical work, it is a mistake, attested by the rubble of failed attempts, to seek permanent binding judgments, and especially judgments couched in terms of types or forms of theory. Theoretic value means value in use, and use value is tied to occasioned want in situated contexts. I would regard it, therefore, as a virtue to have multiple, mutable, and locally validated interpretive schemata rather than setting one up as a privileged metalanguage or metanarrative serving as a supreme court of judgment. (Watson [1984] has compared Habermas's totalizing, unitarian strategy to cope with the modern "crisis" of rational authority with the pragmatic, localizing response of Lyotard along these lines.) For example, and talking once more in the vicinity of Kierkegaard, I would resist drawing a totalizing conclusion from Richard Brown's suggestion that "sociological theory, when it is good theory, illuminates its audience and its subject matter with dialectically ironic insights . . . such a mode of awareness is appropriate not merely for social scientists, but for all who presume to intervene in the conduct of human affairs, that is, for all true citizens of modern states" (Brown, 1983:543). One can, with Kierkegaard, imagine the value of the ironic mode if it is part of a dialectical structure but not as a sufficient form of theory. Brown's own elaboration makes this evident. The ironist is said to regain a freedom of "intentional redefinition" for himself and his reader because what he says relates ambivalently or inversely to what he means and thus brackets the reality effects of ordinary language use. To exercise that freedom, however, it would clearly be necessary to speak responsibly about choices of conduct, which means taking responsibility for what one says, and this the ironic voice cannot do because of its endless self-distancing and evacuation. It is a mode within which positive decision and action are rendered impossible; its own use value is to be a negative supplement of decision and action, and like all use values it is situationally contingent. Good theory is effectively relevant to particular social, cultural, and historical conditions, and is therefore good in situ.

Summing up the discussion, generic evaluation of theory is most viable and fruitful when (a) applied to embodied genres in particular theoretical work, not abstract types, forms, or paradigms; (b) conducted through an interpretive schema explicitly tying purposes to performative styles of theorizing; and (c) oriented to particular demands of theory defined in a social, historical context. I will end illustratively with a statement of demands in our own day that has particular relevance for our chosen theorists, Simmel and Weber.

There has developed in Germany an intellectual movement called "anti-sociology" (Rehberg, 1985). A prominent spokesman is F. H. Tenbruck, well known as an interpreter of Simmel. On closer inspection it turns out that the object of attack is not so much sociology itself as a legacy of the Enlightenment strongly vested in it. This is the belief that society can be intentionally reconstructed by scientific knowledge and planned intervention. The belief has taken shape in social engineering and social revolution, two sides of the rationalist legacy, and has received "scientific" legitimation through social-system models of all kinds. What interests us here is that Tenbruck, having made sociology and its effects an occasion for counteractive theory, invokes Simmel and Weber as allies. We are confronted, therefore, with the seemingly outrageous spectacle of two founding fathers of sociology being enrolled in a battle against it. Tenbruck's own rationale is only that they resisted systems theorizing and respected the historical and cultural particularity of social life. My literary analysis of their compositional methods, however, allows me to say something more specific and convincing. I have shown them to exemplify modes of theorizing, grounded in identifiable literary traditions, that are awkwardly, which is to say counteractively, at a tangent to Englightenment rationalism and nomothetically conceived science. My approach yields a description of just how in working practice they are tangential, and thereby explicates their critical value for those who would use it. One of the benefits of my approach, apart from a closer understanding of the meaning and significance of particular work, is that by identifying the performative methods of exemplary theorists, we can say more definitely and fully which way they lead and what it means to follow them.

Appendix 1

Sectional Distribution of Three Kinds of Text Work in Simmel's *Philosophy of Money*

I have assigned numbers to the sections in Simmel's text as an aid to referencing. The column headings are terms used and explained in chapter 5. Blanks indicate weak or negligible signs of the activity rather than complete absence.

	Section Number	Expression of Ontological Anxiety	Affirmation of Absolute Presence	Deconstruction of Dichotomies
Chap. 1	1	X	X	
	2		X	
	3			
	4		X	
	5		X	
	6		X	
	7			
	8		X	
	9			
	10		X	
	11			
	12	X		
	13			
	14	X		
	15	X		
	16	X	X	X
	17			
	18		X	X
	19			
Chap. 2	20			
	21			
	22			
	23			
	24			
	25	X		
	26	X	X	
	27	X		
	28			
	29			X
	30			
	31		X	
	32			
	33			
	34			

	Section Number	Expression of Ontological Anxiety	Affirmation of Absolute Presence	Deconstruction of Dichotomies
	35			
	36			X
	37		X	
Chap. 3	38			
	39			
	40		X	
	41		X	
	42	X		
	43			
	44			
	45	X	X	
	46		X	X
	47			
	48	X		
	49	X	X	
	50		X	
	51	X		
	52	X		
	53	X		
	54			
	55			
	56			
	57			
	58			
	59			
	60			
	61			
	62		X	
	63			
Chap. 4	64			
	65			
	66			
	67			
	68			
	69		X	
	70			X
	71			
	72		X	
	73			
	74			
	75	X		X
	76		X	
	77			
	78			
	79			
	80			
	81			
	82			

	Section Number	Expression of Ontological Anxiety	Affirmation of Absolute Presence	Deconstruction of Dichotomies
Chap. 5	83			
	84		X	
	85	X		
	86			
	87			
	88			
	89			
	90	X		X
	91			
	92			
	93		X	X
	94			
	95			
	96			
	97			
	98		X	
	99			
	100			
	101		X	
	102			
	103		X	
	104			
	105		X	X
Chap. 6	106	X		X
	107			
	108	X		
	109			
	110		X	
	111		X	
	112		X	
	113		X	
	114		X	
	115		X	
	116		X	
	117	X		X
	118	X		
	119	X	X	
	120	X		
	121	X	X	
	122			
	123			
	124	X	X	X
	125	X		
	126			
	127			
	128			
	129	X		X

Appendix 2

Classification of Major Dichotomies in *The Philosophy of Money*

The classification presented here supplements the discussion in chapter 5 entitled "Deconstruction of Dichotomies." I have assigned numbers to the sections in Simmel's text as an aid to referencing.

Classification	Dichotomy	Section Number
Ontology	Relative/Absolute	10, 12, 13, 16, 18, 46, 48–50, 52, 121, 124, 129
	Passing/Stable	14, 15, 28, 70, 90, 114, 116, 122–25, 127–29
	Contingent/Necessary, Conditioned/Unconditioned	22, 46
	Mutable/Immutable	30, 35
	Being/Nonbeing	25, 90, 128, 129
	Matter/Spirit	32, 36, 113, 116, 118
	Origin/End	38, 39, 46, 47, 49
	Finite/Infinite	48, 49, 51
	Real/Ideal	29, 36, 49, 84, 111–13
	Actual/Potential	76, 105
	Visible/Invisible	92, 117, 124
	Material/Mental	99–103, 117
Epistemology	True/False	14, 15, 22
	Measure/Measured	20–22, 24
	Quality/Quantity	24, 55–57, 60–63, 93, 101, 110
	Unity/Diversity	29, 48, 61, 68, 80, 81, 100, 108, 110, 114, 115, 117, 119, 120, 123, 124
	Continuous/Discontinuous	56–63
	Measurable/Immeasurable	57–59
	Unique/Substitutable	58, 59, 62, 93, 103, 108
	Active/Passive	70, 75
Ethics	Valuable/Valueless	23, 25–27, 37, 48, 52–54, 83, 88, 105, 106, 121
	Necessity/Freedom	34, 36, 39, 46
	Freedom/Bondage	39, 97, 121
	Means/Ends	40–42, 45, 72, 90, 105, 120, 121
	Egoism/Altruism	50, 77, 107
	Obligation/Freedom	64–66, 72–75, 94, 95
	Man/Animal	66, 90, 113
	Dependence/Independence	68, 69, 73, 75, 84

Classification	Dichotomy	Section Number
Linguistics	Symbol/Object	24, 26, 29
	Signifier/Signified	38, 45, 46, 51, 75, 83, 86, 88, 97–99, 102, 117
Social philosophy	Giving/Taking, Losing/Gaining	10, 11, 41, 43, 51, 66, 67, 75
	Collective/Individual	34–37, 40, 45, 84, 90
	Individuality/ Depersonalization	69, 72–75, 90, 94, 108, 109, 114–16, 119
	Self/Non-self	75, 77–83, 90, 117
	Person/Object	90, 92, 106, 111–15, 118, 119
	Public/Private	93, 108, 116

Bibliography

Adorno, T. W. 1973. "Letters to Walter Benjamin." *New Left Review* 81 (Sept.–Oct.): 55–80.

Allison, David B. 1982. "Destruction/Deconstruction in the Text of Nietzsche." In William V. Spanos, Paul A. Bové, and David O'Hara, eds., *The Question of Textuality*, 197–221. Bloomington: University of Indiana Press.

Allison, David B., ed. 1977. *The New Nietzsche*. New York: Dell.

Alpers, Paul. 1982. "What Is Pastoral?" *Critical Inquiry* 8 (Spring): 437–60.

Althusser, Louis. 1969. *For Marx*. London: Allen Lane.

Althusser, Louis, and E. Balibar. 1970. *Reading Capital*. London: New Left Books.

Arato, Andrew, and E. Gebhardt, eds., 1978. *The Essential Frankfurt School Reader*. Oxford: Basil Blackwell.

Axelrod, Charles D. 1977. "Toward an Appreciation of Simmel's Fragmentary Style." *Sociological Quarterly* 18: 185–96.

Balibar, Renée, and D. Laporte. 1974. *Le Français nationale: Politique et pratique de la langue nationale sous la Révolution*. Paris: Hachette.

Barth, John. 1970. *The Sot-Weed Factor*. New York: Grosset & Dunlap, Universal Library.

Barthes, Roland. 1974. *S/Z*. New York: Hill & Wang.

––––––. 1981. "Theory of the Text." In R. Young, ed., *Untying the Text: A Post-Structuralist Reader*. London: Routledge & Kegan Paul.

Bateson, Gregory. 1972. *Steps to an Ecology of the Mind*. New York: Chandler.

––––––. 1979. *Mind and Nature*. New York: Bantam.

Bedell, George C. 1972. *Kierkegaard and Faulkner*. Baton Rouge: Louisiana State University Press.

Bendix, Reinhard. 1960. *Max Weber: An Intellectual Portrait*. New York: Doubleday.

Bendix, Reinhard, and G. Roth. 1971. *Scholarship and Partisanship*. Berkeley: University of California Press.

Benjamin, Walter. 1969. *Illuminations*, ed. Hannah Arendt. New York: Schocken.

––––––. 1973. *Charles Baudelaire: A Lyric Poet in the Era of High Capitalism*. London: New Left Books.

––––––. 1978. *Reflections*. Edited by P. Demetz. New York: Harcourt Brace Jovanovich.

Bentham, Jeremy. 1962. *The Works of Jeremy Bentham*. Vol. 8. Edited by J. Bowring. New York: Russel & Russell.

Bernstein, Basil. 1975. *Class, Codes, and Control*. New York: Schocken.

Bloom, Harold. 1973. *The Anxiety of Influence*. New York: Oxford University Press.

––––––. 1975. *A Map of Misreading*. New York: Oxford University Press.

Bloom, Harold, et al. 1979. *Deconstruction and Criticism*. New York: Continuum.

Bloomfield, Morton W., ed. 1981. *Allegory, Myth, and Symbol*. London: Harvard University Press.

Bretall, Robert, ed. 1946. *A Kierkegaard Anthology*. Princeton: Princeton University Press.

Brooke-Rose, Christine. 1980. "The Evil Ring." *Poetics Today* 1 (Summer): 67–90.

Brown, Richard. 1977. *A Poetic for Sociology*. Cambridge: Cambridge University Press, 1977.

———. 1983. "Dialectical Irony, Literary Form, and Sociological Theory." *Poetics Today* 4, no. 3, 543–64.

Burger, Thomas. 1976. *Max Weber's Theory of Concept Formation*. Durham, North Carolina: Duke University Press.

Burke, Kenneth. 1954. *Permanence and Change*. Indianapolis: Bobbs-Merrill.

———. 1957. *The Philosophy of Literary Form: Studies in Symbolic Action*. New York: Vintage.

———. 1962. *A Grammar of Motives and A Rhetoric of Motives*. Cleveland: Ohio State University Press.

———. 1966. *Language as Symbolic Action: Essays on Life, Literature, and Method*. Berkeley: University of California Press.

Canary, Robert H., and Henry Kozicki, eds. 1978. *The Writing of History: Literary Form and Historical Understanding*. Madison: University of Wisconsin Press.

Carroll, David. 1984. "Rephrasing the Political with Kant and Lyotard: From Aesthetic to Political Judgements." *Diacritics* 14 (Fall): 74–89.

Chambers Twentieth Century Dictionary 1972. London: W. and R. Chambers.

Chamberlain, Houston S. 1900. *Die Grundlagen des neunzehnten Jahrhunderts* Munich: F. Bruckmann.

Condren, Conal. 1985. *The Status and Appraisal of Classic Texts*. Princeton: Princeton University Press.

Cooley, Charles H. 1918. *Social Process*. New York: Scribner's.

———. 1930. *Sociological Theory and Social Research*. Introduction and notes by Robert Cooley Angell. New York: Henry Holt.

Coser, Lewis A. 1978. "American Trends." In *A History of Sociological Analysis*. Edited by T. Bottomore and R. Nisbet. New York: Basic.

Coser, Lewis A., ed. 1965. *Georg Simmel*. Englewood Cliffs, N.J.: Prentice-Hall.

Culler, Jonathan. 1982. *On Deconstruction: Theory and Criticism after Structuralism*. Ithaca, N.Y.: Cornell University Press.

Derrida, Jacques. 1976. *Of Grammatology*. Trans. by G. Spivak. Baltimore: Johns Hopkins University Press.

———. 1978. *Writing and Difference*. Trans. by A. Bass. Chicago: University of Chicago Press.

———. 1982. *Margins of Philosophy*. Trans. by A. Bass. Chicago: University of Chicago Press.

Diem, Hermann. 1965. *Kierkegaard's Dialectic of Existence*. Trans. by H. Knight. New York: Frederic Ungar.

Dilthey, Wilhelm. 1976. *Selected Writings*. Edited and intro. by H. Rickman. Cambridge: Cambridge University Press.

Dummett, Michael. 1973. *Frege: Philosophy of Language*. Cambridge: Harvard University Press.

———. 1978. *Truth and Other Enigmas*. Cambridge: Harvard University Press.

Durgnat, Raymond. 1982. "The Quick Brown Fox Jumps over the Clumsy Tank." *Poetics Today* 3 (Spring): 5–30.

Durkheim, Emile. 1915. *The Elementary Forms of the Religious Life*. Trans. by J. Swain. George Allen & Unwin. [1912] 1915.

———. 1938. *The Rules of Sociological Method*. Trans. by S. Solovay and J. Mueller; ed. and intro. by G. Catlin. Chicago: University of Chicago Press, [1895] 1938.

———. 1951. *Suicide*. Trans. by J. Spaulding and G. Simpson; edited and intro. by G. Simpson. Glencoe, Ill.: Free Press of Glencoe, [1897] 1951.

———. 1961. *Moral Education*. Trans. by E. Wilson and H. Schnurer; edited and intro. by E. Wilson. New York: Free Press of Glencoe, [1925] 1961.

———. 1983. *Pragmatism and Sociology*. Trans. by J. Whitehouse; edited and intro. by J. Allcock. Cambridge: Cambridge University Press, [1955] 1983.

Dworkin, Ronald. 1982. "Law as Interpretation." *Critical Inquiry* 9 (Sept.): 179–200.

Eco, U. 1980. "Two Problems in Textual Interpretation." *Poetics Today* 2 (Autumn): 145–62.

Edmondson, Ricca. 1984. *Rhetoric in Sociology*. London: Macmillan.

Eschholz, Paul, A. Rosa, and V. Clark, eds. 1982. *Language Awareness*. New York: St. Martin's.

Fish, Stanley E. 1972. *Self-Consuming Artifacts*. Berkeley: University of California Press.

———. 1980. *Is There a Text in This Class?* Cambridge: Harvard University Press.

———. 1984. "Fear of Fish: A Reply to Walter Davis," *Critical Inquiry* 10 (June): 695–705.

Fokkema, Douwe W., 1982. "A Semiotic Definition of Aesthetic Experience and the Period Code of Modernism." *Poetics Today* 3 (Winter): 61–80.

Foley, John Miles. 1983. "Genre(s) in the Making." *Poetics Today* 4, no. 4, 683–706.

Foucault, Michel. 1970. *The Order of Things*. Trans. by A. Sheridan. London: Tavistock.

———. 1972. *The Archeology of Knowledge*. Trans. by A. Sheridan. London: Tavistock.

———. 1973. *Madness and Civilization*. Trans. by R. Howard. New York: Vintage.

———. 1977. *Discipline and Punish*. Trans. by A. Sheridan. London: Allen Lane.

———. 1980. *Power/Knowledge*. Edited by C. Gordon. New York: Pantheon.

Freud, Sigmund. 1938. *Basic Writings*. Edited, trans., and intro. by D. A. Brill. New York: Random House.

Frisby, David. 1976. "Introduction to the English Translation." In T. Adorno et al., *The Positivist Dispute in German Sociology*. London: Heinemann.

———. 1978. "Introduction." In G. Simmel, *The Philosophy of Money*. Trans. by T. Bottomore and D. Frisby. London: Routledge & Kegan Paul.

———. 1981. *Sociological Impressionism: A reassessment of Georg Simmel's Social Theory*. London: Heinemann.

———. 1984. *Georg Simmel*. London: Tavistock.

Gadamer, Hans-Georg. 1975. *Truth and Method*. London: Sheed & Ward.

Garfinkel, Harold. 1967. *Studies in Ethnomethodology*. New York: Prentice-Hall.

Garfinkel, Harold, and H. Sacks. 1970. "On Formal Structures of Practical Activities." In E. Tiryakian and J. McKinney, eds., *Theoretical Sociology*, 338–66. New York: Appleton-Century-Crofts.

Gellner, Ernest. 1974. *Legitimation of Belief*. Cambridge: Cambridge University Press.

Gibson, Walker. 1982. "Must a Great Newspaper Be Dull?" In P. Eschholz, A. Rosa, and V. Clark, eds., *Language Awareness*, 137–46. New York: St. Martin's.

Goffman, Erving. 1959. *The Presentation of Self in Everyday Life*. New York: Doubleday Anchor.

———. 1975. *Frame Analysis: An Essay on the Organization of Experience*. New York: Harper.

Gorman, David. 1983. "Discovery and Recovery in the Philosophy of Language." *Diacritics* 13 (Winter): 43–62.

Green, Bryan S. 1977. "On the Evaluation of Sociological Theory." *Philosophy of the Social Sciences* 7:33–50.

———. 1983. *Knowing the Poor*. London: Routledge & Kegan Paul.

Greenblatt, Stephen J., ed. 1981. *Allegory and Representation*. Baltimore: Johns Hopkins University Press.

Habermas, J., 1971. *Knowledge and Human Interests*. Boston: Beacon.

———. 1974. *Theory and Practice*. London: Heinemann Educational Books.

———. 1979. *Communication and the Evolution of Society*. Boston: Beacon.

———. 1983. *Philosophical-Political Profiles*. Cambridge: MIT Press.

Hamon, Philippe. 1973. "Un discours contraint," *Poétique* 16:424–45.

Hekman, Susan. 1983. *Weber, the Ideal Type, and Contemporary Social Theory*. Notre Dame, Ind.: University of Notre Dame Press.

Higonnet, Anne, Margaret, and Patrice Higonnet. 1984. "Façades: Walter Benjamin's Paris." *Critical Inquiry* 10 (March):391–419.

Hirst, Paul Q. 1975. *Durkheim, Bernard, and Epistemology*. London: Routledge & Kegan Paul.

Hjelmslev, Louis. 1971. *Essais linguistiques*. Paris: Minuit.

Hobbes, Thomas. 1968. [1651]. *Leviathan*. London: Penguin.

Holland, Norman. 1984. "The Brain of Robert Frost." *New Literary History* 15 (Winter): 365–86.

Hollis, Martin, and Steven Lukes, eds. 1982. *Rationality and Relativism*. Cambridge: MIT Press.

Hübner-Funk, Sibylle. 1976. "Ästhetizismus und Soziologie bei Georg Simmel." In H. Böhringer and K. Gründer, eds., *Ästhetik und Sociologie um die Jahrhundertwende: Georg Simmel*. Frankfurt.

———. 1982. "Aestheticism in Georg Simmel's 'Philosophy of Money.'" Paper given at World Congress of Sociology, Mexico City, August.

Huff, Toby. 1984. *Max Weber and the Methodology of the Social Sciences*. New Brunswick, N.J.: Transaction Books.

Iser, Wolfgang. 1984. *The Implied Reader: Patterns of Communication in Prose Fiction from Bunyan to Beckett*. Baltimore: Johns Hopkins University Press.

Ishiguro, Hidé. 1972. *Leibniz's Philosophy of Logic and Language*. London: Duckworth.

Jakobson, Roman. 1960. "Closing Statement: Linguistics and Poetics." In T. Sebeok, ed., *Style in Language*. Cambridge: MIT Press.

James, William. 1967. *Selected Writings*. Ed. by J. McDermott. New York: Random House.

Jameson, Frederic. 1971. *Marxism and Form*. Princeton: Princeton University Press.

———. 1972. *The Prison-House of Language*. Princeton: Princeton University Press.

———. 1973. "The Vanishing Mediator: Narrative Structure in Max Weber." *New German Criticism* 1, no. 1 (Winter): 52–89.

Janik, Alan, and S. Toulmin. 1973. *Wittgenstein's Vienna*. New York: Simon & Schuster.

Jones, Robert A. 1977. "On Understanding a Sociological Classic." *American Journal of Sociology* 83, no. 2, 279–319.

Kant, Immanuel. 1929. *Selections.* Edited by T. Greene. New York: Scribner.

Kierkegaard, Søren. 1939 [1843]. *Fear and Trembling.* Trans. by Robert Payne. Oxford: Oxford University Press.

———. 1946. *Anthology.* Edited by R. Brettall. Princeton: Princeton University Press.

Kirk, Russell. 1974. "Is Social Science Scientific?" In G. Ritzer, ed., *Social Realities.* Boston: Allyn & Bacon.

Labov, W. 1970. "The Logic of Non-Standard English." In F. Williams, ed., *Language and Poverty.* London: Markham.

La Capra, Dominick. 1983. *Rethinking Intellectual History: Texts, Contexts, Language.* Ithaca: Cornell University Press.

Lang, Berel. 1978. "Style as Instrument, Style as Person." *Critical Inquiry* 4 (Summer): 715–40.

Lazarsfeld, Paul F. 1972. *Qualitative Sociology.* Boston: Allyn & Bacon.

Leitch, Vincent B. 1980. "The Lateral Dance: The Deconstructive Criticism of J. Hillis Miller." *Critical Inquiry* 6 (Summer): 593–608.

Levine, Donald N. 1971. "Introduction." In Georg Simmel, *On Individuality and Social Forms.* Chicago: University of Chicago Press.

Lima, Luiz C. 1985. "Social Representation and Mimesis." *New Literary History* 16 (Spring): 447–66.

Locke, John. 1964 [1690]. *Essay on Human Understanding.* Edited by J. Yolton. London: Dent.

Löwith, Karl. 1982 [1932]. *Max Weber and Karl Marx.* Ed. and intro. by T. Bottomore and W. Outhwaite. London: Allen & Unwin.

Lukács, Georg. 1971. *History and Class Consciousness.* Trans. by R. Livingstone. Cambridge: MIT Press.

Lukes, Steven. 1968. "Methodological Individualism Reconsidered." *British Journal of Sociology* 19:119–29.

MacKey, Louis. 1971. *Kierkegaard: A Kind of Poet.* Philadelphia: University of Pennsylvania Press.

Marcuse, Herbert. 1968. "Industrialization and Capitalism in the Work of Max Weber." *Negations.* 201–26. Boston: Beacon.

Martindale, Don. 1981. *The Nature and Types of Sociological Theory.* 2d ed. Boston: Houghton Mifflin.

Marx, Karl. 1954. *Capital.* Vol. 1. Moscow: Progress Publishers.

Meiland, J. 1978. "Interpretation as a Cognitive Discipline." *Philosophy and Literature* 11 (Spring): 24–48.

Menzies, Ken. 1982. *Sociological Theory in Use.* London: Routledge & Kegan Paul.

Merton, Robert K. 1967. *On Theoretical Sociology.* New York: Free Press.

Miller, J. Hillis. 1976. "Stevens' Rock and Criticism as Cure, II." *Georgia Review* 30 (Summer): 330–48.

———. 1980. "The Figure in the Carpet." *Poetics Today* 1 (Spring): 107–18.

Mills, C. Wright. 1959. *The Sociological Imagination.* New York: Oxford University Press.

Mitzman, Arthur. 1970. *The Iron Cage: An Historical Interpretation of Max Weber.* New York: Knopf.

Mommsen, W. J. 1974. *The Age of Bureaucracy: Perspectives on the Political Sociology of Max Weber.* New York: Harper & Row.

Moran, Michael. 1970. "The Style of the Dialectic." *The Listener,* 29 October, pp. 577–78.

Mueller, Claus. 1973. *The Politics of Communication.* New York: Oxford University Press.

Mueller, Gert H. 1982. "Socialism and Capitalism in the Work of Max Weber." *British Journal of Sociology* 33 (June): 151–71.

Munch, Peter. 1975. "'Sense' and 'Intention' in Max Weber's Theory of Social Action." *Sociological Inquiry* 45:59–66.

Nehamas, Alexander. 1981. "The Postulated Author: Critical Monism as a Regulative Ideal." *Critical Inquiry* 8 (Autumn): 133–50.

Nietzsche, Friedrich. 1967a. *The Will to Power.* Trans. by W. Kaufmann and R. Hollingdale; edited by W. Kaufmann. New York: Random House.

———. 1967b. *The Genealogy of Morals* and *Ecce Homo.* Trans. and edited by W. Kaufmann. New York: Vintage.

Nisbet, Robert. 1976. *Sociology as an Art Form.* London: Oxford University Press.

Novak, Mark. 1976. "An Introduction to Reading Georg Simmel's Sociology." *Sociological Inquiry* 46, no. 1, 31–40.

O'Neill, John. 1982. *Essaying Montaigne: A Study of the Renaissance Institution of Writing and Reading.* London: Routledge & Kegan Paul.

Overington, Michael. 1981. "A Rhetorical Appreciation of a Sociological Classic: Durkheim's *Suicide.*" *Canadian Journal of Sociology* 6:447–61.

Parsons, Talcott. 1969. *Politics and Social Structure.* New York: Free Press.

Partridge, Eric. 1966. *Origins.* London: Routledge & Kegan Paul.

Pêcheux, Michael, and C. Fuchs. 1982. "Language, Ideology, and Discourse Analysis: An Overview." *Praxis* 6:3–36.

Peirce, Charles S. 1955. *The Philosophical Writings.* Edited by J. Buchler. New York: Dover.

———. 1958. *Selected Writings.* Ed. by P. Wiener. New York: Doubleday.

Prendergast, Christopher. 1985. "Madame Aubain's Barometer, or The Referential Illusion." *Paragraph* 5 (March): 27–55.

Prown, Jules. 1980. "Style as Evidence." *Winterthur Portfolio.* 15 (Autumn): 197–210.

Quilligan, Maureen. 1979. *The Language of Allegory: Defining the Genre.* Ithaca: Cornell University Press.

Rabinow, Paul. 1985. "Discourse and Power: On the Limits of Ethnographic Texts." *Dialectical Anthropology* 10 (July): 1–14.

Rabinowitz, Peter. 1985. "The Turn of the Glass Key: Popular Fiction as Reading Strategy." *Critical Inquiry* 11 (March): 418–31.

Radbruch, Gustav. 1950. "Legal Philosophy." In *The Legal Philosophies of Lask, Radbruch, and Dabin,* 47–224. Trans. and edited by K. Wilks. Cambridge: Harvard University Press.

Rehberg, Karl-Siegbert. 1985. "'Anti-Sociology': A Conservative View on Social Sciences." *History of Sociology* 5 (Spring): 45–60.

Reiss, Albert J., ed. 1968. *Cooley and Sociological Analysis.* Ann Arbor: University of Michigan Press.

Reiss, Timothy. 1982. *The Discourse of Modernism.* Ithaca: Cornell University Press.

BIBLIOGRAPHY

Rex, John. 1974. *Sociology and the Demystification of the Modern World*. London: Routledge & Kegan Paul.

Reynolds, Paul. 1971. *A Primer in Theory Construction*. New York: Bobbs-Merrill.

Rhea, Buford, ed. 1981. *The Future of the Sociological Classics*. London: Allen & Unwin.

Ricoeur, Paul. 1976. *Interpretation Theory: Discourse and the Surplus of Meaning*. Fort Worth: Texas Christian University Press.

Riffaterre, Michael. 1980. "Syllepsis." *Critical Inquiry* 6 (Summer): 625–38.

――――. 1983. "Hermeneutic Models." *Poetics Today* 4, no. 1, 7–16.

――――. 1984. "Intertextual Representation: On Mimesis as Interpretive Discourse." *Critical Inquiry* 11 (Sept.): 141–62.

Ritzer, George. 1980. *Sociology: A Multiple Paradigm Science*. Rev. ed. Boston: Allyn & Bacon.

――――. 1981. *Toward an Integrated Sociological Paradigm: The Search for an Exemplar and an Image of the Subject Matter*. Boston: Allyn & Bacon.

Ritzer, George, ed. 1974. *Social Realities*. Boston: Allyn & Bacon.

Rorty, Amelie. 1983. "Experiments in Philosophical Genre: Descartes' *Meditations*." *Critical Inquiry* 9 (March): 545–64.

Rorty, Richard. 1980. *Philosophy and the Mirror of Nature*. Princeton: Princeton University Press.

――――. 1984. "Deconstruction and Circumvention." *Critical Inquiry* 11 (Sept.): 1–23.

Rossi-Landis, F. 1980. "On Linguistic Money." *Philosophy and Social Criticism* 7 (Fall/Winter): 345–72.

Runciman, W. 1965. "Sociologese." *Encounter* 26 (Dec.): 45–47.

Said, Edward. 1978. "The Problem of Textuality: Two Exemplary Positions." *Critical Inquiry* 4 (Summer): 673–714.

Saussure, Ferdinand de. 1959. *Course in General Linguistics*. New York: Philosophical Library, [1916] 1959.

Scholes, Robert. 1977. "Towards a Semiotics of Literature." *Critical Inquiry* 4 (Autumn): 105–20.

Schor, Naomi. 1984. "Detail and Realism: *Le Curé de Tours*." *Poetics Today* 5, no. 4, 701–10.

Schroyer, Trent. 1973. *The Critique of Domination*. New York: G. Braziller.

Seidman, Steven, 1983. "Beyond Presentism and Historicism: Understanding the History of Social Science." *Sociological Inquiry* 53 (Winter): 79–94.

Simmel, Georg. 1908. *Soziologie: Untersuchungen über die Formen der Vergesellschaftung*. Leipzig: Duncker & Humlot.

――――. 1950. *The Sociology of Georg Simmel*. Trans. and edited by Kurt H. Wolff. Glencoe, Ill.: Free Press.

――――. 1955. *Conflict and the Web of Group Affiliation*. Trans. by K. Wolff and R. Bendix. Glencoe, Ill.: Free Press.

――――. 1968. *The Conflict in Modern Culture and Other Essays*. Trans. by K. P. Etzkorn. New York: Columbia Teachers' College Press.

――――. 1971. *On Individuality and Social Forms*. Edited by D. Levine. Chicago: University of Chicago Press.

――――. 1977. *The Problems of the Philosophy of History*. Trans. and edited by G. Oakes. New York: Free Press.

──────. 1978. *The Philosophy of Money*. Trans. by T. Bottomore and D. Frisby. London: Routledge & Kegan Paul.

──────. 1980. *Essays on Interpretation in Social Science*. Trans. and edited by G. Oakes. Totowa, N.J.: Rowman & Littlefield.

Slights, Camille. 1981. *The Casuistical Tradition*. Princeton: Princeton University Press.

Smelser, Neil, and R. Warner. 1976. *Sociological Theory: Historical and Formal*. New York: General Learning Press.

Smith, Barbara H. 1978. *On the Margins of Discourse*. Chicago: University of Chicago Press.

Spivak, Gayatri C. 1981. "'Draupadi' by Mahasveti Devi." *Critical Inquiry* 8 (Winter): 381–402.

──────. 1984. "Love Me, Love My Ombre, Elle." *Diacritics* 14 (Winter): 19–36.

Spykman, N. J. 1964. *The Social Theory of Georg Simmel*. New York: Russell & Russell, [1925] 1964.

Starr, G. A. 1971. *Defoe and Casuistry*. Princeton: Princeton University Press.

States, Bert O. 1983. "The Dog on the Stage: Theater as a Phenomenon." *New Literary History* 14 (Winter): 373–88.

Steiner, George. 1971. *Extraterritorial*. New York: Atheneum.

Strauss, Leo. 1963. "Natural Rights and the Distinction between Facts and Values." In Maurice Natanson, ed., *The Philosophy of the Social Sciences: A Reader*. New York: Random House.

Thulstrup, Marie, ed. 1980. *Concepts and Alternatives in Kierkegaard*. Copenhagen: C. A. Reitzels Boghandel.

Thulstrup, Neils. 1967. *Kierkegaard's Relation to Hegel*. Princeton: Princeton University Press.

Todorov, T. 1973. *The Fantastic: A Structural Approach*. Cleveland: Case Western University Press.

Watson, Stephen. 1984. "Jürgen Habermas and Jean-François Lyotard: Post Modernism and the Crisis of Rationality." *Philosophy and Social Criticism* 10 (Fall): 1–24.

Waugh, Linda. 1980. "The Poetic Function in the Theory of Roman Jakobson." *Poetics Today* 2 (Autumn): 57–82.

Weaver, Richard. 1970. *Language Is Sermonic*. Baton Rouge: Louisiana State University Press.

Weber, Marianne. 1975. *Max Weber: A Biography*. New York: Wiley, [1926] 1975.

Weber, Max. 1946. *From Max Weber*. Trans. and ed. by H. Gerth and C. Wright Mills. New York: Oxford University Press.

──────. 1947. *The Theory of Social and Economic Organization*. Trans. and edited by A. Henderson and T. Parsons. New York: Free Press.

──────. 1947. *The Methodology of the Social Sciences*. Trans. by E. Shils and H. Finch. New York: Free Press.

──────. 1958. *The Protestant Ethic and the Spirit of Capitalism*. Trans. by Talcott Parsons. New York: Scribner's.

──────. 1975. *Roscher and Knies: The Logical Problems of Historical Economics*. Trans. and intro. by G. Oakes. New York: Free Press.

──────. 1977. *Critique of Stammler*. Trans. and intro. by G. Oakes. New York: Free Press.

———. 1978a. *Selections*. Edited by W. Runciman; trans. by E. Mathews. Cambridge: Cambridge University Press.

———. 1978b. *Economy and Society*. 2 vols. Edited by G. Roth and C. Wittich; intro by G. Roth. Berkeley: University of California Press.

Wilks, K., trans. and ed. 1950. *The Legal Philosophies of Lask, Radbruch, and Dabin*. Cambridge: Harvard University Press.

Wolff, Kurt. 1950. "Introduction." In *The Sociology of Georg Simmel*. Glencoe, Ill.: Free Press.

Wolff, Kurt, ed. 1958. *Essays on Sociology, Philosophy, and Aesthetics by Georg Simmel, et al.* Columbus: Ohio State University Press.

Young, R., ed. 1981. *Untying the Text: A Post-Structural Reader*. London: Routledge & Kegan Paul.

Index

Adorno, T. W., 126
Allegory, 126–29, 135, 176; and allegoresis, 128–29, 133, 176
Allison, David B., 37–38
Alpers, Paul, 187
Althusser, Louis, 65, 67, 115
Angell, Robert Cooley, 42
Antirealism, 170–74
Antisociology, 281
Arato, Andrew, 131
Archiv für Sozialwissenschaft und Sozialpolitik, 184–85, 229
Aristotle, 170–71
Autocontextualization, 254
Axelrod, Charles D., 125

Balibar, E., 65, 115
Balibar, Renée, 15
Barth, John, *The Sot-Weed Factor,* 97–98
Barthes, Roland, 25, 136–37, 273–74
Bateson, Gregory, 34, 39
Baxter, Richard, 187
Bedell, George C., 125, 277
Bejerholm, Lars, 270
Bendix, Reinhard, 180–81, 221
Benjamin, Walter, 95, 125–26, 129–33, 159–61, 171, 175–76
Bentham, Jeremy, 166
Bergson, H., 106, 109
Bernstein, Basil, 15
Biad, 167
Bloch, Ernst, 102
Böhme, Jacob, 110, 131
Bottomore, T., 117, 118
Bloom, Harold, 42, 67–69, 256–57
Bloomfield, Morton, 127, 128
Bretall, Robert, 107
Brooke-Rose, Christine, 61
Brown, Richard, 212, 241, 243, 245, 278, 280
Bühler, Charlotte, 214
Bühler, Karl, 214
Burger, Thomas, 216
Burke, Kenneth, 37, 153, 212, 269

Canary, Robert, 126
Capital (Marx), 21–22, 115, 119, 127, 136–37, 139–41, 272–73
Carrol, David, 266
Casuistry: conditions of degeneration, 189–90, 249, 253–54, 258–63; generative tensions of, 198–203, 215, 224, 249, 254, 261–62; indicative, denominative, and ethical dimensions of, 183, 184, 194, 216, 224, 238, 242, 249; legal concept of, 186, 188–91; legal science and, 204, 207–12; as literary genre, 187–88, 194–98, 215, 224, 234–35, 246, 248, 256–57; Protestant tradition of, 186–88, 193–95, 199–200, 202, 218, 232–35, 248; situated versus formal, 188–93, 253, 258, 265; sociological, 185, 188, 192, 193, 200–203, 212–15, 226, 235–36, 238–40, 245–46, 266. *See also* Weber, Max, casuistic theorizing of; casuistic writing style of
Chamberlain, Houston, 237
Chambers Twentieth Century Dictionary, 86, 232
Classical theory. *See* Sociological theory, classical
Company of texts, 81. *See also* Simmel, Georg, company of texts
Condren, Conal, 167
Cooley, Charles, 38–45, 59, 63–64, 72, 200–203; *Social Process,* 43–44
Coser, Lewis A., 84, 86, 89, 90, 108
Culler, Jonathan, 45, 113

Deconstruction, 45, 71, 111–16, 135, 142, 166. *See also* Derrida, Jacques
Defoe, Daniel, 186, 194–96
Demetz, Peter, 132
De Quincey, Thomas, 191–92, 199
Derrida, Jacques, 45–47, 72–74, 110–13, 135, 141–42, 151, 153–54, 156, 158, 166, 270
"Dialectic" (R. S. Thomas), 143
Diem, Hermann, 108, 270

Dilthey, Wilhelm, 208
Discourse analysis, 64–67
Disraeli, B., *Sybil*, 26
Dummett, Michael, 170–73
Durgnat, Raymond, 79, 80
Durkheim, Emile, 12, 29, 55–59, 69–71, 75, 86, 90, 94, 151, 224, 275; *Elementary Forms of the Religious Life*, 70–71; *The Rules of Sociological Method*, 69–71
Dworkin, Ronald, 27

Eckhart, Meister, 110
Eco, U., 280
Economy and Society (Weber): casuistic text work in, 235–46, 264–65; degenerate casuistry in, 247–58, 260–62
Edifying discourse, 226, 269
Edmondson, Ricca, 212
Elementary Forms of the Religious Life (Durkheim), 70–71
Eliot, George, 191
Encyclopaedia Britannica (11th ed.), 188
Eschholz, Paul A., 259

Fish, Stanley, 29–31, 103–4, 275
Fokkema, Douwe W., 99, 101, 102
Foucault, Michel, 20, 27, 45–46, 113, 159–63, 171, 175
Freud, Sigmund, 68, 71, 87–88, 129, 184–85
Frisby, David, 84, 93, 95, 96, 99, 100, 108, 117, 118, 122, 125
Frost, Robert, 35–37
Fuchs, C., 80
Fuchs, Edward, 130

Gadamer, Hans-Georg, 75, 213–14
Garfinkel, Harold, 79, 259, 260
Gassen, Kurt, 102
Gebhardt, E., 131
Generic recognizability, 26, 59–62, 166
Genre: and comparative evaluation, 274–81; definitions of, 27, 59, 60, 136; intrinsic, 247, 264–65
Gibson, Walker, 61
Goethe, W., 224
Goffman, Erving, 54, 84
Goldscheid, R., 95, 96, 98, 101, 119, 123, 136
Gorman, David, 171
Green, Bryan S., 15, 46, 66
Greenblatt, Stephen J., 128

Habermas, J., 126, 130, 131–32, 157, 159, 175, 276
Hamann, R., 94, 100, 102
Hegel, G., 107, 109, 110, 131, 159, 175, 213, 266, 268
Hekman, Susan, 216
Higonnet, Ann M., 126, 132
Higonnet, Patrice, 132
Hirst, Paul Q., 64–67
Hjelmslev, Louis, 79
Hobbes, Thomas, 16
Holland, Norman, 35–36
Hollis, Martin, 104
Hübner-Funk, Sibylle, 93, 95
Huff, Toby, 216

Ibsen, H., 211
Ideal type method. *See* Weber, Max, ideal type method of
Idiolect, 82
Intertextuality, 81–82, 136–37, 141, 154
Intrinsic genre. *See* Genre, intrinsic
Iser, Wolfgang, 63
Ishiguro, Hidé, 170

Jakobson, Roman, 104; model of communicative act, 62, 97, 99–100, 270
James, Henry, 152
James, William, 106, 172–73
Jameson, Frederic, 53, 71–73, 260–61
Janik, Alan, 72
Joel, Karl, 118
Jones, Robert A., 29, 81
Joyce, James, *Ulysses*, 61

Kafka, F., 47–48
Kant, Immanuel, 33, 157, 266
Keyserling, H., 119, 133, 169
Kierkegaard, S., 107, 108, 116, 125, 160, 276–80; *Concluding Unscientific Postscript*, 269, 276; dialectical writing in, 116, 268–71; *Edifying Discourses*, 269; *Either/Or*, 277–78; *Fear and Trembling*, 107; *Philosophical Fragments or a Fragment of Philosophy*, 269; *The Sickness unto Death*, 277
Kirk, Russell, 15
Knapp, G., 91
Knies, Karl, 217–18
Kozicki, Henry, 126
Kracauer, S., 93, 98, 117

Rex, John, 15
Reynolds, Paul, 15–17
Rhea, Buford, 11, 17–20
Rickert, H., 204, 225
Ricoeur, Paul, 49–52, 53–54, 59, 79
Riffaterre, Michael, 61, 81, 82
Ritzer, George, 267
Rorty, Amelie, 14
Rorty, Richard, 53, 112–13, 229, 269
Roscher, W., 222–23
Rossi-Landis, F., 137–38
Roth, G., 188, 195, 221, 227, 247–48, 254–55, 262
Rules of Sociological Method (Durkheim), 69–71
Runciman, W., 15, 259

Sacks, Harvey, 79
Said, Edward, 45, 46
Sanderson, Robert, 231–35, 240
Saussure, Ferdinand de, 71, 73, 79, 87, 138–39, 146–47, 151, 155
Schaefer, E., 86–87, 91
Schmidt, Conrad, 119
Schmoller, Gustav, 118
Scholes, Robert, 62
Schor, Naomi, 129, 134
Schroyer, Trent, 20
Seidman, Steven, 29
Sign, semiotic theory of, 35, 71–73, 79, 138–39, 146–47
Simmel, Georg, 33–34, 62, 74–75, 267, 270, 281; aestheticism in style of, 92, 95–101, 125; allegory and allegoresis in text work of, 133–35; brilliance in style of, 84–92; dialectical writing in, 104–10, 175, 268, 278–79; immanent degeneration of style in, 268, 271–74; and Jewish mysticism, 131, 132, 175, 268; and modernism, 101–2; objective attitude of, 92–96; *The Philosophy of Money,* 20, 91, 96, 100, 101, 107, 116, 274; receptive epithets around work of, 83–84, 174–75; and relativism, 93–94, 101–2, 172; reflexive and deconstructive writing in, 114–15, 125, 133, 175, 278–89; *Soziologie,* 88–90; "The Stranger," 114–15; textual companions of, 107, 131, 151, 171
Simmel, Hans, 90
Slights, Camille, 186–87, 193–94, 197, 199, 202, 231–32, 234–35, 248
Smelser, Neil, 10–12, 34

Smith, Barbara H., 53
Social semantemes, 24, 26, 58, 82–83
Sociolect, 82
Sociological theory, 55, 74, 245; classical, 5–13, 17–20, 22–23, 38, 62, 129, 166; literary nature of, 6, 8, 11, 18, 38, 74, 265–67; and research, 4–5, 16; as social practice, 5, 6, 45–46, 58, 76; as substantive area, 3, 22–23; valuation of, 3, 9, 13, 16, 23, 46, 212, 247, 260, 263–64, 267–68, 274–81; ways of studying, 6–9. *See also* Text work, of sociological theory; Sociological writing
Sociological writing: aesthetic ideals and, 20–23, 267; generic specificity of, 15, 21, 23–27, 32, 41, 58, 62, 166, 267; natural science ideals and, 15–17, 20; truth and, 38–40, 42, 52, 57–58, 267; valuation of, 27, 46, 267–68. *See also* Genre, and comparative evaluation
Sociology, 74, 188, 190, 192, 199; as art, 21–22, 24–26; as science, 16, 21–22, 24–25, 57–59, 225; treatment of writing style in, 14–15. *See also* Casuistry, sociological
Spencer, Herbert, 38–41
Spivak, Gayatri C., 142, 270–71
Spranger, Eduard, 212, 215
Spykman, N. J., 84
Stammler, R., 206
Starr, G. A., 186–87, 196, 199, 248
States, Bert O., 25
Steiner, George, 72
Strauss, Leo, 181, 194, 241
Style: analysis of, 36–37; and content, 29–31; definitions of, 27, 28, 30–32, 41; as person, 32–41
Stylistics, 30–31

Taylor, Jeremy, 193–94
Tenbruch, F. H., 281
Text work, 67–68, 91, 136, 175; and dream work, 67–68; of sociological theory, 64; system of tendencies in, 43–44, 49, 63–64, 69–74; tensing elements in, 44, 46–49; tentative process and, 42–44, 49, 63–64, 200; and wit work, 67–68, 87–88
Textual meaning: and authorial intention, 44–45, 47, 49, 63; interpretation of, 49–52, 273–74
Thulstrup, Marie, 107, 268, 270–71
Time (magazine), 61
Todorov, T., 61